FILE ORGANIZATION AND ACCESS

FROM DATA TO INFORMATION

Richard H. Austing
University of Maryland

Lillian N. Cassel
Villanova University

D. C. Heath and Company
Lexington, Massachusetts   Toronto

Copyright ©1988 by D. C. Heath and Company.

All rights reserved. No part of this publication may be reproduced or transmitted in any form or by any means, electronic or mechanical, including photocopy, recording, or any information storage or retrieval system, without permission in writing from the publisher.

Published simultaneously in Canada.

Printed in the United States of America.

International Standard Book Number: 0-669-12375-7

10 9 8 7 6 5 4 3 2 1

CONTENTS

Preface, xiii

1 Introduction to Data: A Logical View and Its Physical Organization   1

INTRODUCTION 1
REPRESENTATION OF DATA 2
DATA TYPES: THE LOGICAL REPRESENTATION OF DATA 3
   Simple Data Types 4
      Integer 4
      Real 6
      Character 7
   Composite Data Types 7
      String 7
      Array 8
      Record 12
STORAGE MAPPING; A PHYSICAL REPRESENTATION OF DATA 13
   Integer, Real, and Character Data Types 14
   String, Array, and Record Data Types 16
FILE SYSTEMS 18
   Text, Binary, and Code Files 18
   Master, Transaction, and Temporary Files 19
   Program Files 21
   File Interactions and Overlap 24
SUMMARY 26
EXERCISES 27

2 Searching and Sorting Data — 29

INTRODUCTION	29
SEQUENTIAL SEARCH	31
Method	31
Algorithm	32
Example 2.1	32
Programs	33
Analysis	36
INTERNAL SORTING	37
Selection Sort	37
Method	37
Algorithm	38
Example 2.2	39
Programs	40
Analysis	42
Insertion Sort	42
Method	42
Algorithm	43
Example 2.3	43
Programs	45
Analysis	46
Exchange Sort	47
Method	47
Algorithm	47
Example 2.4	49
Programs	50
Analysis	52
BINARY SEARCH	52
Method	53
Algorithm	53
Example 2.5	54
Programs	56
Analysis	57
SUMMARY	58
EXERCISES	59

3 Faster Sorting 61

INTRODUCTION	61
TREES AND BINARY TREES	62
Trees	62
Binary Trees	64
LIMITS TO COMPARISON-BASED SORT ALGORITHMS	66
A DIVIDE-AND-CONQUER SORT	68
Quicksort	68
Method	68
Algorithm	69
Example 3.1	70
Programs	71
Example 3.2	74
Analysis	80
A TREE-BASED SORT	81
Creating a Heap	83
Heapsort	85
Method	85
Algorithm	86
Example 3.3	86
Program	87
Analysis	89
SUMMARY	90
EXERCISES	91

4 Storing Data 93

INTRODUCTION	93
LEVELS OF STORAGE	93
Registers	94
Cache	95
Main Memory	96

Online Bulk Storage 97
Remote File Storage 98
Offline Bulk Storage 98

SEQUENTIAL STORAGE DEVICES 98
Tape Drives 99
Card Readers 105
Printers 107

DIRECT ACCESS STORAGE DEVICES 108
Disk Storage 108

SUMMARY 114

EXERCISES 114

5 Responsibility: Protecting a Critical Resource 117

INTRODUCTION 117

DEFINITIONS 117

SECURITY 118
Physical Security 119
Legal Security 119
Administrative Security 120
Technological Security 120
    Passwords 121
    Encryption 122
        The Data Encryption Standard 123
        Public Key Systems in Networks 124
Control of Access 125

DATA INTEGRITY 128

PRIVACY 133

SUMMARY 137

EXERCISES 137

6 Sequential File Processing   139

INTRODUCTION	139
SEQUENTIAL FILES: A PHYSICAL ORGANIZATION	140
SEQUENTIAL FILES: A LOGICAL ORGANIZATION	140
Access Times	142
USES OF SEQUENTIAL PROCESSING	142
Batch Versus Sequential Processing	143
Batch Processing With Direct Access	143
Interactive Processing and Sequential Access	144
Batch Processing and Sequential Access	144
MERGING AND SORTING WITH SEQUENTIAL PROCESSING	144
Introduction	144
Merging Files	145
Two-Way Merge	145
Method	145
Algorithm	146
Example 6.1	146
Programs	147
Sorting by Merging	149
N-Way Natural Merge	149
Method	149
Algorithm	150
Example 6.2	150
Programs	151
Analysis	154
Other Methods	154
Balanced Merge	154
Polyphase Merge	155
Cascade Merge	157
APPLICATIONS OF SEQUENTIAL FILE PROCESSING	158
Summary Reports: The Control Break Problem	159
Defining the Problem	159
Presorted Order	160

viii Contents

    Formatting 160
    Method 161
    Algorithm 162
    Programs 164
  Sequential File Update: The Balance Line Algorithm 170
    Programs 173
SUMMARY 178
EXERCISES 179

7 Random File Processing   181

INTRODUCTION 181
DEFINITIONS 182
  Access Time 182
  Overhead 182
ORGANIZATION AND ACCESS 183
  Addressing Random Files 184
    Absolute Addresses 184
    Relative Addresses 185
    Indexed Addresses 185
  Selecting a File Organization 186
RANDOM ACCESS IN DIRECT FILE ORGANIZATION 186
  Directory Lookup 186
  Hashing 188
    Address Calculation 189
      Truncation 190
      Folding 191
      Multiplication 192
      Division-Remainder 192
    Relative File Access 194
    Collision Handling 195
      Open Addressing 195
      Chaining 199
  Dynamic Hashing 200
  Algorithms and Programs 203
    Algorithm for Address Calculation 203
    Programs for Address Calculation 204
    Algorithm for Collision Handling: Linear Probing 205

Contents   ix

    Programs for Collision Handling: Linear Probing 207
    Algorithm for Collision Handling: Chaining 209
    Programs for Collision Handling: Chaining 211
  Analysis of Collision Handling Methods 215

SUMMARY 216

EXERCISES 217

8 Indexed Sequential Access   219

INTRODUCTION 219

OVERVIEW 220

INDEXED SEQUENTIAL ACCESS METHOD (ISAM) 221
  Primary Data Area 222
  The Track Index 223
  Record Insertion 224
  Cylinder Overflow 224
  Independent Overflow Area 226
  Record Deletion 226
  Cylinder Index 227
  Master Index 227
  Summary of ISAM Index Levels 227

VIRTUAL BULK STORAGE 229
  SCOPE Indexed Sequential (SIS) Files 229
  Virtual Storage Access Method (VSAM) Files 229
    Entry Sequenced and Relative Record Data Sets 231
    Key Sequenced Data Sets 231
      Control Intervals and Control Areas 231
      Control Interval Definition Field, Record Definition Field 231
    Index Control Intervals 233
    Random Access 233
    Insertion and Deletion 234
    Control Interval Split 234
    Control Area Split 235
  VSAM-SIS Overflow Handling 235

B-TREES 236
  Balanced Trees 236
  B-Tree Properties 238
  Retrieval 238
  Tree Capacity 240

x Contents

    Insertion 242
    Deletion 245
B⁺-TREES 247
    Insertion 248
        Algorithm for Insertion 251
    Deletion 252
        Algorithm for Deletion 255
B*-TREES 256
    Properties 256
    Capacity 258
    Overflow Handling 258
SEARCH TIME COMPARISON 259
SUMMARY 259
EXERCISES 261

9 Multiple-key File Organizations   263

INTRODUCTION 263
INVERTED LISTS 264
    Duplicate Keys 265
    Structures for Inverted Lists 266
    Search Time 268
    Maintenance 268
    Inverted Lists in Indexed File Organizations 269
    Program Access to Inverted Lists in Indexed File Systems 269
LINKED LISTS IN FILES 271
    Multilists 271
        Maintenance 272
        Doubly Linked Lists 273
        Controlled Length Multilist 273
        Cellular Multilists 274
QUERY ALGORITHMS 275
    Conjunctive Queries 275
    Disjunctive Queries 279
    Compound Queries 280
SUMMARY 282
EXERCISES 283

10 Database Processing Concepts — 285

INTRODUCTION	285
BASIC TERMINOLOGY AND CONCEPTS	287
A Database's Three Levels of Abstraction	287
The Internal Level	289
The Conceptual Level	289
The External Level	290
The Human Components	290
The DBMS	292
DATA MODELS	293
Hierarchical Models	293
Network Models	297
Relational Models	299
CREATING A DATABASE	304
QUERY LANGUAGES	306
SQL-Based Systems	307
SECURITY AND PRIVACY MEASURES	309
APPLICATIONS AND TRENDS	311
Online Databases	311
Expert Systems	312
Fourth-Generation Languages	312
SUMMARY	313
EXERCISES	314

11 File Processing In Computer Networks — 317

INTRODUCTION	317
DEFINITIONS	317
COMPUTER NETWORKS	318
File transfer	320
Security, Integrity, and Privacy	320
REQUIREMENTS OF FILE SHARING	321
Movement of Files	321

xii   Contents

    Microhost Connection 323
    Storage Limitations 323

THE NETWORKED COMPUTER ENVIRONMENT 323
    Local Nets: Tokens versus Contention 324
    More General Network Communication 330
    Open Systems Interconnection 331

SUMMARY 331

EXERCISES 333

Appendix A—COBOL From Pseudocode   335

Appendix B—COBOL for Pascal Programmers: An Introduction   341

IDENTIFICATION DIVISION 342

ENVIRONMENT DIVISION 342

DATA DIVISION 343

PROCEDURE DIVISION 345
    Input/Output 345
    Data Manipulation and Computation. 346
    Control Structures 347

Appendix C—Pascal for COBOL Programmers: An Introduction   349

    Control structures 354

References, 357
Index, 361

PREFACE

INTRODUCTION

Computing, and the knowledge it involves, is such a broad field that two main approaches to its study have developed: computer science and information systems. While there are many differences between these two areas of study, there is a core of knowledge which is critical to both. Among the topics in the beginning level of this core are problem solving and programming methods, including the design, development, and analysis of algorithms; and methods for structuring, storing, retrieving, and manipulating data. In recent years, several course recommendations addressing the programming part of the core have emerged. Among them are the College Board 1983 recommendations for an advanced placement course in computer science, the ACM's CS1 and CS2 a few years later, and the DPMA's more recent model curriculum. Excellent textbooks based on these guidelines are available.

Curriculum recommendations of the ACM and DPMA also consider the data handling part of the core. The ACM's Curriculum '78 describes the course "Principles of File Processing" and the DPMA's model curriculum includes material on data files and programming techniques for file access. A preliminary version of a report by the ACM task force on the core of computer science has listed "Database and Information Retrieval" as one of nine core topic areas. Relatively few textbooks exist that address either the ACM's or the DPMA's guidelines, and no textbook attempts to incorporate the interests of both professional organizations.

Traditionally, computer science courses emphasize data structures, algorithms for sorting, searching, and manipulating the structures, and analysis of the algorithms. At the beginning level, courses usually assume data is stored in main memory. Pascal is an effective language for implementing algorithms on data stored internally. Information systems courses, on the other hand, concentrate on the storage of data on bulk storage devices, and on appropriate programming techniques for accessing such data. Combining individual units of data into records and files is emphasized. Analysis is concerned primarily with the storage space required and the time needed to retrieve a specific piece of data. COBOL is an effective language for implementing file processing in the information systems context.

We believe that both approaches have merit, and that all students in any type of computer science or information systems curriculum need to be exposed to the material of both. Consequently, this text includes algorithms for data manipulation, and complexity analyses of those algorithms. It includes physical characteristics of storage devices, organizations of large files on the storage devices, and access modes applied to those organizations. It includes the design, development, and programming illustrations of efficient algorithms, as well as explanations of the underlying methods of available file systems. The text provides for computer science students the knowledge of file processing methods they will need for designing systems that handle large amounts of data, such as the knowledge bases required for expert systems. It provides for information systems students the ability to develop and analyze algorithms that are fundamental to applications, such as providing online, interactive responses to information requests.

ORGANIZATION

As the title indicates, this text explores ways of organizing and accessing files so that useful information can be obtained from large collections of data. The text takes the reader from basic ideas about data, through techniques for manipulating records and organizing files, to databases and networks that incorporate the techniques so that users can obtain information.

Chapter 1 considers data from a logical and a physical perspective. Simple data types, such as integer, real, and character, and combination data types, such as arrays and records, are discussed from the two perspectives. An introduction to the kinds of files common to computer systems and to file processing is included.

Elementary search and sort methods are covered in Chapter 2. Only internal methods are treated. For each method, we give a description, an algorithm, an example to show how the algorithm works, programs in COBOL and Pascal, and an analysis of the algorithm in terms of the number of comparisons and the amount of memory required.

In Chapter 3, we establish a lower limit on the efficiency of sort methods based on comparisons and then discuss two internal sort methods—quicksort and heapsort—that reach the limit. Because heapsort is tree-based, basic properties of trees and binary trees are included.

Most of the topics in the first three chapters are often presented in programming courses. The topics are part of *this* text for several reasons. Internal search and sort methods are incorporated into external methods. Also, the material can provide a helpful review for some students and an introduction to new concepts for others. Instructors can cover the material as appropriate for their students and can be assured that all students have similar backgrounds before studying the concepts, techniques, and issues pertaining to large data files in the remaining chapters.

Chapter 4 represents a departure from the topics presented in earlier chapters. We address the physical characteristics of memory media, including magnetic tape and disk. Distinctions between absolute and relative addressing are identified. The ways in which files of records are stored on different media and how one or more than one record is accessed are illustrated.

Security, integrity, and privacy issues constitute Chapter 5. These issues are critical matters in file systems containing large amounts of data. Consequently, the topics are placed centrally in the text. Measures taken to maintain the security and integrity of data files help to protect individual privacy, and, more generally, confidentiality and accuracy of data. The issues in this chapter should be considered throughout the design and implementation of file organization and access, not as an afterthought.

Chapters 6–9 form the core of material dealing specifically with different file organizations and searching, sorting, and accessing records in large files stored externally. Chapter 6 treats access in sequential organizations. Because this organization permits only sequential access, sorting records in a file is done by merging. Combining two or more files into one sorted file also requires merging. Two applications of general interest are included—the control break problem for producing a summary report and the balanced line algorithm for sequentially updating a master file.

Chapter 7 deals with the random file organization. Files are organized to facilitate random access, in which a record is obtained directly by specifying an absolute or relative address. Static and dynamic hashing techniques are stressed.

The third type of access, indexed sequential, is the focus of Chapter 8. The corresponding file organization provides a compromise between sequential and random access. Indexed sequential access methods such as ISAM, SIS, and VSAM illustrate how the file organization supports both random and sequential access. B-trees and two variants, B^*- and B^+-trees, are discussed. Algorithms are included for inserting and deleting records in B^+-trees because of the importance of these structures in commercial products like SIS and VSAM, and in databases.

In Chapter 9, we depart from a discussion of file access based on one key and introduce multiple key access. To enable users to obtain information efficiently from a file by specifying values of more than one key, a file must have an organization for each key. Any organization discussed in Chapters 6–8 could be used, but other organizations such as inverted lists and multilists, which are introduced in this chapter, are also possible. Algorithms for handling multiple key queries, specifically the Hsiao-Harary algorithm, are included.

Database designers have available to them all of the concepts, methods, and organizations included in the first nine chapters. They must select and implement an appropriate combination of these techniques and organizations for the large amount of data in a database's multiple files so that different users can readily obtain information. Chapters 1–9, therefore, provide essential material for the discussion of databases in Chapter 10. Basic terminology and concepts of databases are covered. Hierarchical, network, and relational databases are illustrated, with more emphasis given to relational than to the other two architectures. Examples of security measures contained in several database languages are included. By the end of Chapter 10, students have a firm foundation for an advanced database course.

The last chapter in the text addresses the implications of networks on file processing. As computer networks become the norm rather than the exception, ordinary data access considerations must be expanded to include access to data on remote computing systems. File sharing between hosts and between microcomputers and hosts is considered, and use of common file transfer programs is demonstrated in Chapter 11.

LANGUAGES

There are many algorithms developed in the text. Each is developed with a top-down approach, with levels of detail increasing as the development progresses. Each algorithm is fully specified in a language-independent pseudocode. Nearly all are also illustrated in Pascal and COBOL. These two languages are selected to provide familiarity to the largest number of students using the text. The language implementations can be ignored, however, without any loss of any material in the algorithm development and analysis. We urge students to read the programs in both languages for the following reasons: to gain an idea of the diversity of languages for computer programming, to sense that different approaches can be used to solve the same problem, and to see that some problems are solved more easily in one language than in another because of the nature of the language. Three appendices are included to help in understanding the languages used.

Using this Text

This text is intended for college and university students in their second or third semester. It can be used to support very different courses, depending on the emphasis of the instructor. For instance, a course that emphasizes file organization and access will include some appreciation for the B$^+$-tree that supports the most common indexed file systems. A course that concentrates on data structures and efficient algorithms will include indexed file organization and access as an example of the B$^+$-tree being applied.

Material covered in Chapters 1–3 of this text is frequently included in first and second semester programming classes. It can be used as a review and summary. These chapters also serve as convenient references when the methods and concepts are needed in later chapters. Chapters 4–9 contain topics that belong to any course in file processing. Material in the last two chapters can be covered in whatever depth is allowed by the time available in the course.

Features

Introductions and Summaries. The introduction to each chapter provides students with an overview of the topics included in the chapter. The summary helps students to recall the important topics and concepts treated in depth in the chapter and serves as a bridge to the following chapter.

Chapter Highlights. Several chapters contain features that are usually not found in books on file processing. Insertion and deletion algorithms are given for B$^+$-trees rather than the simpler algorithms for B-trees found in a number of books. B$^+$-trees are more commonly used than B-trees in today's database implementations. The database chapter is included to illustrate a practical use of files and to provide, along with Chapters 1–9, suitable background for an advanced course in databases. Chapter 11 contains examples of the use of microcomputer-to-mainframe file uploads and mainframe-to-mainframe file transfers. These are important applications in networks.

Algorithms. Top-down design is used in the development of an algorithm. Several levels of refinement are included as appropriate. In addition, a prose description is given of each method before the algorithm is specified and an example is included to show how the algorithm works. Then the algorithm is implemented in COBOL and Pascal. An analysis is conducted to show the number of comparisons required by the algorithm and the amount of storage needed by the program.

Programming Languages. Algorithms in the text are implemented in both COBOL and Pascal. This enables instructors to use either language throughout the course. They can reference the second language implementation explicitly, or urge students to read the programs independently, or omit the second language entirely. One advantage in referencing both languages is that issues can be discussed that relate to choosing a language that is best suited to a particular application.

Appendices. Two appendices are included to facilitate the understanding of COBOL and Pascal by students who know one but not both of the languages. Because the pseudocode used for algorithms in the text adapts more readily to Pascal than to COBOL, a third appendix is included to illustrate the mapping of the pseudocode to COBOL.

Exercises. At the end of each chapter, there is a set of problems and questions of the following types:

- Thought questions to help students assimilate their knowledge of the material in the chapter. Some of these questions also require the integration of topics from other chapters.
- Problems containing sets of data that students can use to implement algorithms and programs included in the chapter.
- Questions that require students to design algorithms specifying problem solutions and then to write programs implementing and testing the algorithms.

Reference List. An extensive list of papers and books is included to encourage students to read additional material about topics in the book.

Instructor's Guide. A supplement to the book, the *Instructor's Guide* contains teaching notes, answers to exercises, a case study, and syllabi for three suggested course implementations. The case study incorporates most of the methods discussed in the book. The course implementations assume different amounts of programming language backgrounds—one semester of either COBOL or Pascal, two semesters of either language, and one semester of both languages. This text can be adapted for use in a second or third semester course for majors, or in an advanced level service course for students in other disciplines.

Acknowledgments

We are grateful to many people for their help in making this text a reality. The following reviewers contributed valuable suggestions: Robert P. Burton; Jack Cook; Alton R. Crawley, Ouachita Baptist University; Cindy Hanchey, Oklahoma Baptist University; Yedidyah Langsam, Brooklyn College; Kouros Mohit, University of the Pacific, and Vince Smith, DeKalb College.

A colleague at the University of Maryland, Roger Eastman, provided helpful ideas and approaches during numerous discussions.

Pam Kirshen believed that we could produce a book and committed D. C. Heath to the project. Lee Ripley managed to keep us working and on track. Her encouragement and sense of humor were invaluable.

There would not have been a book without the professional and timely assistance of Peggy J. Flanagan, Mark Fowler, Kim Wallin, and the rest of the staff of D. C. Heath.

How can we thank our families enough? Their encouragement, patience, and willingness to postpone activities are deeply appreciated.

Lillian Cassel
Richard Austing

CHAPTER 1

INTRODUCTION TO DATA: A LOGICAL VIEW AND ITS PHYSICAL ORGANIZATION

INTRODUCTION

There was a time when merchants knew most of their customers by name; goods were usually paid for with cash; the few credit accounts that did exist were small enough to maintain by hand; employers knew their employees personally; suppliers, workers, and distributors of the finished product were all familiar with each other; all payments, including salaries, were made in cash; and bookkeeping was done by hand. As time went on, however, businesses grew in size, attracted more customers, hired more employees, handled a larger variety of products, and dealt with more suppliers. With the change in scale of operations, it became necessary to systemize methods of record keeping. Large files were created to maintain and process the immense collections of information. Techniques were developed for organizing data in the files and the files themselves, first on paper in file cabinets, and later, on computer storage media such as tapes and disks. Today file organization and processing are major computer application areas, and they are the main concern of this book.

In Chapter 1 the basics of data representation and the most important types of files for computer use are reviewed. The chapters that follow include methods of keeping files in order so that they can be searched efficiently, techniques for storing files so that data can be retrieved effectively, and kinds of file organizations for handling the ever-growing volume of data. Issues of security, integrity, and privacy of critical data are treated early in the book to emphasize their importance. The final topics—computer networks and data base systems—incorporate files in more complex systems.

Perhaps the most obvious uses of file processing techniques are in the business world, but large collections of data are accumulated and must be examined, sorted, searched, retrieved, protected, and communicated in many other areas as well. Data from satellites helps us understand the origin and future of our universe, and predict tomorrow's weather. Scouting reports and other data are incorporated into game strategies to produce effective game plans. Data on rainfall, temperatures, and soil characteristics provides the means for determining how to feed the world's population. Data on the incidence of disease helps in identifying causes and searching for cures. Some data collection seems frivolous to most of us; some is critical to all of us. In any case, data must all be stored, searched, sorted, retrieved, updated, manipulated, communicated, and combined with other data to make a meaningful whole. That is the subject of this book.

REPRESENTATION OF DATA

An understanding of data is of fundamental importance in the study of file processing. After all, files consist of data and it is data that is manipulated when files are processed.

In computing, there are two aspects of data—one logical and the other physical. The logical representation of data refers to a class of objects (such as integers), their attributes, values, and the operations that can be performed with them. Logically, each specific instance of integer is a whole number with attributes sign, size, and so forth. For example, the integer 3 has the value 3 and the attribute "positive." The integer with value –3 has the attribute "negative." We can add, subtract, multiply, and divide integers. Their range of values is infinite. The physical representation of data pertains to how data is represented within storage. For example, an integer may be stored as a binary number in a fixed-length word of memory. The size of the memory location restricts the range of values that an integer can take within a program.

The following analogy may make the distinction between logical and physical representations of data clearer. The term "human being" is a logical representation. It distinguishes one class of objects from other classes such as insects, plants, and rocks. Elements of this class—that is, human beings—have specific attributes, values, and operations. Each specific instance of human being is a person (value) with attributes that include name, height, and the ability to think. Each individual person is a value that a human being can take. The attributes describe the value, that is, the person who is a member of the class human being. Operations among human beings might include communicating, working together, and marrying. The physical representation of human beings has to do with how a human being is depicted. For example, a human may be shown as having hands, feet, head, muscles, veins, etc. Different levels of detail may be used for different purposes.

DATA TYPES: THE LOGICAL REPRESENTATION OF DATA

A commonly used term for the logical representation of data in a programming language is **data type**. A data type is a class of objects together with a set of attributes and operations for creating and manipulating the objects. **Integer** and **record** are examples of data types. "Human being" would also be a data type if it were part of a programming language. To specify a data type, we identify the attributes that distinguish its data objects, the values they can take, and the operations used to manipulate them.

Data types existed in the early versions of programming languages, such as FORTRAN and BASIC, but were not always explicitly declared. In FORTRAN, for example, variable names beginning with I, J, K, L, M, or N were assumed to take integer values. ALGOL 60 was the first language to require explicit type declarations.

Explicit type declaration simplifies compiler design. Another advantage of explicitness is that the consistency of statements can be checked by ensuring that variables take correct values. That is, a statement can be identified as inconsistent if two or more of its variables have different data types explicitly declared earlier in the program. For example, if x and j are declared *character* and *integer*, respectively, then the statement $j = j+x$ is inconsistent.

Some data types play greater roles than others in file processing. Specifically, integer, real, character, string, array, and record are some of the data types in files and in operations involving files. Some of the characteristics of these data types are reviewed in the following sections.

Three data types—integer, real, and character—are called **simple data types** because each value occupies a single memory location. There are more complex data types—string, array, and record—whose specifications incorporate multiple occurrences of a simple data type or a combination of data types. These are referred to as **composite data types.** For example, a string is a number of characters, and a record can consist of integers, characters, strings, and arrays.

Simple Data Types

Integer

The data type **integer** is common to most programming languages. A representative of type integer is one of the whole numbers from the set

$$\{0, \pm 1, \pm 2, \pm 3, \ldots, \pm n\}$$

where n is the largest integer (whole number) that can be implemented on a specific computer. In Pascal, this largest value is available as the constant MAXINT, and the range of integer values, then, is −MAXINT (or −MAXINT−1 in implementations using 2's complement arithmetic) to MAXINT. The actual value of MAXINT depends on how integers are represented on any specific computer.

In COBOL, integers are stored in one of several ways, depending upon how they are to be used. An integer may serve as a piece of identification, such as a social security number, a part number, the house number in a street address, or the identification of a particular farm field or lab specimen. Operations performed on these descriptive integers are reading and writing, and possibly comparison. Such integers are used most efficiently if treated as strings of characters.

An integer that is to be used in computations is stored differently from the character representation. COBOL provides two forms for numeric storage of integers: binary representation and packed decimal representation. Pure binary representation occupies one word of storage and has the same characteristics as an integer stored in a Pascal program. The binary representation is much more efficient for calculations and is especially useful for index and subscript values that are seldom printed. Packed decimal representation consists of a string of digits, each coded in binary. The packed decimal form is more efficient for computations, but is a more complex representation. On the other hand, packed decimal values are easily converted to and from character form for display. The choice of form is dependent upon use. An integer that is mainly used for display, but must have some calculations performed on it, is best stored as a packed decimal. An integer that is used as a loop index or an array subscript should be stored as a binary value.

Pascal requires that all integer constants and variables (i.e., named objects that take integer values) be declared at the beginning of a program or procedure. For example,

```
const minimumage = 21;
var j,k : integer;
```

declares MINIMUMAGE to be the name of a constant that has the integer value 21 throughout its life in the program, and j, k to be the names of variables that will take integer values. Presumably, the values of j and k will change from time to time when the program is executed.

COBOL uses a PICTURE clause in its DATA DIVISION to declare integer variables. All variables must be declared explicitly. For example,

```
TOTAL     PICTURE 99999
DOLLARS   PICTURE X(8)
```

declares TOTAL to be a variable that takes a five-digit numerical value, such as 34231, and DOLLARS to be a string of eight alphanumeric characters. This string, therefore, could appear as an integer, but it could also be any other string of letters and numbers.

Operations on integers in Pascal include the usual binary operations of +, −, and *, as well as the unary operation −. Pascal also has the two functions **div** and **mod**, which produce the integer quotient and remainder, respectively, of a division of two integers. Relational operators are =, <>, >, ≥, <, and ≤. The functions **ord, pred,** and **succ** are also available. If the parameter x of these functions is an integer, say 24, then **ord**(x) returns the integer itself (the value 24), **pred**(x) returns the predecessor of x (the value 23), and **succ**(x) returns the successor of x (the value 25).

COBOL allows addition, subtraction, multiplication, and division to be written in statement form; for example,

```
ADD J,K GIVING L
MULTIPLY LENGTH BY WIDTH GIVING AREA .
```

or, more concisely,

```
COMPUTE L = J + K
COMPUTE AREA + LENGTH * WIDTH .
```

COBOL also allows the form

```
DIVIDE A BY B GIVING C REMAINDER D
```

where C and D, respectively, correspond to the results of **div** and **mod** of Pascal. Relational operators are IS EQUAL TO (or =), IS GREATER THAN (or >), and IS LESS THAN (or <).

Real

Another data type for numbers is called **real**. A real number is a number that can be expressed as a whole number followed by a fraction, either or both of which could be zero. Attributes, values, and operations for objects having data type real vary more than integers in their language and hardware implementations.

In Pascal, real or **floating-point real** numbers can be written in two forms—as decimal numbers (e.g., 34.5, 0.07, 1864.0, −567.8) or in scientific notation (e.g., 3.45e1, 7.0e−2, 1.864e3, −5.678e2). Scientific notation is a shorthand version for writing powers of ten. That is, 1.864e3 is the same as $1.864*10^3$; both have the value 1864.0. The range of possible values depends on the hardware implementation.

COBOL has the capacity for floating-point real operations, but also implements **fixed-point real** numbers, which are represented by a fixed-length digit sequence with a decimal point located between two of the digits. For example, using the PICTURE clause, a variable described as

```
PIC 999V99
```

would hold values such as 287.43, 027.09, or 000.01. The clause reserves space for five digits. The logical position of the decimal point is defined by the placement of the V.

Declarations of reals in both languages are similar to integers. In Pascal, for example,

```
const pi = 3.14159;
var x,y,percent: real;
```

declares a real constant *pi* with the value 3.14159 throughout its life in the program, and the real variables *x*, *y*, *percent*, that will be assigned values within the program. COBOL requires a PICTURE clause as described earlier.

The same arithmetic and relational operations for integers are provided for reals except for **ord, pred,** and **succ.** These three functions have no meaning for real numbers; there is no unique predecessor or successor of 2.3456, for example. The operator / represents ordinary division. In Pascal, **div** and **mod** are not used with reals. COBOL allows both integers and fixed-point reals in the form

```
DIVIDE A BY B GIVING C REMAINDER D
```

In addition to the arithmetic operations, Pascal includes a number of predefined functions such as **sqrt** (square root) and **log** (logarithm).

Character

A data object of type **character** is one member of the set of available characters provided by the language or hardware implementation. Usually the set includes letters of the alphabet (upper and lower case), digits, and special symbols such as *, $, :, !, and @.

Pascal declarations of constants and variables of type character are similar to those of integers and reals. For example,

```
const star = '*';
var ch1,ch2,first: char;
```

declare *star* to have the value * throughout its life in the program and *ch1*, *ch2*, *first* to take values that are single characters. Similar declarations in COBOL would appear in the WORKING-STORAGE SECTION as follows:

```
01 SINGLE-CHARACTERS.
   03 CH1     PIC X.
   03 CH2     PIC X.
   03 FIRST   PIC X.
```

There are no arithmetic operations on objects of data type character. Relational operations are provided, however, and are based on the ordering in a specific character set, for example, ASCII (American Standard Code for Information Interchange). That ordering is called the **collating sequence** for the character set. Thus, alphabetical sorting can be accomplished by such statements as IF CH1 < CH2 ..., where < now means "comes before in the collating sequence." The functions **ord**, **pred**, and **succ** are also available for characters. If a, b, c are successive characters in a collating sequence, then **ord**(b) < **ord**(c), **pred**(c) = b, and **succ**(b) = c.

Composite Data Types

String

A **string**, or **character string**, is a sequence of characters. Examples of strings include

```
ABCD
926.tk
```

and any word, sentence, or paragraph. An attribute called **length**, the number of characters in a string, is declared in a program or may vary dynamically during program execution. The values of strings are sequences of characters. Operations on strings include concatenation (joining the beginning of one string to the end of another to make one string), and substring selection (identifying consecutive characters that are contained in a string). Strings can also be compared and ordered using relational operations.

The string data type is implemented in some Pascal compilers (e.g., UCSD Pascal and TURBO Pascal), but not in standard Pascal. Strings in standard Pascal are handled in one of two ways: either each character in a string is considered an element of a file of type **text** and is processed one character at a time, or the entire string is a value of the type **packed array**. For example, the declarations

```
const stringsize = 5;
type string = packed array [1..stringsize] of char;
var zipcode: string;
```

create a five-character string variable (or packed array) named *zipcode*. When a statement such as

```
zipcode := '12345';
```

is executed, the string value '12345' is stored in the packed array *zipcode*.

In COBOL, all data objects are stored as strings at run time, except numeric data declared with a USAGE IS COMPUTATIONAL or USAGE IS INDEX clause. Strings are declared with a PICTURE clause, as we illustrated in previous examples.

Array

Logically, an **array** is an ordered collection of like objects arranged in a pattern that allows easy reference and retrieval. A **linear array** or **vector** is a simple list such as

27, 33, 14, 9, 18, 38, 29, 14, 17

A **two-dimensional array**, or **matrix**, is organized into rows and columns by some common features. For example, the number of pupils at each grade level (1–6) in three schools could be listed as

40, 26, 27, 33, 14, 9, 18, 38, 29, 14, 17, 18, 20, 43, 19, 16, 34, 40

where the first six numbers correspond to grades 1 through 6 of the first school, the next six numbers are from the second school, etc. More commonly this data is displayed in an arrangement of rows and columns, as shown here:

	Grade Level					
	1	2	3	4	5	6
School 1	40	26	27	33	14	9
School 2	18	38	29	14	17	18
School 3	20	43	19	16	34	40

In addition to making it easier to find the enrollment in grade 4 of the second school, such an arrangement facilitates other operations, such as row sums (total enrollment in school 1) and column sums (total enrollment in sixth grade).

A three-dimensional array is a collection of related tables. Suppose the enrollment data is repeated for each of four districts in a county. Then the data could be displayed as four pages of tables, as in Figure 1.1. In general, arrays of many dimensions can be defined and used as required by an application. All of the pages of tables for a county could be placed in a box, with another box next to it containing tables for another county. To retrieve a particular value, a user would specify the box (county), page (district), row (school), and column (grade). Regardless of how large the number of dimensions grows, the data object stored in each position remains a simple integer.

An array has three attributes: the number of objects, their data type, and subscripts to select each data object. Subscripts are normally of data type integer. For one-dimensional arrays, subscripts are a set of consecutive integer values in which the *j*th subscript indicates the *j*th

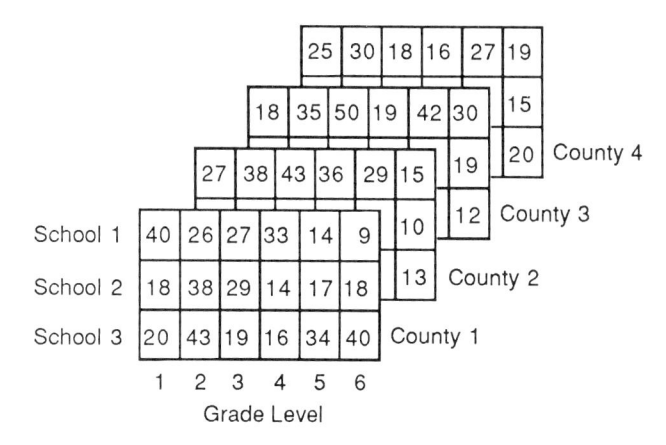

Figure 1.1 *A three-dimensional array.*

object. The number of subscripts in the set is the number of data objects. For example, the set 0, 1, 2, 3, ..., 9 represents an array that has ten data objects, and the fourth subscript, 3, identifies the fourth object. An array of higher dimensions has a set of subscripts for each dimension and a number of objects equal to the product of the numbers in the sets. Thus, a two-dimensional array with subscripts 1, 2, 3, 4 and 1, 2, 3, 4, 5, 6 has 4*6 = 24 data objects. Only one data type, either simple or composite, is specified for an array's objects, because they all must be of the same type.

Operations on arrays include subscripting, which selects a data object from an array, and replacing, which changes the value of a data object. Insertion and deletion cannot be done because arrays are of fixed size. Some languages include operations such as addition and subtraction of whole arrays.

In Pascal, the one-dimensional array *grades* containing data objects 90, 58, 87, 76, and 65 could have been declared as follows:

```
type gradearray = array [1..5] of integer;
var grades : gradearray;
```

This declaration specifies the array type *gradearray* as a one-dimensional array containing five integers and *grades* as a variable of type *gradearray* (i.e., *grades* is an array with five integers). In particular, *grades[1]* has the value 90, *grades[2]* the value 58, ..., *grades[5]* the value 65. The declaration

```
var grades : array [1..5] of integer;
```

has a similar implementation.

Multidimensional arrays can be declared in Pascal in two ways:

```
var counts: array [1..counties] of
                array [1..districts] of
                    array [1..schools] of
                        array [1..grades] of
                            integer;
```

or

```
var counts: array [1..counties, 1..districts,
                   1..schools, 1..grades] of integer;
```

Both cases declare a structure containing integer values. The first description corresponds more closely to the logical view of the data. An array of boxes (counties) is declared in which each box is an array of tables (districts), each table is an array of rows (schools), and each row is an array of integers (grade levels). The second description is a shorthand form for the same declaration. It simply specifies that there are four subscripts required to access each integer in this array. The choice of names for array bounds gives clues as to the significance of each subscript.

Strings can be implemented as a one-dimensional character array in Pascal. For example,

```
var address : array [1..13] of char;
```

contains a string of thirteen characters, one character per memory location. With this declaration, the *j*th character in the string is referenced by *address[j]*. The declaration of a string as a packed array in the previous section is implemented by some compilers by storing more than one character in a memory location.

In COBOL, arrays, also called **tables**, are declared by means of OCCURS clauses. The previous *gradearray* example would appear as follows:

```
01  GRADE-LIST.
    03  GRADES OCCURS 5 TIMES    PIC 99.
```

Because each subscript in COBOL ranges from 1 to the number of times specified in the OCCURS clause, this declaration sets up an array that could contain the five grades in the example above. GRADE-LIST is the name of the one-dimensional array or vector.

A two-dimensional array is declared by including an additional level of nesting. For example,

```
01  ARRAY.
    03  ROW OCCURS 5 TIMES.
        05  COLUMN OCCURS 6 TIMES    PIC 999.
```

declares a five-row by six-column array of three-digit integers. Higher dimensional arrays are declared in a similar manner. For example, our enrollment information would appear in a form similar to the first version of the Pascal declaration:

```
01 ENROLLMENTS.
   03 COUNTY OCCURS 2 TIMES.
      05 DISTRICT OCCURS 4 TIMES.
         07 SCHOOL OCCURS 3 TIMES.
            09 GRADE OCCURS 6 TIMES.
               11 ENROLLMENT    PIC 9(5).
```

In general, each OCCURS clause can declare a one-dimensional array with objects of simple or composite data type.

Record

A **record** is a group of related data objects contained in **fields**. Each field is referred to by a name and contains an object of simple or composite data type. For example, an employee's record may have a social security number field containing a nine-digit integer; a last name field and a first name field, each containing a character string; a salary field containing a real number; and so on. The employee's record can also have a positions field which holds a record containing fields for position titles, descriptions, and dates of employment.

Attributes of a record data type include the number and types of fields and how they are organized. Operations on records include changing and selecting, or accessing, a field's contents.

Records can be fixed-length (all records are the same size) or variable-length. Only fixed-length records are included below.

In Pascal, a record is declared in one of two ways.

```
(i)   type
         name = packed array [1..20] of char;
         grades = array [1..6] of integer;
         gradebook = record
            studentname : name;
            studentid : integer;
            finalgrade : char;
            finalaverage : real;
            testgrades : grades;
         end;
      var cmsc100 : gradebook;
```

or

```
(ii)  var cmsc100 : record;
            studentname : packed array [1..20] of char;
            studentid : integer;
            finalgrade : char;
            finalaverage : real;
            testgrades : array [1..6] of integer;
         end;
```

Both versions specify a record named *cmsc100* whose fields could contain values such as 'John J. Johnson' for *studentname*, 765432 for *studentid*, 'B' for *finalgrade*, 82.5 for *finalaverage*, and 72, 85, 93, 80, 90, 75 for *testgrades[1]*, *testgrades[2]*, ..., *testgrades[6]*. Version (i) is considered to be better style than version (ii).

In Pascal, a sequence of elements of the same type—for example, integers, reals, strings, records—can be combined to form a structure called a **file.** The declaration

```
type gradefile = file of gradebook;
```

names "gradefile" as a file type. It contains records specified as in "gradebook" above. Variables can then be declared to be of file type. For example,

```
var cmsc100grades, cmsc201grades : gradefile;
```

declares two files of records specified by "gradebook".

In COBOL, the record is the fundamental data structure. Records are declared in a program's DATA DIVISION by putting other data type declarations (one for each field) in an outline format. Level numbers are used as in the specification of an array in the previous section.

COBOL also allows declarations of mixed structures containing both records and arrays (as does Pascal). For example,

```
01   UNIVERSITY-ENROLLMENT.
     03   STUDENT-TOTAL   PICTURE   9(5).
     03   COLLEGE OCCURS 10 TIMES.
          05   COLLEGE-NAME   PICTURE   X(20).
          05   COLLEGE-ENROLLMENT   PICTURE   9(4).
          05   NUMBER-DEPARTMENTS   PICTURE   99.
```

is a record named UNIVERSITY-ENROLLMENT. It contains a five-digit field for the total number of students in the university, and a one-dimensional array (vector) COLLEGE of ten objects, each of which is a record having three fields.

STORAGE MAPPING; A PHYSICAL REPRESENTATION OF DATA

The transition of logical to physical representation can be expressed as a mapping of a data type into storage. The physical representations of simple data types are considered first because their mappings are the most direct—one value of the data type into one memory location. Composite data types are then shown to have mappings which require decisions from among several choices.

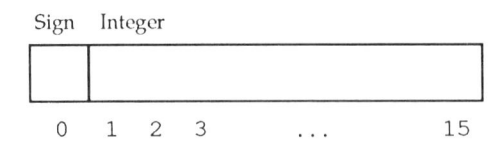

Figure 1.2 Physical representation of an integer in a 16-bit memory location.

Integer, Real, and Character Data Types

In Pascal, a value of data type integer, namely, an integer, is stored in one memory location (Figure 1.2). The first bit in the location or cell is the sign bit, which indicates whether the integer is positive or negative. The sign bit for 0 is usually the same as for positive integers. The remaining bits in the cell represent the integer's value. This representation restricts the range of values of integers to the maximum value (minimum value in the case of negative integers) that can be represented in binary using the number of bits in the memory cell. In particular, the set of integer values cannot be infinite.

In COBOL, integers declared with a USAGE IS COMPUTATIONAL clause are represented in the same way as just noted. Otherwise, an integer is stored as a character string. In the latter case, each digit is represented by eight bits according to the code (e.g., ASCII) being implemented, and large integers span two or more memory cells. Alternatively, an integer can be stored as a string of digits, the packed decimal form mentioned earlier. The advantage of this approach is that the number of digits used to make one integer is variable. If a number is known to need only one or two digits, an appropriate PICTURE clause reserves the space. If a longer number is required, the PICTURE clause specifies more digits. Because each digit is stored separately rather than merged into a binary value, the transition to and from display form is easily accomplished.

The physical representation of a value of data type real is different for floating-point and fixed-point reals. Storing a floating-point real number—for example, 52.125—involves the following steps:

Step 1. Convert the number to binary: 110010.001

Step 2. Normalize so that the point is just to the left of the first 1:
$110010.001 = .110010001 \times 2^6$

Step 3. Store the mantissa and exponent in the form required by a particular computer, such as

Introduction to Data   15

```
Sign  Sign
of    of
no.   exp.  Exponent                Mantissa

 0    0   000110   110010001000000000000000
```

There are many variations on this basic form, but they are the subject of other courses. The important points are the following:

1. The exponent and mantissa are stored as two separate entities, and each has a limited range of possible values. The exponent determines how *large* a value can be. The mantissa determines how many places of *precision* can be maintained.
2. The format of a floating-point real number is very different from the format of an integer stored in binary. If we ask that the integer 52 and the floating point 52.125 be added, the computer will have to copy the integer into another storage location, convert it to floating-point form (as 52.0), and then do the addition. The extra steps slow down the mathematical operations considerably.
3. The floating-point form is not similar to the display form and requires significant conversion effort.

COBOL includes the option of floating-point real storage also. In IBM COBOL, for example, the option is selected by specifying USAGE IS COMPUTATIONAL-1 (single precision) or COMPUTATIONAL-2 (double precision). However, because of the nature of the applications most frequently coded in COBOL, the fixed-point real form is more frequently used.

In fixed-point form, the real number 52.125 would be stored as follows. First, the COBOL declaration should include the number of places (a 9 for each digit) and the location (V) of the decimal point:

```
PICTURE 99V999.
```

The number 52.125 begins in display form, with each digit occupying an 8-bit byte (in hexadecimal):

```
F5 F2 F1 F2 F5
```

Note that the decimal point does not appear. The compiler will generate code to account for the location of the point in any computations. The number is then converted to packed decimal form for computing:

```
52 12 5F
```

Only three 8-bit bytes are needed now, and all the "zone" fields (the F's) have been removed, except one. Adding this number, 52.125, to the packed integer 52 is simply a matter of lining up the digits correctly. Returning the fixed decimal representation to display form is straightforward:

```
52 12 5F
F5 F2 F1 F2 F5
```

All computations require a numeric form of the operators. Any data name defined in DISPLAY form represents a value that must be converted to a computational form before any arithmetic operations can be carried out. Computations involving operands of different computational forms (i.e., binary integer, floating point, and packed decimal) require that conversions be done before the computation is carried out. Program execution is more efficient if data fields to be combined are defined consistently.

Computations in packed decimal are done digit by digit and are much slower than the corresponding binary operations. On the other hand, every decimal value can be represented accurately. Floating-point representations in binary cannot encode such common decimal values as 0.20 exactly. The approximations they use are very close to the correct value, but can lead to small errors. Applications that process dollars and cents are more conveniently processed with fixed-point representation.

Characters (values of data type character) are represented in memory by the 8-bit code defined for a particular character set. For example, the letter k is 01000111 in ASCII and 01100110 in EBCDIC (Extended Binary Coded Decimal Interchange Code). More than one character can be packed into the same memory location in computers with memory cells of 16 bits or more.

String, Array, and Record Data Types

The mapping of composite data types into storage is determined by the hardware implementation and by the programmer's declaration. Underlying any implementation is the fundamental fact that memory locations are addressed by consecutive integers. This implies that values stored in contiguous locations can be accessed (by the system or under program control) successively by incrementing an integer. In the following discussion, composite data types are mapped into contiguous locations.

In both COBOL and Pascal, strings are stored in consecutive locations. The declarations in the languages,—PICTURE clause in COBOL and packed array in Pascal—specify the length of the string. This determines

```
    A    B    C         (a)  A          (b)  A
                              B               D
    D    E    F              C               G
                              D               B
    G    H    I              E               E
                              F               H
                              G               C
                              H               F
                              I               I
```

Figure 1.3. *A two-dimensional array and its mapping into (a) row-major and (b) column-major order.*

how many locations are allocated. For example, in COBOL, if X(6) were declared, the string ABCDE would be stored in six consecutive bytes, including a blank in the sixth byte. In Pascal, on a 16-bit machine, if **packed array[1 . . 6] of char** were declared, the string would be stored in three consecutive 16-bit locations as follows:

```
    AB    CD    Eb
```

where b represents a blank.

Arrays are stored in consecutive memory locations as if they were one-dimensional. This means that the components of arrays of one dimension are mapped into locations in the same order as they appear in the array. However, arrays of two or more dimensions must be mapped into a linear order for storing. This can be accomplished by using row-major or column-major order, as illustrated in Figure 1.3. Implementations utilizing row-major order for a two-dimensional array store all components in the first row, then the components in the second row, then the third, and so on. Column-major order consists of storing all components in the first column, then the components in the second column, and so on. Storage of arrays of three or more dimensions follow similar patterns. In high-level languages like Pascal, programmers reference components by specifying subscripts (row and column numbers). The system converts them into a single integer value to obtain the component's address in storage.

Records are stored in a contiguous block of memory locations. The contents of any location within the block depends on how the record was specified in a declaration. In COBOL, for example, a record that does not involve an item declared as COMPUTATIONAL is nothing more than a character string. In both Pascal and COBOL each field within a record is of a data type such as integer, real, character, string, array, or another record.

File Systems

As we have seen, data is stored and used in different ways for different purposes. The requirements of a particular application affect the way data is viewed and used. In the previous section, the logical and physical representations of data were viewed at a microscopic level. The principal concerns were with bits, bytes, and words; with numbers, characters, and strings; and with individual values and arrays of related values. It is now time to take a macroscopic view and consider **files**, which frequently are large collections of related pieces of information. This larger view looks at the common characteristics shared by many types of files and includes ways to separate files into different types. The perspective here will be logical. Later, in Chapter 4, the perspective shifts to the physical constraints imposed by a number of file storage media.

Text, Binary, and Code Files

One way to classify files is by the amount of machine intervention required to get to the information stored in the file. Three types of files in this category are text, binary, and code files. These files can contain the same information, but in different forms, as suggested by their names.

All computer-usable data is encoded in zeros and ones. Some devices are able to accept and use any combination of bits given to them. Disk and tape media, for example, store bits without regard to what they represent. Other devices, however, are able to use only specific combinations of bits. For instance, a printer prints a particular symbol depending on the code given it; a particular string of bits represents the letter A; another string of bits represents the number 7, etc. When a printer is given a string of bits that does not correspond to any code it is able to translate, it is unable to print meaningful characters. A printer or a terminal display screen is able to use only bit strings representing data encoded as characters—that is, **text data**.

A file consisting of text data is called a **text** file. It may be stored on disk or tape. When a text file is to be printed, the bit representations of characters are transferred to the printer where they are used to select the right symbol to put on paper. The transfer involves very little interpretation and is quickly and easily done. Text files are very convenient when the data will be displayed frequently.

Unlike text files, **binary** files contain data that is meaningful only if interpreted properly. The data is represented in a way that does not correspond to the codes recognized by display devices. In general, the number of bits required to store data in binary form is significantly smaller than the number of bits needed to store the same data as characters. Numbers stored in straight binary representation, therefore, can be read faster by a program and can be used more easily to do calculations. Binary files are appropriate for data that must be used by programs, but does not need to be displayed. To print the contents of a file of binary data, it is necessary to read the data with a program, convert the data to display (text or character) form, and then print it. Since very few files need to be displayed without being formatted by a program first, binary files are important for storing frequently-used data.

A third form of file contains neither text nor binary-coded numbers. A **code** file contains the executable version of a program. This is the program in machine language, the form that the computer actually uses. It does not contain recognizable statements of COBOL, Pascal, or any other language. In fact, once a program is in code form, it is impossible to determine the language in which it was originally written. This is a very useful feature, for it makes it possible to write modules of a program in different languages and link them together to make a final executable code file. When a program is run, it is the code file that is loaded into the computer's memory and executed. In its code file form, a program is meaningful only to the computer for which it was translated.

Unfortunately the file names **text**, **binary**, and **code** are not uniformly used. Though all computers use and recognize files of these general descriptions, the names vary according to the computer manufacturer. For example, the compiled version of a program in an IBM VM/CMS system is given a name such as PROG.TXT, where the TXT stands for text, but indicates an executable, rather than a printable, file. Distinguishing the three files in a particular computer system requires careful reading of the manufacturer's documentation.

Master, Transaction, and Temporary Files

In addition to the form in which their contents are stored, files can be classified according to their use. The classification into master, transaction, and temporary files is common (Figure 1.4). These names and divisions are not intended to be all-inclusive, but to describe some common file types.

A **master** file is used to store data that is used continuously in some application area. A master file might be a list of magazine subscribers, including their addresses, dates of subscription expiration, and other useful information. Another example is an employee master file containing information about employees and used for many purposes such as payroll, insurance information, etc. Another master file might contain information about airline schedules. In general, master files need to last a long time and need to be kept up-to-date. A master file plays a key part in one or more applications, and its integrity is of critical importance to its owners. Because a master file must be kept up-to-date, it is vulnerable to damage during the updating process. Therefore, one or

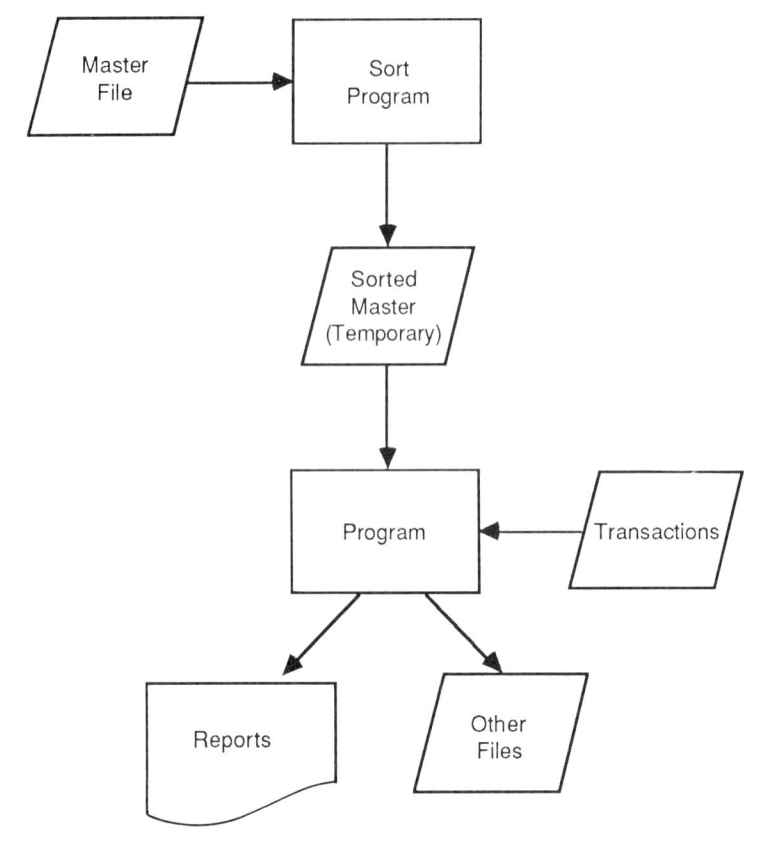

Figure 1.4 The relationships among file types.

more back-up copies of the master file are kept to minimize the danger of loss.

Transaction files are used to collect data to be used in updating a master file. A transaction file is frequently created by data entry operators keying information originally recorded on forms. The possibility of error in a transaction file is high; error can result from a mistake in the way the form was filled out or from a keying error. Since the content of the transaction file will be used to update the master file, some preprocessing is frequently done to verify the contents of the transaction file. An **edit** program will read the transaction file and examine each field for reasonable values. Not all errors can be found, but many will be. A name entered as John R. Jomes, instead of John R. Jones, will probably escape detection. However, if a time of day is listed as 12:95 instead of 12:45, a program can easily detect the out-of-range value. A field claiming 85 hours of work in one week may be correct, but is suspicious. An edit program will print out a warning of this value to be reviewed by human monitors. The number can be verified and allowed to remain, or corrected, whichever is appropriate. Verifying the data in transaction files is tedious and difficult, but it is very important if the master file is to remain uncorrupted.

Unlike transaction files, which are frequently preserved for back-up purposes, **temporary** files are intended to hold intermediate results for short-term use. In some cases, the temporary, or **scratch**, file is created by a program to hold data that does not fit into memory and that will be used later by the same program that created it. Temporary files are common to sort/merge techniques for sorting large files.

Some temporary files are created by one program in order to be used almost immediately by another program as part of a system. For instance, suppose a college soccer coach acquires one file containing data on students in high schools in a particular area, and a second file containing a list of players in a local soccer league. Because the coach is interested in recruiting soccer players who are also good students, he or she uses a program to pick out from the high school file those students who are juniors or seniors and whose grades meet specified criteria. (Examples of this nature involve issues pertaining to the privacy rights of individuals.) The program selects eligible students and records their names, addresses, and grades in a temporary file. The file is sorted to match the order of the file of soccer players. Now a search begins to match names in the two files. Each time a match occurs, the information about that student is recorded in a new file of good students/soccer players. When complete, this new file is kept for use in sending letters and glossy brochures. The temporary file can then be discarded because it is no longer needed. Figure 1.5 illustrates the flow of data and the use of the files.

Program Files

Files associated with programs are also important. A program frequently involves three different files: a **source** file, a **code** file, and a **listing** file. The **source** file contains the original program in text form. It is easily displayed on a terminal or dumped to a printer. The file is created with an editor and can use the editor again to make changes in the program. Once the program is compiled, the source file is no longer needed on a regular basis. The source file cannot be executed by the computer; it exists only as a vehicle by which the programmer enters statements in a high-level language.

When programs are purchased, the source file is frequently not included. This means that the buyer can run the program exactly as it was written, but cannot make any modifications in the way in which it operates. If the program does not exactly suit the way the buyer performs a particular function, the buyer has a choice of modifying practices to

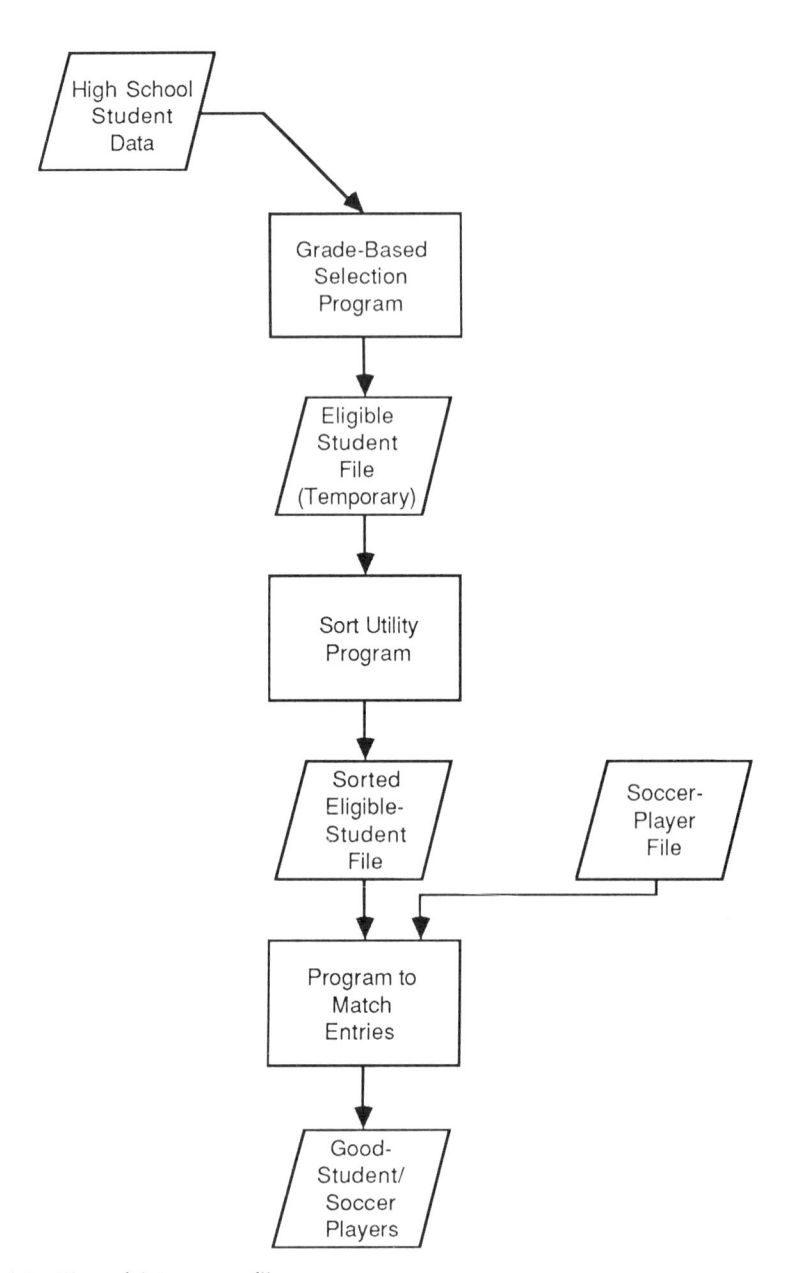

Figure 1.5 Flow of data among files.

match the program or writing a program. When the source code is included in the purchase, the buyer can make changes to the source file, recompile it, and then proceed to use the new version of the program. Of course, if the modifications are not done carefully, the new program may not work at all!

Once the source file has been submitted to a compiler, a **code** file (also called an **object** file) is produced. As already noted, this file contains representations of instructions the computer is to carry out in a form that is usable by a computer, but not readable by humans. (In some systems, the code file generated by a compiler must be linked to actual machine locations before being executed.) The instructions encoded in this file are what the computer will carry out each time the program is run. Since the time needed to compile a program is often substantial, programs are written so that modifications are seldom needed. Thus the source file can be stored offline and largely ignored. The code file, however, is kept accessible so that it will be ready whenever the program is to be run.

A third file associated with programs is the **listing** file. This file is produced by the compiler while it is translating the source into object code. Not all compilers produce a listing, and in some cases it is an option. When the listing file is produced, it contains a copy of the original statements of the program with some additions. In the early stages of program entry and testing, the listing file will show any errors in syntax with whatever error message the compiler produces. The listing file may show the program with each line numbered. It may include an alphabetical list of variable names complete with the numbers of the lines on which each variable is referenced. Some COBOL compilers include a list of paragraph names and the locations at which each name is used. The listing file may be much longer than the source statements of the program but the information it contains can be useful in checking the execution of a program, and as part of the program documentation. Figure 1.6 shows a source file and its corresponding listing file.

Of the files associated with a program, only the code (or object) file needs to be kept online once the program is in production. It is not necessary to keep the listing and source files online. The listing file is useful in debugging and testing, and a printed copy is probably kept for reference by maintenance programmers in planning changes to the program. The source file is very important, but will not be needed again until the program is to be modified. If the programmer is careful in designing and writing, later modification will be an unusual occurrence. The source file will be kept safe and used sparingly.

(a)

```
program copy (input,output);
var   infile,
      outfile: text;
      filename,
      outname,
      inline:  string;
      num,
      lines,
      count:   integer;

begin
      writeln('What is the name of the file to be copied?');
      readln(filename);
      writeln('To where is the file to be copied?');
      readln(outname);
      writeln('How many copies?');
      readln (num);
      rewrite(outfile,outname);
      reset(infile,filename);
      for count := 1 to num do
          begin
             lines:=0;
             while not eof(infile) do
                 begin
                     readln(infile,inline);
                     writeln(outfile, inline);
                     lines := lines + 1;
                 end;
             if count < num then reset(infile);
             if (outname = 'printer:')
                 then while lines < 66 do
                     begin
                         writeln(outfile);
                         lines := lines + 1;
                     end;
          end;
end.
```

Figure 1.6 (a) A source file and (b) its listing file.

File Interactions and Overlap

In considering the several types of files, we must remember that there is a great deal of interaction among various files and file types. Files that contain data, whether they are master files, transaction files, or temporary files, are not totally independent of files that contain programs. Most programs read data. In fact, the program has some knowledge of the form in which the data is stored built into it. When a decision is made to alter the content of a data file, the change must be reflected in all of the programs using that data.

A notable example of the scope of the changes that must be made when a data file is altered is the decision to change from five to nine-digit

(b)

```
 1   1  1:D     1  (*$L COPY.LST*)
 2   1  1:D     1  program copy (input,output);
 3   1  1:D     3  var   infile,
 4   1  1:D     3        outfile:  text;
 5   1  1:D   605        filename,
 6   1  1:D   605        outname,
 7   1  1:D   605        inline:   string;
 8   1  1:D   728        num,
 9   1  1:D   728        lines,
10   1  1:D   728        count:    integer;
11   1  1:D   731
12   1  1:0     0  begin
13   1  1:1     0     writeln('What is the name of the file to be copied?');
14   1  1:1    89     readln(filename);
15   1  1:1   109     writeln('To where is the file to be copied?');
16   1  1:1   163     readln(outname);
17   1  1:1   183     writeln('How many copies?');
18   1  1:1   219     readln(num);
19   1  1:1   238     rewrite(outfile,outname);
20   1  1:1   250     reset(infile,filename);
21   1  1:1   263     for count := 1 to num do
22   1  1:2   282        begin
23   1  1:3   282           lines:=0;
24   1  1:3   286           while not eof(infile) do
25   1  1:4   297              begin
26   1  1:5   297                 readln(infile,inline);
27   1  1:5   317                 writeln(outfile,inline);
28   1  1:5   335                 lines := lines + 1;
29   1  1:4   343              end;
30   1  1:3   345           if count < num then reset(infile);
31   1  1:3   362           if (outname = 'printer:')
32   1  1:3   378              then while lines < 66 do
33   1  1:5   387                 begin
34   1  1:6   387                    writeln(outfile);
35   1  1:6   394                    lines := lines + 1;
36   1  1:5   402                 end;
37   1  1:2   404        end;
38   1  1:0   414  end.
```

Figure 1.6   continued

zip codes. A company that has gone to the considerable trouble of changing all of its stored addresses to include the new zip codes, must also change each program that accesses that data. In order to do this, the source file for each program must be located and the address description field changed. If the program includes any tests based on zip codes, the tests must be reviewed to see if they are still correct, and changes made if necessary. The program must then be recompiled; extra modules that had been linked to the original program must be included in the new version; and the new object code must replace the old one in the company's software collection. In addition, someone must be sure that any programs that are run only occasionally or under special circumstances do not get overlooked. A program that reads the employee master file and produces

W-2 forms ready for mailing at the end of the year could easily be overlooked when the employee master file is being reformatted in July.

Overlapping of data fields occurs between and among data files. For example, the name of a supplier may occur in a parts file to facilitate reorders. The same name may appear in a separate supplier file that contains addresses, additional information about what that supplier provides, and perhaps a record of performance. An accounts payable file may contain the supplier name also. If the name of that supplier changes, it must be changed everywhere it occurs. If the accounting department is maintaining its own accounts payable file separate from the supplier information kept for stocking parts, and if the notice of a change of name of the supplier is sent to accounting only, the company may find itself submitting orders to one supplier name and paying invoices to another. Chapter 9 introduces a large category of techniques for addressing this type of problem.

An obvious solution to this problem is to keep the name of the supplier in one file only, perhaps the supplier master file, and refer to the supplier by identification number elsewhere. This certainly aids in consistency, but may make it inconvenient for a given department to obtain information. A news bulletin that ACME Widgets has just filed for bankruptcy may cause the manufacturing and accounting departments to check their records to see what orders are outstanding and what the status of payments to and from that company is. Both departments would have to check the supplier master file to find the identification number, then check other files for information about that supplier. The inconvenience may be slight, or it may be considerable. Chapter 11 shows how these problems are compounded in a distributed computer system.

The types of data and files included in this chapter are fundamental to an understanding of file processing. Techniques for manipulating data in files, as well as for storing and accessing files, are also important concerns. They will be addressed in the next several chapters.

SUMMARY

Data is the basic entity in computing. It can be represented in a variety of ways and can be combined into different kinds of files for processing. Data representation and file types are building blocks for constructing effective computer applications.

This chapter considers both the logical and the physical representation of data. The logical view pertains to how a person sees the data; the physical view relates to how data is stored in a computer.

With respect to the logical representation of data, we specify a number of simple and composite data types which occur in COBOL and

Pascal. The simple types are integer, real, and character; composite types are string, array, and record. All of these types are commonly used in file processing. We identify the characteristics of each type as a class of objects, and the operations for manipulating the objects.

Any one data type can be mapped into storage in different ways. The representation of data types in storage, that is, the physical representation, is important in methods for processing data in files. Some of the possible ways to store objects of each data type are identified, and representative implementations in COBOL and Pascal are given.

We then look at types of files common to data processing. Files are divided into three major categories according to the form in which data is stored, their use, and their relation to programs. In each classification, three types of files are introduced. Text, binary, and code files differ in the ways in which data is represented within them. Master, transaction, and temporary files are used differently in applications. Source, code, and listing files are generated from programs for different purposes. These files occur frequently in a study of techniques and in programs for storing, retrieving, and manipulating files.

EXERCISES

1. Give a physical representation of yourself as seen by
   a. yourself,
   b. a detective,
   c. a doctor,
   d. a designer of car interiors.
2. Give a logical representation of yourself as seen by
   a. yourself,
   b. a teacher,
   c. a parent,
   d. an employer.
3. Assume that floating-point numbers are represented in binary as follows: a sign bit followed by a 6-bit field for the exponent, and a sign bit followed by a 24-bit field for the number. Express the numbers −50.125 and 37.1 according to this representation.
4. Express $25.30 in the representation of Exercise 3 and in packed decimal form.
5. Assume a social security number has been stored as a nine-digit integer. Design a set of computations that will produce the two-digit middle field (i.e., the fourth and fifth digits).
6. Describe the steps necessary to take a string consisting of <firstname><lastname> and convert it to <lastname><firstname>. How would

your description be affected if <middleinitial> were allowed, but not required, in the name?

7. Design a three-dimensional structure (similar to Figure 1.1) to represent a car manufacturer's distribution of new cars given the model, color, and dealer location for each car. Each entry in the structure is the number of cars of the specific model and color at a location.

8. Specify an appropriate type for each of the following data items:
   a. a student's grade point average,
   b. a salary,
   c. a telephone number,
   d. a shoe size,
   e. a checker/chess board,
   f. a mailing address.

9. For each of the data types in Exercise 8, give a declaration in a programming language.

10. What file types are available on the computer system to which you have access? How are these file types distinguished from each other? (For example, .EXE designates a file of system commands in MS-DOS.)

Note: In addition to working the above exercises, you should review more extensive treatments of the topics included in this chapter in COBOL or Pascal texts.

CHAPTER 2

SEARCHING AND SORTING DATA

INTRODUCTION

We are inundated with data in our society. We collect it, store it, process it, transmit it, and destroy it. Much of the data is disorganized and can remain that way without causing serious problems (for example, collections of memorabilia, photographs, or newspaper clippings). For many applications, however, data must be organized—into personnel records, financial reports, statistical summaries, bibliographies, hospital records, and so on. When data is organized, it becomes more usable. For example, data about a person becomes a personnel record; personnel records of a number of people become a file. It is easier to obtain information by accessing a file than by sifting through piles of data.

Records are collected into a file to make the information more accessible. In the simplest sense, records are accessed by searching the file in some order until the desired record is either found or determined not to be in the file. If there is no reason to access one or more records, then there is no need to organize and store a file of records. Some of the reasons for searching files are to:

  a. Delete/insert/modify one or more records
  b. Count the number of records
  c. Determine all records of a particular type
  d. Determine the contents of one or more records
  e. Sort the records
  f. Combine the file with another file

A specific application usually involves several of these actions. For example, we might sort a file of records, then combine (merge) it with an already sorted file, and delete/insert/modify records in the process.

Maintaining files containing large numbers of records presupposes that the records are organized in some manner. One of the common ways to organize records is to sort them in a predetermined order (for example, alphabetical, chronological, increasing, decreasing). Generally, sorting is done to facilitate searching. Imagine how aggravating it would be to try to find a telephone number if names in the telephone book were not sorted in alphabetical order. Thus, sorting and searching are integrally related, and elementary methods for both topics are included in this chapter. For each method, there is a short discussion, an algorithm, an example, a program segment in both Pascal and COBOL, and an analysis.

In any study of searching and sorting it is important to consider how efficient or time-consuming different methods may be. The results of such an analysis help us decide whether to sort a file before searching it and which search/sort method to choose for a particular application. For example, it may be more efficient to spend time sorting a large file because searching it will then be much faster and more convenient. On the other hand, a file that is accessed infrequently, or one that is constantly changing, may be better left unsorted. Definitive answers cannot be given without knowledge of the application and even then choices may not be clear-cut.

Search/sort methods are either **internal** or **external**, depending on whether the entire file is in internal memory when the search/sort is performed or some records remain in external memory (for example, on disk) while that part of the file in internal memory is being searched/sorted. Internal methods are usually faster than external ones and easier to analyze. Internal search/sort methods are the focus of Chapters 2 and 3. An external sort method called merge sort is covered in Chapter 6.

The following notation, definitions, and interpretations are assumed in the discussion of searching and sorting. A file is a collection of records $r_1, r_2, \ldots, r_n$, where the subscript specifies the record's location in the file. Every record in a given file contains the same set of fields, one of which is the key field. A key identifies the record containing it, or some property of that record. Driver license number is a key in a car registration record. A key value, such as A222777555, identifies a driver of the car. A key is the only field included in discussions, algorithms, examples, programs, and analyses.

Commonly, the term "key" is used to refer to the key value as well as the key itself. The context in which the term appears resolves any confusion. Thus, records $r_1, r_2, \ldots, r_n$ have keys $k_1, k_2, \ldots, k_n$, respectively. Sorting a file of records is accomplished by sorting keys; searching a file is the same as looking for a given key k_0, or looking for one or more keys k_j

equal to/less than/greater than k_0. Specifically, each search algorithm, example, program, and analysis is based on the assumption that only the first occurrence of a key k_j is sought, such that $k_j = k_0$. When a search is conducted on a sorted file, the file is assumed to be in nondecreasing order; its keys have the same value or are increasing in value. For example, the keys 10,20,30,30,40,40,50 are in nondecreasing order. The final assumption is that the file to be searched/sorted is stored as a one-dimensional array of records (actually, keys of records). A record or key is referenced by specifying its index in the array.

SEQUENTIAL SEARCH

Sequential search is the easiest and most straightforward search or sort method to implement and analyze. For that reason, we discuss it first; it demonstrates the treatment of other methods.

Historically, large files were stored on magnetic tape, a sequential medium similar to cassette tape. Not surprisingly, both sorted and unsorted files were then searched sequentially. After random access storage devices (disks and drums) appeared as part of mainframes and minicomputers, records of a file could be stored nonsequentially and other search methods became possible. However, sequential search was, and is, often used as part of another method—for example, to search for a key on a track of the disk or drum after the track has been identified by another method.

Method

A sequential search of a file on a given key k_0 involves comparing k_0 to the key k_j for each record r_j (for $1 \le j \le n$), one after the other in the order in which they appear in the file. The search continues until the record with key equal to k_0 is found or determined not to be in the file. It is the kind of methodical search we make when looking through a pile of old magazines for one of a certain date. We look at the first magazine (record) in the pile (file), and check its date (key) against the specified date (k_0). If that magazine has the desired date, we stop the search. Otherwise, we look at the second magazine, then the third, and so on, each time checking the date, until the desired magazine is found or the pile is empty.

Sequential search can be done on a file whether the file is sorted or unsorted. The basic process is the same: we compare with k_0 the key of one record after another in the order in which they appear in the file. However, if the file is already sorted, there is no need to search to the end if no record has a key equal to k_0. The search continues only until the record is found or until the first record r_j is found such that $k_j < k_0$ or $k_j > k_0$, depending on whether the file is sorted in nondecreasing or nonincreasing order, respectively. In the magazine example, if the pile were ordered chronologically, with the most recent date on top of the pile, then the search would continue until the exact date or the first earlier date were found.

Algorithm

The algorithm for sequential search consists mainly of a single loop to compare keys. If the file is sorted in nondecreasing order, exit the loop either when the key is found or when the first key greater than k_0 is encountered. If the file is unsorted, exit the loop either when the key is found or when no more keys are in the file.

A first cut at writing an algorithm to search a sorted file sequentially is as follows:

Input: File R of n records $r_1, r_2, \ldots, r_n$ sorted in nondecreasing order on keys $k_1, k_2, \ldots, k_n$.
Key k_0.
Output: The index of the first key k_j such that $k_j = k_0$ or 0 if the key is not in the file.
1) Read the first key.
2) While $k_j < k_0$ and $j \leq n$, read the next key k_j.
3) If $k_j = k_0$, then return j; otherwise return 0.

The following refinement is a more precise statement of the algorithm.

```
j = 1
while kj < k0 and j ≤ n do
    j = j + 1
if kj = k0
    then return j
    else return 0
```

For an unsorted file, the algorithm is very similar. Simply replace $k_j < k_0$ in the **while** condition with $k_j \neq k_0$.

EXAMPLE 2.1

Before writing a program from the algorithm, let's "walk through" the algorithm with specific examples for sorted and unsorted files.

1. Assume R is sorted so that its keys are as follows:

    4, 9, 12, 13, 13, 19, 23

(a) Let $k_0 = 12$.
Then
$k_1 = 4. j = 1$.
$k_1 < k_0$ and $j < n$
$j = 2; k_2 = 9$ ($k_2 < k_0$)
$j = 3; k_3 = 12$ ($k_3 \not< k_0$).
$k_3 = k_0$
12 is printed.

(b) Let $k_0 = 10$.
Then
$k_1 = 4. j = 1$.
$k_1 < k_0$ and $j < n$
$j = 2; k_2 = 9$ ($k_2 < k_0$)
$j = 3; k_3 = 12$ ($k_3 \not< k_0$)
$k_3 \neq k_0$
a "not found" message is printed.

2. Assume R is unsorted and that its keys are as follows:

13, 19, 9, 12, 4, 13, 23

(a) Let $k_0 = 12$
Then
$k_1 = 13$ and $k_1 \neq k_0$
$k_2 = 19$ and $k_2 \neq k_0$
$k_3 = 9$ and $k_3 \neq k_0$
$k_4 = 12$ and $k_4 = k_0$
12 is printed.

(b) Let $k_0 = 10$
Then
$k_1 = 13$ and $k_1 \neq k_0$
$k_2 = 19$ and $k_2 \neq k_0$
$k_3 = 9$ and $k_3 \neq k_0$
. . .
$k_7 = 23$ and $k_7 \neq k_0$
"not found" is printed.

Programs

Programs for the sorted file are included in both Pascal and COBOL. In this Pascal program, and in all others requiring arrays, the following declarations are assumed:

```
const n = <any appropriate positive integer>;
type  arraytype = array [1..n] of integer;
```

In Pascal, sequential search of a sorted file can be implemented as the following function:

```
function SEQUENTIALSEARCH (var R : arraytype;
                  keysubzero : integer) : integer;
  { SEQUENTIALSEARCH searches the keys in the sorted
      array R for a key equal to KEYSUBZERO. If the
      key is found, its index is returned;
      otherwise, 0 is returned. }

var j : integer;      { Index of keys in the file. }
begin   { SEQUENTIALSEARCH }
```

```
{ Compare keys to KEYSUBZERO until key is found or
  is not in file. }

j := 1;
while  R[j] < keysubzero and j <= n do
   j := j + 1;
if R[j] = keysubzero
  then sequentialsearch  := j { Key is found.
                                Return its index. }
  else sequentialsearch  := 0   { Key is not found.
                                  Return 0. }
end;    { SEQUENTIALSEARCH }
```

Pascal Program 2.1 *Sequential Search*

Because searching is one of the operations performed very frequently by COBOL programs, the language includes a SEARCH verb that implements the sequential search algorithm. The verb operates on an array (table) stored in memory. It cannot be used to search a file stored on disk or tape. In general, a sequential search of a file would be time-consuming and inefficient. Methods for accessing specific records in a file are discussed in later chapters.

Details of the sequential search algorithm are provided in the SEARCH verb in COBOL; they are hidden to the user. To illustrate sequential search, an implementation of the SEARCH verb must be given for a specific application.

Assume the table to be searched consists of building codes and their associated full names, rather than the short representations such as k_0. It is likely that building codes are used in files to save space, but full building names are printed for the purpose of making reports.

In the WORKING-STORAGE SECTION, the following table is defined:

```
01 BUILDING-CODES-AND-NAMES.
   03 FILLER             PIC X(25)         VALUE
      "DAN DANIELS HALL".
   03 FILLER             PIC X(25)         VALUE
      "WEB WEBSTER LABORATORY".
   03 FILLER             PIC X(25)         VALUE
      "BEA BEACON HALL".
   03 FILLER             PIC (25)          VALUE
      "RIC RICHARDS AUDITORIUM".
   03 FILLER             PIC X(25)         VALUE
      "MOR MORRIS LECTURE HALL".
   03 FILLER             PIC X(25)         VALUE
```

```
                "RIL RILEY READING CENTER".
        03 FILLER                   PIC X(25)          VALUE
                "STE STEVENS SPORTS COMPLEX".
        03 FILLER                   PIC X(25)          VALUE
        "MCK MCKELVEY CONSERVATORY".
        03 FILLER                   PIC X(25)          VALUE
                "ASH ANNA ASH LIBRARY".
        03 FILLER                   PIC X(25)          VALUE
                "DEW DEWEY OBSERVATORY".

    01 BUILDING-CODES-TABLE REDEFINES
        BUILDING-CODES-AND-NAMES.
        03 BUILDING-ENTRY OCCURS 10 TIMES
                          INDEXED BY BLDG-IDX.
            05 BUILDING-CODE     PIC XXX.
            05 FILLER            PIC X.
            05 BUILDING-NAME     PIC X(21).
```

In the PROCEDURE DIVISION, the code to carry out the sequential search of this table is:

```
SET BLDG-IDX TO 1.
SEARCH BUILDING-ENTRY
        AT END MOVE 'NO' TO BUILDING-FOUND
                MOVE SPACES TO OUT-BUILDING-NAME
        WHEN IN-BUILDING-CODE = BUILDING-CODE(BLDG-IDX)
                MOVE 'YES' TO BUILDING-FOUND
                MOVE BUILDING-NAME(BLDG-IDX) TO
                            OUT-BUILDING-NAME.
```

COBOL Program 2.1 Sequential Search of a Table

It is important to set the table index to 1 before each search through the table. Otherwise, the search will continue from wherever it left off the last time. This corresponds to the instruction to set $j = 1$ in the algorithm. The **while** loop of the algorithm is hidden in the SEARCH statement of the COBOL program. The SEARCH statement causes the table index, named in the table with the OCCURS clause, to be incremented repeatedly until one of the two stopping conditions has been met: either the end of the table has been encountered without finding the item sought (called IN-BUILDING-CODE here) or the matching value has been found. Specific actions are defined for each case, just as in the algorithm. The algorithm returns the location at which the desired value was found, or a 0 if the value was not found. In the COBOL version, the value returned is a YES or NO value in a flag variable BUILDING-FOUND. The building name is moved to the output area when it has been found. These details are not part of the search itself, but are reasonable actions to be taken as a consequence of the search.

Analysis

The analysis of the amount of time to carry out a sequential search is straightforward. It amounts to counting the number of key comparisons, because they represent the major time-consuming operations in the program implementing an algorithm. In the best case, the number of comparisons is one—the key is found in the first record. In the worst case, the number is n (the same as the number of keys in the file)—the key is in the last record or not in the file at all.

To obtain an estimate for the average search length, observe that finding a key in the first record is just as probable as finding it in the last one, in the second as in the second last, in the third as in the third last, etc. Thus, if a file of n records is searched m times, where m is a large number, then the key should be found in the first record at least once, in the second record at least once, and so on. The average search length for $m=n$ searches, then, is

$$(1 + 2 + 3 + \ldots + n)/n = n(n+1)/2/n = (n+1)/2.$$

The same analysis applies to sequential search of both sorted and unsorted files. In practice, however, the average search time for a sorted file is less than that for an unsorted one, because the entire file is not searched in every case in which a key is not found.

For large values of n, the dominating term in the estimate $(n + 1)/2$ of the average number of comparisons in sequential search is n. It follows that

$$(n + 1)/2 \leq c * n$$

for some constant c. The "big-oh" notation $O(n)$ is commonly used to represent this relationship. It is read, "the number of comparisons is of the order of n." Formally, if $f(n)$ represents the number of comparisons for a file of n records, then $f(n)$ is of order n, written $O(n)$, if and only if there exists a constant c such that

$$f(n) \leq c * n.$$

By the end of the chapter, it should become apparent that the big-oh notation helps to categorize search and sort methods in terms of their approximate number of comparisons. Of course, these results are only approximations of the actual time required by the program to complete a search.

INTERNAL SORTING

Now that we have seen the simplest way to search files, we turn to methods for sorting records in a file. One of the primary reasons for sorting a file is to speed up the search process. Sorting a file, say, in nondecreasing order, involves rearranging records into an order $r_1, r_2, r_3 \ldots, r_n$, such that $k_1 \leq k_2 \leq k_3 \leq \ldots \leq k_n$.

In general, there are two classes of sort methods: internal and external. For an internal sort, all records of a file to be sorted must be in main memory (RAM on a microcomputer) while the sort is being done. This memory is in addition to that which is required for the sort program and any structures, such as arrays, to store copies of all or part of the records or keys.

An external sort is accomplished by periodically reading into memory parts of the file, sorting them, and then storing the sorted portion on one or more auxiliary storage devices, such as disks or tapes. Although external sorts of large files may require less memory than internal sorts, with more memory available for the sort, more records can be accessed and sorted in one pass, and the sort can be completed faster. External sort methods will be discussed in later chapters.

Three kinds of internal sorts are studied in this section: selection, insertion, and exchange. Only one method of each kind is included; additional methods appear in Chapter 3. The same approach taken for sequential search is taken for each of the three kinds of internal sorts. In all internal sort discussions, assume that every record in the file being sorted can fit into internal memory.

Selection Sort

All **selection sorts** search through a file to find (select) the right record for a particular position. The specific sort chosen to begin the treatment of internal sorts is the easiest one to implement and analyze. It is the kind of sort that could be used when arranging cards of the same suit in a hand of cards, or when sorting a short list of names.

Method

This simplest version of a selection sort of a file of n records involves looking through all the records to find the one with the largest key, then moving that record to the end of the file (assuming the file is being sorted in nondecreasing order). During the next pass, we look through all but the last record to find the largest remaining key, and then move that record to the next-to-last position in the file. The next (third) pass places the record with the third largest key in the third last position in the file, and so on until all records are in order. This type of sort is called the **straight**

selection sort. It is the type of sort to use when sorting a short list of numbers. We scan the entire list to find the smallest (largest) number. After writing down the number, we repeat the process, each time with one less number in the list to search, until we end up with a sorted list. Try it with lists of different lengths to see that the method is more appropriate for short, rather than long, lists.

Algorithm

Assume that initially the file is unsorted and stored in memory as an array R of n records. After the sort, the file is in nondecreasing order. As before, let r_j be the jth record and k_j be its key, for $j=i,\ldots,n$. Let *max* be the value of the currently largest key, and i its index, during each pass through the file. A separate array A contains the sorted file.

Input: Array (file) R of n records $r_1, r_2, \ldots, r_n$, unsorted, with keys $k_1, k_2, \ldots, k_n$.
Output: The array (file) A with records sorted in nondecreasing order.
Repeat the following steps until R is sorted:
a) $max = k_1$; $i = 1$.
b) Compare *max* with keys $k_2, \ldots, k_n$ until a key k_m is found such that $k_m > max$ or until the end of the file is reached.
c) If $k_m > max$, then let $max = k_m$, and continue comparing keys in the rest of the file. Each time a key is greater than the current value of *max*, assign its value to *max* and its index to i.
d) When the end of the file is reached, insert the value of *max* into the last available position in A. Mark the key so it cannot be *max* again.

A refinement of this algorithm uses an outer loop to keep track of the available position in A. An inner loop controls the search for *max* in R. Replace the value of the largest key at the end of each pass with *nokey*, a value to guarantee that the key will not appear as the value of *max* more than once. For example, *nokey* would be smaller than the least expected key value in a file that is to be sorted in nondecreasing order.

Straight Selection Sort

```
for j = n down to 1 do
    i = 1
    max = k₁
    for m = 2 to n do
        if kₘ > max
            then
                max = kₘ
                i = m
    aⱼ = max
    kᵢ = nokey
```

Searching and Sorting Data 39

EXAMPLE 2.2

Assume that the file R of n records is already stored as an array. The records are not displayed, however, only the keys on which the file is to be sorted and their indices (subscripts) in the array. Because all keys are positive integers, let *nokey* = −1. Set $a_1, \ldots, a_n$ to 0. Assume the file to be sorted in nondecreasing order is as follows:

index	1	2	3	4	5	6	7
keys	21	15	62	48	21	39	30

First pass: $j = 7$
 $max = 21; i = 1$
 $m = 2; k_2 \not> max$
 $m = 3; k_3 > max$
  $max = 62; i = 3$
 $m = 4; k_4 \not> max$
 $m = 5; k_5 \not> max$
 $m = 6; k_6 \not> max$
 $m = 7; k_7 \not> max$
 $a_7 = 62$
 $k_3 = -1$

Second pass: The file is now 21,15,−1,48,21,39,30.
 $j = 6$
 $max = 21; i = 1$
 $m = 2; k_2 \not> max$
 $m = 3; k_3 \not> max$
 $m = 4; k_4 > max$
  $max = 48; i = 4$
 $m = 5; k_5 \not> max$
 $m = 6; k_6 \not> max$
 $a_6 = 48$
 $k_4 = -1$

Third pass: The file is now 21,15,−1,−1,21,39,30.
 $j = 5$
 $max = 21; i = 1$
 $m = 2; k_2 \not> max$
 $m = 3; k_3 \not> max$
 $m = 4; k_4 \not> max$
 $m = 5; k_5 \not> max$
 $m = 6; k_6 > max$

40 Chapter 2

$$max = 39; i = 6$$
$$m = 7; k_7 \not> max$$
$$a_5 = 39$$
$$k_6 = -1$$

Fourth pass: The file is now 21,15,−1,−1,21,−1,30.
...

Fifth pass: The file is now 21,15,−1,−1,21,−1,−1.
...

Sixth pass: The file is now −1,15,−1,−1,21,−1,−1.
...

Seventh pass: The file is now −1,15,−1,−1,−1,−1,−1.

At the end of this pass we end up with the sorted file in the array A.

index	1	2	3	4	5	6	7
keys	15	21	21	30	39	48	62

Programs

The following procedure implements the straight selection sort in Pascal:

```
procedure selectionsort(var R, A : arraytype;
                       n : integer)
{ Selectionsort sorts an array by selecting each
    element from an array R of N keys and placing
    it into the proper place in a new array, A. }

const nokey = -9999;     { any value that cannot occur
                           in the original array }
var
    i,j,                 { Loop counters. }
    m,                   { Array position indicator }
    max    : integer;    { Largest unselected array
                           value seen so far }
```

```
begin    { Selectionsort }
{ Find the proper value to place in
         position j in the sorted file. }
  for j := n downto 1 do
    begin
        i:= 1;
        max := R[1];
        for m := 2 to n do      { Find the largest }
          if R[m] > max         { value in the     }
             then               { unsorted array   }
                begin
                    max := R[m];
                    i := m;
                end;
        A[j] := max;
        R[i] := nokey;
    end;
```

Pascal Program 2.2 *Straight Selection Sort*

The COBOL implementation follows the logic described in the language-independent algorithm, but uses the building codes table as a specific example.

```
PERFORM SELECT-VALUE
         VARYING J FROM N BY -1
         UNTIL J = 0.

SELECT-VALUE.
    SET I TO 1.
    MOVE R(1) TO MAX.
    PERFORM FIND-LARGEST
         VARYING M FROM 2 BY 1
         UNTIL M > N.
    MOVE MAX TO A(J).
    MOVE NOKEY TO R(I).

FIND-LARGEST.
IF R(M) > MAX
         MOVE R(M) TO MAX
         SET I TO M.
```

COBOL Program 2.2 *Straight Selection Sort*

Analysis

To determine the number of comparisons in a straight selection sort, observe that the outer loop is executed n times, and each time there are $n-1$ comparisons. Thus, the total number of comparisons is $n * (n-1) = n^2 - n$. For very large n, the value of n^2 is considerably greater than the value of n and the term $n^2 - n$ can be approximated by $c*n^2$, where c is a positive constant. Straight selection sort, then is $O(n^2)$. The same number of comparisons are made regardless of the file's initial ordering, so this result applies to the best, worst, and average cases.

There are other versions of the sort, but none are better than $O(n^2)$. For example, it is possible to eliminate the need for the second array by exchanging the next-to-last key in the unsorted portion of the file R at the end of each pass with the key whose value is in MAX. The analysis of this version is different from the one above, but the result is still $O(n^2)$. Also, there are $n - 1$ interchanges, one for each pass.

Straight selection sort requires memory locations for two arrays: one for the original file and the other for the sorted file. In addition, locations are needed for the maximum key and its index. Memory for only one array is required in the version involving interchanges within the file.

As shown later in this chapter, an $O(n^2)$ method is not the best choice for large files. For small files, straight selection sort is a reasonable alternative, and sometimes even the best choice, because its program overhead is very small. That is, the program includes relatively few additional statements or subprogram calls to be executed other than those involving comparisons.

Insertion Sort

An **insertion sort** chooses a record and searches for the right place in which to put it. There are a number of sort methods that fit this general heading, and some of the methods have several versions. The basic characteristic of all of them is that at each stage a key, along with its record, is placed in its correct position in an already sorted portion of the file.

Method

Initially, assume that the record represented by the first key is a sorted file of one element. Compare the second key to the first, interchange the records if necessary, and end up with a sorted file of two elements. The third key is then compared to the two already sorted ones and inserted so that the result is a sorted file of three elements. This may require shifting one or both keys to make room for the third one. Continue the process, moving keys as necessary at each stage, until the last (*n*th) key in the original file is inserted into its position and the entire file is sorted. This method could be used to sort all cards of the same suit in a hand of cards. Given the 7, 3, J(jack), 9 and 4 of clubs, in that order, first consider the 7 as a sorted file. Then place the 3 before the 7; leave the J where it is; place the 9 between the 7 and the J by shifting the J; and place the 4 between the 3 and the 7 by shifting the 7, 9, and J.

Algorithm

Assume the file R of n records is unsorted and stored as an array. The algorithm sorts the records of R in nondecreasing order. During each pass, the value of the key of the record to be inserted into the already sorted file is assigned to the variable *key*. The index m indicates the length of the sorted file at the end of each pass; that is, the keys in locations 1 to m are sorted. Because the record whose key is k_1 is a sorted file of one key, the algorithm begins by inserting the second key, then the third, and so on. The index j controls the keys that must be moved to insert *key*.

For $m = 2$ to n do the following steps:
a) $key = k_m$.
b) Compare *key* successively with $k_1, k_2, \ldots, k_j$ where k_j is the first key in the sorted file greater than k_m.
c) Insert k_m before k_j.

The algorithm can be refined as follows:

Insertion Sort

```
for m = 2 to n do
    key = km
    i = 1
    while ki ≤ km and i < m do
        i = i + 1
    for j = m–1 downto i do
        kj+1 = kj
    ki = key
```

EXAMPLE 2.3

Consider the same file as in the example for selection sort. The goal is the same: a file in nondecreasing order. The original file is 21,15,62,48, 21,39,30.

$m = 2$
   $key = 15; i = 1$
   $21 > key$
   $j = 1$
      $k_2 = 21$
   $j = 0 < 1$
   $k_1 = key$
$m = 3$ (The file keys are now 15,21,62,48,21,39,30.)
   $key = 62; i = 1$
   $15 < key$ and $1 < 3$
      $i = 2$
   $21 < key$ and $2 < 3$
      $i = 3$
   $3 \not< 3$
   $j = 2 < 3$
   $k_3 = key$
$m = 4$ (The file did not change.)
   $key = 48; i = 1$
   $15 < key$ and $1 < 4$
      $i = 2$
   $21 < key$ and $2 < 4$
      $i = 3$
   $62 > key$
   $j = 3$
      $k_4 = 62$
   $j = 2 < 3$
   $k_3 = key$
$m = 5$ (The file keys are now 15,21,48,62,21,39,30.)
   $key = 21; i = 1$
   $15 < key$ and $1 < 5$
      $i = 2$
   $21 = key$ and $2 < 5$
      $i = 3$
   $48 > key$
   $j = 4$
      $k_5 = 62$
   $j = 3$
      $k_4 = 48$
   $j = 2 < 3$
   $k_3 = key$
$m = 6$ (The file keys are now 15,21,21,48,62,39,30.)
   . . .
$m = 7$ (The file keys are now 15,21,21,39,48,62,30.)
   . . .

The file keys become 15, 21, 21, 30, 39, 48, 62 and the sorting is completed.

Programs

In Pascal, insertion sort can be implemented as the following procedure:

```
procedure INSERTIONSORT (var R : arraytype;
                             n : integer);
{ INSERTIONSORT sorts an array R of N keys into
    nondecreasing order by inserting a key into an
    existing sorted file. }
var
  i,j,m,                          { Loop counters. }
  keyvalue        : integer;

begin    { INSERTIONSORT }
{ Find the proper place for KEYVALUE in the
    existing sorted file.  Initially, R[1] is the
    sorted file.  After each pass through the
    loop, R[1]. .R[M] is sorted. }
for m := 2 to n do
  begin
    keyvalue := R[m];   { KEYVALUE is the value to
                          be inserted into the
                          sorted file. }
    i := 1;      { Initialize counter for the
                   sorted file. }
    while (R[i] ≤ keyvalue) and (i < m) do
      i := i + 1;
    for j := m-1 downto i do
      R[j+1] := R[j];   { Move all keys > KEYVALUE. }
    R[i] := keyvalue;   { Insert KEYVALUE in its  }
  end                   {   proper place. }
end;    { INSERTIONSORT }
```

Pascal Program 2.3 *Insertion Sort*

As before, the COBOL implementation follows the logic described in the language-independent algorithm, but uses the building codes table as a specific example.

```
        PERFORM FIND-POSITION
            VARYING M FROM 2 BY 1
            UNTIL M EXCEEDS NUMBER-OF-BUILDINGS.

FIND-POSITION.
    MOVE BUILDING-CODE(M) TO KEY
    SET I TO 1
    PERFORM LOOK-FOR-SPOT
        UNTIL BUILDING-CODE(I) > BUILDING-CODE(M)
            OR I IS NOT < M.
    PERFORM MAKE-ROOM
        VARYING J FROM M - 1 BY  -1 UNTIL J < I.
    MOVE KEY TO BUILDING-CODE(I).

LOOK-FOR-SPOT.
    SET I UP BY 1.

MAKE-ROOM.
    MOVE BUILDING-CODE(J) TO BUILDING-CODE(J+1).
```

COBOL Program 2.3 *Insertion Sort*

Analysis

Analysis of insertion sort is more involved than analysis of selection sort. The actual number of comparisons depends on the ordering of keys (records) in the original file. If it is already in nondecreasing order, then only one comparison is needed for the first time through the outer loop, two for the second, three for the third, and so on. The loop is executed $n-1$ times, so the total number of comparisons in this case is

$$1 + 2 + \ldots + n-1 = n(n-1)/2 = n^2/2 - n/2$$

For reasons similar to those given in the analysis of straight selection sort, insertion sort is an $O(n^2)$ method. Keys are not shifted in this case.

When the original file is in reverse order, only one comparison is required each time through the loop. In this case, insertion sort is $O(n)$. However, the number of key movements in this case is the same as the number of comparisons in the case of the file already in order. If the file is in random order, the sum of comparisons and key movements during the pth time through the loop ($p = 1,2,\ldots,n-1$) is p if there is no shifting of keys, and $p+1$ otherwise. On the average, we can expect insertion sort to behave as an $O(n^2)$ method. In terms of comparisons alone, then, insertion sort is $O(n)$ (based only on comparisons) in the best case and $O(n^2)$ in the worst and average cases. Other insertion sorts—for example, the shell sort (also referred to as the diminishing increment sort)—are more efficient, but not enough so to recommend them.

Memory requirements are similar to those in the version of selection sort with interchanges. Keys (records) are moved entirely within the original array and only one extra location is needed for *key*.

Exchange Sort

An **exchange sort** repeatedly exchanges records in the file until the file is sorted. Exchange sorts are so called because in each pass pairs of key values are successively interchanged (or exchanged) as necessary until one key attains its proper position in the file. In this section a popular exchange sort called the **bubble sort** is examined, and in Chapter 3 a more efficient one called **quicksort** is studied. Bubble sort probably derives its name from bubbles rising to the surface of a liquid.

Method

During the first pass of a bubble sort the largest key is "bubbled-up" to the rightmost position of the file (assuming, as in previous sorts, that the method sorts the file in nondecreasing order). Each successive pass, if necessary, "bubbles-up" the next largest key not already in its proper position. The "bubbling" is accomplished by comparing, and interchanging when necessary, successive pairs of keys.

Apply this method to sort a pile of magazines so that the one with the latest date is on the bottom. (In computing, we can "bubble-down" as well as "bubble-up.") Compare the date of the first magazine on the pile with that of the second and interchange them if the first date is later than the second. Compare the date of whichever magazine is second with the date of the third one and interchange them if the second magazine's date is later than the third. Continue this process of comparing and (possibly) interchanging successive pairs of magazines until the magazine with the latest date is at the bottom of the pile. Repeat the process on the remaining magazines until the one with the next latest date is in its proper position, and so on until all magazines are in order.

Algorithm

Assume the file R of n records is to be sorted in nondecreasing order and that it is stored as an array. The algorithm consists of two loops: an outer one to control the pass and an inner one to control the keys being compared. The variable *pass* indicates the pass number, and the index j identifies the key being compared. After the ith pass, keys in positions $n - (i - 1)$ to n are in order.

Input: Array (File) R of n records, unsorted.
Output: The array R sorted in nondecreasing order.
For *pass* = 1 to $n-1$ do the following steps:
  For $j = 1$ to $n - pass$ do the following steps:
  Compare the jth and $j+1$st keys.
  Interchange them if they are out of order.

This algorithm is the most commonly programmed sort method. It is easy to visualize and reasonably simple to program. Rather than refine it, however, consider the following modified version which is also frequently implemented.

Assume a file is already sorted. On the first pass of the above algorithm compare successive pairs of keys but make no interchanges. There isn't any reason to make additional passes, but the algorithm continues until $n - 2$ more of them are completed. Nothing useful is accomplished; the passes (and the comparisons during them) simply consume time. In this case the algorithm should terminate after the first pass. Further investigation shows that for an arbitrary (unsorted) file, a bubble sort algorithm can terminate after the pass in which no interchanges are made. The file is sorted at that time. Thus, the algorithm should be modified as follows:

1) *pass* = 1.
2) For $j = 1$ to $n - 1$ do the following steps:
  Compare the jth and $j+1$st keys.
  Interchange them if they are out of order.
3) While *pass* < n and at least one interchange occurred in the previous pass do the following steps:
  For $j = 1$ to $n - pass$ do the following steps:
    Compare the jth and $j+1$st keys.
    Interchange them if they are out of order.

To refine the algorithm, note that steps 2 and 3 can be combined, provided there is a way of determining whether an interchange took place in a previous pass. One way to keep track of interchanges is to include a boolean variable in the loop and in the condition for executing the loop. It can be set to "false" when no interchanges are made in a pass. Then the condition is "false" and the loop is not executed again. Let *exchange* be the boolean variable.

Exchange Sort

  pass = 1
  exchange = true

```
while (pass < n) and (exchange = true)
  do
    exchange = false
    for j = 1 to n − pass
      do
        i = j + 1
        if kⱼ > kᵢ
          then
            exchange = true
            Interchange kⱼ and kᵢ
    pass = pass + 1
```

EXAMPLE 2.4

Assume R is the same file as in the previous two examples—namely, the file of records with keys in the order 21,15,62,48,21,39,30 stored as an array. Sort the file in nondecreasing order.

Pass = 1. Exchange = TRUE.
WHILE condition is TRUE;
  Exchange = FALSE; j = 1;
    i = 2; IF condition is TRUE (21 > 15);
      Exchange = TRUE; k_1 = 15 and k_2 = 21; j = 2;
    i = 3; IF condition is FALSE (21 ≯ 62); j = 3;
    i = 4; IF condition is TRUE (62 > 48);
      Exchange = TRUE; k_3 = 48 and k_4 = 62; j = 4
    i = 5; IF condition is TRUE (62 > 21);
      Exchange = TRUE; k_4 = 21 and k_5 = 62; j = 5;
    i = 6; IF condition is TRUE (62 > 39);
      Exchange = TRUE; k_5 = 39 and k_6 = 62; j = 6;
    i = 7; IF condition is TRUE (62 > 30);
      Exchange = TRUE; k_6 = 30 and k_7 = 62.
Pass = 2; (The file is now 15,21,48,21,39,30,62.)
WHILE condition is TRUE;
  Exchange is FALSE; j = 1;
    i = 2; IF condition is FALSE (15 ≯ 21); j = 2;
    i = 3; IF condition is FALSE (21 ≯ 48); j = 3;
    i = 4; IF condition is TRUE (48 > 21);
      Exchange = TRUE; k_3 = 21 and k_4 = 48; j = 4;
    i = 5; IF condition is TRUE (48 > 39);
      Exchange = TRUE; k_4 = 39 and k_5 = 48; j = 5;
    i = 6; IF condition is TRUE (48 > 30);
      Exchange = TRUE; k_5 = 30 and k_6 = 48.

Pass = 3; (The file is now 15,21,21,39,30,48,62.)
WHILE condition is TRUE;
   Exchange is FALSE; j = 1;
      i = 2; IF condition is FALSE (15 $\not>$ 21); j = 2;
      i = 3; IF condition is FALSE (21 $\not>$ 21); j = 3;
      i = 4; IF condition is FALSE (21 $\not>$ 39); j = 4;
      i = 5; IF condition is TRUE (39 > 30);
         Exchange = TRUE; k_4 = 30 and k_5 = 39.
Pass = 4; (The file is now 15,21,21,30,39,48,62.)
WHILE condition is TRUE;
   Exchange = FALSE; j = 1;
      i = 2; IF condition is FALSE; j = 2;
      i = 3; IF condition is FALSE; j = 3;
      i = 4; IF condition is FALSE.
Pass = 5;
WHILE condition is FALSE.

Programs

In Pascal, the bubble sort algorithm can be implemented as the following procedure:

```
procedure BUBBLESORT (var R : arraytype;
                         n : integer);

{ BUBBLESORT sorts the file R into nondecreasing
  order by successively exchanging adjacent keys. }

var
  j, pass    : integer;    { Loop counters. }
  i          : integer;    { Index of key after R[j]. }
  temp       : integer;    { Needed for interchanges. }
  exchange   : boolean;    { exchange is true when an
                             exchange is to be made. }
begin      { BUBBLESORT }
  pass := 1;          { Initialize pass and exchange. }
  exchange := true;

{ Search the unsorted part of the file for a key
  that's out of order and exchange it with the
  adjacent key. )
```

```pascal
while (pass < n) and (exchange = true) do
  begin
    exchange := false;
    for j := 1 to n - pass do
      begin
        i := j + 1;
        if R[j] > R[i]
          then
            begin
              exchange := true;
              temp := R[j];        { Interchange. }
              R[j] := R[i];
              R[i] := temp
            end;
      end;
    pass := pass + 1
  end;
end;      { bubblesort }
```

Pascal Program 2.4 *The Bubble Sort*

The COBOL version of the bubble sort follows the algorithm description, with only the necessary changes to adapt to the language requirements:

```cobol
        MOVE 'TRUE' TO EXCHANGE-FLAG.
        PERFORM SORT-PASS
            VARYING PASS FROM 1 BY 1
            UNTIL PASS = NUMBER-OF-BUILDINGS - 1
                OR EXCHANGE-OCCURS.

SORT-PASS.
    MOVE 'FALSE' TO EXCHANGE-FLAG.
    PERFORM COMPARE-ITEMS
        VARYING J FROM 1 BY 1
        UNTIL J> NUMBER-OF-BUILDINGS - PASS.

COMPARE-ITEMS.
    IF BUILDING-CODE(J) > BUILDING-CODE(J+1)
        MOVE 'TRUE' TO EXCHANGE
        MOVE BUILDING-CODE(J) TO HOLD-BUILDING-CODE
        MOVE BUILDING-CODE(J + 1) TO BUILDING-CODE(J)
        MOVE HOLD-BUILDING-CODE TO BUILDING-CODE(J + 1).
```

COBOL Program 2.4 *Bubble Sort*

Analysis

The number of comparisons in a bubble sort, as in other exchange sorts, depends on the ordering of keys (records) in the original file. Consider a file whose keys are already in nondecreasing order. Only one pass is made through the keys because no interchanges occur. In this case, $n - 1$ comparisons are required, so we can say that in the best case bubble sort is an $O(n)$ method. If the file's keys are in reverse order, then $n-1$ comparisons are required to place the largest key in position, $n-2$ for the next largest, and so on. The total number of comparisons, then, is

$$(n - 1) + (n - 2) + \ldots + 1 = n*(n-1)/2$$

It follows that in this, the worst case, bubble sort is an $O(n^2)$ method. The average case is also considered to be $O(n^2)$ although, as the example suggests, fewer passes are usually required than in the worst case. This could reduce the number of comparisons considerably if the original file were almost sorted.

Testing to determine if an interchange occurs during a pass is time-consuming. It must be measured against executing additional comparisons in the first bubble sort algorithm we specified. Although the method that terminates after no interchanges are made appears to be more efficient than the other method, testing could involve a significant enough overhead to make it less efficient, especially for randomly ordered files.

Memory requirements for bubble sort are the same as for the insertion sort described in the previous section. The file is sorted within the original array and only one additional location is needed for interchanges.

The number of interchanges in an average case bubble sort makes it less efficient than an insertion sort, and much less efficient than a selection sort. But the selection sort requires twice as much memory. In the worst case—that of a file with keys in reverse order—bubble sort has as many interchanges as comparisons. In general, interchanges are fewer in number than comparisons, but are significant enough so as not to recommend bubble sort unless the file is known to be almost sorted.

BINARY SEARCH

The final method in this chapter is a search of files which are already sorted. The method is called **binary search**. It is similar to a method we frequently use quite naturally when searching a large file. Binary search is reasonably easy to program and is much faster for large sorted files than sequential search.

Method

A binary search splits the original file into two halves, sees if the key k_0 is the middle value and, if not, determines which half could possibly hold a record containing k_0. The search then splits that part of the file into two halves. Again, it determines in which of those halves the key might be located, then splits that half, and so on until the key is found or it is determined that it is not in the file. A less formal version of binary search is often used to look for a specific word in a dictionary (or a telephone number in a phone book, or a specific magazine in a sorted pile of magazines). Open the book at approximately the halfway point and determine whether the word occurs at that point or appears earlier or later in the book. Ignore one of the two halves and open the other part to about the halfway point. By repeating these steps, the correct page is eventually found and the word is obtained, possibly by a sequential search through the words on the page. Binary search is efficient because, at each stage, it eliminates half of the remaining portion of the file by making only one comparison of keys. Of course, the search's efficiency depends on the entire file being stored in random access memory. The method would not work at all on an unsorted file.

Algorithm

Assume the file is sorted in nondecreasing order and terminate the search after finding the first occurrence of the given key k_0. At each stage, assign to *left* and *right*, respectively, the values of the lowest and highest numbered subscripts of keys in that portion of the file to be searched. Its midpoint is the key with subscript equal to the greatest integer in (*left* + *right*)/2. Initially, *left* = 1 and *right* = n.

Input: Array (File) R of n records $r_1, r_2, \ldots, r_n$ sorted in nondecreasing order on keys $k_1, k_2, \ldots, k_n$. Key k_0.
Output: The first key k_j such that $k_j = k_0$ or a message that the key is not in the file.

1) If *left* > *right*, then key is not in file; return 0.
2) m = greatest integer in (*left* + *right*)/2.
3) If $k_0 = k_m$, then return the key's index.
4) Otherwise, do one of the following:
   a) If $k_0 < k_m$ then let *right* = m − 1 and repeat steps 2–4 (that is, search the left half of the subfile).
   b) if $k_0 > k_m$ then let *left* = m + 1 and repeat steps 2–4 (that is, search the right half of the subfile).

Before refining the algorithm, note that there are two ways to carry out step 4. Both (a) and (b) repeat the same set of steps, but with different values of the variables *left* and *right*. This suggests that the steps could be implemented with iteration. Alternatively, recursion could be used. A recursive implementation involves naming the procedure, specifying parameters, and then using the name with parameter values in the steps of the algorithm. The refinement involves the recursive approach. It is followed by an illustration of how the recursive algorithm can be written as an iterative one.

Binary Search (Recursive)

```
searchr(array,left,right)
   if left > right
      then return 0
      else
         m = (left + right) div 2
         if k₀ = kₘ
            then return m
            else
               if k₀ < kₘ
                  then searchr(array,left,m–1)
                  else searchr(array,m+1,right)
```

Binary Search (Iterative)

```
searchi(left,right)
   while (left < right) and (k₀ ≠ kₘ)
      do
         m = (left + right) div 2
         if k₀ < kₘ
            then right = m – 1
            else left = m + 1
   if k₀ = kₘ
      then return m
      else return 0
```

EXAMPLE 2.5

Assume R is sorted so that its keys are as follows:

4,9,12,13,16,19,23,25,30,34,38.

Then $k_1 = 4$, $k_n = 38$, $n = 11$, left = 1, and right = 11. The recursive algorithm proceeds as follows:

Let $k_0 = 25$.
  searchr(R,1,11)
  left $\not>$ right
  m = (1 + 11) DIV 2 = 6   ($k_6 = 19$)
  $k_0 \neq 19$
  $k_0 \not< 19$
  searchr(R,7,11)   (i.e., search between keys 23 and 38)
    left $\not>$ right
    m = (7 + 11) DIV 2 = 9   ($k_9 = 30$)
    $k_0 \neq 30$
    $k_0 < 30$
    searchr(R,7,8)   (i.e,. search between keys 23 and 25)
      left $\not>$ right
      m = (7 + 8) DIV 2 = 7   ($k_7 = 23$)
      $k_0 \neq 23$
      $k_0 \not< 23$
      searchr(R,8,8)   (i.e,. search between keys 25 and 25)
        left $\not>$ right
        m = (8 + 8) DIV 2 = 8   ($k_8 = 25$)
        $k_0 = 25$
        Return 8.   (Key is found.)

Applying the recursive algorithm to the case when the key is not in the file is left as an exercise.

With the same data, the iterative algorithm proceeds as follows:

  Assume $k_0 = 10$.
  left < right and $k_0 \neq k_m$
    m = (1 + 11) DIV 2 = 6   ($k_6 = 19$)
    10 < 19
      right = 6 – 1 = 5
    left < right and $k_0 \neq k_m$
    m = (1 + 5) DIV 2 = 3   ($k_3 = 12$)
    10 < 12
      right = 3 – 1 = 2
    left < right and $k_0 \neq k$
    m = (1 + 2) DIV 2 = 1   ($k_1 = 4$)
    10 $\not<$ 4
      left = 1 + 1 = 2
    left $\not<$ right
  $k_0 \neq k_m$
    Return 0.   (Key is not found.)

Applying the iterative algorithm to the case when the key is in the file is left as an exercise.

Programs

Both the iterative and the recursive algorithms can be implemented in Pascal. Only the recursive one is included because it is more readable. The iterative algorithm is implemented in COBOL.

In Pascal, binary search is implemented as the following recursive procedure:

```
procedure binarysearch (var R : arraytype;
                        keysubzero : integer;
                        left, right : integer;
                        keylocation : integer): integer;

{ binarysearch is a recursive procedure. It takes a
sorted array R of integers with subscripts
LEFT. .RIGHT, does a binary search to find a key
equal to KEYSUBZERO, and returns the subscript
KEYLOCATION of the found key or 0 if the key is not
found. }

var midpoint : integer;   { Subscript of key at
                            midpoint of interval. }
begin   { binarysearch }
  if left > right
  then keylocation := 0   { Return. keysubzero is
                            not in file. }
  else
    begin
      midpoint := (left + right) div 2;
      if keysubzero := r[midpoint]
        then keylocation := midpoint   { return.
                              keysubzero is found }
        else
          if keysubzero < R[midpoint]
            then binarysearch(R,keysubzero,left,
                              midpoint-1,keylocation)
                    { search the left subarray. }
            else binarysearch(R,keysubzero,
                     midpoint+1,right,keylocation)
                    { Search the right subarray. }
  end;   { binarysearch }
```

Pascal Program 2.5 *Binary Search*

The COBOL version of the binary search should look familiar. It is very much like the linear search in appearance. All of the complexities of the binary search are hidden in the extra word "ALL" in the SEARCH command. The SEARCH ALL command does require that the table to be searched be sorted. Furthermore, an additional clause is required in the table definition, telling whether the table is sorted in ascending or descending order, and on what key. The revised version follows.

```
01 SORTED-BUILDING-CODES.
   03 SORTED-BUILDING-ENTRY OCCURS 10 TIMES
              ASCENDING KEY IS SORTED-BUILDING-CODE
                            INDEXED BY SORTED-BLDG-INDEX.
      05 SORTED-BUILDING-CODE    PIC XXX.
      05 FILLER                  PIC X.
      05 SORTED-BUILDING-NAME    PIC X(21).

      . . . . .

SEARCH ALL SORTED-BUILDING-ENTRY
   AT END MOVE 'NO' TO BUILDING-FOUND
          MOVE SPACES TO OUT-BUILDING-NAME
   WHEN IN-BUILDING-CODE = SORTED-BUILDING-CODE(BLDGIDX)
          MOVE 'YES' TO BUILDING-FOUND
          MOVE SORTED-BUILDING-NAME(BLDG-IDX) TO
                   OUT-BUILDING-NAME.
```

COBOL Program 2.5 *Binary Search of a Table*

Analysis

After each comparison of k_0 and k_m, the remaining portion of the file is split in half. Only (1/2) the keys remain to be searched after the first comparison, $(1/2)^2 = 1/4$ after the second comparison, $(1/2)^3 = 1/8$ after the third comparison, and so on. If the key is not in the file, or if it is found when only one key remains to be checked, as in the example, the algorithm will terminate one comparison after the difference in values of *left* and *right* is 1. The worst case occurs after j comparisons, where j is the largest value such that $2j \le n$, the number of records in the original file. In the example, $j = 3$. Solving the inequality $2j \le n$ for j, we get $j \le \log_2 n$. Therefore, binary search is an $O(\log n)$ algorithm. (In big-oh notation, it is not necessary to specify the base of a logarithm. Why?) This is a worst-case estimate, whether or not the key is in the file. The best case occurs when the key is found with the first comparison. On the average, the key will be found after about half the number of comparisons between 1 and j have been made.

The following table illustrates the relative efficiencies of algorithms that are $O(n)$, such as sequential search, and $O(\log n)$.

n	$O(n)$	$O(\log n)$
2	2	1
4	4	2
8	8	3
16	16	4
1024	1024	10
65,536	65,536	16
262,144	262,144	18
1,048,576	1,048,576	20

It is evident from the table that binary search is more efficient than sequential search, especially for large files. However, other factors may influence a choice between the two methods. Binary search is possible only with the key on which a file is sorted and when the file's records are stored so that they can be accessed randomly. For example, a binary search can be performed on a sorted file of records stored as an array, but not as a one-way linked list. Sequential search may be preferred for applications requiring extensive file updating, including insertions and deletions.

Summary

Large quantities of data are managed by organizing them into records and files. Files are searched to locate one or more records. The search process involves comparing a given key k_0 of a record with the keys of the other records in the file. Eventually, a key k_i is found such that $k_0 = k_i$ (or $k_0 > k_i$ or $k_0 < k_i$), in which case the record is either found or determined not to be in the file. The process can be followed whether or not the file is sorted, but it is appreciably faster for sorted files.

There are many search and sort methods. Sequential search is the simplest and applies to both sorted and unsorted files. Binary search is faster—$O(\log n)$ versus $O(n)$ for sequential search—but requires a sorted file.

Some of the basic sort methods fall into three categories: selection, insertion, and exchange sorts. A selection sort searches through the file to find (select) the right record for a particular position. An insertion sort chooses a record and searches for the right place to put (insert) it. An exchange sort repeatedly exchanges records in the file until the file is sorted. The representative methods from each category—straight selection, insertion, and bubble, respectively—are the most straightforward and easy-to-implement sort methods available. They are also some of the slowest. All three methods are $O(n^2)$. They are considered appropriate only for small files, including the files that appear toward the end of methods that are faster for large files. Two of the faster sorts are considered in the next chapter.

EXERCISES

1. In the introduction to this chapter, six reasons for searching files were given. For each reason, give an example in which a large file would be searched.
2. Verify the analysis of the sequential search algorithm for unsorted files by running the following experiment:

    Create an unsorted file of 500 or more keys (preferably randomly generated). Randomly generate fifty or more values. Write a program that will search the file sequentially for each value and count the number of comparisons. Average the number of comparisons.
3. Repeat the experiment in Exercise 2 after first sorting the file.
4. Write the straight selection sort without using the second array. Compare/contrast your algorithm with insertion sort.
5. Develop a recursive algorithm and write the program for the straight selection sort.
6. Can the bubble sort algorithm be rewritten to eliminate unnecessary executions of the statement *exchange* = **true**. Explain.
7. In the bubble sort example, keys near the beginning of the file also seem to become sorted (not just at the end) as the sort proceeds. Is this behavior expected of the algorithm? Can you give an example in which the behavior does not occur?
8. Design an experiment to verify the results of the analysis of any one of the sort methods included in this chapter.
9. For each of the three sort methods, give an example in which one method would be more appropriate than the other two.
10. Could linked lists be used instead of arrays to implement selection, insertion, and exchange sorts? If so, list advantages and disadvantages. If not, give a reason.
11. Use the recursive binary search algorithm to determine whether the key 17 is in the example file.
12. Use the iterative binary search algorithm to determine whether the key 25 is in the example file.
13. Write an iterative function in Pascal for binary search.
14. Design and conduct an experiment to compare the efficiencies of the sequential and binary searches on large sorted files.

CHAPTER 3

FASTER SORTING

INTRODUCTION

Internal sorts in the last chapter were all characterized by $O(n^2)$ comparisons. In each case the $O(n^2)$ estimate was a direct result of involving the entire unsorted portion of the file at the beginning of each pass. Because, in general, only one key was placed in its proper position during each pass, the unsorted portion required $n-j$ comparisons for the jth pass, $j = 1,2,\ldots,n-1$. Addition of these comparisons led to the $O(n^2)$ result.

There is no reason to expect any significant improvement in efficiency unless, for example, less than the entire unsorted file is involved during a pass. That this might be a reasonable approach is suggested by the effects on searching efficiency achieved in the binary versus the sequential search methods. Working with roughly half of the file at any one time reduces comparisons from $O(n)$ for sequential search to $O(\log n)$ for binary search.

In this chapter we discuss a sort method called **quicksort** which uses the strategy of dividing a file into two parts at each stage. For this method efficiency is improved from $O(n^2)$ to $O(n \log n)$, which is the best estimate (that is, it is a lower bound) for sorts involving comparisons. A second $O(n \log n)$ method called **heapsort** is also presented. The discussion of this sort uses the concept of a **tree**—and more specifically, a binary tree. Some pertinent information about trees and binary trees is given prior to introducing the two sort methods.

TREES AND BINARY TREES

Trees

A tree is a data structure that includes storage of a value (or values) and the explicit representation of connection, or association, between pairs of values. Figure 3.1 shows a tree structure representing relationships in a family. The values stored in boxes are the names of people. The lines connecting boxes represent the relationships of ancestors/descendants. For example, Karen is an ancestor of Judy; Judy is a descendant of Karen. The structure facilitates locating the parent, or child, of any individual. It does not provide an easy way to identify siblings, that is, other values at the same level of the tree.

The tree structure is useful in a wide variety of areas of computing (for example, artificial intelligence, databases, decision support systems, and languages). Trees are studied as special cases of the abstract structures called **graphs** (which allow more relationships to be represented), usually in discrete mathematics or theoretical computer science courses. We treat trees as data structures (without reference to graphs), define them, establish notation and terminology, and then consider binary trees as the topic most relevant to the study of faster sort methods.

> DEFINITION. A **tree** is a finite set of one or more nodes such that:
> (i) there is a specially designated node called the root;
> (ii) the remaining nodes are partitioned into $n \geq 0$ disjoint sets $T_1, \ldots, T_n$, where each of the sets is a tree. ($T_1, \ldots, T_n$ are called **subtrees** of the root.)

This is a recursive definition; that is, tree is defined in terms of itself. Part (ii) of the definition introduces the concept of a partition, that is, the separation of a set of elements into subsets such that each element appears in and is a member of only one subset. To get a better idea of a partition, consider the problem of putting together a jigsaw puzzle. A usual first step involves finding all the border pieces. At the end of this step, the set of puzzle pieces is partitioned into two subsets, one containing all the

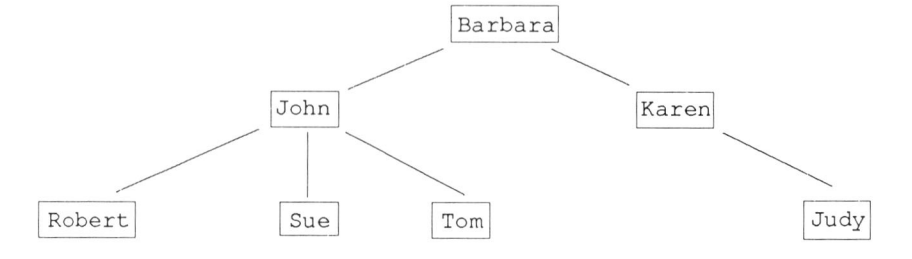

Figure 3.1 A family tree.

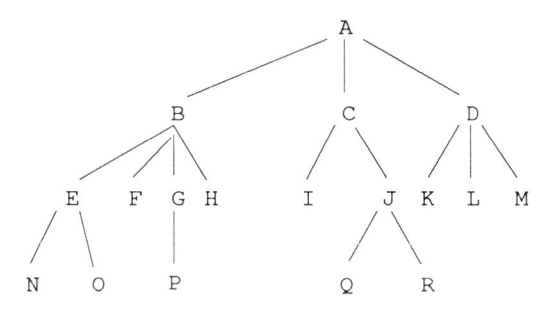

Figure 3.2 An example of a tree.

border pieces, and the other containing the rest of the pieces. Other partitioning is possible as work on the puzzle develops. For example, a partition into four subsets might include all sky pieces, all pieces with part of a house, all pieces with yellow on them, and all the remaining pieces. There are many examples of partitions, although the actual term is rarely used. In a high school, for instance, all students are partitioned into freshmen, sophomores, juniors, and seniors. All merchandise in a store is partitioned into departments such as sportswear, toys, furniture, and electronics.

Figure 3.2 is an example of a tree as it is typically portrayed, with its root at the top. We refer to this tree to review common terminology.

    a. A,B, ... R are **nodes.**
    b. A is the **root.**
    c. The root A has three **subtrees**: the set of nodes B,E,F,G,H,N,O,P (T_1), the set C,I,J,Q,R (T_2), and the set D,K,L,M (T_3). These sets are disjoint and constitute a partition (a set of disjoint sets).
    d. B is the root of the tree (subtree) T_1.
    e. J is the root of the tree (subtree) consisting of the nodes J,Q,R.
    f. The tree has four **levels.** Level 0 consists of the root A; level 1, the nodes B,C,D; etc.
    g. A is the **parent** of B,C,D; B is the parent of E,F,G,H; etc.
    h. B,C,D are **offspring** of A; E,F,G,H, of B; I,J, of C;. . .; Q,R, of J.
    i. B,C,D are **siblings** as are E,F,G,H, but E is not a sibling of D because they have different parents.
    j. The **degree** of A is 3, the number of subtrees. The degree of B is 4; of C, 2; . . .; of J, 2.
    k. Nodes of degree 0, such as F,H,I,K,L,M,N,O,P,Q, and R, are called **terminal**, or **leaf**, nodes; others are **nonterminal**, or **branch,** nodes.
    l. The **height,** or **depth,** of the tree is 3, the length of the longest path from the root to a terminal node.

Binary Trees

DEFINITION. A **binary tree** is a finite set of nodes which either is empty or consists of a root and two disjoint binary trees called the **left** and **right subtrees** of the root.

In Figure 3.3(a), the root A has the left subtree B and the right subtree C. The left and right subtrees of both B and C are empty. In part (b), the root A has the left subtree B,D,E,H, whose root is B, and the right subtree C,F,G,I, whose root is C. D, when considered as the root of a binary tree (the left subtree of B), has the left subtree H and an empty right subtree. In part (c), the left subtree of the root A is empty, and the right subtree consists of nodes B,C,D,E,F,G. Thus, any node in a binary tree has two binary subtrees, but one or both of them can be empty. The terminology in the preceding list (a)–(l) applies to binary trees as well. Although binary trees, by definition, are not trees (binary trees can have zero nodes; trees must have at least one node, the root), it is possible to transform any tree into a binary tree and the process is reversible. This, and the fact that binary trees have significant applications, make them worthwhile structures to study.

As discussed earlier, binary search can be described in terms of a binary tree. In the example on pages 54–55, the keys that divided (partitioned) the file at each stage were 19, 30, 23, and 25. Let 19 be the root of a binary tree. Then the search is conducted in the left or right subtree when the key value is, respectively, less than or greater than 19. The same pro-

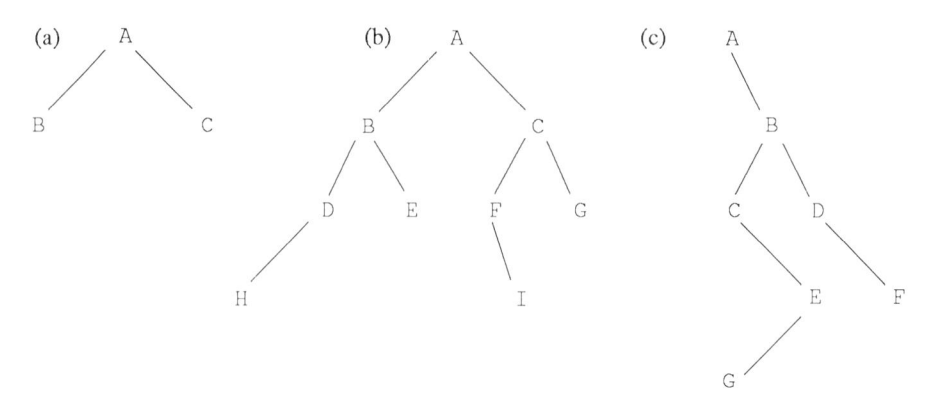

Figure 3.3 Examples of binary trees.

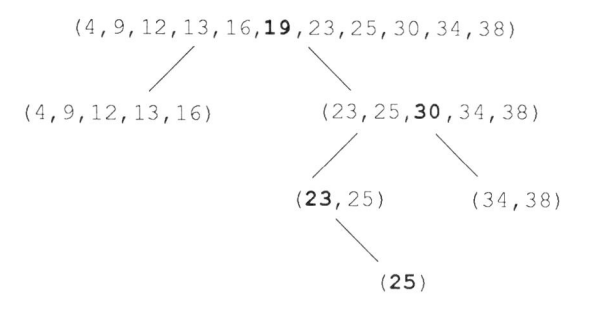

```
            (4,9,12,13,16,19,23,25,30,34,38)
           /                                \
   (4,9,12,13,16)                    (23,25,30,34,38)
                                      /             \
                                  (23,25)          (34,38)
                                       \
                                       (25)
```

Figure 3.4 A tree version of the binary search.

cess is followed at each root until either the key is found or an empty subtree is encountered. The binary tree is shown in Figure 3.4, with boldface numbers representing the keys actually compared in the example search.

This representation shows the partitioning of the file. In particular, it shows that half of the remaining file is ignored at each stage. The maximum number of comparisons is the depth of the binary tree.

Analysis of the binary search algorithm is somewhat easier to follow with the aid of this representation. The analysis is considered here and then referred to when sort methods are presented later in this chapter. At level 0 (the root) of the binary tree, there are n keys to search. The first comparison divides the n keys approximately in half, leaving $\lceil n/2 \rceil$[1] keys to be searched at level 1. After the comparison at level 1, at most $\lceil n/4 \rceil = \lceil n*(1/2)^2 \rceil$ keys remain to be searched at level 2. In general, at most $\lceil n*(1/2)^j \rceil$ keys remain at level j. The total number of comparisons, then, is that value of j such that $\lceil n*(1/2)^j \rceil \leq 1$. Thus, in the worst case, $j \leq \log n$, as established earlier.

Two additional results for binary trees are needed in the analysis of faster sort methods:

    a. The maximum number of nodes at level j of a binary tree is 2^j.
    b. The maximum number of nodes in a binary tree of depth m is $2^{m+1} - 1$, $m \geq 0$.

The example in Figure 3.5 illustrates these results.

The binary tree in Figure 3.5 illustrates both results. It contains the maximum number of nodes and is called a **full binary tree**. All nodes, except those at the last level, have two nonempty subtrees. The maximum number of nodes at level 0 is $1 = 2^0$; at level 1 is $2 = 2^1$; at level 2 is $4 = 2^2$; and, in general, at level j is 2^j. Proof of this result requires mathematical

---

1. $\lceil x \rceil$ = the smallest integer not less than x. For example, $\lceil 5.2 \rceil = 6$ and $\lceil 3 \rceil = 3$.

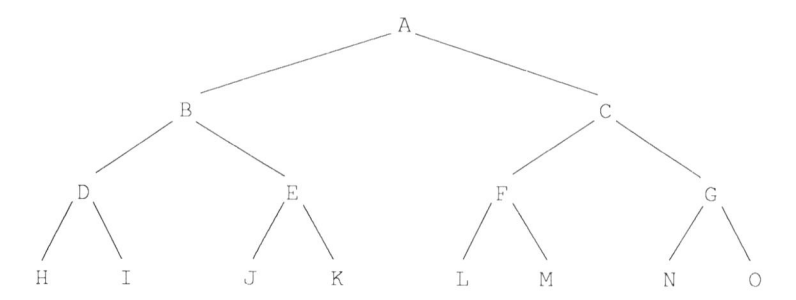

Figure 3.5 *A full binary tree.*

induction; it is left as an exercise. Result (b) is obtained by adding together the maximum number of nodes at each level.

LIMITS TO COMPARISON-BASED SORT ALGORITHMS

The results from the previous section are used in the analysis of the two sort methods in this chapter. Before discussing those methods, however, we address the general question of how efficient a sort based on comparisons can be. Is $O(n^2)$, as in the three sort methods of Chapter 2, the best we can expect from a sort method? If the answer is yes, then there is little need to consider additional sort methods; any of one the three methods is simple enough, and all of them are $O(n^2)$.

The answer is that there are comparison-based sorts which are better than $O(n^2)$. In fact, some of them sort in time $O(n \log n)$. The improvement is analogous to sequential versus binary searches—$O(n)$ to $O(\log n)$—and for a similar reason. That is, when a sort divides a file into two parts at each stage, there is a dramatic decrease in number of comparisons from $O(n^2)$ to $O(n \log n)$. The amount of difference, especially for large values of n (that is, for large files), is apparent in the following table:

n	$O(n^2)$	$O(n \log n)$
1024	1,048,576 (10^6)	10,240 (10^4)
8192	67,108,864 (10^7)	106,496 (10^5)
65,536	4,294,967,296 (10^9)	1,048,576 (10^6)
262,144	687,194,767,736 (10^{11})	4,718,592 (10^6)
1,048,576	(10^{12})	20,971,520 (10^7)

(The powers of 10 shown are approximations of the magnitudes of the numbers.)

There have been extensive study of and experimentation with sort techniques leading to an answer to this question (some of the references are included in the list at the end of the book). We give a result which establishes a limit on the efficiency of any comparison-based sort. After indicating why it is a reasonable conclusion, we present two methods, quicksort and heapsort, whose sort times approximate the result.

In particular, the following result can be proved:

> Every comparison-based sort requires a minimum of $c(n \log n)$ comparisons on the average, for some constant $c > 0$.

The proof is based on the assumptions that all orderings of the file to be sorted are equally likely and that all keys are distinct (if not, the algorithm will take less time). Then each comparison in which the key is not found involves determining that the key is less than or greater than the key in the file. But this is equivalent to deciding whether to follow the left or right branch of a binary tree.

For example, consider the file of three keys, t,u,s. Let $t:u$ denote a comparison of t and u. Figure 3.6 displays the comparisons required to sort the file in any possible order. The binary tree is based on the assumption that when a comparison, for example, $t:u$, is made at each node, the left subtree is followed if the first element is less than the second; otherwise, the right subtree is followed. The correct path for the specific ordering t,u,s is shown in boldface.

Given any three keys, a similar binary tree could be constructed. The terminal nodes would represent every possible ordering of the three keys. Only one path would lead to a correct ordering.

The binary tree representation provides an example of two general results needed in the proof. One result is that there are $n!$ nodes representing possible orderings of a file of n keys. (In the example, there are $3! = 6$ possible orderings of three keys.) The other result was discussed previously—namely, that there are at most 2^j nodes at level j. (In the example, there are at most $2^2 = 4$ nodes at level 2 and $2^3 = 8$ nodes at level 3.) Because the maximum number of nodes at the bottom level is greater than or equal to the number of possible orderings of a file, it follows that $2^{(C(n))} \geq n!$

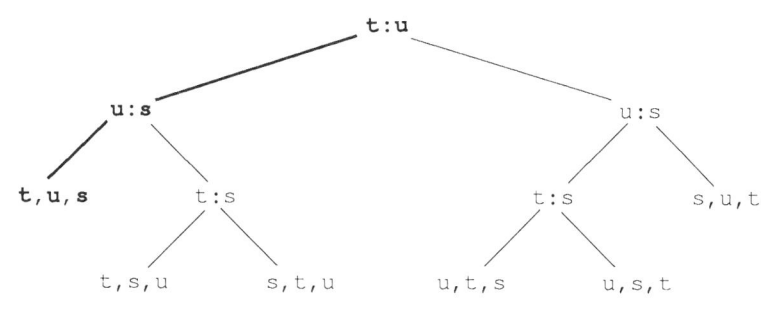

Figure 3.6 All possible comparisons of three keys.

where $C(n)$ = the depth of the binary tree, including the nodes representing file orderings as part of the binary tree. Since $C(n)$ is an integer, we get

$C(n) \geq \lceil \log(n!) \rceil$.

The mathematical formula known as Stirling's approximation can be applied to show that $\lceil \log(n!) \rceil$ is greater than or equal to an expression that is $O(n \log n)$. Since the depth of a binary tree of comparisons (also called a comparison tree or decision tree) is equal to the number of comparisons, it follows that $C(n)$ is $O(n \log n)$, which implies that the number of comparisons in a comparison-based sort method is no less than $O(n \log n)$. Furthermore, this bound can actually be obtained, as shown in the analyses of the two internal sort methods, quicksort and heapsort.

A DIVIDE-AND-CONQUER SORT

Divide and conquer describes a class of methods that involve solving (conquering) problems by successively splitting (dividing) them into smaller problems until the smaller problems can be readily solved. Binary search is an example of a divide-and-conquer method for searching files. One of the most efficient divide-and-conquer sort methods is called **quicksort**.

Quicksort

The sort method known as quicksort appeared in 1962 in a paper by C. A. R. Hoare (see Reference List). It is considered to be one of the fastest sort methods for large files whose records are randomly arranged.

Method

In quicksort, one key, called the "pivot," is chosen initially. All other keys are compared to it; the lesser ones end up to the left of the pivot and the greater ones to the right. Keys equal to the pivot end up on one side. At the end of the first pass, the pivot key is in its proper position and the original file is divided (partitioned) into two subfiles, one with keys less than (and equal to, if our comparisons are ≤ rather than <) the pivot, and the other with keys greater than (and, possibly, equal to) the pivot. Place one subfile (actually only the indices of the subfile's first and last keys) on a stack. Choose a new pivot for the other subfile and repeat the process. The pivot key ends up in its proper position with respect to the final sorted file, and two new subfiles are created, one of which may be empty. Continue the process until one subfile is empty. Then remove the top file on the stack and process it as before. Repeat until the stack is empty, at which time the original file is sorted.

Algorithm

The description above indicates that an algorithm for quicksort requires iteration and the operation of a stack. These can be implemented directly or through recursion. When a program written from a recursive algorithm is run, both the iteration and the stack mechanisms are automatically established. The recursive version is developed here because it more clearly depicts the quicksort process. As in previous algorithms, assume an unsorted file of n records whose keys are stored as an array, R.

Input: An array R of n keys, unsorted.
Output: The array R sorted in nondecreasing order.
Repeat the following steps until R is sorted:
1) Choose one key as the pivot. For simplicity, assume the leftmost (first) key is chosen.
2) Establish a pointer (subscript) i for the leftmost key that has not yet been compared to the pivot.
3) Establish a pointer (subscript) j for the rightmost (last) key in the array being searched.
4) Repeat the following steps until each key in the array has been compared to the pivot:
   (a) Compare the key, indicated by pointer i, to the pivot and move right to the next key until a key G is found that is greater than the pivot, or pointer i becomes greater than j.
   (b) Compare the key, indicated by subscript j, to the pivot and move the pointer j to the left until a key L is found that is less than the pivot, or the pointer j becomes less than i.
   (c) If the pointer to G, i, is less than j, exchange the positions of the two keys G and L.
5) Exchange the positions of the pivot and L.
6) Place on a stack the value of subscript i and of the rightmost array position. These define a part of the array still to be sorted.

Now sort the leftmost part of the array that is still to be sorted; this subarray has leftmost index equal to the leftmost index of the array just used. Its rightmost index is just to the left of (that is, 1 less than the index of) the position in which the pivot was just placed. The sort continues from step (1) using these new array bounds. If the new array bounds represent an empty array (an array with zero elements), then another set of array bounds is popped from the stack and the sorting continues. When the stack is empty, the array is sorted.

In this form, the algorithm explicitly specifies iteration and a stack. The refinement that follows will simplify the description by using recursion. The recursive version is shown in Pascal; the iterative version is then refined and illustrated with COBOL code.

Let P be the index of the pivot. For simplicity, the value of the leftmost (first) key is used for the pivot. Indices i and j keep track of the array elements being compared, with i being the index of the key on the left and j being the index of the key on the right. The variable k is used to refer to the elements of the array that is to be sorted, and the parameters, *left* and *right*, define the left and right edges (beginning and end) of the array. Initially, *left* = 1 and *right* = n to sort the entire array.

```
quicksort(left,right)
   begin
      p = left
      i = left + 1
      j = right
      repeat
         while (k_i ≤ k_p) and (i ≤ j) do
            i = i + 1
         while (k_j > k_p) and (i ≤ j) do
            j = j - 1
         if i < j
            then
               Interchange k_i and k_j
               i = i + 1
               j = j - 1
         until j < i
         Interchange k_p and k_j
         p = j
      quicksort(left,p-1)
      quicksort(p+1,right)
```

EXAMPLE 3.1

Assume the same file as in the previous internal sort examples is to be put into nondecreasing order. Initially, then, the file contains keys 21, 15, 62, 48, 21, 39, and 30. Choose the pivot as the leftmost key in the file to be sorted.

quicksort(1,7)
 $p = 1$
 $i = 2; j = 7$a
 $k_2 < k_p$ (15 < 21) and 2 < 7
  $i = 3$
  $k_3 > k_p$ (62 > 21). Exit the loop.
 $k_7 > k_p$ (30 > 21)
  $j = 6$
  $k_6 > k_p$ (39 > 21)
  $j = 5$
  $k_5 \not> k_p$ (21 = 21). Exit the loop.

3 < 5. Interchange the third and fifth keys.
(The order of the keys is now 21, 15, 21, 48, 62, 39, 30.)

  $i = 4$
  $j = 4$
  $k_4 > k_p$ (48 > 21). Exit the loop.
 $k_4 > k_p$ (48 > 21)
  $j = 3$
  $i \not< j$ (4 < 3). Exit the loop.
 $i \not< j$ (4 > 3). Exit the repeat loop.

Interchange the first and third keys.
$p = 3$

The file is now 21 15 <u>21</u> 48 62 39 30. The pivot, shown underlined, partitions the file into two disjoint subfiles, as intended. The algorithm continues by recursively applying this same partitioning process to the subfile to the left of the pivot [quicksort(1,2) is called] and then to the right of the pivot [quicksort(4,7) is called].

(If this array actually holds keys to records in a file, there would not usually be duplicate values, like the two 21s shown here. In general, of course, an array to be sorted might have duplicate values, and the way the sorting algorithm treats the duplicates is an important characteristic of the algorithm. See the exercises at the end of this chapter for more about how sort algorithms treat duplicates.)

Programs

The recursive algorithm is illustrated below in Pascal. The iterative version is then further refined and shown in COBOL on page 78.

```
procedure quicksort(var R :arraytype;
            left, right :integer);
{ Quicksort is a recursive procedure that sorts the
file R with indices left. . .right into
nondecreasing order. }
var
  p,                { Index of pivot                  }
  i,                { Index values from left          }
  j,                { Index values right              }
  TEMP : integer;   { Temporary, for interchanges     }

begin   { quicksort }
  if left < right then
    begin    { Partition the array into two
              subarrays, one  with key values less
              than or equal to the pivot, the
              other with key values greater than
              the pivot. }
      p := left+1;   { Pivot is leftmost key. }
      i := left;     { Initialize i to index of
                       leftmost key. }
      j := right;    { Initialize j to index of
                       rightmost key. }
    repeat    { Until i becomes less than j }
              { Find the next key value greater
                than the pivot. }
        while (R[i] <= R[p]) and (i <= j) do
          i := i + 1;
        { Find the next key value less than the
          pivot. }
        while (R[j] > R[p]) and (i <= j) do
          j := j - 1;
        if i < j then  { Interchange keys that are
                         out of order. }
          begin
            TEMP := R[i];
            R[i] := R[j];
            R[j] := TEMP;
            i := i+1;
            j := j-1;
          end;
      until j < i;
```

```
        { Interchange keys. }
        TEMP := R[j];
        R[j] := R[p];
        R[p] := TEMP;
        { Reset pivot index. }
        p := j
      end;           { Pivot partitions the array }
    quicksort(R,left,j-1);
    quicksort(R,i+1,right)
  end;    { quicksort }
```

Pascal Program 3.1 *Recursive Quicksort*

In the iterative implementation of the quicksort method, the stacking operations implied by recursion must be specified explicitly.

```
iterative-quicksort:
while (last – first) > 0
   pivot = first
   left = first + 1
   right = last
   repeat
      while R_left <= R_pivot and left <= right do
         left = left + 1
      while R_right > R_pivot and left <= right do
         right = right – 1
      if left < right
         interchange R_left and R_right
         left = left + 1
         right = right – 1
   until left > right
   Interchange R_right and R_pivot
   If (right – first) > 1
      then
         if last > left
            then push left, last onto stack
         last = right – 1
      else
         if (last – left) > 1
            then first = left + 1
            else
```

74 Chapter 3

>   if stack empty
>   then
>   last = 0
>   first = 0
>   else pop last, first from stack

When the pointer moving from the right crosses the pointer moving from the left, all values greater than the pivot have been placed to one side, and all values less than the pivot have been placed to the other side. The pivot is then moved into position between the two sections. The beginning and ending place of the right side, currently marked by values stored in left and last, are placed on the stack while the left side is sorted. When all left sides have been sorted, the limits will be popped from the stack and used to define the endpoints of a subarray that still must be sorted. When the attempt to pop the stack yields no endpoints, the values of last and first are set to zero. This indicates that there are no more subarrays to sort, and the outer while loop is terminated.

Example 3.2 has the same set of key values used in previous examples, but it is expanded to force enough use of the stack to demonstrate its role.

EXAMPLE 3.2

The following table indicates how we execute the iterative version of quicksort.

Array to be sorted: 21 15 62 48 21 39 30 25 10 54 60 12 9 4

Assignment or comparison made	Key values in comparison	Comments
last = 14		
first = 1		
pivot = 1		
left = 2		
right = 14		
$R_2 < R_1$	15 < 21	
and left ≤ right	2 < 14	Enter while loop
left = 3		
$R_3 > R_1$	62 > 21	Exit while loop
$R_{14} < R_1$	4 < 21	Exit while loop
left < right	3 < 14	Interchange R_3, R_{14}

New order of array: 21 15 4 48 21 39 30 25 10 54 60 12 9 62

left = 4
right = 13

left ≠ right	4 < 13	Continue repeat loop
$R_4 > R_1$	48 > 21	Exit while loop
$R_{13} < R_1$	9 < 21	Exit while loop
left < right	4 < 13	Interchange R_4, R_{13}

New order of array: 21 15 4 9 21 39 30 25 10 54 60 12 48 62

left = 5		
right = 12		
left ≠ right	5 < 12	Continue repeat loop
$R_5 = R_1$	21 = 21	
and left ≤ right	5 < 12	
left = 6		
$R_6 > R_1$	39 > 21	Exit while loop
$R_{12} < R_1$	12 < 21	Exit while loop
left < right		Interchange R_6, R_{12}

New order of array: 21 15 4 9 21 12 30 25 10 54 60 39 48 62

left = 7		
right = 11		
left < right		Continue repeat loop
$R_7 > R_1$	30 > 21	Exit while loop
$R_{11} > R_1$	60 > 21	
and left ≤ right	7 < 11	
right = 10		
$R_{10} > R_1$	54 > 21	
and left ≤ right	7 < 10	
right = 9		
$R_9 < R_1$	10 < 21	Exit while loop
left < right	7 < 9	Interchange R_7, R_9

New order of array: 21 15 4 9 21 12 10 25 30 54 60 39 48 62

left = 8		
right = 8		
left ≠ right	8 = 8	Continue repeat loop
$R_8 > R_1$	25 > 21	Exit while loop
$R_8 > R_1$		
and left ≤ right		
right = 7		
right < left	7 < 8	Exit while loop
left > right		Do not interchange
left > right		Exit repeat loop
Interchange R_7, R_1		

New order of array: 10 15 4 9 21 12 <u>21</u> 25 30 54 60 39 48 62

(The pivot, 21 (underlined), is in its final position. Everything to the left of the pivot is less than or equal to the pivot. Everything to the right of the pivot is greater than the pivot.)

right − first > 1	7 − 1 > 1	There is more array to sort to the left of the pivot.
last > left	14 > 8	There are values to the right of the pivot to be stored for later sorting.
Push 8, 14 onto stack	Stack contains: 8 14	
last = 6		

(Begin outer while loop again with endpoints of left side of array.)

last − first > 0	6 − 1 > 0	
pivot = 1		
left = 2		
right = 6		
$R_2 > R_1$	15 > 10	Exit while loop
$R_6 > R_1$	12 > 10	
and left ≤ right	2 < 6	
right = 5		
$R_5 > R_1$	21 > 10	
and left ≤ right	2 < 5	
right = 4		
$R_4 < R_1$	9 < 10	
left < right	2 < 4	Interchange R_2, R_4

New order of array: 10 9 4 15 21 12 <u>21</u> 25 30 54 60 39 48 62

left = 3		
right = 3		
left ≯ right		Exit repeat loop
$R_3 < R_1$	4 < 10	
and left ≤ right	3 = 3	
left = 4		
left > right		Exit while loop
left > right		Skip while loop
left ≮ right		Do not interchange
left > right		Exit repeat loop
Interchange R_3, R_1		

New order of array: 4 9 <u>10</u> 15 21 12 <u>21</u> 25 30 54 60 39 48 62

The second pivot (10) is now in place. Everything to the left is less than or equal to 10, everything to the right is greater than 10.

right − first >1	3 − 1 > 1	More sorting may be needed to the right of the pivot.
last > left	6 > 4	More sorting may be needed to the right of the pivot in the current subarray.
Push 4, 6 onto stack	Stack contains: 8 14 4 6	
last = 2		

Begin the outer while loop again.

last − first > 0	2 − 1 > 0	
pivot = 1		
left = 2		
right = 2		
$R_2 > R_1$	9 > 4	Exit while loop
$R_2 > R_1$		
and left ≤ right	2 = 2	
right = 1		
left > right	2 > 1	Exit while loop
left ≯ right		Do not interchange
left > right		End repeat loop
Interchange R_1, R_1		

New order of array: <u>4</u>   9   <u>10</u>   15   21   12   <u>21</u>   25   30   54   60   39   48   62

Another pivot is in place.

right − first ≯ 1	1 − 1 = 0	
last − left ≯ 1	2 − 2 = 0	
Stack is not empty.		
last = 6	Pop stack	
first = 4	Pop stack	
Stack now contains	8 14	

Begin outer while loop

last − first > 0	6 − 4 > 0	
pivot = 4		
left = 5		
right = 6		
$R_5 > R_4$	21 > 15	Exit while loop
$R_6 < R_4$	12 < 15	Exit while loop
left < right	5 < 6	Interchange R_5, R_6

New order of array: <u>4</u>   9   <u>10</u>   15   12   21   <u>21</u>   25   30   54   60   39   48   62

left = 6
right = 5
left > right   Exit repeat loop
Interchange R_5, R_4

New order of array: <u>4</u>   9   <u>10</u>   12   <u>15</u>   21   <u>21</u>   25   30   54   60   39   48   62

right − first $\not> 1$
last − left $\not> 1$
Stack is not empty
last = 4   Pop stack
first = 8   Pop stack

Begin outer while loop and sort the array from positions 8 through 14 in the same way that the left side of the array was sorted.

The COBOL implementation of the iterative version of the quicksort algorithm follows:

```
DATA DIVISION.
WORKING-STORAGE SECTION.
01 FILE-KEYS.
    03 R         OCCURS 50 TIMES
                 PICTURE 9(5).
01 ARRAY-INDICES.
    03 PIVOT          USAGE IS INDEX.
    03 LEFT           USAGE IS INDEX.
    03 RIGHT          USAGE IS INDEX.
    03 FIRST          USAGE IS INDEX.
    03 LAST           USAGE IS INDEX.

01 STACK-STRUCTURE.
    03 STACK     OCCURS 50 TIMES   USAGE IS INDEX
                 INDEXED BY S-PTR.

PROCEDURE DIVISION.

QUICKSORT.
    SET S-PTR TO 0.
    PERFORM MAIN-QUICKSORT UNTIL (LAST - FIRST) > 0.
```

```
MAIN-QUICKSORT.
    SET PIVOT TO FIRST.
    SET LEFT TO FIRST. SET LEFT UP BY 1.
    SET RIGHT TO LAST.
    PERFORM MOVE-POINTERS UNTIL LEFT > RIGHT.
    MOVE R(RIGHT) TO TEMPORARY.
MOVE R(PIVOT) TO R(RIGHT).
    MOVE TEMPORARY TO R(RIGHT).
    IF (RIGHT - FIRST) > 1
        PERFORM STACK-RIGHT-AND-USE-LEFT
      ELSE
        IF (LAST - LEFT) > 1
            SET FIRST TO LEFT  SET FIRST UP BY 1
          ELSE
            IF S-PTR = 0
               SET LAST TO 0
               SET FIRST TO 0
              ELSE
                POP-FROM-STACK.

MOVE-POINTERS.
    PERFORM ADD-LEFT
        UNTIL (R(PIVOT) > r(LEFT)) OR (RIGHT < LEFT).
    PERFORM SUBTRACT-RIGHT
        UNTIL (R(PIVOT) > R(RIGHT)) OR (RIGHT < LEFT).

ADD-LEFT.
    SET LEFT UP BY 1.
SUBTRACT-RIGHT.
    SET RIGHT DOWN BY 1.

STACK-LEFT-AND-USE-RIGHT.
    IF LAST > LEFT
        PERFORM PUSH-ON-STACK.
    SET LAST TO RIGHT. SET LAST DOWN BY 1.

PUSH-ON-STACK.
    SET S-PTR UP BY 1.
    MOVE LEFT TO STACK(S-PTR).
    SET S-PTR UP BY 1.
    MOVE LAST TO STACK(S-PTR).

POP-FROM-STACK.
    SET LAST TO STACK(S-PTR).
    SET S-PTR DOWN BY 1.
    SET FIRST TO STACK(S-PTR).
    SET S-PTR DOWN BY 1.
```

COBOL Program 3.1 *Quicksort*

Analysis

A detailed analysis of quicksort involves recurrence formulas and algebraic manipulation. Some authors also incorporate calculus or probability-based arguments to obtain bounds on the number of comparisons. A complete proof that quicksort is an $O(n \log n)$ method in the average and best cases is beyond the scope of this book. However, quicksort is no better than $O(n \log n)$; it is evident from the sketch of the proof in the section "Limits to Comparison-Based Sort Algorithms" that any comparison-based sort is at least $O(n \log n)$.

Consider the best case situation for quicksort, namely, when the pivot at each stage divides the file (subfile) into two equal parts. Then the comparison activity in quicksort can be illustrated with a binary tree as in Figure 3.7, where the fraction represents the approximate size of the subfile in relation to the original file and the quantity in parentheses is the approximate number of comparisons required to move to the next level of the tree.

At the jth level there will be 2^j nodes, each representing $1/2^j$ of the original file and requiring $n/2^j$ comparisons. The number of comparisons, then, for the best case of quicksort is less than or equal to

$$(n-1) + 2(n/2 - 1) + 4(n/4 - 1) + \ldots + 2^j(n/2^j - 1)$$

But this sum is less than or equal to $n * j$, where j is the depth of the binary tree. From before, $n * j \leq c(n \log n)$; hence quicksort is $O(n \log n)$ in the best case.

The worst case of quicksort occurs when the pivot is the least (or greatest) key value at each stage. In this case, the first pivot divides the

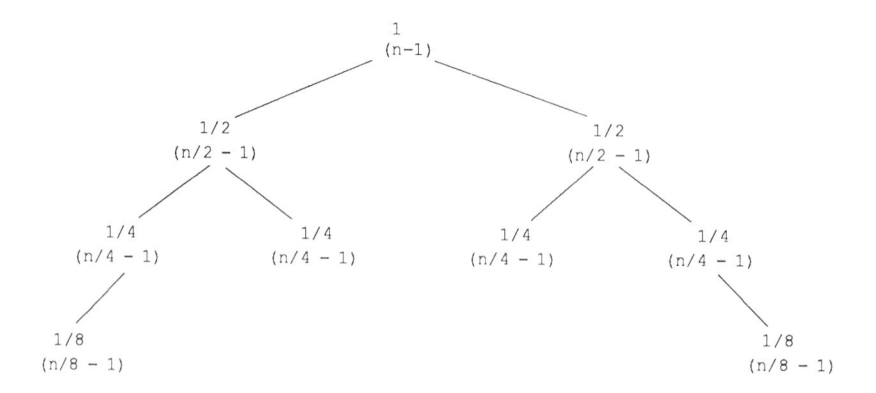

```
                        1
                      (n-1)
                   /         \
               1/2             1/2
             (n/2 - 1)       (n/2 - 1)
             /     \         /      \
          1/4     1/4      1/4      1/4
       (n/4 - 1)(n/4 - 1)(n/4 - 1)(n/4 - 1)
         /                              \
       1/8                              1/8
    (n/8 - 1)                        (n/8 - 1)
```

Figure 3.7 The number of comparisons in quicksort when the pivot equally divides the file at each step.

original file into an empty subfile and a subfile of $n - 1$ keys. The second pivot divides the file of $n - 1$ keys into an empty subfile and a subfile of $n - 2$ keys, and so on. The number of comparisons is the sum of the first $n - 1$ integers (the same as in the straight selection sort), and the method is $O(n^2)$ in the worst case. Curiously, this case occurs when the original file is already sorted and the pivot is chosen to be the first key at each stage. It can also occur, but is not likely, when the file is unsorted and the pivot is chosen randomly. The pivots would have to appear in the same order in which the file is to be sorted.

There are various ways to modify quicksort to approach best-case efficiency. Generally, they involve selecting pivots or changing to another sort method for small subfiles. Experimental evidence has shown that selecting the first key (the one with the lowest array index) at each stage tends to produce a slower quicksort than randomizing the choice. Two suggested ways to select pivots involve using a random number generator or the median of three keys (such as the first, middle, and last). Switching to a straight selection or insertion sort when small subfiles are encountered can also make quicksort faster (but not better than $O(n \log n)$). For subfiles of sixteen or fewer keys, quicksort has large overhead, while insertion sort, for example, is relatively fast.

Memory requirements for quicksort are greater than those for previous methods. In addition to space for the array (file) of records and a location to handle interchanges, memory is needed for a stack and two pointers (indices). The stack size depends on how many subfiles (pairs of indices) are placed on it during a specific implementation, but the maximum size will be one-half the number of nodes on the binary tree. From before, that number is $(2^j - 1)/2$. Of course, each entry in the stack is a pair of indices. A location for the pointer to the top of the stack is also required. The stack size can be minimized by placing the larger partition on the stack and processing the smaller one immediately. Small subfiles are partitioned fewer times than large ones, so the stack does not contain as many subfiles.

A TREE-BASED SORT

A second category of sort methods that are $O(n \log n)$ is based on tree structures. One specific method, **heapsort,** is discussed in detail. Its effectiveness is due to the properties of a type of complete binary tree called a heap. In order to understand how heapsort works we must know what a complete binary tree is and how it can be made into a heap.

A complete binary tree with n nodes and depth k is best described in terms of a full binary tree of depth k. A full binary tree of depth k has $2^k - 1$ nodes numbered as in Figure 3.8. A complete binary tree with n nodes and depth k corresponds to the nodes numbered 1 to n in the full

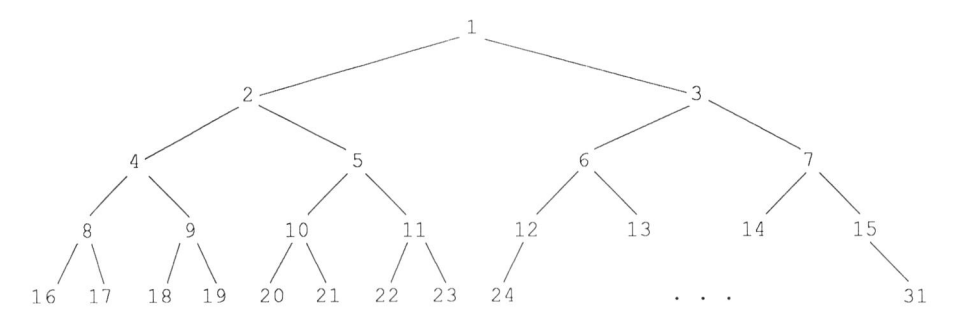

Figure 3.8 A full binary tree with thrity-one nodes.

binary tree of depth k. For example, the first twenty-two nodes in Figure 3.8 constitute a complete binary tree, where $n = 22$ and $k = 5$.

Both complete and full binary trees can be stored as one-dimensional arrays because of the way the nodes are numbered—that is, the left and right offspring of the kth node are numbered $2k$ and $2k+1$, respectively. In terms of the array, if the index of the kth node is k, then $2k$ and $2k+1$ are the indices of its left and right offspring, respectively. Of course, if $2k > n$, then there is no left offspring of the kth node. Similarly, if $2k + 1 > n$, then there is no right offspring.

> **DEFINITION:** A **heap** is a complete binary tree such that the value at each node is greater than or equal to the values at its offspring (if they are not empty).

According to the definition, only one of the binary trees in Figure 3.9—part (i)—is a heap. The binary tree in part (ii) is complete, but the node with value 30 is less than one of its offspring. The binary tree in part (iii) meets the value of nodes requirement but is not complete. As previously noted, a complete binary tree requires a particular ordering of nodes in a full binary tree.

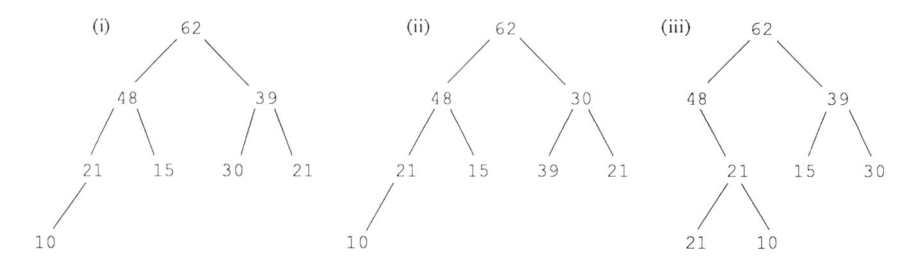

Figure 3.9 Binary tree (i) is a heap; (ii) and (iii) are not.

Creating a Heap

There are several ways to construct a heap from an array of n keys. One way involves inserting each key in turn into a heap consisting of all previous keys. This approach proceeds as follows. The first key is already a heap. Add the second key to the bottom level of the heap (that is, as the left offspring, in this case). Compare it to the parent and interchange, if necessary, to maintain the heap property, namely, that the value of the parent node at position k is not less than the values of its offspring nodes at positions $2k$ and $2k+1$. Add the third key to the bottom level of the heap just created (as the right offspring), and compare and interchange with the parent, if necessary. Add the fourth key to the bottom level of the heap just created, and compare and interchange it with its parent, if necessary. Then compare it with its new parent and interchange, if necessary. Continue the process until all keys in the array constitute a heap. This approach can be expressed as a recursive algorithm.

A second, and better, way to construct a heap from an array of n keys assumes that all keys in the array are stored as if they were in a complete binary tree. Each step involves combining two heaps into one, until the entire binary tree is a heap. Initially, every leaf is considered to be a heap. The process begins at the bottom level by comparing the greater of the keys at positions $2k$ and $2k+1$ with its parent at position k and interchanging the two keys if the parent is less than the greater offspring. The process systematically works up the binary tree, level by level, by comparing the greater of two offspring with its parent and interchanging as necessary. Each time a parent at level m is interchanged with its greater offspring, it becomes a parent at level $m+1$. It must then be compared with the greater of its offspring at level $m+2$, and so on, until a heap results.

As an illustration, the following steps create a heap from the file in Figure 3.10(i).

(i)

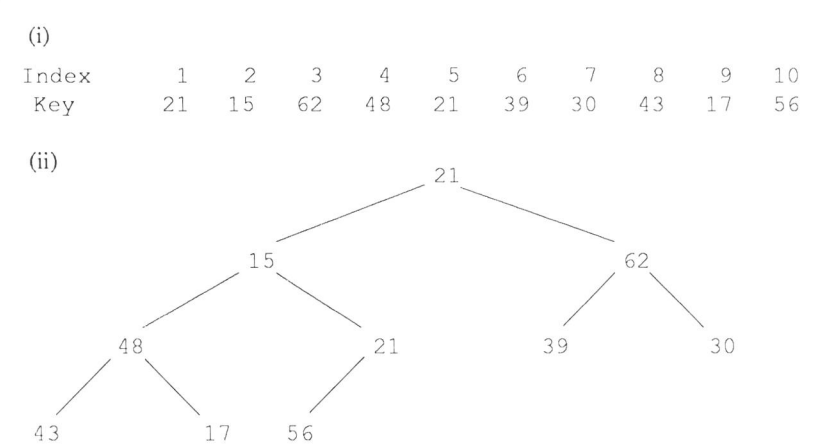

Index	1	2	3	4	5	6	7	8	9	10
Key	21	15	62	48	21	39	30	43	17	56

(ii)

```
                          21
                 /                  \
              15                     62
            /    \                  /    \
          48      21              39      30
         /  \    /
        43  17  56
```

Figure 3.10 A file of ten keys (i) as an array and (ii) as a complete binary tree.

Compare 56 with 21. Interchange.
Compare 17 with 43 and then 43 with 48. No interchange. After the lowest level has been processed, the tree is as shown below:

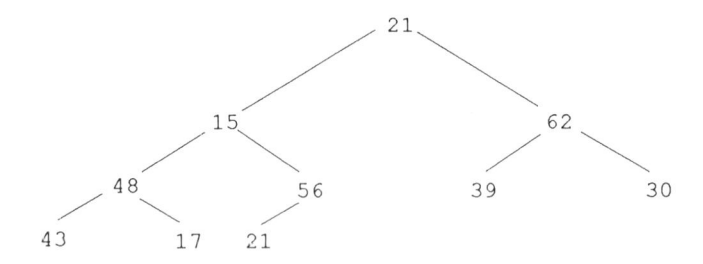

```
                    21
           15                62
       48        56       39      30
    43    17  21
```

Now continue with the next lowest level.

Compare 30 with 39 and then 39 with 62. No interchange.
Compare 56 with 48 and then 56 with 15. Interchange.
Compare 15 with 21 (in the bottom level). Interchange. Keys at level 2 have been processed (recall that the root is level 0) and the tree is now

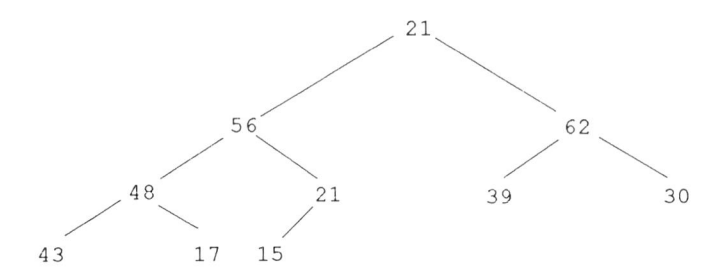

```
                    21
           56                62
       48        21       39      30
    43    17  15
```

Now process keys at level 1 with their parent.

Compare 62 with 56 and then 62 with 21. Interchange.
Compare 39 with 30 and then 39 with 21. Interchange. The process stops. The following heap has been created:

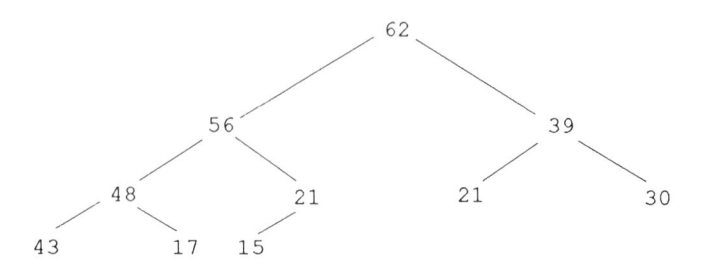

```
                    62
           56                39
       48        21       21      30
    43    17  15
```

We express the process more formally as an algorithm named *createheap*. It consists of repeated calls to another algorithm, *heapmaker*, one call for each key in the file. The key with index j is the root of the heap to be made (at each step). Then $2j$ and $2j+1$ are indices of its offspring. The index *last* determines whether j is the index of a leaf. In particular, j is the index of a leaf if $j > last/2$.

Createheap:

Input: An array R of n records with keys in the order $k_1, k_2, \ldots, k_n$
Output: The array R arranged as a heap.

```
createheap:
for j = n down to 1 do
    heapmaker(j,n)
```

Heapmaker is the following recursive routine.

```
heapmaker(j,last)
    if (kj not a leaf) and
       (kj < its greater offspring ki, where j ≤ i ≤ last)
    then
        interchange kj and ki
        heapmaker(i,last)
```

The loop in this algorithm *createheap* cycles through all keys in the file from the last to the first. It is not necessary to do so because all keys after the one with index equal to the greatest integer in $n/2$ are leaf nodes. Consequently, the algorithm's efficiency is improved by having the loop begin with the greatest integer in $n/2$, rather than n.

Heapsort

The sort method called **Heapsort** appeared originally in 1964 in a paper by J. W. Williams (see Reference List). Heapsort involves alternately creating a heap and performing an interchange. The method is $O(n \log n)$ in the best, worst, and average cases.

Method

The **createheap** algorithm initially converts any file into a heap. The key with the greatest value is the root of the heap, and the root is in the first position in the array. By interchanging the first and last (nth) keys, the greatest key goes to the end of the array. Using the algorithm again, create a heap of the $n-1$ remaining keys and then interchange the root and the n–1st key. Repeat this process j times, for $j = n, n-1, \ldots, 2$, each time

86   Chapter 3

placing the next largest key in its position in the array. The result is an array of keys sorted in nondecreasing order.

Algorithm

The algorithm for heapsort relies heavily on the algorithm *heapmaker* developed in the preceding section.

Input: An array R of n records with keys $k_1,\ldots,k_n$.
Output: The array R with keys sorted in nondecreasing order.
1. Convert R to a heap.
2. Repeat the following steps until the keys are sorted:
   (a) Interchange the root and the last remaining unsorted key.
   (b) Make a heap of the remaining unsorted keys.

Refine the algorithm as follows:

```
heapsort(R,n)
    createheap(R,n)
    for j = n down to 2 do
        interchange k₁ and kⱼ
        heapmaker(1,j–1)
```

EXAMPLE 3.3

Continuing from the steps on pages 83–84, which converted the original file of ten keys 21,15,62,48,21,39,30,43,17,56 into the heap, we now sort the file. (Underlined keys are in their final positions.)

```
Index  1   2   3   4   5   6   7   8   9   10
Key   62  56  39  48  21  21  30  43  17  15

j=10  Interchange       15 56 39 48 21 21 30 43 17 62
      heapmaker  Compare 15 56 39
        (1,9)    Result  56 15 39
                 Compare    15     48 21
                 Result     48     15 21
                 Compare           15         43 17
                 Result  56 48 39 43 21 21 30 15 17 62
j=9   Interchange        17 48 39 43 21 21 30 15 56 62
      heapmaker  Compare 17 48 39
        (1,8)    Result  48 17 39
                 Compare    17     43 21
                 Result     43     17 21
```

		Compare		17		15		
		Result	48 43 39 17 21 21 30 15 56 62
j=8	Interchange		15 43 39 17 21 21 30 48 56 62
	heapmaker	Compare	15 43 39
	(1,7)	Result	43 15 39
		Compare	15	17 21
		Result	43 21 39 17 15 21 30 48 56 62
j=7	Interchange		30 21 39 17 15 21 43 48 56 62
	heapmaker	Compare	30 21 39
	(1,6)	Result	39 21 30
		Compare	30	21
		Result	39 21 30 17 15 21 43 48 56 62
j=6	Interchange		21 21 30 17 15 39 43 48 56 62
	heapmaker	Compare	21 21 30
	(1,5)	Result	30 21 21 17 15 39 43 48 56 62
j=5	Interchange		15 21 21 17 30 39 43 48 56 62
	heapmaker	Compare	15 21 21
	(1,4)	Result	21 15 21
		Compare	15	17
		Result	21 17 21 15 30 39 43 48 56 62
j=4	Interchange		15 17 21 21 30 39 43 48 56 62
	heapmaker	Compare	15 17 21
	(1,3)	Result	21 17 15 21 30 39 43 48 56 62
j=3	Interchange		15 17 21 21 30 39 43 48 56 62
	heapmaker	Compare	15 17
	(1,2)	Result	17 15 21 21 30 39 43 48 56 62
j=2	Interchange		15 17 21 21 30 39 43 48 56 62

Program

Only the Pascal implementation of heapsort is included because the algorithm is recursive. Iterative implementations of the method are left as exercises.

```
procedure heapmaker(var R: arraytype;
                j, last: integer);
{ Heapmaker is a recursive procedure that converts
a binary tree stored in array R, and rooted at
position j, into a heap. Last is the location in
the array at which the last node of the tree is
stored. }

var i,           { Index of offspring of node at j }
    TEMP: INTEGER;  { Used for interchange          }
```

```
begin {  heapmaker   }
  if (2 * j <= last)              { j is not a leaf    }
    then
      begin
        i := 2 * j;        { Find i = index of the }
        if (i + 1 <= last) { greater offspring }
          then                    { of R[j]            }
            if (R[i] < R[i + 1])
              then i:= i + 1;
        if (R[j] < R[i])
          then
            begin
              TEMP := R[j];       { Interchange }
              R[j] := R[i];
              R[i] := TEMP;
              heapmaker(R,i,last);{ Make tree
                                    rooted at i
                                    into a heap }
            end
      end
end;

procedure createheap(var R: arraytype;
                         n: integer);
var j: integer;
begin
    for j := (n div 2) downto 1 do
        heapmaker(R, n);
end;

procedure heapsort (var R: arraytype;
                        n: integer);
var  j, TEMP : integer;
begin
    for j := n downto 2 do
        begin
          TEMP := R[1];
          R[1] := R[j];
          R[j] := TEMP;
          heapmaker(1, j-1);
        end
end;
```

Pascal Program 3.2 *Heapsort*

Analysis

The analysis of heapsort is best done in two stages—one for the creation of the heap and the other for sorting the file once the heap is created. We begin with the latter part; it is the less complex of the two.

Let m be the depth of the complete binary tree containing the n keys of the file. Assume this binary tree is a heap. Each stage in the process of obtaining a sorted file involves interchanging the root with the last node in the remaining unsorted file. The new root is then moved down the binary tree until it is not less than its offspring. The maximum number of moves is equal to the depth m of the binary tree. Each move requires at most two comparisons. This process is done $n-1$ times, the number of times through the outer loop in the algorithm. Thus, the number of comparisons to obtain a sorted file after the initial heap has been created is

$$2 * m * (n-1)$$

From the analysis of binary search we know that $m \leq \log n$. Thus,

$$2 * m * (n-1) \leq 2(n-1)(\log n)$$

It follows that this part of the algorithm is $O(n \log n)$.

Consider now the algorithm for creating a heap from the original file of n keys. No comparisons are made at level m because every node at that level is a leaf. Each node at level $m-1$ is compared with the greater of its offspring after the offspring are compared with each other. Consequently, there are two comparisons for each node at level $m-1$. From the previous discussion of binary trees there are at most 2^{m-1} nodes at that level. In general, there are $2 * 2^{j-1}$ comparisons for each level j, where $j=1,2,\ldots,m-1$. Working up the complete binary tree then, requires at most

$$2*2^{m-1} + 2*2^{m-2} + \ldots + 2*2^1 + 2$$

comparisons, where $m \leq \log n$. Since $2^{m-k} = 2^m/2^k$ and $2^m \leq n$, the sum is no greater than

$$2*(n/2 + n/2^2 + n/2^3 + \ldots + n/2^m) \leq 2*n$$

Also, each time a parent node is interchanged with its greater offspring, it could be moved subsequently to lower levels. From the above, we see that the number of comparisons in that number of moves for all possible nodes is $O(n \log n)$.

Thus the total number of comparisons to create a heap from the original file is at most the sum of three terms, two of which are $O(n \log n)$, while the other is $2*n$. It follows that heapsort is $O(n \log n)$. The result applies to the best, worst, and average cases.

Memory requirements for heapsort are minimal. All interchanging is done within the original array locations. Only one location for interchanging is needed in addition to the original array. However, heapsort does involve interchanges—one each time a node is moved down one level, and $n-1$ to place keys in their final position in the sorted file.

Summary

In this chapter, we introduced two of the fastest internal sort methods available for large unsorted files. The methods, quicksort and heapsort, are $O(n \log n)$, an efficiency measure that is the best possible for comparison-based sort methods.

Quicksort is a divide-and-conquer method that derives its efficiency from successively dividing a file into two files of approximately equal size. It proceeds by selecting a key, called a pivot, and comparing it to the other keys until the pivot is located in its proper place in the file. This creates one unsorted file of all keys less than or equal to the pivot, and a second file of keys greater than the pivot. One of the two files is placed on a stack; the other is processed as before. Eventually, files are popped from the stack and processed. The sort can be implemented in a language that supports recursion by repeated calls of a recursive subprogram. In other languages, iteration is necessary. When subfiles get relatively small, quicksort becomes less efficient because of the computation that does not involve comparisons. The program should then switch to simpler internal sorts, such as selection, to complete the sorting of the original file.

Heapsort is a tree-based sort that derives its efficiency from properties of the structure called a complete binary tree. The sort method limits comparisons to those keys along a path in the binary tree, rather than to all keys. Initially, the file is reorganized into a heap, a complete binary tree in which each parent node is greater than or equal to its offspring. Then the last remaining key in the unsorted file is compared to its sibling, and the larger of the two is compared to the parent. The parent and largest sibling are interchanged as necessary to maintain the heap property. The sibling-parent comparison and interchange are repeated until the largest key reaches the top of the heap (becomes the root). This key is then interchanged with the last unsorted key, and the process is repeated until the original file is sorted.

The methods in Chapters 2 and 3 provide efficient searching and sorting techniques for internal files. Later chapters address methods and applications related to searching and sorting external files. These topics are easier to understand with a knowledge of the physical characteristics of storage devices, which is the subject of Chapter 4.

EXERCISES

1. A sorting algorithm is stable if it preserves the order of elements with equal sort key values. Is either quicksort or heapsort stable? Explain your answer.
2. Convert (by hand) the following into a heap:

    80 60 40 70 10 20 30 40 50
3. Write a program in COBOL or Pascal for the iterative version of heapsort.
4. Assume R is the array

    45 25 90 20 15 40 65 35 30 5 60 95 9 10 1.

    a. Use quicksort to sort R into ascending (increasing) order, and count the number of moves and comparisons required.
    b. Repeat (a) using heapsort.
5. Assume S is the sorted version of R from Exercise 4. Repeat 4(a) and 4(b) using S.
6. Assume that T is S (from Exercise 5) in reverse order. Repeat 4(a) and 4(b) using T.
7. Compare the time, expressed in the number of moves and comparisons, for running the iterative versions of quicksort and heapsort, with the time for running the recursive versions. Use R, S, and T.
8. Assume you have decided to run quicksort (and heapsort) but will change to a simpler sort (from Chapter 2) when subfiles get below a specifed minimum size, m. Using R, S, and T, plot the time (moves and comparisons) as a function of m, for m = 1,2,3,4,5,10.
9. Compare the number of operations (comparisons and moves) required for the following four situations:
    a. Quicksort (consider worst and best cases) of an array of 1000 items.
    b. Bubblesort of an array of 1000 items.
    c. Quicksort (best and worst cases) of an array of five items.
    d. Bubblesort of an array of five items.

10. Make a graph. On the x axis, show the number of items in an array. On the y axis show the number of operations required for a sort on the y axis. Plot the curves for bubblesort, exchangesort, quicksort, and heapsort. Do all sorts assuming worst-case performance, and again for best-case performance. What can you say about the appropriate selection of a sort algorithm?

CHAPTER 4

STORING DATA

INTRODUCTION

Previous chapters presented basic ideas about data types and files of data elements, and about searching and sorting files on the assumption that a large amount of data is stored and accessible. This chapter considers physical devices for storing data. It concentrates on those aspects of greatest importance in the effective use of files, but does not go into great detail about the architecture of the various storage devices.

Many end users of computers are able to create files and access their data without knowing anything about the topics in this chapter. However, this material forms a very important foundation for those people who

- need to know the most efficient use of storage devices;
- are concerned with the speed of access to very large files;
- make decisions concerning the purchase of storage devices; or
- are concerned with sharing data over different computers.

LEVELS OF STORAGE

There are many ways to store information. When a person works on a project, such as preparing a tax statement or writing a term paper, some important, often-used information is kept in the person's head for immediate recall: the number of hours in a day, the number of months in a year, the deadline for completing the task, and many other details. Other information is readily at hand, but is not in the person's head. For instance, a watch or clock has the time, and a calendar has the date and the number of days remaining until the project deadline. One glance gives the information very quickly. For quick reference, a notebook or manual contains project requirements: how information is to be combined, what rates apply, and what items must be accompanied by receipts. Other information—facts, dates, exact amounts—is stored in a folder in a file drawer, or a book on a shelf, to be retrieved as needed. Old receipts and old papers may be packed in boxes and stored in the attic, in case they are needed again. Additional information—perhaps some receipts and more extensive references—are stored elsewhere: in an associate's office or a library. They can be retrieved when needed, but retrieval requires more effort.

Data in a computer system is similarly stratified into six levels of storage. The key features of these levels that set them apart from each other and determine when each is to be used are access time, addressability, and cost.

- **Access** time is the total time required to make a piece of data available for use by a program executing in a computer.
- **Addressability** is the size of a data item that is accessible. An address may refer to a single character or to a large block of data. If a program test condition requires only one bit of data, and a storage device allows data to be accessed only in 512 Kbyte blocks, considerable filtering is necessary to retrieve exactly what is needed. (For instance, a person may need to know a particular tax rate. Asking for the information might result in getting a book of tax tables.)
- **Cost** includes the original purchase price of equipment and also the cost of operation, floor space, and human operators.

An overview of the six levels is shown in Figure 4.1.

Registers

A **register** is a fixed-size data storage device located in the control unit of the CPU and immediately available for manipulation by a program. Access time is negligible. A register address specifies which register is to be used and always refers to the entire register. Some machine-level instructions access particular bits of the specified register. The number and size of registers is an important design feature of a computer. Typically, a computer has eight or sixteen general-purpose registers. Like facts stored in a person's head, the data that can be kept in registers is severely limited.

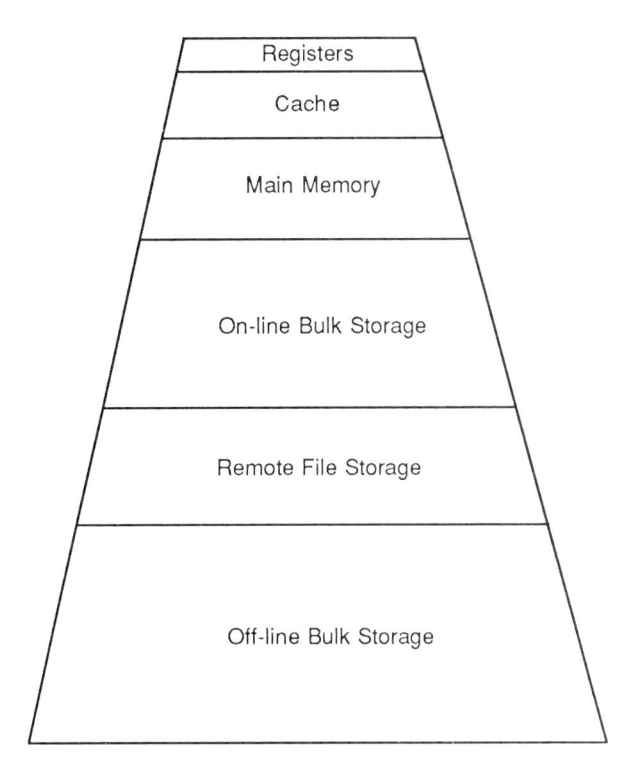

```
                  ┌─────────────────┐
                  │    Registers    │
                  ├─────────────────┤
                  │      Cache      │
                ┌─┴─────────────────┴─┐
                │    Main Memory      │
              ┌─┴─────────────────────┴─┐
              │                         │
              │  On-line Bulk Storage   │
            ┌─┴─────────────────────────┴─┐
            │                             │
            │    Remote File Storage      │
          ┌─┴─────────────────────────────┴─┐
          │                                 │
          │     Off-line Bulk Storage       │
          └─────────────────────────────────┘
```

Figure 4.1   *A storage hierarchy.*

Cache

Cache is a term used to mean a hiding place, especially one used by explorers to store provisions. In computing systems, cache refers to a small amount of very high-speed memory. Cache is a "hiding place" in the sense that it is not available to the computer user directly, but is used by the operating system to store data needed for its proper operation. In modern multi-user computing systems, each user's program and data are stored wherever there is space available, and that space may change frequently. The user does not need to know where the actual storage is as long as the operating system is keeping track of it. The computer must be able to find the next instruction or the required data whenever it is required. An important use of cache is for keeping track of the current location of anything the operating system is likely to need soon. The use of cache memory is transparent to the user, but allows the computer to execute programs faster by reducing the time needed to access main memory. The size of cache is generally a few (1 to 32) Kbytes.

Main Memory

The next layer in the hierarchy of computer storage is commonly called **main memory,** or just memory. The term **core storage,** still used occasionally, is a remnant of a particular type of memory device in which tiny magnetic cores were used to represent bits.

Memory may be byte- or word-addressable. Byte addressing allows access to individual characters in memory and facilitates use of character-oriented data. When each byte of memory has its own address, a larger number of different addresses must be available to give a program access to all of memory than if each address refers to a larger portion of memory.

In a word-addressable memory, each address refers to a number of bits that is usually equal to some number of bytes. In the DEC (Digital Equipment Corporation) PDP-11 series of minicomputers, for instance, a word is 16 bits and a byte is 8 bits. Thus, a given size memory has half as many words as bytes and therefore requires half as many addresses to access all of memory. The address field of an instruction, which is 16 bits long, can identify 2^{16} = 64K different word addresses and have access to 128K bytes of memory. Though memory is addressed by words, some machine-level instructions specify that only one byte is to be used. The large computers of the Burroughs Corporation address 48-bit words, the equivalent of 6 eight-bit bytes. CDC (Control Data Corporation) computers have 60-bit words and use 6-bit bytes. Like DEC's PDP-11 computers, IBM's 360/370 architecture is both byte- and word-addressable. The IBM word size is 32 bits. While DEC's design accesses a word and allows the program to limit use to one byte at a time, IBM's design addresses a byte and allows several bytes to be used together as a word. The difference in emphasis is a result of orientation toward numeric processing (word-oriented) or text processing (character- or byte-oriented). While both types of problems can be solved on both types of computers, each computer will execute more efficiently the type of program for which it was designed. The more recent DEC VAX computers also address a 32-bit word. Double-word instructions exist to allow two full words of memory to be referenced together, an important feature for numerical problems which require high accuracy.

In general, word-oriented memory access is more appropriate when binary-encoded real and integer numbers are to be used. A longer word size provides a wider range of integer values and a greater degree of accuracy in real values being stored.

Before an instruction can be carried out, the instruction and every related data item stored in main memory must be transferred to the central processing unit. Access time for memory is the time required to make the transfer. Since each byte or word of memory can be addressed directly, access to main memory is the fastest of the large-scale storage devices.

In microcomputers, main memory is usually referred to as RAM (Random Access Memory). Early microcomputers had word sizes of 8 or 16 bits. More recent ones have 32 bit words consisting of 4 bytes.

ROM (Read Only Memory) is memory that is written on only once, when it is manufactured. ROM is inexpensive to produce if many identical copies are required. Since its contents are never moved or modified they are easily located and used by the computer. ROM may be used to hold program steps that are frequently used, such as a particular numeric conversion, or the steps involved in loading the rest of the operating system when the computer is turned on. Most personal computers have a BASIC interpreter installed in ROM. Special-purpose computers, such as the controllers for appliances and toys, are equipped with inexpensive mass-produced ROM chips.

Online Bulk Storage

The types of storage that are of most direct interest to users are those that store files online and offline. Registers, cache, and memory contain the instructions and data for an executing program. Programs that have not begun to execute, and data that has not yet been called for, are much too extensive to be kept in these memory forms. Online bulk storage is used to hold those programs and data that will be needed soon or that are known to be needed frequently. Like a file drawer or a book on a shelf, it holds data that is accessible with a little effort. Many types of online storage devices are available. Important differences include cost and the time needed to access information stored on the device. Disk drives are the dominant form of online storage. They are described in some detail later in this chapter.

An interesting device intended to provide large quantities of online storage is IBM's 3851 Mass Storage Facility (MSF), part of the IBM 3850 Mass Storage System. The MSF stores data on cartridges consisting of magnetic tape rolled on cylinders and stored in cells resembling a honeycomb. To access the data, the device moves an arm (accessor) to the appropriate cell, removes the cartridge, and places it on a Data Recording Device. Each of 4720 cartridges has a capacity of up to 50 megabytes of data. The MSF is not used for ordinary input/output operations. It is used to provide a place to store large quantities of data that are not being used frequently and are occupying space needed on disk systems. The contents of the disk are copied to a mass storage device, and the disk space reused. When a request for the data is issued, the data is restored to disk and used as if it had been there all along. The migration of the data from the disk to mass storage device and back is transparent to the program, unless I/O time is noted. For various reasons, the mass storage device has been discontinued, and the search for inexpensive, high-volume, automatic storage continues.

Remote File Storage

With advances in computer communications systems, it has become feasible to use files that are associated with different computers, from a session at one computer. The files are online, but not to the computer that is running the program or process that calls for the data. The request for data is communicated from one computer to another over a communications link. The computer that has the file storage device attached passes on the request for data made by the user computer. The file is then transferred to the user. No human intervention is required to make the data available, as in the case of offline files, but the transfer takes longer than when the data is stored on devices attached to the user's computer. Remote files are addressed in Chapter 11.

Offline Bulk Storage

The slowest, least expensive storage media is offline bulk. Records on storage devices in this category cannot be accessed by the computer without intervention by a human operator. Some offline storage media, such as Computer Output Microfilm, cannot be reused by the computer at all. Removable disks, such as floppy disks for microcomputers, are offline storage media, but most offline storage is in the form of magnetic tape. The tapes can be read by a computer, and their data can be used only when mounted on tape drives connected to the computer. Tapes hold back-up copies of critical files and archives—files that provide records of past events and which are used only when necessary to reconstruct a past situation. Like cancelled checks, back-up and archival tapes may never be used again, but nevertheless are indispensible for many purposes. The need for a human operator to fetch and mount a tape, then demount and store it, is a severe bottleneck in tape file processing. However, data on a tape or disk that has been removed from the computer and locked up cannot be accessed by unauthorized computer users. This is important in the context of security issues discussed in the next chapter.

SEQUENTIAL STORAGE DEVICES

A **sequential storage device** is one which stores data in such a way that it can be used only in one order. A familiar example of such a storage medium is the common audio or video tape. A collection of songs recorded on tape is heard in the same order every time the tape is played. To play the first, third, and second recording, in that order, it is necessary to play the first, then fast forward past the second, play the third, then rewind the tape to the beginning of the second song and play it. There is no way to go from the first to the third piece without passing the second through the playing mechanism. By contrast, a phonograph record is made in a way that allows the user to position the tone arm at the beginning of whichever recording he or she wants to hear. It is often convenient, but not necessary, to play the intermediate pieces. If someone wants to hear the first and fifth recordings on a record, the fastest way is to play the first and then move the tone arm to the fifth. If someone wants to hear all of the pieces on the record, the fastest and most convenient way is to start with the first and play all of them in the order in which they appear. If lifting and repositioning the tone arm were required for each recording, this "feature" would be considered very inconvenient. A similar situation occurs in accessing data stored on sequential and direct-access devices.

Tape Drives

Magnetic recording tape has been in common use for decades. The media used for computer input/output is the same as for audio/video recording. Quality must be extra fine because of the density with which data is packed on the tape.

Reels of tape come in varying lengths, with 2400 feet being the most common. The tape is one-half inch wide, and coated with a metallic oxide substance to hold a magnetic imprint. Figure 4.2 shows features of a reel of tape. A plastic ring removed from the hub of the tape reel allows a tape to be write protected, that is, read only. Cartridges are gaining in popularity, but reels continue to dominate the market.

Tape leader is needed to start the tape on the take-up reel. Usable tape begins with a **tape mark**—a piece of aluminum that is sensed by the tape drive.

A **tape label** is a computer-readable record describing the tape's contents. (The term tape label is also used for an external, printed or handwritten stick-on label used by a human operator to identify a particular reel of tape.) A tape may be (internally) labelled or unlabelled. An unlabelled tape contains data as written by a program, but contains no information about the data. Such a tape is suitable for moving data from one type of computer to one or more others. A labelled tape contains records in addition to the actual data. These records describe what is on the tape and are used by the computer's input/output subsystem.

A **volume table of contents** (VTOC) is a record on the tape that contains information about the entire reel of tape. It includes the name,

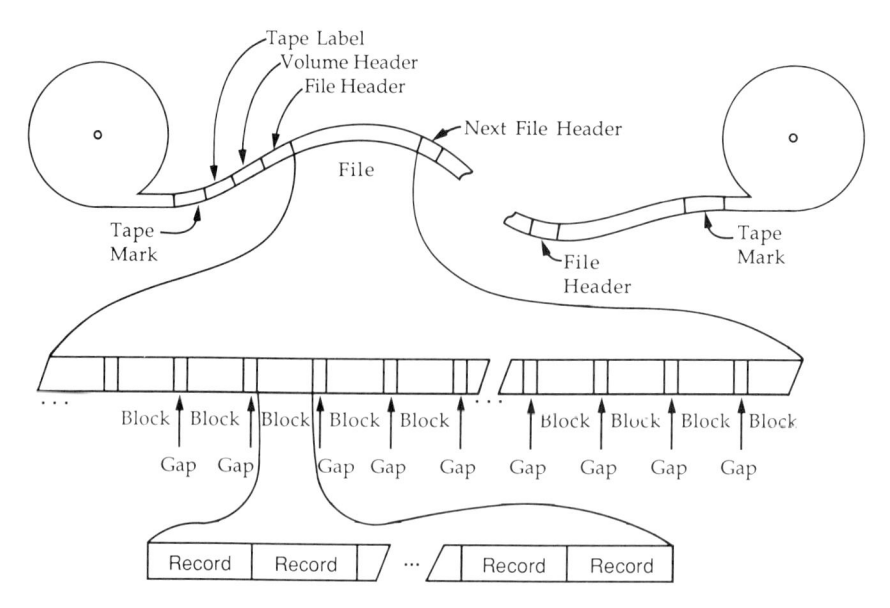

Figure 4.2 "Exploded" view of a reel of tape.

length, creation date, and other data about each file currently on the tape. An I/O system can be used in conjunction with the VTOC to identify an owner for each file and to deny access to the file to anyone who is not an owner. This is not a very secure system, but may prevent accidental use of the tape and can be protection from a casual user. It is useful in verifying that the correct reel of tape is actually mounted on the drive.

A **file header** is a record that contains descriptive information about a particular file. This includes the file name, the size of records and the number of records that are combined in blocks, the file creation and expiration date, and perhaps other information. Generally, the operating system's I/O subsystem writes a standard label on the tape unless the user specifies something else to be written.

A COBOL Program Note

In COBOL, the File Description entry

```
LABEL RECORD IS STANDARD
```

tells the I/O system to write (or expect on input) a standard label. A user specifies a label by writing

```
LABEL RECORD IS TAPE-LABEL
```

Storing Data 101

where TAPE-LABEL is a data name defined in the program. When a user specifies a tape label, program code can be written to use fields in the label. With this facility, a user of one operating system can write a label that is recognized by another operating system, or read one produced by another system. Thus, tapes are a flexible way to share data between different types of systems.

The clause

```
LABEL RECORD OMITTED
```

describes an unlabelled tape. This option causes the program to treat everything on the tape as data and not look for any descriptive record.

After the file label, the tape contains data. Data is written on the tape according to the format used by the recording device. Data written on incompatible devices cannot be shared. The number of tracks on a tape is an important characteristic. Most tapes are nine-track, as illustrated in Figure 4.3.

Consider a length of tape. Imagine that a very short piece has been cut from it. Eight bits of data are written across this section of tape. If EBCDIC characters are written on the tape, the letter A (EBCDIC 1100 0001) appears as shown by the top eight tracks of the tape section. The bits could also be made to represent data in ASCII, or a portion of a computer word containing a binary number. The meaning of the bits is not important to the tape system. The ninth bit on the tape section is a parity bit. **Parity checking** is a simple technique for locating errors that can occur in transferring data. The parity bit is set by the I/O system when the tape is written. Either EVEN or ODD parity may be used. If even parity is used, the parity bit is set so that the total number of 1's across the tape is even. The example in Figure 4.3 shows the parity bit set in the bottom track. Even parity is used. Note that a totally blank section of tape, with

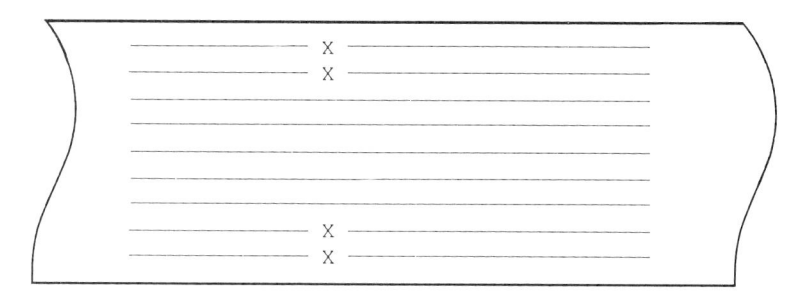

Figure 4.3 One character encoded on a nine-track tape.

no bits encoded, has even parity, and a data character represented by all 0 bits cannot be distinguished from blank tape. If odd parity is used (that is, the parity bit is set so that the total number of 1's across the tape is odd), a section with no data bits must have a 1 bit in the parity position. Then data consisting of eight 0's can be distinguished from unrecorded tape.

The number of such 9-bit sections found in a length of tape determines the recording density. The density is measured in bpi units. The b refers to bytes when the eight data bits across the section are considered, or to bits when a single track is considered. Thus, 800 bpi tapes have 800 bytes of data per inch of tape (800 bytes is equivalent to ten full lines on a terminal screen). Tape density of 1600 bpi is common, but 6250 bpi is not unusual. Newer tape systems, such as the IBM 3480 tape drive, record at 38,000 bpi.

Tape drives in a computer system work much like audio/video tape units. The tape passes a head that either reads (plays) or writes (records). When a data tape is being read, a computer is doing some processing. On input, for instance, the computer reads some amount of data from the tape, uses the data in some way specified by a program, and then reads more data. Just as a video tape must be played at the correct speed to produce proper images, a data tape must be moved past the head at the proper speed in order to be interpreted correctly. Since the tape motion cannot change from full speed to complete stop instantaneously, some amount of tape passes the head at less than proper speed every time a read (or write) operation starts or stops. This small space on the tape, called a **gap**, is unusable but very important, as the following example illustrates.

Suppose a file exists containing data about all employees of a company as of December 31, 1987. Current data is kept in accessible form, but a history tape is made once a year for future reference. The company employs 14,730 people worldwide. Data on each employee consists of an identification number (9 digits); a name (30 characters); the dates of birth, hire, last promotion, changes in classification, and termination (6 digits per date); an address (45 characters); education level (2 digits); a classification (2 digits); and so on. Assume that there is a total of 120 characters of data for each employee. Then a total of 1,767,600 characters (bytes) of data is required to record all employees. This amount of data covers approximately 92 feet of tape at 1600 bpi, assuming no gaps between records.

$$1767600 \text{ bytes} * \frac{1 \text{ inch}}{1600 \text{ bytes}} = 1104.75 \text{ inches of tape}$$

$$1104.75 \text{ inches} * \frac{1 \text{ foot}}{12 \text{ inches}} = 92.0625 \text{ feet of tape}$$

Now, assume a one-half inch gap between records. Then the number of gaps is approximately the same as the number of records. The length of tape needed for gaps is:

$$14730 \text{ records} * \frac{1 \text{ inch}}{2 \text{ records}} = 7365 \text{ inches}$$

$$7365 \text{ inches} * \frac{1 \text{ foot}}{12 \text{ inches}} = 613.75 \text{ feet of gap}$$

Then, not counting header records,

$$92.0625 + 613.75 = 705.8125 \text{ feet of tape}$$

are required to store the file. Of that,

$$\frac{613.75}{705.8125} \cong 87\%$$

is unused gap! At that rate, a great deal of storage space is wasted. How can the waste be reduced?

Remember how the gaps came to exist. They are needed to distinguish sections of tape used for separate read (or write) operations. If a program could read (or write) two records without stopping the tape drive, only half as many gaps would be required. What changes would be required to process such data? The computer would have to set aside space in memory to build two complete records before issuing the command to write (or space to accept two complete records whenever it reads). This holding area between a program and an I/O device is called a **buffer**. A large buffer requires a large section of memory to be reserved. Something else is required. A program has to "know" that there are two types of read operation. One type of read actually causes data to be transferred from the tape to memory; the other must just change the part of the buffer the program is using so that the other record read becomes available. The process is illustrated in Figure 4.4.

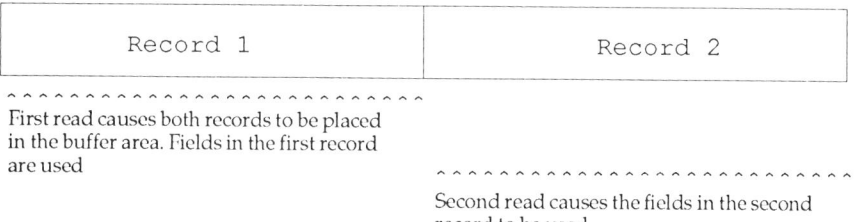

Record 1	Record 2

First read causes both records to be placed in the buffer area. Fields in the first record are used

Second read causes the fields in the second record to be used.

Figure 4.4

104   Chapter 4

This second type of read is extremely fast. The program execution does not have to stop and wait for the data to be transferred—the data is ready and waiting. Not only is space saved on the tape, but also the time lost by the program to an I/O bottleneck is reduced. The additional program complexity—deciding which type of read (or write) operation is required at a given time—can be put into the operating system's I/O handling routines. The need for large buffer areas cannot be ignored, but the space savings on the tape, the processing time reduction to the program, and the decreasing cost of RAM combine to make the transfer of multiple records a reasonable solution to the gap problem.

The number of records read or written together is called the **blocking factor** of a file. Once a file is created, its blocking factor is a permanent part of its design. If a file has a blocking factor of 30, each data transfer will refer to 30 records. It is not possible to move fewer than 30 records to memory at any one time. The best choice of block size depends on the equipment in use and the size of individual records. Applying a blocking factor of 30 to the sample file has the following effect: the space required to store data does not change; it is still 92.0625 feet of tape. Now, however, only one gap occurs for each 30 records (1 block).

$$14730 \text{ records} * \frac{1 \text{ gap}}{30 \text{ records}} * \frac{1 \text{ inch}}{2 \text{ gaps}} * \frac{1 \text{ foot}}{12 \text{ inches}} = 20.46 \text{ feet}$$

The total space required is now

$$\begin{array}{ll} 92.0625 & \text{feet for data} \\ \underline{20.46} & \text{feet for gap} \\ 112.5225 & \text{feet of tape} \end{array}$$

of which

$$\frac{20.46}{112.5225} \cong 18\% \text{ is gap}$$

To hold 30 records in memory, 120 * 30 = 3600 bytes of buffer space must be set aside. In the days when a moderate size computer system had 32 Kbytes of memory, that number of records would have consumed about ten percent of available memory for buffer space. A medium-size computer today may have 4 Mbytes (mega, or million, bytes) and this buffer is less than 0.1 percent of memory.

The increased execution speed of a program that does not have to wait for an actual data transfer each time it issues a read or write request is so significant that buffering has been carried a step farther. Many multiprogramming computer operating systems provide two or more buffers for I/O operations. On a read request, the operating system fills the first buffer. On subsequent read operations, the operating system gives the program access to successive records. At some time when the I/O subsystem has an opportunity, it anticipates further reads and moves the next block of data into another buffer. Thus, it is possible for the program to execute without ever having to pause for the actual transfer of data from an external device into memory.

A COBOL Program Note

The COBOL option

    RESERVE NO ALTERNATE AREAS

informs the operating system that this extra buffer space is not to be allocated, and thus reading ahead is not to be performed. The program executes more slowly using one buffer but consumes less memory.

When every record in a file is to be used, a blocked file organization is ideal. Most reads and writes are accomplished by changing the reference to another part of the buffer. Access time is very small. However, if it is necessary to use only a small portion of the file for a program, timing advantages of blocking are lost and the cost in terms of memory use is retained.

In summary, combining many records into one block for I/O purposes has the following effects:

(a) Program execution time is reduced by decreasing the number of actual data transfers that must occur.
(b) Storage of data on a tape is compressed by reducing the number of interblock gaps.
(c) Main memory requirements are increased by using large buffer areas.

Card Readers

Cards were the dominant form of computer storage, but have finally become more of an exception than the norm in computing centers. Cards are discussed briefly here for two reasons: there are still a number of operating card systems, and the "card image" has an enduring effect on other forms of computer I/O.

The standard 80-column card is shown in Figure 4.5. Holes punched in cards were used to store data by Joseph Marie Jacquard in the early

1800s. Herman Hollerith used the idea to record census data in 1890. The company he formed, Tabulating Machine Company, produced equipment to process data stored on cards. After three mergers and a renaming, the company became International Business Machines (IBM).

Data is encoded on a card in character form. Each card column holds one character. A code punched on a card consists of holes punched in a particular column. A column with no holes punched represents a blank. The top two positions in each column are called "zone" punches and are labelled 12 and 11, respectively. The remaining positions are numbered from 0 through 9 and are referred to as the numeric portion of the code. Each digit is encoded by punching a hole in the appropriate numeric position. Letters are punched with one hole in a zone position and another in a numeric position. The codes for the letters and numbers and some special characters (/, *, &) are shown in Figure 4.5. When a card is read, the holes allow an electrical contact to be made and a signal is sent to the reading device. The code is then converted to one recognized by the computer in use, and the data is available for processing.

Cards all have the same number of columns and thus the size of a card record is fixed. Though a compact 96-column card was introduced, the dominant image in card-encoded data is the 80-column record. If more than 80 characters are needed for a record, then more than one card must be used. The terms "physical" and "logical" record refer to the fixed actual record size (80 bytes) and the number of bytes of data that constitute one record. Many files stored on tape or disk are designed around an 80-column record, perhaps because the file was originally stored on cards. Terminal screens are designed to display 80 columns, and many printers have 80-character lines. The shadow of the 80-column card will endure long after the last card reader is retired.

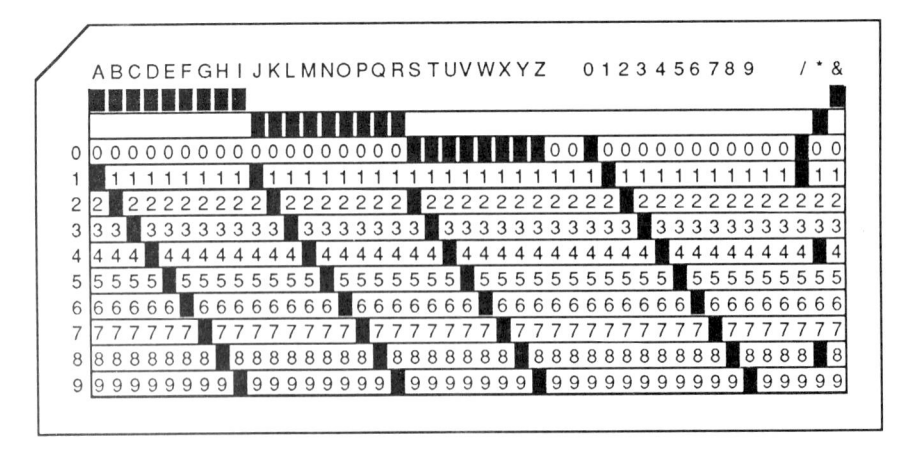

Figure 4.5 Card codes for letters, numbers, and some special characters.

Card systems have fallen out of favor for several reasons:

- Cards are bulky and heavy. One inch of 1600 bpi tape will hold the equivalent of 20 cards.
- Cards are inflexible. If a record requires 81 characters, and no fewer will do, you must use two cards to hold the data.
- Cards are vulnerable to moisture and tearing. The warning: "Do not bend, fold, spindle, or otherwise mutilate this card" was no joke to computing centers trying to get mistreated cards through card readers. At one university computing site a sign was posted during the rainy season: "Do not attempt to read any cards that have been taken out of this building."
- Card handling equipment is slow and prone to errors. Reading cards requires a lot of mechanical motion and card jams occur often.
- Cards cannot be erased. People frustrated by the inability to get to a card punch machine used to joke about filling in the holes. A punching error in a card means that the card must be replaced.
- Cards cannot be reused. After the cards have been used and their contents are no longer needed, they cannot be used again with new data. Some imaginative people have designed holiday decorations from used cards, but most of the cards ended up in the trash or paper recycling centers.

Printers

A printer is a sequential storage device. The data stored by a printer is not usually in machine-readable form, but has important uses in communication among people. In a computing system where many users share devices, the printer may be kept very busy by print requests. Suppose that two or three programs that send output to the printer are running simultaneously. Program 1 completes the processing needed for a line of output and sends it to the printer. While the output operation is being completed, Program 1 goes to sleep and Program 2 begins to execute. After a while Program 2's print request is served.

If such a scenario were continued for the length of time needed for processing both programs, and if each program were actually printing, the result would be a useless hodgepodge with alternating sections of output from the two programs hopelessly mixed. To prevent that situation without having to schedule programs that use the printer to run at separate times, the I/O subsystem takes care of getting printed output to the printer without interference between users. The process is called **spooling** (simultaneous peripheral operation online) and involves intermediate storage of records that are sent to the printer. See Figure 4.6.

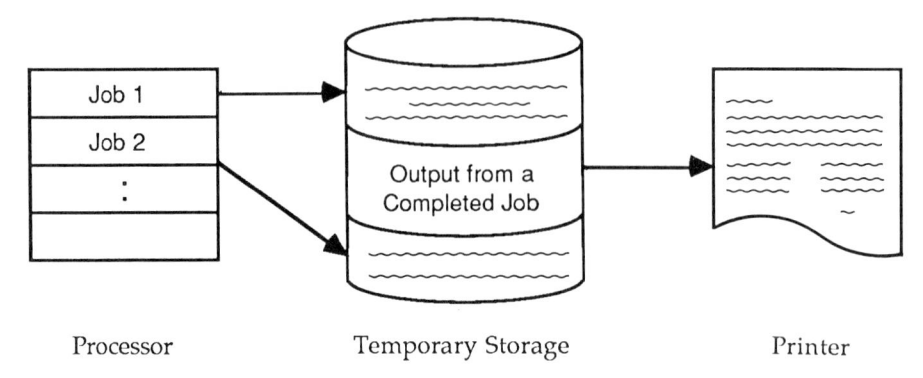

Figure 4.6 Spooling.

Records are stored in the proper order in separate disk areas. When a program has finished running, the print images stored for it are queued for sending to the printer.

DIRECT ACCESS STORAGE DEVICES

Two extremes of accessibility in computer storage have been presented. In one, memory is addressed at the byte or word level, and the programmer has control over the use of storage to a large extent. In the other, sequential storage devices such as tapes not only restrict access to whole records, or blocks, at a time, but they require that the records be used in a particular order. Program control is severely restricted.

Between these two extremes is a class of storage devices called direct access storage devices (DASD, pronounced *Das-d*). Direct, or random, access storage allows the programmer to access a particular record without having to process all the records that were stored before it in a file. In the DASD environment each record is equally accessible conceptually, and random motion through the file is feasible. In Chapter 7 it becomes evident that this flexibility exists to varying degrees in different systems. In all cases, however, access to an arbitrary individual record in a direct access storage device is more convenient than in sequential storage systems.

Disk Storage

Many people are now familiar with some forms of disk storage, in particular, the "floppy" disk popular with microcomputer users. A disk is a flat, round platter with a coating made of Mylar, the same substance used for magnetic tape. The disk is, in fact, another shape for this familiar magnetic recording technology. The disk is mounted in a disk drive, where it spins continuously. The disk spins under the read/write head, which in turn moves between the outer and inner edges of the platter. With the read/write head in a fixed position, the area of the disk that passes under the head forms a circle on the surface of the disk. This circle is called a track (see Figure 4.7). A disk surface has one track for each possible position of the head. Whenever a particular portion of a track passes under the head, that portion can be accessed.

Since the disk moves constantly, there is no need for interblock gaps to allow for start-up and slowdown of the medium. Increased speed of execution of programs using blocked data remains an important consideration, however, and many disk files are blocked. Characteristics of disk systems vary considerably, and some can be used most efficiently if the data is stored in blocks of particular sizes.

Some disk systems employ a **fixed-block architecture**, which means that a constant physical block size is associated with the device. Data is transferred to and from the device in these physical blocks. "Logical blocks" and records defined by the program cannot span the physical blocks. Thus, use of the media is most efficient if record and block sizes are chosen to conform to the units of the fixed block size. For example, if a record contains 100 bytes and the fixed block size is 512, then 5 records fit in the physical block and the remaining 12 bytes are wasted.

Floppy disks used with microcomputers are inexpensive, removable, and easily moved. Removable disks offer an advantage in that the amount of disk storage space on a computer system is essentially unlimited. More and more disks can be bought, used, stored and reused as needed. This same feature, however, makes the storage of data on removable disks risky. If the disk is not stored and handled properly, data is lost. In the case of small floppy disks, the disk itself may be lost through careless handling.

Large computer systems also use removable disks, though not commonly. Removable disk packs allow a single disk drive to provide access to more data than if a permanent, fixed disk were used. Removable

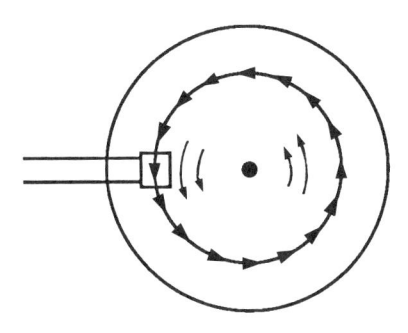

Figure 4.7 One track on a disk.

disks are vulnerable to damage if not carefully stored and are bulky and inconvenient to store. They do provide the advantage of security. When complete assurance that data cannot be accessed is needed, there is no alternative but to remove the data storage media from the computer system. A removable disk, like a tape, can be removed from the computer system and locked away.

The **Winchester disk**, sometimes called a fixed or hard disk, is a disk and access mechanism permanently and completely enclosed as a unit. Reliability of such disks is much greater than of removable disks because dust contamination is eliminated. Modern disk devices for large computers operate so precisely that the smallest particle of dust or smoke can cause serious damage. Enclosed disk systems cannot be removed from the computer system, and thus all the data stored there is always online. Because of the protected environment, however, extremely high density and access speeds are possible.

Speed of access to data stored on a disk is affected by three characteristics of the storage mechanisms: Seek time, latency, and data rate. See Figure 4.8. **Seek time** is the time needed to position the read/write head over the area of the disk containing the data. Seek times are on the order of 20 to 40 milliseconds (ms). **Latency**, also called **search time**, is the time required for the disk to spin around so that the desired data is under the read/write head. Once the head is in position at the right track, the data may be under it almost immediately, or it may have been "just missed" and have to rotate all the way around before becoming available. The average latency time (about 10 ms) is half the time of one revolution. Finally, the **data rate** is the speed with which the data can be read (or written) by the head. This time depends on the density with which data is stored on the device. The more bits there are stored on an inch of disk, the more bits will pass under the head during a given period of time. Data rates are measured in kilobytes (KB) per second, and values of 1000 to 3000 KB are typical.

As with the head on a tape drive, it is important that a disk head access the disk at the proper speed in order for the data to be interpreted correctly. Consequently, the head reads data at the same rate at both the outermost and innermost tracks. Data is stored much more densely on the smaller, innermost circle in order to present the same number of bits per second as the outermost circle.

The read/write head "floats" over the surface of the disk and can be moved in and out to access data on various tracks. Moving the head (seeking) is a time-consuming operation in disk access. Fastest retrieval of data occurs by using all the data stored under the current head position, then moving to an adjacent track and using all the data stored there. As when listening to a phonograph record, we have the flexibility to skip around at will, but it is not always the most convenient way to use the device. This is discussed further in Chapters 7 and 8.

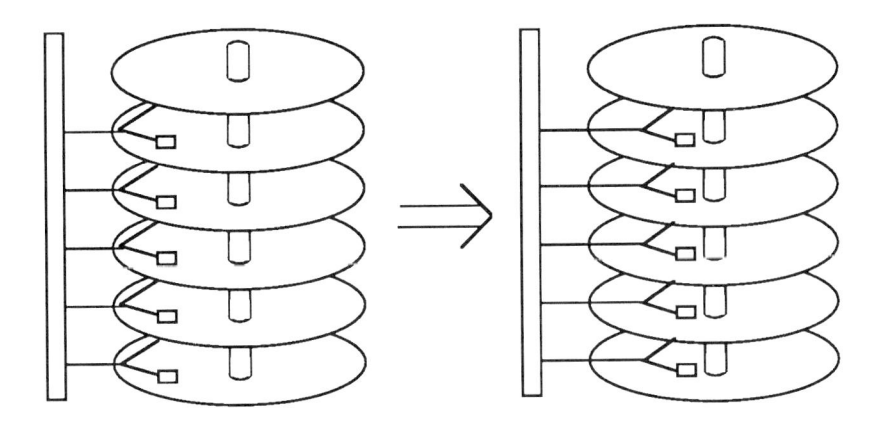

Seek time:
The read/write heads move from one position to another to access data.

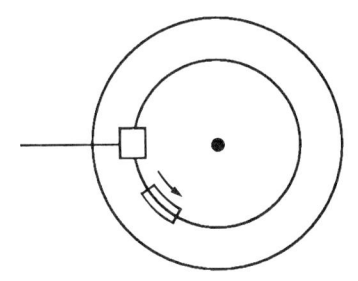

Latency:
The read/write head waits while the disk surface rotates and the data area comes under the head.

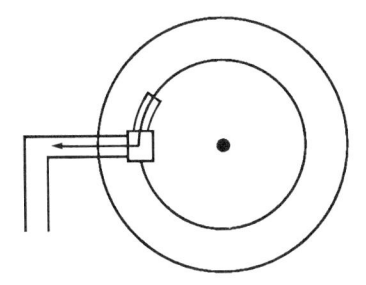

Data transfer rate:
The rate at which bits are copied to or from the storage medium.

Figure 4.8 Disk access times.

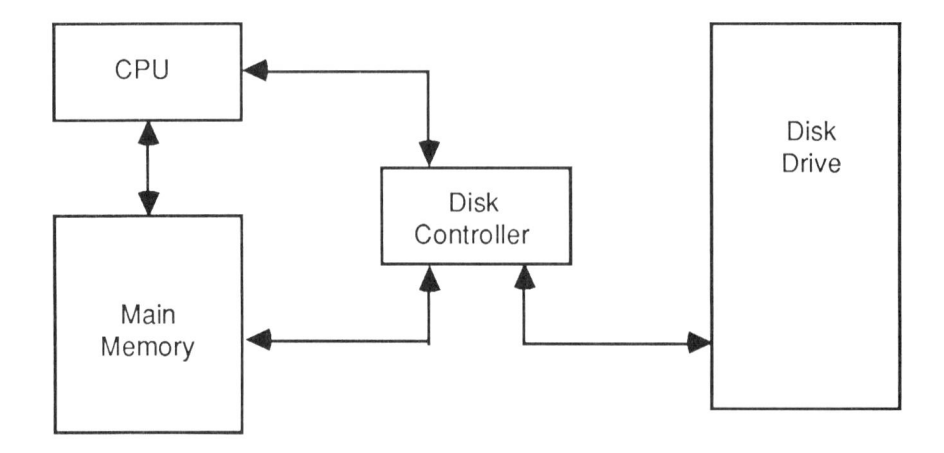

Figure 4.9 *CPU-Memory-Controller-Disk communication.*

Disk access speed is affected by characteristics of the disk drive, and also by a controller (see Figure 4.9). The **controller** is a special-purpose processor that coordinates communication between the computer and the disk drives. An intelligent controller can reduce average access time considerably from the raw times associated with the disk drive. (Digital Equipment Corporation advertises 35% speedup due to optimization provided by a controller.)

Among the methods for speeding up read access is prefetching data. The processor in the controller guesses what data will be requested next based on the past history of data requests. That data is read from the disk and stored in the controller, ready for fast transfer to the computer if and when the request actually comes. Such intelligent access mechanisms are important in retrieving data from very large files stored in sections over a number of disks. Improving the algorithms that do the guessing is a significant research area in computer system development.

A disk device may consist of a stack of disks, commonly called a pack. A disk pack is illustrated in Figure 4.10. Each pack contains some number of disk surfaces. A separate read/write head is used for each surface. All the heads move together as a single unit. When a disk pack is used, the access strategy is planned so as to use all of the surfaces of the pack at one position for the read/write arms before moving the arms to another position. As shown in Figure 4.11, the space defined by all of the disk area available without moving the arms resembles a cylinder, and it is called just that.

Figure 4.10 Disk pack. (Courtesy of BASF Systems Corp.)

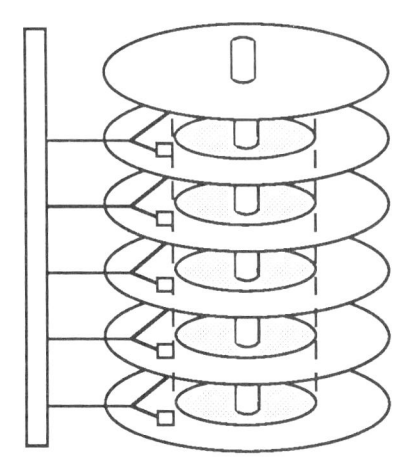

Figure 4.11 A disk pack and a cylinder defined by one position of read/write heads.

A 5 ¼ inch floppy disk for a personal computer has only one platter and a typical capacity of approximately 360 Kbytes to 1.2 Mbytes. They may be single or double sided. "Hard" (Winchester) disks available for use with personal computers, provide storage of from 5 to 60 Mbytes. The 3 ½ inch "rigid" disk is popular because it is less vulnerable to damage than the floppy and is easy to transport. The smaller disk drive needed to access these disks is easier to fit into the smaller cases of portable computers.

In a large computer installation, disk capacity is frequently measured in Gigabytes (billions of bytes). The IBM 3380 disk with double capacity will store 5 Gigabytes per unit. Digital Equipment Company's RA81 Winchester drive has a capacity of 456 MB per drive. Three RA81s can be mounted in one cabinet to provide 1.4 Gigabytes of storage.

These numbers, although accurate today, will soon be out-of-date, as the advances in storage technology are proceeding at a rapid rate. They are offered simply to give some idea of the size and speed of important storage devices.

Summary

This chapter reviews some of the physical characteristics of the data storage devices that hold records and files for processing. The treatment is light, but thorough enough to give some sense of why users must put up with certain constraints. The reason for, and the implications of, data blocking are highlighted. Also noted is the greater flexibility provided by disks for skipping around in the data and retrieving records in an arbitrary order. These storage devices provide the physical environment for discussing organization and the processing of files in subsequent chapters.

Exercises

1. What are the physical characteristics of storage devices accessible to you?
2. Discuss the advantages and disadvantages of tape versus disk storage in a large computer center.
3. What factors determine the block size in a particular application?
4. Why should the block size be neither "too small" nor "too large?"

For Exercises 5–9, assume the following specifications:

Record size = 200 characters
Tape: 2400 feet, 6250 bpi, 780KB/sec. data transfer rate.
IBG = 0.3 inches Blocking factor = 10.

5. a. What size buffer is required to read the tape?
   b. How many records can the tape hold?
   c. How much space is wasted by interblock gaps?
   d. What percentage of the tape holds data?
   e. Approximately how much time is required to read the tape if the start/stop time is 10.6 ms.?
6. How many double-sided, double-density floppy disks (5 ¼") are needed to hold the same amount of data?
7. What blocking factor is necessary to have 90 percent of the tape holding data?
8. How much space on the tape is required to store a file of 50,000 records? (Include interblock gaps.)
9. Assume the blocking factor is n. Create a table showing the number of records, space for interblock gaps, and percentage of tape holding data, for n = 1, 3, 5, 10, 20, 50, 100.
10. Estimate the number of 2400-foot, 6250-bpi tapes needed to store Volume A of the *Encyclopedia Britannica*? List all specifications you assume. Ignore illustrations and tables.
11. How many double-sided, double-density floppy disks are required to hold the data in Exercise 10?

CHAPTER 5

RESPONSIBILITY: PROTECTING A CRITICAL RESOURCE

INTRODUCTION

Previous chapters dealt with fundamental concepts and techniques pertinent to file processing: data types and structures, sorting and searching, and storage devices. Security, integrity, and privacy—the subjects of this chapter—are equally important aspects of file system applications and are of concern to anyone involved in the development, maintenance, use, or management of files.

Files and collections of files in databases contain vast amounts of data. That data must be accurate (integrity), must be kept safe from destruction and unauthorized access (security), and must be protected from individual rights violations (privacy). Though it is not feasible to expect 100 percent protection in any of these areas, a number of measures must always be taken toward reaching these goals. These measures toward security, integrity, and privacy in file processing applications are relevant to every implementation of files in the other chapters, even though attention is not always specifically given to their impact.

DEFINITIONS

Security, integrity, and privacy are three distinct, but related, topics. **Security** involves the mechanisms and techniques that control access to a computer system. It is the protection given to the system, including its data, against unauthorized access or modification, misuse, and violence. Security also includes provision for recovery if disaster does strike. In general usage, **integrity** is the quality of being reliable. Applied to data in a file, **data integrity** is the condition that exists when the file data is the same as the source data. **Privacy** pertains to the right of an individual to decide what information to share with, and accept from, others. Security and integrity relate to technological matters, privacy to personal ones.

Concerns about security, integrity, and privacy are not limited to computers. Security is essential to relationships among countries and businesses. Damage resulting from an information leak or an intercepted message varies from embarrassment to financial disaster, or even a threat to national security. Terrorist attacks succeed, at least in part, because of inadequate security. Data integrity is expected of the news media. Statistics reported, such as the number of people injured in a crash or the number of senators voting in favor of a bill, must conform to reality. Privacy is an individual right. Confidential data about a student or hospital patient is not accessible to the to public.

What make security, integrity, and privacy potentially more serious issues when computers are involved are the facility with which data can be accessed from exceedingly large collections, and the difficulties in preventing and detecting violations.

SECURITY

No computer system can be made totally secure. Nevertheless, elaborate efforts to safeguard the system and data are sometimes taken for a number of reasons. Business and industry need secure systems in order to:

- Prevent the loss of trade secrets (for example, proprietary information and sensitive technology).
- Prevent unauthorized and destructive entry into systems.
- Comply with federal legislation on privacy and security.
- Assure the integrity of data and transactions.

The federal government also requires protection for information exchange with other countries and a secure back-up communications network.

The extent of security implementation is proportional to the perceived value of the system and data, and to the vulnerability of the file's environment. Fewer security measures are needed for a file containing a bibliography than for a file of bank transactions. On a personal computer in the home, the only protection necessary is against unintentional damage, such as erasing the contents of a disk, or a sudden power surge or outage. Microcomputer files in business, education, and government, and in multiuser systems, are subject to malicious, as well as unintentional, damage. Either type of damage can affect multiple users. Because security measures can be costly, and usually cause some inconvenience to a user, they are enacted in proportion to individual system requirements.

A periodic **security risk analysis** keeps security measures current and appropriate. This process determines the potential effects of unauthorized modifications to data, identifies threats to the system, and specifies countermeasures. The analysis includes a plan of action to implement reasonable measures. The risk analysis heightens the security consciousness of employees and management. This is especially important because people's awareness is one of the best safeguards against security violations. Another process some companies have used to detect problems with their security is to authorize certain individuals to attempt to penetrate a system. Knowing how security can be breached helps determine which preventative measures to implement.

Physical Security

As the words suggest, physical security measures are concerned with protecting computer hardware and facilities from damage and destruction. They are only indirectly related to security of data; if physical destruction occurs, programs and data are also lost.

Physical security methods include installing computers in windowless rooms to deter break-ins, using special locking devices and identification badges to restrict access, and connecting terminals to mainframes with dedicated lines to prevent unauthorized dial-ups from remote sites. Checking inventories frequently, and fastening microcomputers and other portable equipment to tables or floors, are other forms of physical security.

Locks installed on microcomputers prevent unauthorized use, but require any legitimate user to carry a key. A user who forgets to bring the key has the same problem as a driver who doesn't have the key to a locked car—neither the microcomputer nor the car can be operated. To avoid this inconvenience, users frequently leave the microcomputer unlocked or tape the key to the back of the machine. In either case, the intended security measure is subverted, because anyone can use the microcomputer.

Legal Security

Legal security measures refer to those legislative acts intended to protect individuals and organizations against security violations. Although most states have laws that penalize computer crimes, enforcement is difficult.

Legal definitions of computer components and placing a value on data have been hard problems to resolve. Also, companies such as banks have been reticent about prosecuting computer criminals for fear that customers will lose confidence and not do business with the institution.

Two examples of federal legislation are the Privacy Act of 1974 and the Federal Computer Systems Protection Act of 1983, the first federal act to deal with computer crime. The Privacy Act gave citizens the right to access data about themselves in government and private sector databases. The Computer Systems Protection Act made it illegal to tamper with federal government computers and computers used in interstate commerce. Prior to 1983, computer crime was prosecuted under laws that applied to theft or fraud.

Administrative Security

Administrative means to increase security include personnel policies for hiring, promoting, and retaining loyal employees; employee training programs; and organizational policies and procedures. Unannounced financial audits and the offering of incentives for appropriate conduct are helpful. Specifying and imposing penalties for violations are effective measures as well.

An organization's personnel constitute both the greatest threat and the best safeguard to its security system. Most computer-related losses in organizations are traceable to employees' actions. Employees' knowledge of the computer system and ease of access to data give plenty of opportunity to modify data or manipulate it for their own purposes. Security violations by employees are not always intentional. An employee may write the combination of an electronic lock on the wall near the lock's push buttons, or a password next to a terminal. An employee may prop open a computer room door to let fresh air in or may allow another person to enter a secure area at the same time without asking to see appropriate identification.

Familiarity with an organization's computer system also makes personnel the greatest potential safeguard against security violations. They have the best view of ways in which to breach security and are in positions to notice any irregularities. Consequently, administrative measures taken by employers constitute the most effective security for systems and data.

Technological Security

Technological measures have a direct effect on users because they restrict interaction with a system. Primarily, these means are intended to limit user access to parts of the system, including data.

Passwords

The most common security tool is the password following a user identification for signing onto a system. Only when a person's identification and password match a combination stored in the computer system is access permitted. One variation of this method includes an automatic dial-back procedure. A user dials into a computer system, provides identification (such as a last name) and a password, then hangs up. Search of a file in the computer produces a telephone number of the site where the terminal is located and the number is automatically dialed. Connection between the terminal and the computer is established only when the computer calls back. Otherwise, no access is possible. In another variation, a system automatically disconnects a user after a set number of incorrect attempts at entering a password. In some systems the user is informed at a successful login that attempts have been made to logon to the account with failed attempts at the password. A user with sensitive files is thus warned that an attempt has been made to obtain access to the account. A transaction log is usually maintained in conjunction with passwords so that a record is available of when the system was used, by whom, and at what level.

An effective password system includes provisions for changing the password frequently. Unauthorized access into otherwise secure systems has been traced to failure to change passwords or to change them often enough. In a number of instances, unauthorized users have broken into systems with passwords that were never changed from the default settings, such as PASSWD or SYSTEM. Similarly, the choice of easily guessed or easily typed passwords (like the popular QWERTY) compromise security of the system.

The password is an easily implemented and commonly available security measure. An effective password is one that is easily remembered by the proper user (it is not written down), is difficult for others to guess (it is not a nickname, birth date, or family name), and is frequently changed.

Some environments call for a sequence of passwords, each one providing access to another level of the system. Users must remember the passwords and their sequence or be denied access to a particular level. Writing the passwords on paper violates security, but it is not uncommon to find passwords taped to walls near terminals to help authorized users remember the correct passwords. A security system that employs sequences of passwords is especially troublesome to users when it also includes frequent changes of passwords.

A password authenticates a user to the computer system, but not the system to the user. Consequently, someone could program a system to respond the same as the one the user intends to access. That person, referred to as an intruder, intercepts transmissions, primarily the user's

```
Original Alphabet
A B C D E F G H I J K L M N O P Q R S T U V W X Y Z

Substitution Rule
M N O P Q R S T U V W X Y Z A B C D E F G H I J K L
```

Figure 5.1 *A table of values for encoding letters of the alphabet.*

identification and password, and terminates the exchange with an error message. The intruder has the password, and the user does not realize it.

Passwords are standard security tools, even though they cannot prevent all problems. More sophisticated user identification methods are needed, but are not yet commonly available. Some attempts, such as fingerprints or scanning devices, are not socially acceptable, or present operational difficulties. Voice identification appears to have merit, but it introduces a different technology and has not yet been perfected.

Encryption

Encryption transforms data and programs so that they are difficult to access or understand without proper authorization. The simplest type of encryption involves substituting different letters and digits according to a predetermined rule. For example, the word SECURITY is written EQOGDUFK when the substitution rule in Figure 5.1 is applied. To be used effectively, the substitution method requires that the sender and receiver of the message have a copy of the substitution rule, but that no one else has it.

Encryption of messages was common practice long before computers. Extensive efforts were made for some time to create codes that were difficult to break, or decipher, and to find ways to break codes.[1] A noted code-breaking operation during World War II involved Americans and British secretly acquiring the sophisticated German encoding device called "enigma." With it the Allies were able to decipher German war plans and attack strategies. This example points out one of the dangers of encryption, namely, that the user may not know when the code is broken. In such cases, the user has a false sense of security.

Encryption can also be used for two-way authentication. A table of passwords and encryption transformation keys is stored in the computer system. A user transmits a password, causing a table look-up. The corresponding transformation key is found and is sent to the system's

---

1. It is significant to note that work in the area of encryption by the mathematician Claude Shannon and others in the 1930s influenced the design and development of the first computers several years later.

enciphering mechanism. Communication is established with the user, who has loaded a transformation key into the terminal's enciphering mechanism. If the two keys have the same value, then the user knows the correct system is at the other end of the communication. Also, the system "knows" the correct user is communicating.

The Data Encryption Standard

In 1973, the United States National Bureau of Standards began a program that resulted in the Data Encryption Standard (DES) four years later. Its criteria, listed below, are desirable goals for any encryption system.

- Provide a high level of data protection against unauthorized disclosure or undetected modification of data.
- Simple to understand, but complex enough to cost more to break than the gain would warrant.
- Method of protection based on encryption key rather than on secrecy of the algorithm.
- Economical to implement.
- Efficient to operate.
- Adaptable for different applications.
- Available to all users and suppliers at reasonable cost.

The DES satisfies these requirements. A microcomputer version exists for under $100, attesting to its being readily available at reasonable cost. A hardware implementation maximizes the execution speed of the algorithm. The algorithm's complexity prohibits a full treatment in this book, but a brief description is given to indicate that the process is understandable even though the details are complex.

Input to the DES consists of data in binary form, in blocks of 64 bits. Keys are 56 bits in length, expanded to 64 bits to provide error detection capabilities. Each block goes through an initial permutation (rearrangement), and the permuted block is split into two 32-bit blocks—call them $L0$ and $R0$ for the left and right halves, respectively. $L0$ and $R0$ are transformed into 32-bit blocks $L1$ and $R1$ as follows:

$$L1 = R0 \quad \text{and} \quad R1 = L0 \oplus f(R0, K1)$$

where $\oplus$ is an operator that combines two 32-bit blocks, and $f(R0,K1)$ is a 32-bit block obtained by combining $R0$ with a key $K1$. The combination involves a number of permutations. $R0$ is expanded into a 48-bit block by duplicating half of its bits and rearranging the result. The bits in $K1$ are rearranged, split in half, shifted, and then recombined into a 48-bit block.

The two 48-bit blocks are combined and passed through 8 distinct selection functions, each of which takes 6 bits as input and yields a 4-bit block as output. The outputs form a 32-bit block that is combined with $L0$ to form $R1$.

The process is repeated with $L1$, $R1$, and a different key $K2$ to produce

$$L2 = R1 \quad \text{and} \quad R2 = L1 \oplus f(R1, K2).$$

Then $L3$ and $R3$ are obtained and so on, until $L16$ and $R16$ are determined. Finally, $L16$ and $R16$ are subjected to an inverse initial permutation whose output is the 64-bit block encrypted version of the input block. Each permutation of bits and each combination of blocks follows a well-defined pattern.

From its inception, the DES has been controversial. Objectors claim that the key length should be expanded to 128 bits or that multiple encryption should be employed to make the system less susceptible to being compromised. However, no new standard has replaced the DES.

Public Key Systems in Networks

The existence of computer networks has increased the need for encryption and other security techniques. In networks, data can be in numerous storage facilities, and access can be gained from thousands of locations. Security problems related to user identification and authorization are compounded. Safeguarding valuable data and important messages by encoding becomes almost a necessity, although an expensive alternative. Concerns about security of computer equipment are secondary in networks because multiple paths are possible; if one computer system is down, then communications are maintained through an alternate system. The focus of security issues in networks is to protect data rather than computers.

One encryption technique implemented in networks is public key systems, a concept proposed by Diffie and Hellman in the mid 1970s (see Reference List). Public key systems make encryption of messages (data files) in networks feasible. The traditional approach, which requires each user to maintain the secret encoding-decoding keys of every other user, breaks down in networks. The number of users is too large to expect anyone to remember all of the secret key values without keeping a written record of them and thus compromising security. The public key system provides a viable alternative for maintaining security of data files.

In a public key encryption system, each user chooses an encoding-decoding (E,D) pair of keys. The E key value is placed in a directory with the user's name and address; the D value is kept secretly by the user. When USER1 wants to send a message to USER2, USER1 looks up the public key of USER2 in the directory, and then encodes and sends the message. *USER2* receives the message, decodes it with the secret *D* key, and reads it. By following this process, any user in the network can send an encoded (secret) message to any other user. Everyone on the network can see the encoded message, but only the addressee can decode it. Users are required to remember only their own secret key.

In order for this method to be effective, the *E* and *D* keys must meet the following criteria:

- *E* and *D* must be inverse functions; that is, if *E* encodes a message, then *D* must decode the encoded version and produce the original message. (The original message must be sent and received.)
- Both *E* and *D* must be easily found, and computation of the encoded and decoded messages must be efficient. (The overhead in sending and receiving the message must be minimal.)
- When *E* is known, finding *D* must be computationally infeasible. (Only the intended receiver should be able to decode and read the message. No one else in the network should be able to discover the decoder *D*.)

Four classes of public key encryption systems are discussed by Lakshmivarahan (see Reference List). They are all based on mathematical results beyond the level of this book.

Control of Access

Encryption and passwords are means of safeguarding files against unauthorized access. An encryption system is designed primarily to protect messages from being read by intruders. A password system is designed primarily to control user access to specific files. This section describes a method of using passwords to control user access.

Assume files of data are stored in mutually exclusive collections so that it is possible for users to gain access to one set of files but not to others. The computer system, then, must be programmed to identify a user and determine what files the user can rightfully access. Conceptually, this is accomplished through an access control matrix, also called a user authorization table, as shown in Figure 5.2. Column headings of the matrix are file names; row headings are user identifiers. Entries in the matrix specify the type of access permitted—read only, read and write, delete, etc. Blank entries indicate no access rights. For example, *USER2* has the right of access to *FILE3* for the purposes of reading and writing, and to *FILEN* for reading only, but does not have the right to access *FILE1* or *FILE2* for any reason.

An access control matrix dynamically specifies which users have access rights to files. It also provides data to an operating system for

	FILE1	FILE2	FILE3	...	FILEN
USER1	read	read, write			read, delete
USER2			read, write		read
...					
USERK	read, write		read, delete		read

Figure 5.2 Access control matrix.

enforcing file-sharing mechanisms in which two or more users need the same file.

Storing access control information as a matrix is not space efficient because the matrix is sparse. One alternative is to store with each file a list of authorized users and their access rights to that file. Entries in this access control list are pairs, of the form

<user identifier, access rights>

For example (see Figure 5.2), the access control list stored with FILE3 is

USER2, read, write
USERK, read, delete

In this representation, the absence of a user identifier means that the user does not have access rights to the file. Another alternative is capability-oriented, where a capability is a set of access rights and the file name. For each user, this method stores capabilities. For example, USER2 has the capabilities

read, write   FILE3
read   FILEN

Implementation of either of these alternatives is handled by the file system within the operating system. With access control lists, when USER2's program specifies a *write* to FILE3, for example, the file system checks USER2's entry in the list for FILE3 and determines that the *write* right is present. A pointer associated with the list gives the physical location of FILE3, and the *write* operation proceeds. With the capability-oriented system, the *write* to FILE3 request is compared to the <rights, file name> pairs in USER2's capabilities. When a match is made, the file system looks up the file name in a directory to find the physical address, and the *write* operation proceeds.

A user having rights to specific files can grant or revoke the rights of others to one or more files. The process is straghtforward in access control lists. If USER2 wants to give USER1 the right to read FILE3, then USER2 provides USER1's identifier and access right to the file system, which simply adds the data to the access control list for FILE3. Revoking of rights is accomplished by deleting the user identifier and corresponding rights. In a capability- oriented system, however, both processes are more complicated. USER2 cannot be allowed to enter USER1's capability directory because, once in, USER2D *has access to all of USER1's* rights or file names. Consequently, an indirect approach is taken. When USER2 gives USER1 the right to read FILE3, both identifiers are exchanged by means not involving their capability directories. USER2's capability to read FILE3 is placed in a separate location designated for USER1. When USER1 attempts to READ FILE3, the file system looks in the location and finds USER2's access rights, and the READ operation proceeds. Revoking of rights must also be done indirectly.

File protection in UNIX[2] is a simple example of these methods. In a UNIX operating system file environment, each file has an owner who establishes access rights to the file. All users fall into one of three categories: owner, group, or world. Each category of user can be given read, write, and/or execute privileges to a file. The owner of the file is the user in whose file space the file resides. A group is established by giving a common identification to a number of users who wish to share access to some files, perhaps because they are working on a project together. The world is everyone else who is entitled to log onto the computer. The file owner specifies access as a nine-bit code described as *rwxrwxrwx*, where r = read, w = write, and x = execute. The leftmost *rwx* is for the owner's privileges. The execute privilege is only enabled for files containing executable code. Deletion comes with write privilege, so an owner may choose to turn off write to protect against accidental deletion. The owner can turn the privilege on and off at will. The middle *rwx* specifies group rights, and the rightmost *rwx* shows the accessiblity to the world. The owner specifies a 1 for each position to be turned on, and a 0 for each off. The chmod (change mode) command specifies the protection as three octal digits, each representing access to one category. For example, a file containing an executable program might be protected as

chmod filename 711

Expanding the octal digits yields 111001001. The owner has full rights to the file; the group and world can execute only.

---

2. UNIX is a registered trademark of Bell Laboratories.

DATA INTEGRITY

By protecting data from unauthorized modification, security measures increase the likelihood of data accuracy. In this sense, the concepts of integrity and security are related. However, methods to improve data integrity are independent of measures to achieve security. As before, many of the issues pertaining to integrity are related to people, including management, data entry personnel, programmers, and anyone involved in processing data.

Accuracy and reliability of data begin with collecting and entering it. If sales representatives enter sales data from the field through terminals to the mainframe at the home office, then they must first obtain, and then enter, it correctly. The data must then be transmitted accurately over communication lines and stored appropriately. If sales representatives send written or telephone reports, then data entry clerks at the home office must enter the data accurately. Most mistakes occur at the entering stage. Either data is initially recorded erroneously or it is missent, or mistakes are made in entering it. Usually these are unintentional errors due to carelessness on the part of over-tired, distracted, or inadequately trained personnel.

Data integrity is especially important where personal data is involved. Entering or storing erroneous data can have serious consequences. For example, a policeman stops a speeder and enters the wrong license number from the terminal in his police car. He receives a report that the car has been stolen and arrests the driver for theft. By the time the error is discovered and corrected, the driver, along with family and friends, has been through a trying ordeal, possibly including jail.

Measures to improve data integrity at the entering stage vary from periodically relieving data entry personnel, to having a second person verify the data, to including error prevention statements in programs. Management also contributes by providing adequate training in data entry operations, including how to fill out forms.

A number of programming techniques are possible, but none of them will prevent all errors. Some techniques pertain to entering data, others to processing data after it has been entered.

When data is entered with the help of forms, the software prompts the person who enters the data. Possible prompts are of several kinds. One kind displays the actual form on the screen, a new form for each set of data, as shown in Figure 5.3. This enables data entry personnel to fill in the blanks as if they were doing it with pencil and paper. Another kind of prompt, shown in Figure 5.4, displays a menu-like list of field names in a record. Data items are then entered for each field, and the program organizes the data into whatever record structure is needed. In both cases, maximum field length is indicated by a number, a shaded bar, or a set of blank lines.

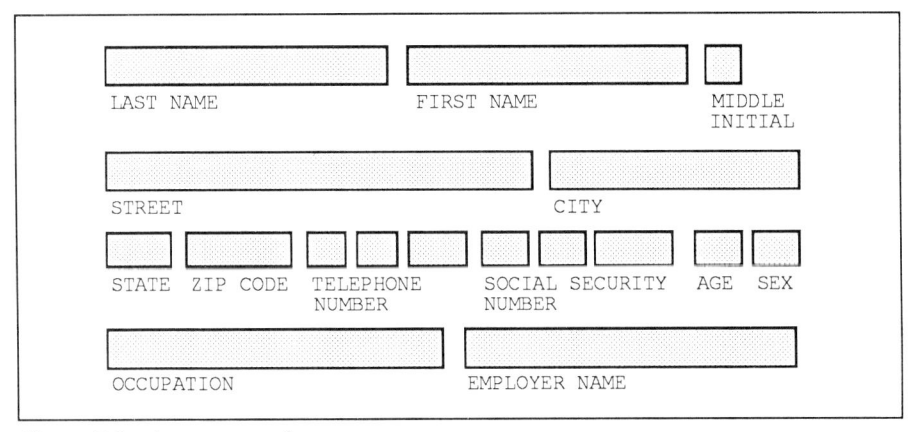

Responsibility: Protecting a Critical Resource   129

Figure 5.3   *An on-screen form.*

Figure 5.4   *A list of fields in menu form.*

In either case, certain protection against entering and processing erroneous data is built into software. Maximum field length and data type can be specified for each data item. In Pascal, this is done when records are declared at the beginning of a program. Figure 5.5 contains an example. COBOL's PICTURE clause allows the use of the designator "*A*" (for alphabetic) or "9" (for numeric) instead of "X." However, if data does not conform to the alphabetic or numeric specification, the program is terminated. For that reason, use of "*A*" or "9" is not recommended. COBOL also provides tests for alphabetic or numeric fields, as illustrated in Figure 5.6. These precautions do not prevent errors such as entering "1987" instead of "1988", or "JANES" instead of "JAMES", but they do catch errors such as entering "198L" instead of "1981".

```
type date = record
          month : (jan,feb,mar,apr,may,jun,jul,
                   aug,sep,
                   oct,nov,dec);
          day   : 1..31;
          year  : integer
          end;
     person = record
          name  : packed array [1..20] of char;
          sex   : (m,f);
          birth : date
          end;
```

Figure 5.5 Specifying data type and field length in Pascal.

```
IF EMPLOYEE NOT ALPHABETIC        IF AGE NOT NUMERIC
   THEN (imperative statement)       THEN (imperative statement)
```

Figure 5.6 Alphabetic and numeric tests in COBOL

A form-based data entry system allows data to be examined as it is entered. In addition to checking for validity of field length and the use of alphabetic or numeric entries, the program accepting the data can verify the reasonableness of some fields. For instance, a new employee's year of birth may be required to be after 1900, the number of hours worked in a week may be expected to be less than 80, or the number of dependents may be compared to a reasonable maximum. An expense report may include a maximum allowable amount for *per diem* expenses. A very large purchase may be refused until a credit check has been done to insure that the account contains sufficient funds or credit to cover the purchase price.

Data entered in batch mode is also checked before any processing (for example, file updates) is done with it. The nature and extent of the verification done by these edit programs varies with the application. Often the edit program is the most complex in the system flow. Some typical checks include the following:

- If a field is only alphabetic or only numeric, then an entry of any other type should be prevented. (see Figures 5.5 and 5.6).
- If the maximum salary for a position is $40,000, then entering "$43,500" should not be possible. It can be prevented by inserting a statement that checks ranges of values, such as

```
If SALARY > 40000
  then <take some action>
```

- If the field contains a department designator for a course—for example, CMSC—then the entry can be checked against a table of valid entries. Action can be specified for invalid entries. This kind of check is reasonable if the table of possible values is limited in size.
- If the field contains a cumulative value, say car mileage, then a new entry can be checked against the previous one. If the field contains the mileage value 30575, then an entry of 39700 after a short trip should be flagged.
- If an entry in one field invalidates an entry in another field, the record should be flagged. For example, if one field indicates that a man is registered as a Democrat, but another field shows he voted in the Republican primary, then the vote should not be counted.
- If a field cannot contain one or more values, then an entry with any of those values should be flagged. For example, if a bank charges a $5.00 monthly fee for maintaining a customer's account, no other value should be permitted in the field for monthly fee.
- If numeric data is especially sensitive—that is, a small error causes significant problems—then a check digit should be added to the number. This digit is computed from the number and changes when the number changes. The following example illustrates one way to obtain a check digit; many other algorithms are possible.
    (1) Multiply each digit of a number by its place in the number, working from right to left.
    (2) Add the products.
    (3) Determine the difference between the sum and the smallest multiple of ten that is not less than the sum.
    (4) The difference is the check digit.
    (5) Rewrite the number with the check digit as the last (first) digit.
Figure 5.7 contains a numerical example for this algorithm

Assuming that accurate data has been entered and reasonable checks are in place for processing, there is still the problem of maintaining data integrity. System (hardware and software) failures and operational mistakes are prime causes of integrity loss. Periodic testing of data in a system is a partial safeguard. It adds to the overhead costs, and the extent to which it is done in a given application must be weighed against the importance of having reliable data. Some of the methods mentioned above can be adapted, or methods of periodically validating data can be used.

Validation is a means of testing the completeness of data. It is practically impossible, and too expensive, to attempt total validation. However, purposeful random checks can be made to give a measure of assurance that the data is all there and is probably accurate. Major problems can also be identified in this way. The following examples indicate the kind of random checks that are helpful.

```
Inventory Number                         456789

Multiply digits by                       9 * 1 =  9
position in number.                      8 * 2 = 16
                                         7 * 3 = 21
                                         6 * 4 = 24
                                         5 * 5 = 25
                                         4 * 6 = 24

Sum the products.                                119

Find the difference                      120 - 119 = 1
between the sum and
the smallest multiple of 10
not less than the sum.

The difference is the                            1
check digit.

Rewrite the number                       4567891
with the check digit
as the last digit.
```

Figure 5.7   Check digit example.

- Records can be sampled at random and printed. Their contents are then checked by hand against what is supposed to be in them. If anything appears suspicious about one or more records, then additional sampling can be done. If errors occur in the same field of a number of records, then a major problem exists; someone is deliberately altering records, or the program is incorrect, or the computer system has a malfunction.
- One or more artificial transactions can be put through a system. The exact results of the transactions are figured in advance. When the transaction has come completely through the system, a careful check of its effects is made, and the results are compared to expectations.
- A record count during processing of a file indicates whether or not all records are included.
- Subtotals for designated fields can be printed. Suppose an accounts system in a bank prints totals for deposits and withdrawals made between opening and 11:00 A.M. each day. If a comparison of these totals shows that bank deposits are unusually low on a given day, or

that withdrawals are remarkably high, then there is reason to check for an error or criminal activity.
- Artificial totals can be computed to verify that all records have been processed. Suppose personnel records contain a field for an individual's height in inches. As all records are processed—say, for a general mailing—a running sum of heights can be kept. When processing is complete, the sum is compared to the total obtained previously. A sum that is 72 less than the true total suggests that the record of a six-foot tall employee did not get processed.

Accurate data can still produce inaccurate results if the program that manipulates it is incorrect. Good programming practices, then, are important integrity measures. Solution design before writing the program, testing modules, using assertions to prove correctness of program segments, and choosing an appropriate programming language for an application, are all means to help insure that correct output results from accurate input.

Privacy

A person's right to privacy is one of the fundamental tenets of the United States. It existed long before computers, and was much easier to sustain before they appeared. With computers, extensive data on an individual can be collected, stored, and manipulated in ways and amounts that are practically impossible by other means. Huge files containing personal data are now maintained by federal, state, and local governments (for instance, the Internal Revenue Service, the Social Security System, the National Crime Information Center, and the Department of Motor Vehicles), financial and educational institutions, credit card companies, department stores, etc. The power and capacity of computers enable large numbers of people to gain access to different collections of data, search them, manipulate the data, and find out more about an individual than previously feasible with noncomputerized files.

Security and integrity help deter misuse of personal data, but cannot prevent it altogether, just as a seat belt protects a driver, but does not eliminate all chance of injury. A secure system makes unauthorized access more difficult than one without security measures. Data in a file which is hard to access is less likely to be obtained or used by unauthorized people. Unfortunately, though, unauthorized access is nearly impossible to eliminate because of the vast collections of personal data that exist, and the large number of people who have terminals and can gain access to systems.

Data that is stored online in a computer system to which there is access by remote terminals can never be considered completely private. Truly private data must be physically removed from such a system (on a tape or removable disk) and locked away. Data that is to be kept online and still be protected must be limited to a system that has no remote access—that is, no terminals that are not in the immediate area and under complete control, no dial-up facility, and no network connection. The price for absolute privacy is very high.

Large collections of personal data that are used as the basis for statistical reports are susceptible to privacy violations. The usual reports generated from these databases contain summaries of data that do not identify specific individuals. For example, a report states that 2,364 people in the area defined by zipcode 33333 voted Republican in the 1980 election. It does not list people's names or any other data that could identify a specific individual. No privacy violations are involved. However, statistical databases can yield personal data about an individual, even though all identifying information (name, address, Social Security number) is removed from each entry. The process involves a sequence of queries and assumes knowledge of a set of properties about an individual.

Suppose we want to find out the annual salary of Agnes Peabody. Assume we know that Agnes is 32 years old, lives in Chicago, is employed as a technical writer, and is not married. We submit the following query to a statistical database: How many people have all of the properties listed below?

Age	32
Sex	Female
Marital Status	Single
City	Chicago
Occupation	Technical writer

The response is 143. This result is not sufficient to identify anyone, so we determine other information about Agnes, through friends or other sources. A second query includes all of the old properties, along with the new ones:

Education	B.A. degree
Year	1975
School	University of Michigan

The response is 5. After getting more information and including it in queries, the response eventually is 1. At this stage, Agnes Peabody has been identified. The next query contains all of the old properties, plus the new one:

$$\text{Salary} \qquad < \$20{,}000$$

If the response is 1, then we have found out that Agnes earns less than $20,000. Additional queries can pinpoint the actual salary. Once the set of properties produces a response 1, any data available in the database can be obtained. Hoffman gives a formal treatment of this technique, as well as more sophisticated ones (see Reference List).

There is no complete protection of individual privacy in statistical databases, but there are several deterrents. One way to discourage numerous queries from the same person is to maintain a log book of query activity. Periodic review of the log can indicate similar queries or queries that have small number counts as responses. Detection of misuse is difficult because the queries are interspersed with legitimate ones and because two or more users can alternate queries so that one person does not appear overly active. A log book provides a psychological deterrent and it has other purposes related to record-keeping.

Another way to reduce unauthorized access to statistical databases is to maintain a link file system. When data is collected, personal identifying information is stored in one file, and the statistical data in a second file. Different arbitrary identification numbers are assigned to the personal information (*IDENT1*) and to the statistical data (*IDENT2*). A third file (table) holds the two identification numbers. The three files are administered separately. For example, a service agency administers the file of identification numbers. The group responsible for analyzing data and generating statistical reports administers the statistical data file. The department responsible for mailing and collecting surveys administers the personal information file. This file is the master file for mailing follow-up surveys. It is updated whenever new survey results are obtained. Then *IDENT1* is assigned to the statistical data and sent to the service agency. The agency finds *IDENT1* and the corresponding *IDENT2* in its file, replaces *IDENT1* with *IDENT2* on the statistical data, and sends it to the analysis- and report-generating group. That group then has both the new and the old data available. This link system can be invaded, but considerable effort is required of an intruder. Potential defects in the system, as in any system, pertain to the people involved and how well they administer the files.

Legislation enacted to help protect personal privacy includes a series of federal laws beginning with the Freedom of Information Act of 1966. These laws are summarized in Figure 5.8. These legal security measures are less effective than intended. Privacy violations are difficult to prove, and the penalty for proven violations is not very severe—only a relatively

Freedom of Information Act

- Passed in 1966, amended in 1967
- Requires federal agencies to make available for public inspection certain aspects of their operations
- Provides individuals legal recourse if an agency refuses to comply to an information request

Fair Credit Reporting Act

- Passed in 1970
- Requires consumer reporting agencies to furnish a consumer report under specified conditions
- Provides some protection against erroneous information and disclosure
- Provides legal recourse for consumers whose rights are violated

Privacy Act of 1974

- Passed as an amendment to the Freedom of Information Act
- Pertains only to federal agencies except law enforcement and intellgence agencies
- Permits an individual to determine what records are collected, maintained, used, or disseminated by federal agencies
- Permits an individual to prevent use of information for purposes other than that for which it was obtained
- Permits an individual to gain access to personal records, to have a copy made, and to amend the records
- Permits exeptions from these requirements in cases of important public policy needs
- Provides legal recourse for individuals whose rights are violated
- Created a Privacy Protection Study Commission

Education Privacy Act

- Passed in 1978
- Permits stored information to be controlled only by those authorized by law to control it
- Permits access to a student's educational records by parents and the student
- Prevents disclosure of educational records except to those granted specific rights to see the data

Right to Financial Privacy Act

- Passed in 1978
- Limits governmental access to certain financial institutions' customer records

Figure 5.8 Highlights of federal acts influencing privacy. From R. Austing and L. Cassel, Computers in Focus. Brooks/Cole, 1986, p. 289.

small fine. The average individual is unaware of what information is in a file and would have a great deal of trouble finding out. Also, it is seldom possible to determine when, or how often, one government agency improperly accesses files maintained by other agencies to crosscheck data on specific individuals.

Computerized mailing lists are common sources of privacy violations. Many organizations offer or use lists without permission of the people whose names are on the lists. For example, a magazine may offer a list of subscribers to one of its advertisers. Companies have rented mailing lists of occupational categories (for example, physicians or lawyers) to the Internal Revenue Service (IRS). Nonfilers of tax returns could be detected by comparing these lists with a master list of taxpayers.

No amount of security or integrity can prevent all privacy violations. The best safeguard is a concern for privacy by everyone who creates, accesses, processes, or enters data.

SUMMARY

In this chapter, the focus shifted from algorithms, language implementations, and hardware to security, integrity, and privacy issues. The three terms were defined and differentiated. Measures for securing systems and data against unauthorized entry were emphasized. Techniques for improving accuracy and reliability of data at entry and during processing were surveyed. Concerns about privacy were raised.

Security, integrity, and privacy are primarily people-oriented topics. They are management responsibilities. Security and integrity also have a technical side, but they cannot be guaranteed by technical measures alone. Influencing people's attitudes and heightening their awareness are the most effective means of achieving security, integrity, and privacy. It is appropriate, therefore, to confront these issues early, so that they affect the design and implementation of files, topics that are discussed in the later chapters of this book.

EXERCISES

1. Discuss relationships among security, integrity, and privacy.
2. Determine what security measures are enforced at the computer installation to which you have access. Which of these measures affects your interaction with the system?
3. Assume that access to a system requires a six-character password containing letters or digits. (For example, ABCDEF, R45JYU, and 123456 are legitimate, but G#HI5J, CAR(4), and KF_MT are not.) If the

microcomputer is capable of performing one million operations per second, how much time is needed to compute all legitimate passwords?

4. Use the algorithm in this chapter (p. 131) to compute the check digit for each of the following account numbers.
   (a) 356789
   (b) 446789
   (c) 455789
   (d) 456788

5. List a minimum set of properties that would uniquely identify you in a statistical database.

6. Identify several sources of error in computerized billing systems. How could they be corrected? What steps can a consumer take when a billing error is identified?

7. Obtain at least five forms (mail-in coupons, questionnaires, etc.). Fill in each form with a different version of your name that you do not normally use. For example, James Henry Robinson could use J. H. Robinson, Jim Robinson, Hank Robinson, Rob Robinson, and Jas Robinson. Send in all of the forms. Watch your mail for advertisements, solicitations, etc., using each version of your name. Compile a list of how your name and address were spread around by each version you used.

8. Try to find out what data on you is contained in files maintained by public agencies. Report on your efforts.

9. What laws that are intended to protect individual privacy exist in your state. Comment on their effectiveness.

10. Is collection of data on individuals ever warranted if it intrudes on their privacy?

CHAPTER 6

SEQUENTIAL FILE PROCESSING

INTRODUCTION

Sequential storage and processing of data is the simplest, most "natural" way to access data. No elaborate methods are required in order to know where each record is located. Minimal physical motion in the recording device is required for each record. All the advantages of blocking, described in Chapter 4, can be realized.

The advantages of sequential file processing generally result from using all, or nearly all, of the records in a file. In working with a sequential file, there is very little overhead in accessing each record; it is the next one in order is accessed. Since files have a tendency to become large, sequential file processing applications frequently involve processing a large number of records. Thus, overall efficiency of the processing to be done is important. The emphasis in this chapter, consequently, will be on producing effective, efficient algorithms for performing some complete task in the sequential processing environment.

This chapter presents a sequential file from two perspectives: that of a physical organization of data, and that of a logical view of data, with storage details hidden. Methods for merging and sorting files are also introduced because the techniques of Chapters 2 and 3 do not apply directly to files that do not fit into memory. Algorithms and programming techniques are included for two common examples: producing summary reports from sequential files, and updating such files.

SEQUENTIAL FILES: A PHYSICAL ORGANIZATION

In a physically sequential file, each record is located adjacent to another record of the same file. The order of the records is based on placement and may not correspond to any significant feature of the data stored. An input or output operation proceeds from where the previous input or output operation left off. There is no key to tell the program where to find a particular record; records are accessed in the order in which they are placed in the file. To process a record other than the next adjacent one, it is necessary to consider each record encountered until the desired one is found. To process a record previous to the current one, it is necessary to return to the beginning of the file. Sequential search in Chapter 2 is an example of this approach.

Physically sequential files occur frequently. Examples include files stored on magnetic tape, a stack of checks to be processed by a bank, and a collection of mark sense or other Optical Character Reader (OCR) records. Historically, a stack of punched cards also provides an example of physically sequential data. (see Figure 6.1).

SEQUENTIAL FILES: A LOGICAL ORGANIZATION

In many instances—for example, when printing a list of employees or customers—it is desirable to process the records of a file as if they were sequentially stored, whether they are or not. When a file is logically sequential, each record appears to the user to be next to another record of

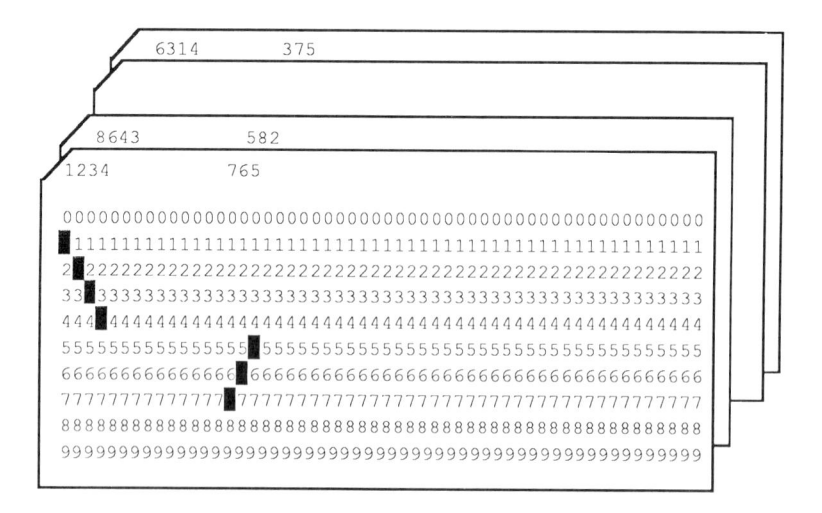

Figure 6.1 Punched cards: physically contiguous records

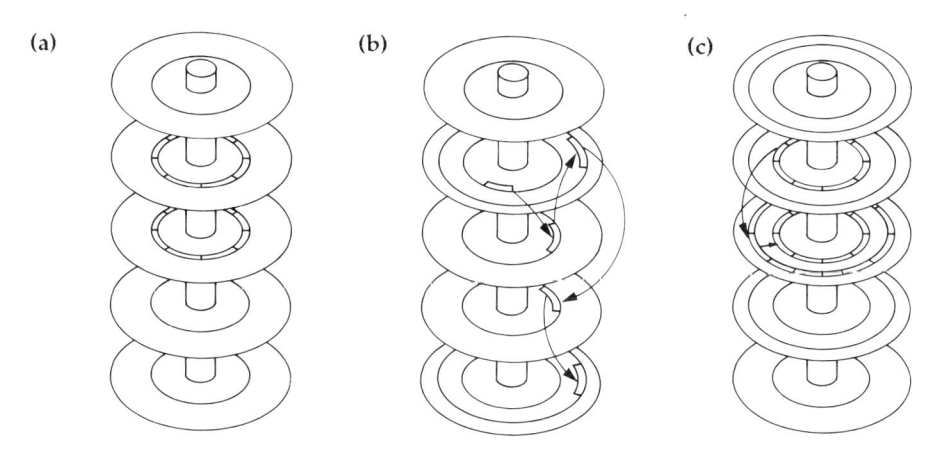

Figure 6.2 (a) *Almost physically contiguous records (Two disk surfaces are needed and the two surfaces are not contiguous.)*
(b) *A logically sequential file in which the records are physically scattered, but each includes an explicit pointer to the record that is logically "next."*
(c) *Logically sequential records with physically contiguous groups linked by pointers.*

the file, even though the records that appear to be adjacent may be widely separated in storage. All of the records are processed, one after another. Input and output operations proceed consecutively according to a predetermined order. As in any sequential file processing operation, skipping from one record to another that is not logically adjacent to it requires some processing of the logically intervening records.

Logically sequential files may be physically sequential as well. Magnetic tape files, a stack of checks, and a collection of OCR forms or punched cards are all both physically and logically sequential. In addition, files stored on a direct access device may be logically sequential. Several possibilities are illustrated in Figure 6.2. In each case the device shown is a disk, but other direct access storage devices could also be used.

In Figure 6.2(a), the records are almost physically, as well as logically, sequential. Records are located in adjacent positions on a track, until the track is filled. Then the next record is placed on a different track—usually on a different surface—so that the read/write heads do not have to move. When all the surfaces are filled, the read/write heads move to another cylinder and the records loaded on its surfaces. The records are as contiguous as possible on the storage device. The number of records per track or per cylinder is not significant for most applications, and the file is treated as if it were actually sequential.

Figure 6.2(b) shows a very different case. Here the records are actually scattered over the available storage space. Each record contains the address of the "next" record, which is frequently not adjacent. The user program will have to wait for any movement needed by the read/write heads before the record can be accessed. However, the program proceeds from one record to a predetermined next record in a logically sequential way. Usually the programmer is not aware of the scattered storage of the file.

In Figure 6.2(c), a number of records are located contiguously. In each collection of records there is an address of the next collection of records. Again the program treats the file as if the records were stored sequentially, processing one record after another in a predetermined order. The user is unaware of which records are stored together and when a transition to another group occurs.

Access Times

An important difference between files that are physically sequential and those that are logically but not physically adjacent is the time needed to access the records in the file. When a record to be read or written is physically adjacent to the previous record,

- No address has to be calculated.
- Minimal physical motion is required. (For example, simply advance the tape, and take the next record or card.)
- The advantages of blocking can be realized, thus saving on external references. (It is only helpful to transfer several records at one time if it is known that these records are likely to be the next ones requested.)

For physically sequential files, the computer's directory system needs to keep very little information in order to permit access to each record. The directory must contain the location of the beginning of the file. From that point on, every other record will be located in turn. If the file is located on a direct access storage device that may contain many files, a directory must identify the beginning of the file to be used. A directory usually contains other information, such as who is allowed to access the file, creation date, expiration date, and so on, but these are not part of the access of individual records.

USES OF SEQUENTIAL PROCESSING

There are many occasions when sequential processing is desirable regardless of the physical storage of the file. For instance, many uses of an employee master file imply access to nearly all records. Among these are:

- Producing the payroll.
- Listing all employees by department, education level, experience, etc.
- Listing all employees who know French, or have some other particular skill.

Customer accounts must frequently be completely processed to:

- Send sale notices.
- Send invoices.
- Send membership or subscription renewal notices.
- Process payments received.

A number of operations are performed on complete files and require that all records be accessed, including:

- Sorting files.
- Merging files.
- Counting records.
- Splitting a file.
- Copying or moving the file.

Sorting and merging files are discussed later in this chapter.

Batch Versus Sequential Processing

A distinction must be made between batch and sequential processing. In **batch processing**, transactions are collected and applied together at a certain time, perhaps overnight or during the weekend. **Sequential processing** refers to an order of using records in a file. The order is predetermined when the file is stored, and it involves some access to each record of the file in turn. These are two distinct approaches to processing data. They can be combined or applied separately, as illustrated in the following cases.

Batch Processing With Direct Access

A batch of transactions may refer to only a small portion of a master file, and access to every record of the master file may not be desirable. For instance, processing subscription renewals that have come in during the week is not likely to require most of the records in the subscriber file.

Reading each record in the master file wastes a great deal of time and effort. This is a batch application, since the transactions were all collected some time before processing, but it is not a suitable application for sequentially processing every record in the file. In this case, direct access to each required master record is more efficient.

Interactive Processing and Sequential Access

A "real time" (that is, with only reasonable or acceptable delay), or interactive, application can be processed sequentially. In this case a transaction, or query, is processed as soon as it is presented. Such a transaction may require the entire file when, for instance, we are directed to: "Find all the students who have completed <some course>". This is an interactive, not a batch, operation, since the request is not held until others are made and serviced together. Sequential files are appropriate since each record must be accessed in turn to see if it meets the criterion.

Batch Processing and Sequential Access

Finally, there are many cases in which transactions are collected into a batch and are then applied to a master file, requiring nearly all the records in the master file. In this case, both batch processing and sequential access are used. This combination is also used in the sequential file update algorithm developed later in this chapter.

Merging and Sorting with Sequential Processing

Introduction

It is not always possible to store an entire file in main memory in order to search or sort it. Very large collections of data, such as student records at a large university, personnel records of a major corporation, transactions in a multi-branch bank or popular department store, and census data, are generally stored as files on auxiliary memory media (tape or disk). When these files are updated, only portions of them can be in main memory at any one time. They are called **external files**, and methods for searching and sorting them are called **external searches** and **sorts**.

The search and sort methods of Chapters 2 and 3 do not apply to these files, with the exception of sequential search. Although the discussion of sequential search assumed that the entire file was stored internally as an array, the method can be adapted easily to search external files. We simply read a portion of the file that fits into memory, search it, and then read the next portion, and the next portion, and so on, each time applying the sequential search algorithm (or binary search, if the file is sorted on the search key). Other external search methods are discussed in later chapters. This chapter treats external sort methods.

As in Chapters 2 and 3, only keys are specified in external sorts. Files are made up of records, and records are represented by their keys. Searching and sorting depend on the key value, not on other fields in each record. Consequently, only the key values appear in descriptions, algorithms, examples, and programs. Each key must be thought of as representing a full record that is read, stored, moved, and written, whenever these operations are indicated for the key values.

Many external sorts include a technique called **merging**. Thus, the notion of merging files is considered next, and then is applied to a sampling of external sorts.

Merging Files

Merging is a common process. Two lanes of traffic merge into one. A list of on-site registrants for a course or conference is merged with the list of those who preregistered to produce a single alphabetized list. A stream merges with a river. Several lines of people merge into one line to enter a theater. In computing, two or more files are merged into one file.

More formally, the term **merging** refers to the combining of two or more ordered files into one ordered file. It is essential that the files have the same order. Combining unordered collections is like shuffling cards—the result is still an unordered collection. Try organizing two unsorted lists of names into one sorted list. It is always easier and more efficient to sort each list first, and then merge them, rather than combine the lists before sorting them. In fact, trying to merge two unordered lists makes no more sense than placing them end-to-end (concatenating them).

Two-Way Merge

Method

When two files are already sorted, say, in nondecreasing order, the simplest way to merge them into one file in nondecreasing order is to compare the first key in each file and put the smaller key into a third file. (Decide in advance how to handle ties.) Then compare the remaining key—the larger one—with the next key in the nonempty file and put the smaller of these two keys as the next key in the third file. Continue this process until one file is empty. Then put all remaining keys from the nonempty file into the third file. At the end of the merge, the third file will contain all keys from both files, in nondecreasing order.

Algorithm

An algorithm for this method, called **two-way merge** because two files are merged, is straightforward.

> Input: File X of records with keys in nondecreasing order.
> File Y of records with keys in nondecreasing order.
> Output: File Z of all records from X and Y with keys in nondecreasing order.
>
> Read record x from X and record y from Y.
> While both X and Y contain records
>   do the following:
>   If key of x < key of y
>   then
>   Write record x to file Z
>   Read record x from X
>   else
>   Write record y to file Z
>   Read record y from Y
> If file X is the one that is empty
>   then transfer rest of Y to Z
>   else transfer rest of X to Z

EXAMPLE 6.1

To illustrate this algorithm, we merge the following files, which contain only names that are also record keys:

F_1: Amy, Dick, Gene, Paul, Sam, Tina
F_2: Andy, Earl, Joy, Mary

Input	*Comparison*	*Output*
Amy, Andy	Amy, Andy	Amy
Dick	Dick, Andy	Andy
Earl	Dick, Earl	Dick
Gene	Gene, Earl	Earl
Joy	Gene, Joy	Gene
Paul	Paul, Joy	Joy
Mary	Paul, Mary	Mary
		Paul
Sam		Sam
Tina		Tina

Variations of two-way merge apply when one file is considerably smaller than the other. However, when the files are approximately the same size (say, m and n records, respectively where m and n are nearly equal), then the method requires no more than $m+n-1$ comparisons and sufficient memory to hold the two records whose keys are being compared. External storage for one output file is required, with the length of the output file = $n + m$. In this situation, the two-way merge is one of the best possible merge techniques.

Programs

Assume the following declarations and program header:

```pascal
program mergeapplication (filex, filey, filez);
type rec = record
           keyfield: <appropriate type>;
           otherfields: <appropriate types>;
           end;

var recx, recy, recz    : rec;
    filex, filey, filez: file of rec;
```

The Pascal procedure follows directly from the algorithm.

```pascal
procedure twowaymerge;
     begin
        read(filex, recx);
        read(filey, recy);
        while not eof (filex) and not eof(filey) do
          begin
             if recx.keyfield < recy.keyfield
               then
                 begin
                    write(filez, recx);
                     read(filex, recx);
                 end
               else
                 begin
                    write(filez, recy);
                    read(filey, recy);
                 end;
          end;
```

```
          if eof(filex)          {File X is empty}
            then                 {Copy rest of file Y}
              while not eof(filey) do
                begin
                  write(filey,recy);
                  read(filey,recy);
                end
              else     {Copy rest of file X}
                while not eof(filex) do   {file Y is
                                                empty}
                  begin
                    write(filey, recx);
                    readfilex, recx);
                  end;
```

Pascal Program 6.1 *Two-way merge*

COBOL includes a command, MERGE, that does the merge operation shown in the algorithm and is illustrated in detail by the Pascal program. The appropriate COBOL statements to merge two files, called FILEX and FILEY, into a new file called FILEZ follow:

```
DATA DIVISION.
FILE SECTION.
SD MERGE-WORK-FILE.
01 WORK-RECORD-LAYOUT.
   03 WORK-KEYFIELD      PIC <as appropriate>.
   03 <other fields of the files>.

FD FILEX.
01 FILEX-RECORD          PIC X(<total record size>).

FD FILEY.
01 FILEY-RECORD          PIC X(<total record size>).

FD FILEZ.
01 FILEZ-RECORD          PIC X(<total record size>).

PROCEDURE DIVISION.
   .
   .
   .
   MERGE MERGE-WORK-FILE
       ON ASCENDING KEY WORK-KEYFIELD
     USING FILEX, FILEY
     GIVING FILEZ.
```

COBOL Program 6.2 *Merging two files*

Operating system libraries frequently include utility programs for such common operations as file merging. The COBOL MERGE statement invokes the system utility program. In most instances, it is preferable to merge files as a separate operation, not as part of a program that has other work to do.

Sorting by Merging

Merging is typically combined with internal sort methods to produce sorted files. One method, called **mergesort**, involves splitting an internally stored unsorted file into two halves, sorting each half, and merging the results. Each half, in turn, is sorted by being split, sorted, and merged. Mergesort is recursive and is $O(n \log n)$.

Other methods require that an external (unsorted) file be split into two or more subfiles, each of which is read into main memory, sorted by an internal sort method, and then written to an external file. The sorted subfiles are then merged into one sorted file.

N-Way Natural Merge

Method

Consider the following situation. At the end of each day, books returned to a large library during that day are sorted in increasing order by the ISBN, a unique number assigned to each book title. Data for each book is entered into a file on an external storage medium as the books are returned. At the end of the day, a large, unsorted, external file exists.

This input file is sorted by the following process. A number of records, corresponding to individual books, are read into memory and sorted by any internal sort method on the key field ISBN. The sorted records are written to an external file, call it F1. The records for the next k books are read, sorted and written to a second external file, F2. The next k are read, sorted, and written to F1, then the next k books to F2 and so on. The groups of k sorted book records are alternately written to F1 and F2 until no more books remain in the input file. Each group of k sorted records is called a run. At this stage, then, book records from the original file are in runs of length k, placed alternately on the two files F1 and F2.

Merging of these runs now occurs. The first runs on each (input) file are merged into a run (sorted file) of length $2k$ and written to a third (output) file, F3. The second runs are merged and written to F3. Each pair of runs is merged and written in a similar way. Eventually, F1 and F2 are empty, and F3 contains all books arranged in runs of length $2k$. These runs are then distributed between the files F1 and F2—the first, third, fifth, etc. runs on F1, and the second, fourth, sixth, etc. runs on F2. As before, the first runs on each file are merged into a run, now of length 2 * 2k, and written to F3. Each pair of runs are merged successively and written to F3, until both F1 and F2 are empty. This process of distributing and merging runs continues until all book records are sorted into one file on F3.

As described, the process is called a 2-way sort merge, because two files (F1 and F2) play the role of input files. The process is also termed a **natural merge** because only one output file is involved.

Algorithm

Only the 2-way sort merge is considered here. The algorithm is in two parts: the initial sorting of records into runs, and the merging of runs.

Input: An unsorted file R of n records, each with an identifying key.
Output: A file, F3, of the n records with keys in nondecreasing order.
Two intermediate files, F1 and F2, to hold runs.

(a) Sorting into runs:
Choose a number k (the size of the initial runs).
Repeat the following steps until R is empty:
Read k records from file R.
Sort them into a run (of length k) by an internal sort method.
Alternately write the run onto F1 and F2.

(b) Merging:
Repeat the following steps until F3 contains only one run, of length n (that is, the whole file is sorted and on F3).
For each pair of runs, one from F1 and one from F2, merge the two runs into a run of twice the length and write the run onto F3.
Distribute the runs from F3 alternately on F1 and F2.

Note that the merging part of the algorithm involves the 2-way merge previously discussed. Also, the choice of k depends on the amount of memory available for an internal sort. The longer the initial runs are, the fewer merging steps will be required.

EXAMPLE 6.2

For convenience, consider a file of 8 records and let $k = 1$ (that is, assume each record is a sorted file of length one). Assume the keys of the records are in the following order:

21,15,62,48,21,39,30,43

Because $k = 1$, the initial sort phase of the algorithm is unnecessary. The process can be portrayed as a binary tree, upside-down. Each level corresponds to a pass. Each level after the first is obtained by applying the merge phase of the algorithm to the pairs of sorted files in the preceding level.

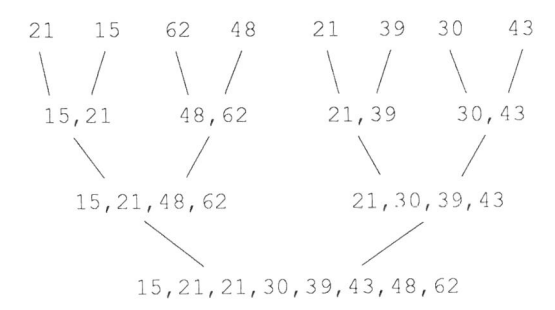

```
        21    15    62    48    21    39    30    43
         \   /       \   /       \   /       \   /
         15,21       48,62       21,39       30,43
             \       /                \       /
             15,21,48,62              21,30,39,43
                       \              /
                    15,21,21,30,39,43,48,62
```

Programs

```
procedure twowaysortmerge (k:integer);
var runcount,              {number of runs on each
                            temporary file (X, Y)}
    j: integer;            {loop counter}

procedure sortrun;
{Read k records from file R into array A and sort A}
var A:array[1..k] of rec;
    j: integer;
begin
    j := 0;
    while not eof(filer) and j<k do
        begin
            j:= j+1;
            read(filer, A[j]);
        end;
    sortrecords(A,j);      {Any of the internal sorts,
                            with complete records
                            exchanged when the keys
                            are out of order }
end;
```

152   Chapter 6

```
procedure distributeruns;
{Read sorted runs of records from file Z and write
alternately on files X and Y}

var outcode,            {=0 for filex, =1 for filey}
    j:integer;          {loop counter}
begin
   reset(filez);
   runcount:=0;
   outcode:= 0;
   while not eof(filez) do
       begin
          j:=0;
          outcode:=(outcode+1)mod 2;  {0=filex,1=filey}
          runcount :=runcount + outcode;
          while j < k and not eof(filez) do
            begin
               read(filez,recz);
               case outcode of
                 0: write(filex,recz);
                 1: write(filey,recz);
               end;      {case}
            end;
       end;
end;

procedure distributearray(A:array[1..k] of rec;
                          var outcode:integer);
begin
   outcode:=(outcode+1) mod 2;  {0=filex, 1=filey}
   runcount:= runcount +outcode;
   for j := 1 to k do
   case outcode of
      0: write(filex, A[j]);
      1: write(filey, A[j]);
   end;            {case}
end;

begin     {twowaysortmerge main procedure}
   outcode := 0;
   runcount := 0;
   while not eof(filer) do
      begin
         sortrun;
         distributearray(A, outcode);
      end;
```

```
    repeat
       twowaymerge;                    {procedure on page 147}
       if (runcount > 1)
          then
               distributeruns
       until runcount = 1;
end;
```

Pascal Program 6.2 *Two way sort merge*

A COBOL program to sort files invokes the system sort utility and uses a sort/merge program. The exact details of the sort merge method used depend on the utility provided in the operating system. The sort merge method shown in the algorithm, and the variations on the sort merge method discussed in the next section, are examples of the type of coding being executed when the COBOL SORT statement is used. In general, it is preferable to invoke the system utility directly, rather than use the SORT statement within a program which has other work to do.

```
DATA DIVISION.
FILE SECTION.
SD  SORT-WORK-FILE.
01  SORT-WORK-RECORD.
      03  WORK-KEYFIELD         PIC (<as appropriate>).
      03  other fields defined as in the file to be sorted.

FD  FILE-R.
01  FILE-R-RECORD               PIC X(total record size).

FD  FILE-Z.
01  FILE-Z-RECORD               PIC X(total record size).
    .
    .
    .
PROCEDURE DIVISION.
    .
    .
    .
        SORT SORT-WORK-FILE
            ON ASCENDING KEY WORK-KEYFIELD
            USING FILE-R
            GIVING FILE-Z.
```

COBOL PROGRAM 6.2 *Sort merge*

Analysis

From the previous results on methods that can be represented as binary trees of n nodes, it follows that the number of passes (which is equal to the depth of the binary tree) required to sort a file using 2-way sort merge is $O(\log n)$. During each pass there are no more than n comparisons. Thus, n-way merge is an $O(n \log n)$ method. Each pass also requires n records being copied (written to new files). In n-way sort merge records are copied into n files each pass, but the number of comparisons is approximately the same as in 2-way sort merge. It can be shown that n-way sort merge is also $O(n \log n)$.

Internal memory requirements consist of space for two records while keys are compared, and room for one additional record for interchanges. There are $n+1$ external files; the original file, which can be written over to become the output file, and n files, each of approximately $1/n$th the length of the original file. The output file has n records, and the other n files have a total of n records. Consequently, external memory requirements are $2*n$.

Other Methods

Numerous methods for sorting by merging are in the literature, but they are mainly variations of n-way sort merge. Some of these methods are included in the following discussion, and examples of how they work are given. No algorithms, programs, or analyses are included. The algorithms and programs are relatively straightforward adaptations of *twowaysortmerge*. Analyses are similar, but more complex, than the 2-way sort merge analysis, but result in the same conclusion, namely that the methods are $O(n \log n)$.

In the descriptions, a run is assumed to be in nondecreasing order. For example, in n-way sort merge, runs of length 1, 2, 4, and 8 are present at the start of the first, second, third, and fourth passes, respectively. On the jth pass, runs are of length 2^{j-1}. In particular, 15,21 is a run of length 2, and 21,30,39,43 is a run of length 4.

Balanced Merge

Assume an unsorted file of n records is in external memory (that is, on tape or disk) and that four contiguous areas are available in external memory. These areas could be on one disk, on different surfaces of a disk pack, or on separate tapes. Two of them are for input files, the other two are for output files. As in the two-way sort merge, sorted runs are alternately written onto the input files until no records remain in the original file. The second pass begins by reading the first runs from the two input files, merging them, and writing the longer run onto one of the output files. The second runs in the input files are merged onto the second output file. The third runs are merged onto the first output file, the fourth runs onto the second output file, and so on, until both input files have been read. The third pass alternately merges pairs of runs from output files onto input files. Each pass lengthens the runs. The last pass merges two runs into one, the sorted file.

When four files are used, this method is more properly called the **balanced two-way merge**. In general, a balanced n-way merge uses $2*n$ external files, n each for input and output, and n-way merges. The balanced merge is much faster than the natural merge, since it does not require the redistribution of records from one output file to n input files in each pass, but it does require almost twice the number of output files.

The following example illustrates the balanced two-way merge by sorting the file whose record keys are 21, 15, 62, 48, 21, 39, 30, 43, 17, and 56. Input files are indicated by (1) and (2); output files by (3) and (4). The mark "|" indicates the end of a run, and "| |" indicates the end of the file.

First pass: (1) 21 | 62 | 21 39 | 17 56 | |
                  (2) 15 | 48 | 30 43 | |

Second pass: (3) 15 21 | 21 30 39 43 | |
                 (4) 48 62 | 17 56 | |

Third pass: (1) 15 21 48 62 | 39 43| |
                 (2) 17 21 30 56 | |

Fourth pass: (3) 15 17 21 21 30 48 56 62 | |
                 (4) 39 43 | |

Fifth pass: (1) 15 17 21 21 30 39 43 48 56 62| |

One way to improve the performance of balanced merge (and the methods that follow) is to increase the length of runs in the first pass. More memory is required to hold records for sorting, but fewer runs are produced, and therefore fewer merge passes are required.

Polyphase Merge

The basic process in the **polyphase merge** is k-way merging, using $k+1$ external files. During the first pass, varying numbers of runs (whose specifications are described below) in the original file are distributed onto k input files. The first runs from each file are merged onto the $k+1$st file (an output file). Then the second runs are merged onto the $k+1$st file, followed by the third runs, then the fourth, and so on, until one of the k input files has no more runs. The empty file becomes the output file, and the previous output file becomes one of the k input files. This process is repeated until the final k-way merge combines the only run from each input file into the entire sorted file on the output file.

This method requires a distribution of runs from the original file onto k input files. Various distributions have been tried, but the most successful one is based on a sequence of integers called the **Fibonacci numbers**. You may be familiar with the Fibonacci numbers of order 2. They are obtained from the recurrence relation

$f_0 = 0$
$f_1 = 1$
$f_n = f_{n-1} + f_{n-2}$ for $n \geq 2$

The numbers in this sequence are 0,1,1,2,3,5,8,13,21,34,55,.... Each number in the sequence (after the first two) is obtained by adding together the two previous numbers. For example, 34 is the sum of 13 and 21. In general, Fibonacci numbers of order k are defined as follows:

$f_n = 0$ for $0 \leq n \leq k-2$
$f_{k-1} = 1$
$f_n = f_{n-1} + f_{n-2} + \ldots f_{n-k}$ for $n \geq k$

After the first k numbers, each number in the sequence is obtained by adding the k previous numbers. When $k = 4$, for example, the sequence is 0,0,0,1,1,2,4,8,15,29,56,....

To see how runs are distributed over the k available input files, consider the case when $k = 4$, that is, a polyphase merge with 4 input files and one output file. The following table gives distributions over the 4 input files a,b,c,d, for different numbers of runs. The first four rows in the table are included to show how the rest of the rows can be obtained; namely, in each column, a number is the sum of the four numbers preceding it in the same column. Fibonacci numbers of order 4 appear in column a, but the other columns are derived in a similar manner.

a	b	c	d	Number of runs
0	0	0	1	
0	0	1	0	
0	1	0	0	
1	0	0	0	
1	1	1	1	4
2	2	2	1	7
4	4	3	2	13
8	7	6	4	25
15	14	12	8	49
29	27	23	15	94
56	52	44	29	181

If the original file contains 94 runs, for example, 29 are put in file *a*, 27 in *b*, 23 in *c*, and 15 in *d*. In the event the file has less than 94, but more than 49, runs, we distribute dummy runs over the input files. During the first pass of the polyphase merge, the first run in each of the files is merged (by means of the 4-way merge) onto the output file, called *e*. Then the second runs are merged onto *e*, and so on, until 15 runs are on *e*. At that point, file *a* contains 14 runs, *b* contains 12, *c* contains 8, *d* is empty, and *e* contains 15. File *d* becomes the output file, and the second pass begins. Runs are merged onto *d* until *c* is empty. At that time, *a*, *b*, *d*, and *e* contain 6,4,8, and 7 runs, respectively, and *c* becomes the output file. The numbers of runs in the five files after each pass are shown in the following table.

Pass	a	b	c	d	e
0	29	27	23	15	0
1	14	12	8	0	15
2	6	4	0	8	7
3	2	0	4	4	3
4	0	2	2	2	1
5	1	1	1	1	0
6	0	0	0	0	1

At the end of the sixth pass, the sorted file is in file *e*.

Cascade Merge

When magnetic tapes were used as input files for polyphase merge, the time required to rewind tapes after each pass delayed the start of the next pass. This decreased the method's efficiency. **Cascade merge** alleviates some of the problem by employing a different merge strategy. It is considered a faster method for more than six tapes, but slower for six or less. In cascade merge, distribution of runs and the *k*-way merge in the first pass are similar to polyphase merge. The second pass, however, uses a (*k*–1)-way merge onto the newly emptied tape. The tape written on in the first pass is being rewound during the second pass. The third pass involves a (*k*–2)-way merge, and so on, until the *k*th pass, when a one-way merge is done (that is, runs are copied from one tape to another). The next pass begins the *k*-way merge again.

The data in the following table illustrates a cascade merge of four tapes, assuming the original file has 70 runs. In the table, *r* indicates that the tape is rewinding.

Pass	a	b	c	d	Merge Order
0	31	25	14	0	
1	17	11	0	14	3
2	6	0	11	14r	2
3	0	6	11r	14r	1
4	6	0	5	8	3
5	6r	5	0	3	2
6	6r	5r	3	0	1
7	3	2	0	3	3
8	1	0	2	3r	2
9	0	1	2r	3r	1
10	1	0	1	2	3
11	1r	1	0	1	2
12	1r	1r	1	0	1
13	0	0	0	1	3

The sorted file is on tape d.

Sorting and merging files stored on disk and tape are very common operations and consume a large portion of the time spent on file maintenance. Files are sorted primarily to provide a known order of records for efficient processing of most or all of the records. There are many applications that require files to be in a known order. Two of the most common applications are described in the next section.

APPLICATIONS OF SEQUENTIAL FILE PROCESSING

This section develops two programs commonly required for the processing of sequential files. Both programs expect a known order to the input files and presorting by one of the methods of the previous sections is assumed. The discussions of these programs are intended to provide more than a cookbook solution to two common problems. They are intended to suggest a methodology for solving problems involving sequential file processing. The programs developed here are correct, of course, but also are straightforward solutions to the problem. There are no subtle tricks, and the methods employed are generally useful.

The two problems selected for this illustration are the control break problem and the sequential file update. Merging sorted files is integral to the method used in sequential file update.

The control break problem prints (or displays on a terminal) selected information from a file. It summarizes certain numeric values by producing subtotals and totals. The problem is illustrated in the context of sales reports, but the logic is applicable to a number of similar situations. The presentation of the data provided by this program is considered, so the data can be easily used by the end user.

The sequential file update problem involves two files, one containing transactions (records to add to the file, and indications of records to be deleted or changed), and a master file to be updated using the transactions. Sequential access to the master file is justified if transactions affect a very large portion of the master file. Otherwise, each master file record affected by a transaction would be accessed directly. An advantage of sequential updating over direct access updating is that the original master file remains after the update is complete; a new file is created with the changes in place. Keeping the old master file allows "backing up" to the pre-update file status, thereby undoing the effects of any bad transactions. There are appropriate situations for each approach: a customer billing system or an employee master file update would be done sequentially. The most recent one or two versions of the file are maintained; older copies are overwritten. On the other hand, an interactive application such as a reservation system does not allow time to back up the whole file each time a change is made. In these cases, backup is accomplished by periodically taking a snapshot of the system; that is, a copy of the file is made showing its status at a particular instant. A log of transactions is also kept so that it is possible to restore the last copy of the file known to be good, and then reprocess all good transactions.

In the sequential file update program, progress through the master file and the transaction files is kept in balance. The basis of the program is a method called the balance line algorithm, and it will be useful whenever there is a need to coordinate the sequential access to two or more files.

The following sections discuss each of these two problems in general terms, and describe some of their important aspects. Each program will then be developed in the top-down style; that is, first the solution is presented in very broad terms, without regard for how each step might be accomplished, and then refinements of each part follow, providing more detail. A language-independent specification provides the overall solution to the problem. Finally, the complete problem solution coded in Pascal and in COBOL provides the full illustration.

Summary Reports: The Control Break Problem

Defining the Problem

A control break problem is one in which input is processed sequentially until condition (control) is encountered. Processing then pauses (breaks) while additional processing occurs. Regular processing then resumes and continues until a control condition is recognized again. In a trivial sense, all sequential processing is control break processing; input is processed until the end of input is encountered. End of input is the control condition.

Generally, however control break programming involves multiple occurrences of the control condition during input processing. One example is the balanced sort merge seen earlier in this chapter. Each time the end of runs was encountered on input (control condition), output was switched to a different unit.

In this section, the control break problem deals with production of a summary report. The control condition is the end of a section of input for which a summary is required. The special processing to be done at each break is the presentation of the summary of the previous section and preparation for processing a new section.

Production of a summary report with appropriate control breaks requires access to each record in a file. Various fields within the records are accumulated, producing subtotals, totals, and possibly averages. Values will be accumulated for records having some feature in common, for instance, all sales made by a particular sales representative, all sales made from a particular district office, all sales made throughout the region, and a total of all the sales. Since access to every record in the file is required, sequential file processing is indicated.

The example used in this section finds the total sales for each sales representative, for each district office, and for each region, and the overall sales total.

Presorted Order

To accumulate the total sales for each sales representative, all the records for a particular sales representative must be found before any record for another sales representative. Similarly, all the records for a particular district must be encountered together, and all region records must be together. Thus, the order of access is important.

Order is guaranteed by presorting the file. Therefore, processing begins with appropriate sorting. For the sales report example, it is assumed that all records for a particular region are logically contiguous; within that collection of records all those for a given district are together; within each district all records for a given sales representative are together.

Formatting

Presenting the results of processing in a form that is easily usable is an important part of preparing a report. All important information must stand out clearly. Extraneous words, lines, numbers, and anything else not contributing to the usefulness of the report must be eliminated. In the sales report, the following format buries significant information in the clutter of too much repetition.

```
REGION 1   DISTRICT 3   REPRESENTATIVE 03217   JOHN JONES   AMOUNT SOLD    257.23
REGION 1   DISTRICT 3   REPRESENTATIVE 03217   JOHN JONES   AMOUNT SOLD   1042.85
REGION 1   DISTRICT 3   REPRESENTATIVE 03217   JOHN JONES   AMOUNT SOLD    762.48
 . . .
REGION 1   DISTRICT 3   REPRESENTATIVE 03217   JOHN JONES   TOTAL SOLD    8324.48
```

By suppressing repetition we produce a more easily read report, but one that is more complicated to produce. For example, the following output is much easier to read.

```
REGION 1
    DISTRICT 3
        Representative                    Amount Sold
        03217    John Jones                   257.23
                                             1042.85
                                              762.48
                                                  .
                                                  .
                        Total Sales          8324.48
```

If the program output is displayed on a screen, the format must include consideration of screen characteristics. Line width and page length are restricted for screen output. Special features such as reverse video and blinking characters are sometimes available for emphasizing particular information. Color may be available. If several different types of terminals are in use, the screen display facilities may vary. Time spent in considering the way the user will see the program output is time well spent.

The example subtotals program includes only basic considerations in output design. A page break does not occur immediately before a total or subtotal is displayed: the identification of levels of information reappears at the top of each new page.

Method

The hierarchy of information in records is important in processing them correctly. In the example, the region is the highest (most inclusive) level of description. There may be a District 3 in Region 1 and also a District 3 in Region 2. These are different districts, despite the shared identification number. Similarly, it may be possible for a sales representative's identification to be repeated. Thus, when region identification changes between two consecutive records, a change in district and representative must also occur. In processing the records in the file, the first condition test is for a change in region. If the region is unchanged between two consecutive records, a change in district is tested.

If the district has not changed, the representative identification is compared. If that has not changed, the program prints a detail line, increments the representative's total sales amount, and gets the next record. A detail line includes the output information associated with one input record. It includes a sales amount and may include the sales representative's identification. The amount of detail included in the detail line varies, depending on its position in the report. However, it always contains at least the detail of data present in the current input record.

Whenever a change in representatives occurs, the program displays the total for the previous representative, updates the district total, and begins the display and accumulation of sales data for the new representative. This continues until a change of district is detected. Then the display includes the last representative's total (the change of district implies the change of representative as well). The representative's total is compared to the district total, which is then displayed. Processing then begins for the new district; the program reinitializes the district total to zero and the representative total to zero. The new district's identification line and the representative's identification line appear in the display. The sales amount read becomes the new representative's total. A change in region is treated similarly, but requires another level of processing.

Algorithm

Briefly stated, the processing is as follows:

```
Initialize
While data remains
   If this region = last region
      then If this district = last district
         then If this rep = last rep
            then write sales amount
                 add sales amount to rep total
            else End Rep Processing
                 Begin New Rep Processing
         else End District Processing
              Begin New District Processing
      else End Region Processing
           Begin New Region Processing
   Input the next data record
Complete processing
```

Notice the check for the same region, then the same district, then the same representative, before writing an ordinary output line containing a single sales amount. The following refinements provide additional detail of steps.

End Rep Processing

(New data is for a different representative than the last data.)

> Write total for last representative.
> Add rep total to district total.
> Reset rep total to zero.
> Make this rep the last rep.

Begin New Rep Processing

> Write rep identification and sales amount line.
> Add sales amount to rep total.

End District Processing

(End of district implies end of last representative in the previous district as well.)

> End Rep Processing.
> Write (with label) total for district.
> Add district total to region total.
> Reset district total to zero.
> Make this district the last district.

Begin New District Processing

> Write district Identification line.
> Begin New Rep Processing.

End Region Processing

(End of region implies end of last district in the previous region which, in turn, implies the end of the last representative in the previous district.)

> End District Processing.
> Write (with label) total for region.
> Add region total to grand total.
> Reset region total to zero.
> Make this region the last region.

Begin New Region Processing

> Write region identification line.
> Begin New District Processing.

Initialize:

> Set all totals to zero (rep total, district total, region total, grand total).
> Read the first data record.
> Begin New Region Processing.
> Read new data record.

Complete Processing

(End of data implies end of the last region, which implies the end of the last district in the region, which implies the end of the last representative in that district.)

> End Region Processing.
> Write grand total line.
> Close files.
> Stop run.

Write Sales Amount

(We assume the existence of a variable called *page length* that holds the number of lines to be printed or displayed on a page. The page length will allow room for any totals that may be needed to print without overflowing the page. The variable *line count* contains the number of lines printed on this page so far.)

> If line count MOD page length = 0
>   then print report heading
>   print region identification line
>   print district identification line
>   print rep identification and sales amount
>   update line count
>   else print sales amount
>   update line count

Programs

The development of the summary report program so far has been independent of language, considering only what has to be done to accomplish the desired results. Now each of the small parts is implemented in a programming language that is available. In COBOL, the parts become paragraphs; in Pascal and most other languages, the parts become procedures. Implementation in both COBOL and Pascal follows.

```
PROCEDURE DIVISION
    PERFORM INITIALIZE.
    PERFORM CONTROL-BREAK-REPORT UNTIL END-OF-INPUT.
    PERFORM END-PROCESSING.
    PERFORM CLOSE-UP.
    STOP RUN.
INITIALIZE.
    MOVE ZEROS TO REP-TOTAL, DISTRICT-TOTAL,
        REGION-TOTAL, GRAND-TOTAL.
    READ SALES-DATA INTO OLD-SALES-DATA
        AT END MOVE 'YES' TO SALES-FILE-DONE.
    PERFORM BEGIN-NEW-REGION.
    READ SALES-DATA AT END MOVE 'YES' TO
        SALES-FILE-DONE.
CONTROL-BREAK-REPORT.
    IF SALES-REGION = OLD-REGION
        IF SALES-DISTRICT = OLD-DISTRICT
            IF SALES-REP = OLD-REP
                PERFORM WRITE-REPORT-LINE
                ADD SALES-AMOUNT TO REP-TOTAL
            ELSE PERFORM END-REP-PROCESSING
                PERFORM BEGIN-NEW-REP
        ELSE PERFORM END-DISTRICT-PROCESSING
            PERFORM BEGIN-NEW-DISTRICT
    ELSE PERFORM END-REGION-PROCESSING
        PERFORM BEGIN-NEW-REGION.
    READ SALES-DATA AT END MOVE 'YES' TO
        SALES-FILE-DONE.
BEGIN-NEW-REP.
    WRITE REPORT-LINE FROM REP-HEADING.
    MOVE SALES-REP-NAME TO REP-NAME.
    MOVE SALES-REP-ID TO REP-ID.
    MOVE SALES-AMOUNT TO REP-AMOUNT.
    WRITE REPORT-LINE FROM REP-LINE.
    ADD SALES-AMOUNT TO REP-TOTAL.
END-REP-PROCESSING.
    WRITE REPORT-LINE FROM SUM-LINE.
    MOVE REP-TOTAL TO REPORT-AMOUNT.
    MOVE REP-STARS TO REPORT-TOTAL-INDICATOR.
    WRITE REPORT-LINE.
    MOVE SPACES TO REPORT-LINE.
    ADD REP-TOTAL TO DISTRICT-TOTAL
    MOVE ZERO TO REP-TOTAL.
    MOVE SALES-REP TO OLD-REP.
BEGIN-DISTRICT.
    MOVE SALES-DISTRICT TO DISTRICT-ID.
    WRITE REPORT-LINE FROM DISTRICT-LINE.
    PERFORM BEGIN-REP.
```

```
    END-DISTRICT.
        PERFORM END-REP.
        MOVE DISTRICT-TOTAL TO REPORT-TOTAL.
        MOVE DISTRICT-STARS TO REPORT-TOTAL-INDICATOR.
        WRITE REPORT-LINE.
        MOVE SPACES TO REPORT-LINE.
        ADD DISTRICT-TOTAL TO REGION-TOTAL.
        MOVE ZERO TO DISTRICT-TOTAL.
        MOVE SALES-DISTRICT TO OLD-DISTRICT.

    BEGIN-REGION.
        MOVE SALES-REGION TO REGION-ID.
        WRITE REPORT-LINE FROM REGION-LINE.
        WRITE REPORT-LINE FROM UNDERSCORE-REGION.
        PERFORM BEGIN-REGION.

    END-REGION.
        PERFORM END-DISTRICT.
        MOVE REGION-TOTAL TO REPORT-TOTAL.
        MOVE REGION-STARS TO REPORT-TOTAL-INDICATOR.
        WRITE REPORT-LINE.
        MOVE SPACES TO REPORT-LINE.
        ADD REGION-TOTAL TO GRAND-TOTAL.
        MOVE ZERO TO REGION-TOTAL.
        MOVE SALES-REGION TO OLD-REGION.

    COMPLETE-PROCESSING.
        PERFORM END-REGION.
        MOVE GRAND-TOTAL TO REPORT-TOTAL.
        MOVE GRAND-STARS TO REPORT-TOTAL-INDICATOR.
        WRITE REPORT-LINE.

    WRITE-REPORT-LINE.
        DIVIDE LINE-COUNT BY PAGE-LENGTH GIVING PART-USED
            REMAINDER LINES-LEFT.
        IF LINES-LEFT = ZERO
            WRITE REPORT-LINE FROM REPORT-HEADING
            WRITE REPORT-LINE FROM REGION-LINE
            WRITE REPORT-LINE FROM DISTRICT-LINE
            WRITE REPORT-LINE FROM REP-LINE
            MOVE ZERO TO LINE-COUNT
        ELSE
            WRITE REPORT-LINE FROM AMOUNT-LINE
            ADD 1 TO LINE-COUNT

    CLOSE-UP.
        CLOSE SALES-FILE, REPORT-FILE.
        STOP RUN.
```

COBOL Program 6.3 *Control break program*

```
program salesreport(salesfile,output);
type rec: record
          iden: integer;
          name: array[1..30] of char;
          district: integer;
          region: integer;
          amount: real;
     end; {record}
var reptotal, districttotal, regiontotal,
    grandtotal: real;
    linecount, pagelength: integer;
    salesfile: file of rec;
    sales, last: rec;
procedure beginregion: forward;
procedure initialize;
    begin
        reptotal       := 0.00;
        districttotal  := 0.00;
        regiontotal    := 0.00;
        grandtotal     := 0.00;
        read(salesfile, sales);
        beginregion;
        read(salesfile, sales);
    end;
procedure beginrep;
    begin
        writeln(' ':10, sales.iden:5,sales.name:30,
                  sales.amount:7:2);
        reptotal := reptotal + sales.amount
    end;
procedure endrep;
    begin
        writeln(' ':50,reptotal:7.2);
        districttotal:=districttotal + reptotal;
        reptotal := 0.00;
        last.iden := sales.iden;
    end;
procedure begindistrict;
    begin
        writeln(' ':5, 'Region',sales.region:2);
        beginrep;
    end;
```

```
procedure enddistrict;
    begin
        endrep;
        writeln(' ':50, districttotal:7.2,
            'District total');
        regiontotal := regiontotal + districttotal;
        districttotal := 0.00;
        last.district := sales.district;
    end;

procedure beginregion;
    begin
        writeln('Region ', sales.region:2);
        writeln('---------');
        begindistrict;
    end;

procedure endregion;
    begin
        enddistrict;
        writeln(' ':50, regiontotal:7:2,
            'Region total');
        grandtotal := grandtotal + regiontotal;
        regiontotal := 0.00;
        last.region := sales.region;
    end;

procedure completeprocessing;
    begin
        endregion;
        writeln(' ':50, grandtotal, 'Grand total');
    end;

procedure writesaleamount;
    begin
        if (linecount mod pagelength) = 0
            then
                begin
                    writeln(appropriate report heading);
                    writeln('Region ',sales.region:2);
                    writeln('---------');
                    writeln(' ':5,'District ',
                        sales.district:2);
```

```
                    writeln(' ':10, sales.iden:5,
                       sales.name:30, ' ':5,
                       sales.amount:7:2);
                    linecount := 0
          end
            else
              writeln(' ':50, sales.amount:7:2)
          end;

begin
     initialize;
     while not eof(salesfile) do
       begin
         if (sales.region = last.region)
            then if (sales.district = last.district)
              then if (sales.rep = last.rep)
                then
                  begin
                    writesaleamount;
                    reptotal:=reptotal+sales.amount;
                  end
                else
                  begin
                    endrep;
                    beginrep;
                  end;
              else
                begin
                  enddistrict;
                  begindistrict;
                end
            else
              begin
                endregion;
                beginregion;
              end;
         read(salesfile,sales);
       end;
     completeprocessing;
end.
```

Pascal Program 6.3 *Control break program*

Sequential File Update: The Balance Line Algorithm

The summary report program of the preceding discussion is a systematic way to step through all the records in a sequential file. The algorithm required knowledge of the order of the records in the file and performed some processing of the data of each record.

Our next example allows us to step through two files concurrently, matching entries where possible and processing the files in parallel. Variations on this technique are appropriate when two files are to be merged and when the common elements of two files are to be identified. Slight modification allows use of more than two files at a time.

The example shown here uses a file of transactions to indicate changes to be made to a master file. It is assumed here that the original master file will remain unchanged, and a new copy of the master will be made, which will contain all the changes indicated by the transactions. Thus, every record in the master file will be accessed, either for exact copying or for updating. Since all master records are used, regardless of the number of transactions, a sequential file update is appropriate. If the master were to be updated without copying, and the number of transactions were small relative to the size of the master file, direct access to the master records for which there were transactions would be more suitable. That situation will be considered later.

The algorithm is called the **balance line** and proceeds by balancing progress through the two files, reading from one and then from the other, as needed. As in the summary report program, knowledge of the order of records is required. Since we are matching transactions in one file to master records in another, some identification field must be common to both. This common field is called a key. Both the transaction file and the master file must be sorted in the same order on the same key.

Let's begin by considering what we have to work with and what we are expected to produce:

Input:
- A file of transaction records sorted in nondecreasing order on some key
- A master file sorted on the same key as the transaction file

Output:
- An updated new master file, containing all the changes indicated by the transaction file, as well as copies of all the unaltered records in the original master file
- A report showing all changes made to the master file
- An exception report showing all errors encountered in the transaction file

Transactions may be one of three types: **adds**, **changes**, or **deletions**. An add transaction must be able to insert a new record in the master file. A change transaction replaces one or more fields in the master record with new values. A delete transaction indicates that a record will not be copied from the old master to the new master.

In the most general terms, we describe the processing to be done as follows:

> Each master record whose key corresponds to the key of a record in the transaction file is to be updated as indicated by the transaction record. Unchanged master records are to be copied to the new master file.

A more explicit description of the processing to be done is expressed as follows:

> Copy each master file record until one is encountered for which a transaction is provided. Apply any valid transactions to the master file. Place the updated master record in the new master file.

More detail is provided in the following description of the processing. The buffer is the file in which the most recently read master record is stored. The work file is the place where the master record is constructed or altered prior to writing to the new master file. This allows the insertion of a new master record if a transaction calls for it. Notice that a newly added master record can be changed by subsequent transactions. Therefore, it is necessary to have an add transaction precede any change transactions for the same record. Finally, if the record is to be deleted, that must be the last transaction against that record. It is not unreasonable for a newly added record to be changed and even deleted. If the transactions are batched for a long time before the run of the update program, such a sequence may well occur. The program should allow it. All the transactions will be reported by the program even though a sequence of add, change, delete would result in no change to the master file. The expanded description of the process is now:

> Read the first transaction record.
>
> Read the first master record into the buffer and work files.
>
> While transactions remain
>   While master records remain AND   { Locate the   }
>   the master key < transaction key   { required   }
>   Write a new master record   { master record   }
>   Get a master record
>   Carry out the transaction, if possible.

172   Chapter 6

>   While master records remain
>   Write a new master record   { copy remaining }
>   Get a master record.   { master file   }

Each of the tasks required in the algorithm (write a new master, get a master record, carry out the transaction if possible) are shown below:

Get a master record:

>   If key of buffer record = key of work file   { the current   }
>   then read master file into buffer.   { buffer record   }
>   Copy buffer into work file.   { has been updated   }

Carry out the transaction, if possible.

>   If transaction key = master key
>   then if transaction code = CHANGE
>   then process change
>   else if transaction code = DELETE
>   then process delete
>   else process error (invalid transaction on matching key)
>   else if transaction code = ADD
>   then process add
>   else process error (invalid transaction – nonmatching key)
>   Read next transaction record

The tasks process change, process delete, and process add are as follows:

Process change

>   Read the next transaction record
>   For every nonempty field in the transaction record
>   replace the corresponding value in the master
>   Print a record of changes made

Process delete

>   {Remove the current master record from the work file so it will
>   not be written to the new master file}
>   Print a record of the deletion
>   Get a master record

Process add

>   {Master currently in the work file has a key value greater than the
>   key value of the record to be added. The same master record also
>   exists in the input buffer file. The copy in the work file is replaced

by the record to be added. The copy in the buffer file remains available for later processing.}
Read the next transaction record into the master work area.
{This next transaction record contains the data for the new master record.}
Print a record of the add transaction.
{Note that the new record does not get written to the new master file until the possibility of changes and of a deletion transaction affecting the new record has been investigated}

The implementations of the algorithm in both COBOL and Pascal follow. Note the features that make file processing in COBOL more straightforward than in Pascal. The READ INTO option allows flexibility in positioning input. Both languages have the features needed, however, and can be used to solve the problem.

Programs

The following program segments assume the existence of the following declarations and program header:

```
program update (master, trans, log, output);
type   rec = record
              key: appropriate type;
              otherfields: appropriate types;
           end;

var transrec, masterrec, work: rec;
    trans, master: file of rec;
    log: text;

procedure getnextmaster;
begin
  if masterrec.key = work.key
     then read(master, masterrec);
  work := masterrec;
end;

procedure processchange;
begin
  read(trans,transrec);
```

<Details depend on the actual format of the records. Each field in the work area is replaced by the contents of the corresponding field in the

transaction record. If the value of the field in
the transaction record is not coded (that is, is
blank or zero or otherwise null) then the
corresponding work area field is not changed.>

<Each changed field is printed or written to a log
file on disk, to document the changes made to the
master file.>
end;

```
procedure processdelete;
    begin
    {Remove the current master record from the work
    area so it will not be written to the new
    master file.}
        write(log,'Record deleted: Key = ',
            work.key);
       getnextmaster;
    end;

procedure processadd;
    begin
        read(trans,work);
         write(log,'Record added: Key = ',
            work.key,'  ', work);
    end;

procedure processerror(errorcode);
    begin
      case errorcode of
         1: write(log, 'Error -- Attempt to add. ',
                'Master record already exists');
         2: write(log, 'Error -- Attempt to ',
                'delete. No such master record. ',
                'Key = ', trans.key);
    end;

procedure dotransaction;
    begin
      if transrec.key = masterrec.key
         then if trans.code = 'C'
              then processchange
              else if trans.code = 'D'
                   then processdelete
                   else processerror(1)
```

```
            else if trans.code = 'A'
                then processadd
                else processerror(2);
      read(trans,transrec);
    end;
begin
    read(trans, transrec);
    read(master, masterrec);
    while not eof(trans) do
      begin
         while not eof(master) do
            begin
                write(newmaster, masterrec);
                getnextmaster;
            end;
          dotransaction;
      end
      while not eof(master) do
        begin
           write(newmaster, masterrec);
           getnextmaster;
        end;
end.
```

Pascal Program 6.4 *Sequential file update*

Exact DATA DIVISION entries depend on the details of the records of the master file that is to be updated. Appropriate descriptions for the master, transaction, and work area records are suggested. Other needed DATA DIVISION entries are shown.

```
01 MASTER-RECORD.
   03 MASTER-KEY              PIC <depends on the file>
   03 <Other fields>

01 TRANS-RECORD.
   03 TRANS-KEY               PIC <same as master>
   03 TRANS-CODE              PIC X.
         88 TRANSACTION-IS-CHANGE   VALUE 'C'.
         88 TRANSACTION-IS-DELETE   VALUE 'D'.
         88 TRANSACTION-IS-ADD      VALUE 'A'.
01 ALTERNATE-TRANS REDEFINES TRANS.
   03 KEY                     PIC <same as master>
   03 <other fields, same as for master>
```

```
      * DELETE transactions have only the KEY and TRANS-CODE.
      * ADD and CHANGE transactions have two records. The first
      * identifies the transaction and the key. The second
      * record contains data to be placed in the master file.
      * The record of the transaction has exactly the same
      * format as the master records.
       01 WORK-AREA-RECORD.
          03 WORK-AREA-KEY          PIC <same as master>.
          03 <Other fields>         PIC <same as master>.

       01 LOG-DESCRIPTION.
       01 LOG-KEY                   PIC <same as master>.
       01 LOG-TRANSACTION-TYPE      PIC XXXXXX.
       01 LOG-ERROR-MESSAGE         PIC X(30).
       01 LOG-DETAILS               PIC <same as master record>.

       01 NEW-MASTER.
          03 KEY                    PIC <same as master>.
          03 <other fields>         PIC <same as master>.

       01 FLAGS.
          03 MASTER-FILE-DONE       PIC XXX.
             88 END-OF-MASTER       VALUE 'YES'.
          03 TRANS-FILE-DONE        PIC XXX.
             88 END-OF-TRANSACTIONS VALUE 'YES'.

       PROCEDURE DIVISION.
       CONTROLLER.
           PERFORM INITIALIZE.
           PERFORM FILE-UPDATE.
           PERFORM CLOSE-UP.
           STOP RUN.

       INITIALIZE.
           OPEN INPUT TRANS, MASTER.
           OPEN OUTPUT NEW-MASTER, LOG-FILE.
           READ TRANS AT END MOVE 'YES' TO MASTER-FILE-DONE.
           READ MASTER AT END MOVE 'YES' TO TRANS-FILE-DONE.

       FILE-UPDATE.
           PERFORM UPDATE-MASTER UNTIL
               END-OF-TRANSACTIONS.
           PERFORM COPY-MASTER UNTIL
               END-OF-MASTER.
```

```
UPDATE-MASTER.
    PERFORM COPY-MASTER UNTIL
        END-OF-MASTER OR
        MASTER-KEY < TRANS-KEY.
    DO-TRANSACTION.

COPY-MASTER.
    WRITE NEW-MASTER FROM WORK-AREA.
    GET-NEW-MASTER-RECORD.

GET-NEW-MASTER-RECORD.
    IF MASTER-KEY = WORK-AREA-KEY
        READ MASTER AT END
            MOVE 'YES' TO MASTER-FILE-DONE.
    MOVE MASTER-RECORD TO WORK-AREA.

DO-TRANSACTION.
    IF TRANS-KEY = MASTER-KEY
        IF TRANSACTION-IS-CHANGE
            PERFORM PROCESS-CHANGE
        ELSE IF TRANSACTION-IS-DELETE
                PERFORM PROCESS-DELETE
            ELSE MOVE 'ATTEMPT TO ADD WHEN KEY EXISTS'
                    TO LOG-ERROR-MESSAGE
                MOVE 'ADD' TO LOG-TRANSACTION-TYPE
                PERFORM PROCESS-ERROR
    ELSE IF TRANSACTION-IS-ADD
            PERFORM PROCESS-ADD
        ELSE MOVE 'NO MATCHING KEY FOUND '
                TO LOG-ERROR-MESSAGE
            IF TRANSACTION-IS-CHANGE MOVE 'CHANGE' TO
                    LOG-TRANSACTION-TYPE
                ELSE MOVE 'DELETE' TO LOG-TRANSACTION-TYPE
            PERFORM PROCESS-ERROR.
    READ TRANS AT END MOVE 'YES' TO TRANS-FILE-DONE.

PROCESS-CHANGE.
    READ TRANS AT END MOVE 'YES' TO TRANS-FILE-DONE.
    <Details depend on the exact record description.
    Each non-blank field in the transaction record
    replaces the corresponding record in the work area.>
    MOVE 'CHANGE' TO LOG-TRANSACTION-TYPE.
    MOVE TRANS-RECORD TO LOG-DETAILS.
    WRITE LOG-RECORD FROM LOG-DESCRIPTION.
    MOVE SPACES TO LOG-DESCRIPTION.
```

```
PROCESS-DELETE.
    MOVE 'DELETE' TO LOG-TRANSACTION-TYPE.
    MOVE TRANS-KEY TO LOG-KEY.
    WRITE LOG-RECORD FROM LOG-DESCRIPTION.
    MOVE SPACES TO LOG-DESCRIPTION.
    GET-NEXT-MASTER.

PROCESS-ADD.
    READ TRANS INTO WORK-AREA
        AT END MOVE 'YES' TO TRANS-FILE-DONE.
    MOVE 'ADD' TO LOG-TRANSACTION-TYPE.
    MOVE TRANS-RECORD TO LOG-DETAILS.
    WRITE LOG-RECORD FROM LOG-DESCRIPTION.
    MOVE SPACES TO LOG-DESCRIPTION.

PROCESS-ERROR.
    MOVE TRANS-KEY TO LOG-KEY.
    MOVE 'ERROR' TO LOG-TRANSACTION-ERROR.
    WRITE LOG-RECORD FROM LOG-DESCRIPTION.
    MOVE SPACES TO LOG-DESCRIPTION.
```

COBOL Program 6.4 *Sequential file update*

Summary

There are many occasions when access to all or nearly all the records in a file is required. In such cases, it is inefficient to specify which record is wanted before each access; we simply want to retrieve each record in turn in whatever order is most appropriate.

In this chapter we look at several matters relevant to the orderly access of records: (1) sequential files as a physical characteristic, as in tape and card storage; (2) logically sequential files, which may be stored in widely scattered, nonsequential order, but which are viewed as a cohesive whole; (3) algorithms for merging sequential files and sorting them by merging.

Finally, we describe in detail two important applications of sequential file access. In both applications we treat the files as if they are stored in sequential order. In the summary report example, we work with one sequential file, and stress the need to presort the file so that the program can make assumptions about the order of records. In the sequential file update example, we coordinate access of two different sequential files. Once again, it is necessary to presort, this time two files, in order to process them in an orderly fashion. Both of these examples are meant to illustrate general methods that are appropriate in a variety of cases.

EXERCISES

1. Develop an algorithm and a program to simulate a sequential search of an external file. Assume that the external file contains at least 100 records, each with an identifying key, and that (internal) memory can handle no more than ten keys at a time. Test the program with an appropriate set of data.

2. Assume two separate mailing lists are sorted in nondecreasing order by last names. Define an appropriate record structure and sets of data for the mailing lists, and then implement the program *twowaymerge* on the data.

3. Develop an algorithm and a program to implement the following variation of the 2-way balanced sort merge.

    Sorted runs of length k are distributed as in the text. During the merge at each pass, whenever the last key value, *last*, in a run R is reached, compare it to the first key value, *first*, of the next run NR on the same file. If *last* > *first* (assuming nondecreasing order), then continue processing as in the text. Otherwise, treat NR and R as one run (that is, append NR to R) and continue processing. For example, suppose two files $F1$ and $F2$ each contain two runs, as shown here:

    ```
    F1    | 2 4 | 6 8 |
    F2    | 3 7 | 4 5 |
    ```

    Then the merge takes place as if 2 4 6 8 were one run on the file F1. One output file would get the run 2 3 4 6 7 8, and then the run 4 5 would be merged with the next run on the file F1.

4. Contrast the 2-way balanced sort merge and the variation given in Exercise 3. Give an example of an initial distribution of runs onto two files that would be processed by the variation as if each file contained only one run (that is, the entire file would be sorted in one pass).

5. Assume that 44 runs have been sorted. For each of the following methods, create a table showing the distribution of runs on each file after each pass through the data.
    (a) n-way (natural) sort merge with $n = 2$
    (b) n-way balanced sort merge with $n = 2$
    (c) n-way balanced sort merge with $n = 3$
    (d) polyphase sort merge with $k = 4$

6. Compare and contrast the methods in Exercise 5 with regard to number of passes, number of files required, and amount of rewriting of records that is necessary.

7. Assume a file of records has two-digit keys in the following order:

    12, 34, 75, 19, 10, 41, 86, 53, 38, 13, 40, 60, 22, 11, 44, 78, 50

For each of the methods in Exercise 5(a)–(e), show the contents of all files after the initial sort distribution (assuming each run contains only one record) and after each merge.

8. Discuss the advantages and disadvantages of the polyphase sort merge relative to:
   (a) the n-way balanced sort merge
   (b) the n-way (natural) sort merge
   Are the numbers of key values (that is, the values of n and k) relevant to the discussion?

9. Develop an algorithm and a program (in Pascal or COBOL) to implement the polyphase sort merge with Fibonacci distribution and $k = 4$. Also, instead of including a procedure to sort the initial data into runs, assume each data item is a sorted run of length 1.
   (a) Choose an unordered set of data consisting of 94 key values, and run the program.
   (b) Insert into the program, statements to print the distribution of runs after each pass. Run the program with the data from part (a) to verify the distribution table in the text.

10. Generalize the program in Exercise 9 to work for any value of k. Using the data in 9(a), run the program and compare sort times for $k = 2, 3, 4, 5, 6,$ and 7.

11. Run the 2-way balanced sort merge program in the text with the data from Exercise 9(a). Compare the sort time with the results of Exercise 10.

12. (a) Determine what sequential file processing is used in the registration system at your school. What reports are generated? How are updates handled? Are history files maintained?
    (b) Are admissions to your school handled in a manner similar to the way in which registrations are handled? Give reasons for any differences.

13. List three different applications that could use the summary report with control breaks program.

14. For one of the applications listed in Exercise 13, design appropriate record and report formats. Then create a file of records and run the report program.

15. List three different applications for the master file update program.

16. For one of the applications listed in Exercise 15, design appropriate record and report formats. Then create transaction and master files and run the program.

CHAPTER 7

RANDOM FILE PROCESSING

Introduction

File storage devices such as tape drives and printers, are limited to sequential access, while others, such as disk drives, provide more flexibility. There are applications for which sequential access is appropriate. These applications are implemented on any storage device discussed in Chapter 4 and require algorithms and programs for sequential access such as those developed in Chapter 6.

In this chapter the focus shifts from sequential to random organization of files. Topics include what random organization means, why it is sometimes beneficial and sometimes not, and how to use randomly organized files effectively to get a particular record as quickly as possible. Two important considerations when using random files are **access time**, which is a function of the disk storage equipment and how it is being used, and **overhead**, which is associated with the organization and access method chosen for the file. All discussions assume that the file is stored on some type of disk drive, as described in Chapter 4.

It is helpful to separate those issues related to random organization that are determined by a characteristic of the storage device from those that are imposed by the organization and access strategy. Though users cannot make changes in the requirements of the storage device except when purchasing new equipment, they *can* make meaningful choices in regard to the organization and access methods.

Definitions

When a file is called *random access*, or *direct access*, its records can be accessed in a somewhat arbitrary, or random, order. It is not necessary to put successive records in contiguous storage locations; nor is it necessary to read or fast-forward over many unwanted records when retrieving others.

Of course, access to a record is not completely direct, except when the record is stored in memory. On a disk drive, for instance, the read/write head is moved directly to the track on which the record is stored without pausing at other tracks. However, once the head is in place, there is a wait, during which the disk rotates until the desired record is under the head. Other records pass under the head during this waiting period. The process is called direct access because it is much more direct than is possible with sequential devices. The term *random access* is also used to indicate that at any time during processing, it is possible to access a randomly chosen record, rather than only the next sequential record.

Access Time

An important consideration in the timely placement and retrieval of records is access time. As we saw in Chapter 3, **access time** on a disk drive has three components: seek time, latency, and data rate. Seek time is required to position the read/write head at the correct track; latency is the waiting period while the disk rotates under the head and positions the desired record; and data rate is the speed with which the data is actually transferred from the disk to the computer for use. Of these, seek time is usually the most significant, and storage methods are designed to minimize access time by limiting head motion.

Overhead

Another important influence on the time needed to reach a record is the amount of overhead required by the file organization and access method. **Overhead** consists of all actions and processing that are required to access data but that do not directly result in obtaining data. Methods for accessing data stored on disk vary in the amounts of overhead they require, and this is an important part of the description of each method.

There are several sources of overhead. The overhead required to locate a record has been implied already. Moving the read/write head to the correct track has been mentioned several times, but with no consideration given to how the right track is determined. That information may be stored externally to the file system, or may be written in machine-readable form in a carefully specified place on the disk itself.

A list that tells where each record can be found is called a **directory**. A telephone directory, for instance, is used to find telephone numbers; a file directory is used to find records in a file. A directory is almost always kept in machine-readable form and is a special kind of file. Accessing a directory to locate a record in another file, rather than accessing the record directly, is an example of overhead.

ORGANIZATION AND ACCESS

Evaluation of random file access methods is done at two levels: the file's organization and the way records are accessed. The organization of a file determines how records are grouped, and what steps are necessary to locate a particular record. Access involves the order in which records are available. The principal file organizations are sequential, relative, and indexed.

A **sequential organization** is characterized by contiguous storage of all records, with no intervening empty space (except as necessary to accommodate equipment, such as the interblock gaps on most tape files). No external information about the location of records within the file is kept.

Relative organization is a special case of direct file organization. Direct file organization allows any individual record to be accessed by specifying its address. Unlike sequential or indexed organization, no sequential processing of intervening records is required. In relative file organization, the address is specified as a relative position of the record within the file, and records are required to be of the same size. Using the relative position number of a record within the file avoids the need to specify a device-dependent physical address, which is required when the absolute addressing form of direct file organization is used.

A relative file organization consists of a sequence of positions where records may be stored. Some of the positions may be empty. Each record in the file must be of the same length, and that length is recorded in a file description maintained by the operating system. With this information, the system calculates the exact location of the nth record by computing $(n-1)$ times the record length, and adding that value to the location of the beginning of the file. Thus, it is possible to access each record in the file directly.

Relative file organization is machine-independent. A number of programming languages support its implementation, including COBOL and some extensions of standard Pascal.

An **indexed organization** consists of groups of records, all in contiguous storage locations. Each group has an address that is maintained externally to the file. Access to a record requires the address of a group of records and sequential examination of the records within the group.

Access is concerned with the order in which records are obtained. The principal access modes are sequential, random, and dynamic (a combination of sequential and random). **Sequential access** means reading or writing each record in some specific order. **Random access** refers to reading or writing a particular record without considering it in relation to other records. **Dynamic access** permits random access to a particular record within a file, and then sequential access to succeeding records in a specified order. Only sequential access is permitted in sequential file organizations. Sequential, random, and dynamic access to records are possible in relative and indexed file organizations.

Addressing Random Files

Both relative and indexed organizations permit random access. Random access requires that the location of a particular record be specified. There are three main techniques for specifying the address of data stored on a direct access device: **absolute addressing, relative addressing,** and **indexed addressing.** The merits and weaknesses of these three types of addressing are briefly discussed to form a basis for the subsequent description of methods for implementing them.

Absolute Addresses

The most straightforward addressing scheme is absolute addressing, in which the actual address of the desired record is provided. On a disk, this means explicit specification of which drive, which cylinder, and which track to access. There is no overhead for this access as far as the I/O system is concerned. No directory needs to be maintained and no extra read to a directory is required. The input/output operation takes place as fast as the actual device allows.

With such benefits to recommend absolute addressing, why isn't it the only kind of addressing in use? In fact, it is rarely implemented. One reason is that it requires someone, somewhere, to know where all the records are located. If this information is not kept in a directory and maintained by the computer I/O system, it must be kept somewhere else and maintained by a programmer. The information must be specified explicitly every time an I/O operation is carried out on the file. Programs that use the file have to be revised whenever the file is reorganized. The result is complication in programs and a reduction in a very valuable resource: programmer productivity. In addition, the chance of error is increased and the integrity of the file is therefore less secure.

Furthermore, because absolute addresses are detailed and specific, they are influenced by the type of equipment being accessed. When DASD units are replaced by newer equipment, programs with absolute addresses must be revised.

For these reasons, absolute addressing is seldom used except in modules of the operating system. Other methods for associating addresses with key values in directory tables are dealt with extensively in this chapter, primarily for ease in expanding the ideas to accessing records in the more common relative access methods.

Relative Addresses

A relative address is specified in terms of some reference point. For instance, "Take the third exit after the state line" is a relative direction to a driver but, "Take Exit 4" is an absolute direction. In a data file, a relative address is expressed as a position within a file, rather than as a specific location consisting of drive, cylinder, and track numbers.

Indexed Addresses

Indexed addressing methods work much like the thumb indices of a dictionary. The index locates the first of a sequence of related items. In a dictionary, the index identifies the first page of words that begin with a particular letter. In a file, the index identifies the location of a record with a particular key value. The record with the next key value is in the next contiguous storage space.

Indexed addressing allows access to the same file for two different purposes: to find a particular record by random access and to process the entire file. To access a particular record, the index is searched, and a record close to the desired one is accessed. Intervening records are processed until the desired record is found. Thus, random access by indexed addressing combines some of the elements of sequential access and direct access. Getting a particular record involves less overhead (processing of unwanted records) than sequential access, but more than locating the record directly by relative access. On the other hand, the file can also be processeed sequentially (for copying, sorting, merging, updating) by using the index to locate successively each group of records; the records within each group are processed sequentially. In this case, there is more overhead (looking up the index) than there is with sequential access, but less than there is when locating each record by direct access.

Indexed addressing has more of the advantages than the disadvantages of sequential and relative file addressing. The next chapter contains details of indexed addressing organizations and access methods.

Selecting a File Organization

The best choice of sequential, relative, or indexed organization for a particular file depends on the application. The physical organization is selected to support the access mode. If accessing every record of a file is the principal requirement, as in processing master and transaction files, then sequential organization is indicated. If accessing individual records, or a small percentage of records, is the major requirement, as in a reservation system, then relative organization is appropriate. If accessing a file for different purposes is necessary, as in a supermarket where the checkout person requires prices of particular items and the manager wants a periodic inventory of all items, then indexed organization is a good compromise.

RANDOM ACCESS IN DIRECT FILE ORGANIZATION

Directory Lookup

When a record is to be read or written, a key value associated with the record is known. To associate that key value with an address in a direct file organization (that is, an absolute or relative address), a directory is often used. The directory is a table with two columns. One column contains a key value; the other contains the corresponding address of the record indicated by the key value. An address is found by searching the directory for the key value. Then the address is used to access the record.

Numerous ways to search a file for one or more records were reviewed in previous chapters. Each method searched for a key value within the record, but in doing so, searched through or moved entire records. At no time was the key value physically separate from the record. The file was stored serially, that is, with records one after the other in contiguous memory locations.

Random file processing allows alternative methods for storing a file's records. In particular, each record is viewed as having two parts; the key field and the rest of the record. All of the key values are stored together in the directory. The records are stored separately in the file. Association of a key value and its record in a directory is illustrated in Figure 7.1.

Searching for a record by first looking up its key value in a separate directory is called directory lookup. It is similar to asking a classmate (the key value) where he lives, then going to the address he gives and meeting his family (the record).

The process of directory lookup has a number of advantages over accessing a record whose key value is not stored separately.

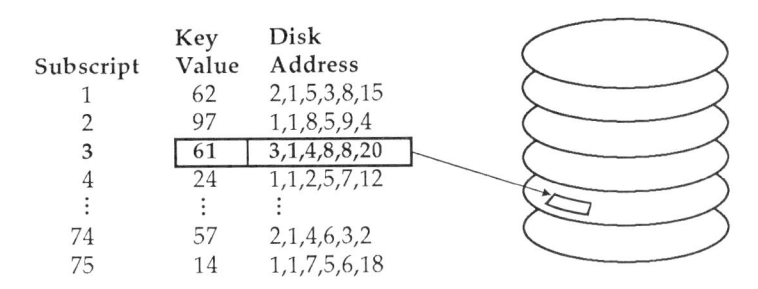

Subscript	Key Value	Disk Address
1	62	2,1,5,3,8,15
2	97	1,1,8,5,9,4
3	61	3,1,4,8,8,20
4	24	1,1,2,5,7,12
⋮	⋮	⋮
74	57	2,1,4,6,3,2
75	14	1,1,7,5,6,18

(Disk Address = Drive, Spindle, Cylinder, Sector, Track, Record Number)

Figure 7.1 *A directory containing the physical addresses of records in a file on a disk.*

- Search time is substantially reduced because the directory for an entire file is read into memory (or is maintained there) for searching. Only the directory must be searched; the record is accessed only after its key value is found.
- Searching is simplified because all directory entries are the same size, even though records in the file may be of variable length.
- Sorting is easier because only directory entries need to be sorted. Records are not moved.
- Inserting is more efficient. Only the directory entry is inserted, the record is added to the end of the file.
- Deleting involves removing the directory entry. The record does not have to be deleted unless space is needed for more records. In that case, the entire file and the directory are reorganized.

A disadvantage of directory lookup is that directories require additional memory for the addresses of records; however, that is insignificant for large files. Additional programming effort is required to provide an address for each read or write operation.

Arrays are the most common structures for storing directories but linked lists or trees are effective in applications in which directory size changes dynamically. As shown in Figure 7.2, for each record in a file, the directory contains the key value and a pointer to the record.

When a directory is stored as an array, any of the internal search or sort methods described in Chapters 2 and 3 can be used to find a key value or to sort the key values. Each array looked very much like a directory, except that it did not include pointer address fields. Because of this similarity it is reasonable to conclude that a directory can be searched

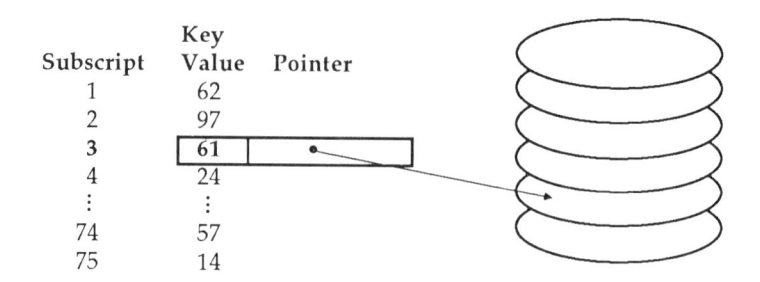

```
              Key
Subscript   Value   Pointer
    1        62
    2        97
    3        61    •───┐
    4        24        │
    ⋮         ⋮        │
   74        57        │
   75        14
```

Figure 7.2 A directory containing pointers to record locations.

in $O(n)$ or $O(\log n)$, depending on the search method. In the worst case, n or $\log n$ comparisons are required to search the entire directory, while in the best case, the key value is located on the first comparison.

The remainder of the chapter deals with a class of methods designed to improve the chance of locating the key value on the first comparison. In the treatment of hashing, a directory is a two-dimensional array of n rows and two columns. Key values and pointers to corresponding records occupy the first and second columns, respectively. Accessing the array row corresponding to a particular record key is accomplished by specifying a subscript $1, 2, \ldots, n$ of the array.

Hashing

Hashing **(scatter storage)** techniques involve performing an arithmetic calculation on the value of a key to produce an integer. This integer is the relative address at which the key value is stored in the directory. When the directory is stored as an array, for example, the relative address calculated is one of the array indices. More precisely, hashing requires the definition of a function or mapping f, of a key k into an address a, written $f(k) = a$. The domain of f is a set of key values and the range is a subset of the set of positive integers (for example, the indices $1, 2, \ldots, n$ of an array). The transformation of a key to an integer value is called a **key-to-address calculation**.

The goal of hashing is to find an easy-to-compute function that maps each key value into an empty location. Searching a directory, or hash table, created in this way is quick and easy. Given a key value, we hash it (that is, perform the same key-to-address calculation as used in creating the table) and then either find it at the address calculated or know that it is not in the table (because the location would be empty). Only one probe is necessary to find a given value. In this ideal case, the search for a key value by hashing is $O(1)$.

This one-to-one mapping occurs, for example, in the case of a company's file of invoices, where the invoices are consecutively numbered. Suppose the numbers contain 5 digits, and the smallest number is 10001. Let

f(keyvalue) = keyvalue − 10000

be a mapping of the record key (invoice number) to the position in the directory that contains the pointer to the record. The directory entry for invoice 10475 is found in directory row 475. Since no two invoice numbers are identical, the transformation produces a unique directory entry for each key value.

Unfortunately, a "one-to-oneness" is seldom attained in practical applications. Seldom are all keys mapped into unique addresses; **collisions** occur. Collisions happen when distinct keys are mapped into the same address. Suppose, for instance, that a file of employee data is available, in which each employee is identified by social security number. To map employee number to directory entry with no collisions, a directory entry for each of the 1,000,000,000 different social security numbers is necessary. Even for a large company, this means reserving much more storage space than is needed to store the information. In practice, the size of the directory is limited to prevent such waste. However, this increases the chance that different social security numbers (key values) map to the same address, regardless of the function. Resolution of these collisions is necessary. Hashing, then, has two major components:

- **Address calculation**, to determine where to place a key value in the directory.
- **Collision handling**, to find a place for a key value when the address calculated already contains a different value.

Address Calculation

Theoretically, any function whose range is a subset of the set of positive integers can be used in hashing. In practice, however, a very limited number of functions is considered. Many functions are eliminated because they are too time-consuming to compute. Some of the advantage of hashing over other methods is lost if too much time is required to produce the relative address of a key value. Other functions fail to meet another desirable criterion of hashing, that is, scattering the key values randomly but uniformly throughout the table. The purpose of scattering key values is twofold: it reduces collisions and it simplifies their handling when they do occur. Hash tables are also referred to as **scatter storage tables** because of this criterion.

Many hash functions are possible, but only four of the most prominent ones are discussed here. They are based on truncation, folding, multiplication, and division. Of these, division is by far the most common. In general, however, no single method is best for all applications. Much depends on the nature of the key values.

Truncation

A number is **truncated** when some of the beginning or ending digits are removed. A truncation function, then, eliminates the first k or last m digits of an n-digit number. For example, if the function f eliminates the last six digits of the nine-digit number 123456789, then

$f(123456789) = 123$

In other words, the hash function f maps the number 123456789 into the address 123. The value is then stored at the hash table location specified by 123.

$f(222345654) = 222$
$f(301657434) = 301$
$f(123882345) = 123$.

From this list, it is evident that this truncation function is undesirable for an application where the key is the nine-digit social security number, because all social security numbers originating in a particular area of the country have the same first three digits. In particular, all numbers beginning with 123 map to the same location, causing too many collisions. However, for a small, local company, truncating the high-order part of an employee's social security number and using the last three digits defines a reasonable hash function. In that case, the four numbers above hash to 789, 654, 434, and 345, respectively.

Truncation is also an appropriate hash function in the following example. Assume that multidigit project numbers are assigned sequentially in a consulting firm, but no more than 60 or 70 projects are ever active at any one time. Then the last two digits of the project numbers can be the address.

The advantages of truncation as a hash function are that it is fast and easy to implement. A disadvantage is that it restricts the size of the address space (that is, the number of distinct storage locations) to a power of 10. If the value produced by the hash function is the relative position of a record within a file, then there must be a position in the file corresponding to each possible hash value. This is sometimes inappropriate. If a company has 192 employees, and the employee file has a relative organization, then a three-digit number is required to specify the position of a record within the file. The smallest address space whose size is a power of 10 is 1000. The relative file, then, requires 1000 positions for 192 entries.

Truncation alone is appropriate only in very restricted circumstances. However, it is effective when used in conjunction with another function, such as folding or multiplication.

Folding

The process of folding involves partitioning a number into two or more sections, then summing the sections. For example, the number 123456 can be partitioned (folded) into two sections of three digits each, 123 and 654 (the order 456 is also possible). The sum of the sections is 777 (or 579 if the order 456 is used), the relative address at which the number 123456 is stored. In functional notation,

$f(123456) = 777$ (or $f(123456) = 579$).

The same process applies to any six-digit number. Thus,

$f(234351) = 387$
$f(222456) = 876$
$f(321654) = 777$

In the last case, a collision occurs, because $f(123456) = f(321654)$.

Often, the sum of two three-digit numbers is a four-digit number. For example, $f(456288) = 1338$. The first digit is not used because it is always 0 or 1, which violates the criterion of scattering keys randomly. In this case, folding is followed by truncation. The result of the key-to-address calculation, 1338 is truncated to 338, and the key 456288 is stored in 338, unless another key is already there.

Many possible hash functions involve folding. For example, assume the key is social security number and the table size is 10,000 (with relative addresses 0 to 9999). One approach folds the key into three parts, each part consisting of three-digit numbers in the order in which they appear in the key. Thus, $f(123456789) = 123 + 456 + 789 = 1368$, and the key 123456789 is stored in location 1368 of the hash table. Similarly, the value 020010056 is stored in location 86 (020 + 010 + 056). Another approach folds the key into two parts, a four- and a five-digit number, and then truncates the sum. The actual choice for folding depends on the data (key values), the table size (which must be a power of 10), and how well the function distributes the key values throughout the table.

Multiplication

Instead of partitioning a key and summing the sections, as in folding, parts of a key can be selected and multiplied. The product, or a truncated version of it, is the relative address of the location where the key is stored. For example, consider the social security number as the key. Define the hash function as follows: multiply the first three and the last three digits of the key, and then truncate the product so that it is within the range of values in the table. The number 123456789 hashes to 123*789 = 97047. This value is truncated to 9704 if the table addresses are 0 to 9999. Other multiplication hash functions are possible, but the range of key values must be a power of 10, as in folding and truncation.

Multiplying parts of keys tends to spread out the relative addresses calculated, and by so doing, reduces the chance of collisions. Of course, the success of any multiplication hash function depends on the nature of the keys. If, for example, the last three digits of six-digit keys are frequently 000 or 001, then a function that multiplies the first three digits by the last three digits does not distribute the key values in a desirable way. Actually, if little is known about the key values, then multiplication is not likely to be as good a hash method as the division method described in the next section.

A variation of multiplication is the method of **squaring**. It involves selecting consecutive digits in a key and squaring the number they represent. For example, if the middle three digits in a social security number are chosen, then $f(123456789) = 456*456 = 207936$. As before, this number must be truncated to obtain the relative address within the table. In a method called **midsquare**, the entire key is squared. Then, instead of truncating the result, the middle digits are used as the relative address. In midsquare, keys tend to be more uniformly distributed than in truncation because more digits are involved in determining the middle part of a product than the end portions. Squaring has advantages and disadvantages similar to multiplication.

Division-Remainder

The most successful and simplest hash method involves division of a key by the table size. The value of the remainder is the relative address at which the key is stored in the table. For example, if the table size is 11 and the key value is 648, then

$f(648) = 648 \bmod 11 = 10$

The value 648 is stored at location 10. Hashing by division is especially easy to implement in any programming language containing a MOD function. The address is the value returned by MOD. Another advantage is that any table size, not just powers of 10, is easily accommodated.

(12 mod 11) + 1 = 1 + 1 = 2; store 12 at 2.
(21 mod 11) + 1 = 10 + 1 = 11; store 21 at 11.
(68 mod 11) + 1 = 2 + 1 = 3; store 68 at 3.
(38 mod 11) + 1 = 5 + 1 = 6; store 38 at 6.
(52 mod 11) + 1 = 8 + 1 = 9; store 52 at 9.
(70 mod 11) + 1 = 4 + 1 = 5; store 70 at 5.
(44 mod 11) + 1 = 0 + 1 = 1; store 44 at 1.
(18 mod 11) + 1 = 7 + 1 = 8; store 18 at 8.

The table is as follows:

Index	1	2	3	4	5	6	7	8	9	10	11
Key Value	44	12	68	—	70	38	—	18	52	—	21

Figure 7.3 Hashing by the division-remainder method.

The remainder in a division is always less than the divisor. If the divisor is n (the table size in hashing), then the remainder has values 0, 1, 2, ..., $n-1$. Because not all programming languages allow 0 as an index, the remainder can be modified by adding 1. This guarantees that the key-to-address calculation always produces a value within the range 1, 2, ..., n of relative addresses in the table. An example of hashing by division (with no collisions) is given in Figure 7.3. In the example, assume a table size of 11 and a file of eight records with the following key values:

12, 21, 68, 38, 52, 70, 44, 18

Truncation is never necessary in the division method. However, the table size t is important. Some choices will lead to more collisions than others. In particular, the most desirable choice for t is a prime number (a number divisible only by itself and 1) greater than n, the number of keys. This claim can be supported as follows.

> The table size t should be at least as large as the number n of key values in the file so that there is space for all of them. If t is an even number, then the remainder after dividing an even- (odd-) numbered key by t is even (odd). This increases the chance of collisions and tends not to distribute keys uniformly throughout the table. Thus, for large values of n, t must be an odd number at least as large as n. The rest of the argument is based on empirical testing of large files. Results of this testing show that prime values distribute key values better, and with fewer collisions, than nonprime values, especially when the latter have small, odd numbers as factors.

Relative File Access

The association of a key value with an address in a directory is important in the use of absolute addresses. Direct calculation of actual storage addresses, including drive, spindle, cylinder, and track numbers, can be done in a program that is to access a record, but should not be. If the location of records were changed, every program that uses the records would have to be changed. It is much more practical to store the addresses in a directory, and keep the directory in a special file. The directory can then be read by any program that needs the data. Changes can be made to the directory as needed, and the changes seen by every program that uses the directory.

Relative files are somewhat different from files accessed by absolute addressing. The address associated with a record in a file is a relative position number for that record within the file. The same hashing techniques that are appropriate for determining the correct row of the directory to examine for a particular key value, are suitable for determining the correct position number for a record within a file. In other words, there is no need to store the address (position number) 234 at row 234 of a directory table in association with a key value. The hash value 234 produced with the key value *is* the address and can be used immediately to access the file.

Since the value produced by the hash function for a given key value is not necessarily unique, it is possible that the read or write operation that uses the hash value for an address will access the wrong storage location. Consequently, reading and writing become more complex operations:

READ: Operate on the key value with the hash function.
            Produce a hash value, to use as an address.
            Fetch the record stored at the address provided by the hash function
            Compare the key value of the record obtained with the key value sought.
            If the key values match, the read operation has succeeded.
            If the key values do not match, a collision condition has occurred: the same address is generated by at least two key values, the one being sought and the one actually stored at the address.

WRITE: Operate on the key value with the hash function.
            Produce a hash value, to use as an address.
            Attempt to read from the address produced by the hash function.
            If the read succeeds, the address is already in use; a collision condition has occurred.

If the read fails, the address is vacant, and the write operation can continue.

Each time a collision occurs, another address must be generated for the key whose associated record is sought. The complete read or write sequence must be repeated. A hashing method that produces a large number of collisions causes the program's input/output operations to take too much time. An effective method for handling collisions is an important aspect of a hashing method.

Collision Handling

For real applications, the hash function maps some distinct key values into the same relative address, no matter how much care is taken when choosing a hashing technique. When a collision occurs, an empty location must be found for the colliding key value. The object of collision handling is to provide a method for placing the colliding key value in an empty location so that it can be found at a later time.

Because collisions are inevitable, and because there is no best way to handle them in all cases, there exist a variety of approaches to collision resolution. The methods are grouped under two main headings—**open addressing** and **chaining**. Descriptions and examples of the techniques are given, followed by a discussion of their performance in specific circumstances. Programming language features and implementations are addressed in a later section.

Open Addressing

Assume a key value is hashed (by any function) to an address already occupied by a different key value. The process called **open addressing** searches the table for an empty location and stores the key value there. There are a number of ways to carry out the process so that the value can be found in a subsequent search. In the following descriptions, assume that a key k is mapped by a hash function h to an address A (that is, $h(k)=A$) in a table of size t. Then A has values in the range 1, 2, ..., t independent of the number of distinct key values.

The simplest open addressing technique is called **linear probing**. Choose a positive integer d (called the **displacement**). If the collision occurs at location A, then search at $A+d$, $A+2d$, $A+3d$, and so on, until an empty location is found. Each address is computed modulo(t) + 1 so that its value does not exceed the maximum table address. The most common choice for d is the integer 1. The search sequence then is

$A, A+1, A+2, \ldots, A+j\,(=t), 1, 2, \ldots, A-1.$

This choice guarantees that all table locations will be probed if necessary and readily determines that the table is full when the sequence returns to A. An example of linear probing is shown in Figure 7.4. For that example, the table size is 11 and the file consists of eight records with the following key values:

12, 21, 68, 32, 56, 77, 91, 18

The initial hash address is found by the division method.

A disadvantage of linear probing is that long sequences of consecutive occupied addresses tend to get longer as the table gets closer to being full. This effect is illustrated in the preceding example (Figure 7.4). By the time the fifth key value, 56, is hashed, the table has a sequence of four consecutive occupied addresses (11, 1, 2, 3). Resolving collisions for the fifth, sixth, and seventh key values extends the sequence to five, six, and seven addresses, respectively. This kind of effect is called **primary clustering**. It increases the probability that the first probe is a collision. For example, if the table size is 11, then the probability is 1/11 that the first insertion will be in a particular location $L1$. The probability is twice as great that the second insertion will be at $L2$ (the position next to $L1$) than at any other other location because a hash to either $L1$ or $L2$ results in the key value being placed at $L2$. Similarly, the probability is three times as

(12 mod 11) + 1 = 1 + 1 = 2; store 12 at 2.
(21 mod 11) + 1 = 10 + 1 = 11; store 21 at 11.
(68 mod 11) + 1 = 2 + 1 = 3; store 68 at 3.
(32 mod 11) + 1 = 10 + 1 = 11; probe at 11; collision.
   (11 mod 11) + 1 = 1; store 32 at 1.
(56 mod 11) + 1 = 1 + 1 = 2; probe at 2; collision.
   (2 mod 11) + 1 = 3; probe at 3; collision.
   (3 mod 11) + 1 = 4; store 56 at 4.
(77 mod 11) + 1 = 0 + 1 = 1; probe at 1;collision.
   (1 mod 11) + 1 = 2; probe at 2; collision.
   (2 mod 11) + 1 = 3; probe at 3; collision.
   (3 mod 11) + 1 = 4; probe at 4; collision.
   (4 mod 11) + 1 = 5; store 77 at 5.
(91 mod 11) + 1 = 3 + 1 = 4; probe at 4; collision.
   (4 mod 11) + 1 = 5; probe at 5; collision.
   (5 mod 11) + 1 = 6; store 91 at 6.
(18 mod 11) + 1 = 7 + 1 = 8; store 18 at 8.

The table is as follows:

Index	1	2	3	4	5	6	7	8	9	10	11
Key Value	32	12	68	56	77	91	—	18	—	—	21

Figure 7.4 Hashing by the division-remainder method with linear probing.

great that the third insertion will be at L3 than at any other location. As the number of insertions increases, the probability of long sequences getting longer increases.

Another disadvantage of linear probing becomes evident from an examination of the collision sequences in the above example. The sequences originating from different hash values intermix, or **coalesce**. In the example, the first instance of coalescing occurs during collision handling of the key value 56. The first collision occurs at location 2. Therefore, 56 should be part of a chain with 12, the key value at 2. However, the next collision is at 3. As a result, 56 is stored in location 4 and becomes part of the chain containing 68, the key value stored at 3. Other instances of coalescing occur during collision handling of 77 and 91. In particular, 77 ends up on the chain with 68 and 56, instead of on the chain with 32. Coalescing contributes to the problem of lengthening the sequences of occupied addresses, which creates longer searches for empty locations or for keys already in the table.

The next method, **random probing**, is a variation of linear probing that reduces primary clustering. Instead of using a constant displacement d, we generate a pseudo-random number r each time a collision occurs, and then probe at the address of the collision plus r. Of course, the generated numbers cannot really be random because the sequence must contain every value $1, 2, \ldots, t$ exactly once, using modulo(t) + 1 where necessary. Also, the same sequence used to find an empty location for a key value must occur every time a search is made for that value. The function $r = (r+m) \bmod t$, where m and t are relatively prime and r is initially the hash address A, is one example of a pseudo-random number generator that meets both criteria.

Although random probing decreases primary clustering, it can cause **secondary clustering**. This kind of clustering happens when two different keys are mapped to the same address. The same pseudo-random number sequence is generated from the two key values, which means that probes are made at the same sequence of addresses. Random probing also suffers from coalescing of collision sequences.

An open addressing technique based on division is called the **linear quotient** method. It is used in conjunction with the division hash function. Let q be the quotient obtained when the key k is divided by the table size t to determine the address A. If $q = 0$, set $q = 1$. If a collision occurs at A, then search for an empty location at $(A+q) \bmod t + 1$. If the location is already occupied by a different key value, then add the most recently computed quotient (or 1 if the quotient is 0) and remainder (the occupied address), divide the sum by t, add 1, and probe at the address (remainder) resulting from the division. Continue this process until an empty location is found or the table is full. This method reduces secondary clustering, but coalesces collision sequences for different hash

(12 mod 11) + 1 = 1 + 1 = 2; store 12 at 2.
(21 mod 11) + 1 = 10 + 1 = 11; store 21 at 11.
(68 mod 11) + 1 = 2 + 1 = 3; store 68 at 3.
(32 mod 11) + 1 = 10 + 1 = 11; probe at 11; collision.($q = 2$)
　((11 +2) mod 11) + 1 = 3; probe at 3; collision. ($q = 1$)
　((3+1) mod 11) + 1 = 5; store 32 at 5.
(56 mod 11) + 1 = 1 + 1 = 2; probe at 2; collision. ($q = 5$)
　((2+5) mod 11) + 1 = 8; store 56 at 8.
(77 mod 11) + 1 = 1; store 77 at 1.
(91 mod 11) + 1 = 3 + 1 = 4; store 91 at 4.
(18 mod 11) + 1 = 7 + 1 = 8; probe at 8; collision. ($q = 1$)
　((8+1) mod 11) + 1 = 10; store 18 at 10.

The table is as follows:

Index	1	2	3	4	5	6	7	8	9	10	11
Key Value	77	12	68	91	32	—	—	56	—	18	21

Figure 7.5 Hashing by the linear quotient method.

values. An example using the same key values and table size as before is shown in Figure 7.5.

Another open addressing method is called **double hashing**. It resolves collisions by generating a new address with a second hash function different from the first. One implementation of this approach is to have the second hash function generate a constant which becomes the displacement for a sequence of probes starting with the initial hash address. This technique differs from linear probing because the value of the constant depends on the address generated by the first hash function. Different addresses are likely to give rise to different constants for the displacements. Double hashing decreases the probability of secondary clustering. Collision sequence coalescing can occur, however.

An open addressing scheme called **quadratic probing** generates a sequence of addresses $A_0, A_1, \ldots, A_t$ as follows:

$A_0 = h(k)$, the initial address generated by hashing
$A_j = (A_0 + j^2) \bmod t$, for $j = 1, 2, \ldots, t$

For example, if a key k is hashed to an address A which is already occupied, then successive probes are made at $A+1$, $A+4$, $A+9$, and so on (all modulo(t) + 1), until an empty address is found. This technique avoids primary clustering, but does allow coalescing of collision sequences.

Two serious problems are associated with any open address method for handling collisions. One stems from the table size t being fixed. In many applications, the number of records may increase beyond t and the table overflows. The only recourse at that point is to declare a larger table size and rehash the entire file of records. The second problem is that collision sequences coalesce, making deletion difficult.

If a key value is deleted from a location in a coalesced list, then any search of a collision address sequence containing that location could reach the empty location before a desired key value is found. The search stops erroneously because the key value does not appear to be in the table. Marking the location "deleted" rather than "empty" and searching past deleted locations could alleviate the problem, provided relatively few deletions are made. Otherwise, long searches through locations, many of which are marked "deleted," could occur.

Chaining

The second kind of collision handling method, **chaining**, resolves the two problems just discussed. It maintains linked lists of key values that hash to the same address. The first value hashing to a particular address, say j, is placed in the table at j along with a pointer to the record and one additional field. This field contains a pointer to the list of key values hashing to the same address. Initially, the pointer is set to null, indicating that the rest of the list is empty. When a different value hashes to the same address, it is compared to the key value already there, and then it is added (chained) to the linked list by changing the pointer. For each key value hashing to that address, the linked list is searched, and the value is either found or added to the end of the list. Each list could be maintained as a sorted list. Then searching for a given key value is more efficient, but only slightly if the lists are short.

A common way to organize the hash table for chaining is to consider each table entry as a listhead (see the example in Figure 7.6). Each listhead can contain information about the list, such as the number of key values, in addition to the pointer to the first value in the list. No key values appear in the table. The example in Figure 7.6 illustrates a table with listheads. The hash function is $k \bmod 5 + 1$, and the key values are 12, 21, 68, 32, 56, 77, 91, and 18.

Chaining requires a smaller table size than open addressing; the table does not hold all of the key values. Also, because list handling is dynamic (that is, spaces are allocated on an as-needed basis) there is no need to

```
1   null
2   ⟶  21  ⟶  56  ⟶  91  null
3   ⟶  12  ⟶  32  ⟶  77  null
4   ⟶  68  ⟶  18  null
5   null
```

Figure 7.6 Collision handling by chaining.

estimate maximum table size in advance. Other memory requirements are space for each key value, its pointer, and its list entry. If lists become long, search efficiency is lost and the purpose of hashing is violated. Rehashing with a different table size may then be appropriate.

Collision handling can be reduced by allocating specific storage areas, or **buckets**, one for all key values hashing to the same address. (All previous hash methods could be considered as having buckets of size 1.) Each key value, sometimes with its entire record, is placed in the next available location in the bucket. When a bucket, sometimes referred to as a **primary bucket**, is full, an attempt to add another value causes overflow. This is analogous to collision handling in a hash table. To resolve an overflow situation, assign the key value, and its record, to a new bucket, called an **overflow bucket**, either by placing the value in the next available location (analogous to linear probing) or by linking (chaining) it to the previous value hashed to the primary bucket. A single overflow bucket generally accommodates all of the primary buckets.

Within each primary bucket, key values may be sorted. Then overflow causes the last value in the sorted sequence to be placed in the overflow bucket. This method, referred to as **open hashing**, is effective when the buckets are located in external memory and their size corresponds to an addressable portion of the memory device—for example, a sector on a disk or a block on magnetic tape. A search can then be conducted efficiently, by simply hashing the given key value, loading the appropriate primary bucket (sector, block) into main memory, and searching its contents. If the key value is not found, and if there is empty space in the bucket, then the value is not present. If the bucket is full, the overflow bucket is loaded and searched. The section entitled "Indexed Sequential File Organization" in the next chapter contains an implementation of this technique.

Dynamic Hashing

A method called **dynamic hashing** incorporates many of the good features of the other hash techniques, including double hashing, dynamic space allocation, and short searches after collisions. The method requires a hash table that serves as an index to a file of primary buckets holding records with their key values. One of its major advantages is that the size of the file grows dynamically as the number of records increases. The size does not have to be known in advance. Another significant advantage pertains to the way in which collisions are handled.

Assume a file of twenty-four records with the following key values:

12, 21, 68, 32, 56, 77, 91, 18, 80, 29, 45, 14, 53, 84, 70, 34, 20, 41, 89, 67, 49, 58, 31, 23

Hash Table			File	
1	1	1	77	
2	2	2	12	56
3	3	3	68	
4	4	4	91	
5	5	5		
6	6	6		
7	7	7		
8	8	8	18	
9	9	9		
10	10	10		
11	11	11	21	32

Figure 7.7 Dynamic hashing file and hash table after 8 key values are entered.

Let the bucket size be 3 and the division-remainder method be the hash function (any key-to-address function can be used) with hash table size of 11. Figure 7.7 shows the hash table and the file after the first eight key values are hashed.

To illustrate the process, consider the first key value 12. By the division-remainder method,

(12 mod 11) + 1 = 1 + 1 = 2

Location 2 of the hash table contains the pointer 2, which is the bucket in the file where 12 is stored. Similarly, the next value, 21, is stored in bucket 11, 68 in bucket 3, 32 in bucket 11, and so on. Hashing continues until the key value 34 is hashed to 2 and the probe at bucket 2 finds three different values already there. Then two activities are carried out to handle this collision. All four values—the three in the bucket (12, 56, 45) and the colliding one (34)—are rehashed with a second hashing function to split the records between bucket 2 and an overflow bucket added to the file. Also, the entry at 2 in the hash table becomes a binary tree with pointers to the two buckets created by the split.

Various criteria could be applied to determine which key values stay in the primary bucket, and which values go to the overflow bucket. For example, if the rehash produces a binary representation of the key values, then values with first bit 0 could stay in the primary bucket and the others could go to the overflow bucket. The criterion is used to determine which path in the binary tree is to be followed. In Figure 7.8, the split is based on a different criterion; namely, values less than 50 (the approximate midpoint of two-digit key values) stay in the primary bucket, while other values go to the overflow bucket.

202 Chapter 7

```
Hash Table                          File
1      1  10-49   2          1     77
2         •<                 2     12    34   45
3      3  50-99   12    3          68
4      4                    4      91    80   14
5      5                    5      70
6      6                    6
7      7                    7
8      8                    8      18    29   84
9      9                    9
10    10                    10     53
11    11                    11     21    32
                            12     56
```

Figure 7.8 Dynamic hashing after the first collision.

Hashing continues. The key value 20 ends up in bucket 10. The value 41 is hashed to 8, causing a collision. The split of the file, and the binary tree in the hash table, are shown in Figure 7.9. The remaining key values are hashed, and the records are inserted into the appropriate buckets by following pointers in the hash table. When the last value, 23, is hashed, a collision occurs because bucket 2 is already filled. The values in the bucket and the value 23 are rehashed to split them into primary and overflow buckets. In the hash table, an additional level of the binary tree at 2 is created, with the node containing the pointer to 2 becoming the root of a subtree, as shown in Figure 7.10. The criterion for the split is that all key values less than 25 (approximately halfway between 1 and 50) stay in the primary bucket.

```
Hash Table                          File
1      1  10-49   2          1     77
2         •<                 2     34    45
3      3  50-99   12         3     68
4      4                     4     91    80   14
5      5                     5     70
6      6                     6
7      7  10-49   8          7
8         •<                 8     18    29   41
9      9  50-99   13         9
10    10                    10     53    20
11    11                    11     21    32
                            12     56
                            13     84
```

Figure 7.9 *Dynamic hashing after the second collision.*

Hash Table				File			
		10–24	2				
1	1 10–49			1	77		
2		25–49	15	2	12	23	
3	3 50–99	12		3	68		
		10–49	4				
4				4	14		
5	5 50–99	14		5	70		
6	6			6	49		
7	7 10–49	8		7			
8				8	18	29	41
9	9 50–99	13		9			
				12	56	89	87
11	11			11	21	32	
				12	56	89	87
				13	84		
				14	58	80	91
				15	34	45	

Figure 7.10 Dynamic hashing after all data is entered.

Algorithms and Programs

Previous sections contained informal discussions with examples of a variety of ways to create and search a hash table. It is now time to formalize the discussion by presenting algorithms and their program implementations for selected methods. Specifically, we discuss the division method for address calculation and two collision handling techniques—linear probing and chaining. These implementations illustrate the use of pointers and other relevant language features.

Algorithm for Address Calculation

The division method of address calculation is straightforward. For each key, assuming the keys are integers, the algorithm simply initializes the table index and then computes a value of the index from the **mod** function. Insertion into the table is a function of collision handling. When the keys are not integers, the algorithm must be modified by converting each key into an integer before the index is calculated. In Pascal, the **ord** function accomplishes this conversion; it returns a character's ordinal number equivalent, which is an integer value, as specified by a particular character code. For example, **ord**('a') = 56 because the character 'a' has the ordinal number 65 in ASCII. Adding the ordinal numbers of the nonblank characters in a key obtains the integer that represents the key. By treating an integer as a character string, the function **ord** could also be used when the keys are integers. Keys are assumed to be character strings in the following algorithm and program.

Algorithm divisionhash

    Variables: index, the hash table index.
               key, the key value of a record.
               stringsize, the maximum length of the key;
               tablesize, the size of the hash table;
               n, the number of records; and
               blank, a single blank character.

    Input: key, a character string of length 1..stringsize.
    Output: index, an integer in the range 1..tablesize.

    Process:
      Initialize index to 0.
      Add to index the ordinal numbers of the nonblank characters
         in key.
      index = (index mod tablesize) + 1.
      Return the value of index.

Programs for Address Calculation

The Pascal implementation of the algorithm is the integer function divisionhash.

```
function divisionhash (key : string) : integer;
{ For a character string key, divisionhash returns
an integer value in the range 1. .tablesize. }
const
  blank = ' ';
var
  j : 1..stringsize;    { Loop control variable for
                 the number of characters in key. }
  index : integer;      { The hash value. }

begin
  index := 0;           { Initialize the sum. }
  { Sum the ordinal values of the nonblank
    characters in key. }
  for j := 1 to stringsize do
      index := index + ord(key[j]); { Compute sum. }
  divisionhash := (index mod tablesize) + 1
end;
```

Pascal Program 7.1 Division hashing

The COBOL implementation is as follows:

```
DATA DIVISION.

WORKING-STORAGE SECTION.

01 CONSTANT-VALUES.
    03 STRINGSIZE         PIC 9(3)      VALUE IS 20.
01 NEW-KEY-ENTRY.
    03 NEW-KEY            PIC X(20).
    03 KEY-CHARACTERS REDEFINES NEW-KEY.
        05 KEY-PART OCCURS 20 TIMES  PIC 9.
    03 NEW-ADDRESSPIC <whatever is needed>.

01 SUBSCRIPTS.
    03 POSITION           PIC 9(3).

01 HASH-FIELDS.
    03 HASH-INDEX         PIC 9(3).
    03 UNNEEDED-VALUE     PIC 9(11).
    03 LEFT-OVER          PIC 9(3).

PROCEDURE DIVISION.

DIVISION-HASH.
    MOVE ZERO TO HASH-INDEX.
    PERFORM CONVERT-KEY VARYING POSITION FROM 1 BY 1
        UNTIL POSITION EXCEEDS STRINGSIZE.
    DIVIDE HASH-INDEX BY TABLESIZE
        GIVING UNNEEDED-VALUE
        REMAINDER LEFT-OVER.
    COMPUTE HASH-INDEX = LEFT-OVER + 1.

CONVERT-KEY.
    ADD KEY-PART(POSITION) TO HASH-INDEX.
```

COBOL Program 7.1   Division hashing

Algorithm for Collision Handling: Linear Probing

The **divisionhash** function provides the initial hash address for any collision handling routine. The function is called from two routines—linear probing and chaining. Algorithms and programs are given for both routines. Once the value is available, the routines follow different steps to store the record whose key was hashed. Each of the methods for locating a key value in the directory is used for three different purposes: to insert the key value for a new record when the record is written to the file; to delete the key value when the record is deleted from the file; and to find the address associated with the key value, for the sake of reading that record from the file.

In any search of the directory, three cases are possible:

1. The initial probe finds an empty location, in which case the key value and associated address are inserted for insert operations, or an error occurs for find and delete operations.
2. The probe finds the same key at the location as the one that was hashed, in which case the corresponding address is returned for find operations, the record is flagged as deleted for delete operations, or an error occurs for insert operations.
3. The probe finds a different key at the location, in which case a search of consecutive locations for an empty or matching one is begun. The search for an empty location in which to insert a new key value stops if the table is full. The search for a matching key value stops when all entries in the table have been examined. To guarantee that the search terminates, increment a counter each time a probe is made after a collision and indicate an error if the counter equals the table size.

An algorithm can be specified as follows:

Algorithm linearprobe

    Variables: hashindex, the table index of the initial probe.
                      newkey, the key to be hashed and inserted.
                      newaddress, the address of a record associated
                          with newkey for insert operations
                      probenumber, the counter to determine when the
                        whole table has been examined.
                      key, the value of a key in the hash table.
                      table, the hash table.
                      tablesize, the size of the hash table.
                      n, the number of keys.
                      empty, a string of blank characters.
    Input: The key newkey.
    Output: Depending on the reason for searching the table:
                      The Address associated with the newkey, that was
                        found in the table
                      The table updated to include newkey, and its
                        associated newaddress
                      The table updated to include a deletion flag set for the
                        entry corresponding to newkey.

Using the division method, calculate hashindex for newkey.
initialize probenumber to 1.
While all three of the following conditions are true
    1. table[hashindex] is not empty
    2. table[hashindex] is different from newkey
    3. probenumber is less than tablesize
do the following:
    increment hashindex (modulo tablesize)
    increment probenumber
If table[hashindex] is empty
    then if the operation is insert, insert newkey
    else indicate error for delete or find operation
if table[hashindex] = newkey
    then if the operation is delete, set the delete flag
        if the operation is find, return the address found
        if the operation is insert, indicate error
if probenumber = tablesize
    indicate error: table full for insert operation
                     newkey not found for find or delete operations

Programs for Collision Handling: Linear Probing

The Pascal procedure for linear probing follows directly from the algorithm. Appropriate definitions of **hasharray** and **addresstype** are assumed.

```
procedure linearprobing (var table  : hasharray;
                         newkey     : string
                         var address: addresstype;
                         operation  : (insert,
                                       delete, find));

{ Linearprobing references the function
divisionhash to hash a character string newkey and
uses the hash value returned to access the hash
table. A key value and address is inserted if the
operation specified is insert; an entry is flagged
as deleted if the operation specifed is delete; the
address in the table that corresponds to the key
value is returned if the operation is find.}
const
  empty = 0;
var
  hashindex  : 1..tablesize; {The hash table index. }
  probenumber : 1..tablesize;  {The number of probes
                                to insert a key. }
```

```
begin  { linearprobing }
  hashindex := divisionhash(newkey);    { Calculates
              the hash address, the table index. }
  probenumber := 1;      { Initialize the counter. }
  while (table[hashindex].key <> empty) and
        (table[hashindex].key <> newkey) and
        (probenumber <= tablesize) do
    begin
      hashindex := hashindex mod(tablesize) + 1;
      probenumber := probenumber + 1
    end;   { While }
  if table[hashindex].key = empty
    then
      case operation of
        insert: begin
                  table[hashindex].key := newkey;
                  { Insert the new key and address }
                  table[hashindex].address:=address
                end
        delete: errorcode:= 1; {deletion error:
                                   no match}
        find  : errorcode:= 2; {find error:no match}
      end;   { case }
  if table[hashindex].key = newkey
    then
      case operation of
        insert: errorcode:= 3;  { insertion error:
                                     matching key }
        delete: table[hashindex].deleteflag := TRUE;
        find  : address :=
                  table[hashindex].fileaddress;
    end; { case }
  if probenumber = tablesize
    then
      case operation of
        insert: errorcode:= 4;  { insertion error:
                                     table full }
        delete: errorcode:= 1;  { deletion error:
                                     no match }
        find: errorcode:= 2; {find error: no match }
      end; { case }
end;   { linearprobing }
```

Pascal Program 7.2 Linear probing

The COBOL implementation of LINEAR PROBING is as follows:

```
    PERFORM DIVISIONHASH.
    PERFORM PROBE-TABLE
        VARYING PROBENUMBER FROM 1 BY 1
        UNTIL TABLE-KEYFIELD(HASH-INDEX) = NULL-VALUE
          OR  TABLE-KEYFIELD(HASH-INDEX) = NEW-KEY
          OR  PROBENUMBER > TABLESIZE.
    IF TABLE-KEY(HASH-INDEX) = NULL-VALUE
        PERFORM EMPTY-TABLE-ENTRY.
    IF TABLE-KEY(HASH-INDEX) = NEW-KEY
        PERFORM MATCHING-ENTRY.
    IF PROBENUMBER > TABLESIZE
        PERFORM END-OF-TABLE.

PROBE-TABLE.
    DIVIDE HASH-INDEX BY TABLESIZE
        GIVING UNNEEDED-VALUE
        REMAINDER LEFT-OVER.
    COMPUTE HASH-INDEX = LEFT-OVER + 1.
    ADD 1 TO PROBENUMBER.

EMPTY-TABLE-ENTRY.
    IF INSERT-KEY
        MOVE NEW-KEY TO TABLE-KEY(HASH-INDEX)
        MOVE NEW-ADDRESS TO TABLE-ADDRESS(HASH-INDEX).
    IF DELETE-KEY PERFORM DELETION-ERROR.
    IF FIND-KEY PERFORM FIND-ERROR-MISSING.

MATCHING-ENTRY.
    IF INSERT-KEY PERFORM INSERT-ERROR-MATCHING.
    IF DELETE-KEY MOVE 'D' TO TABLE-DELETE-FLAG.
    IF FIND-KEY
        IF TABLE-DELETE-FLAG NOT = 'D'
            MOVE TABLE-ADDRESS(HASH-INDEX) TO READ-ADDRESS.

END-OF-TABLE.
    IF INSERT-KEY PERFORM INSERT-ERROR-TABLE-FULL.
    IF DELETE-KEY PERFORM DELETE-ERROR-MISSING-KEY.
    IF FIND-KEY PERFORM FIND-ERROR-MISSING.
```

COBOL Program 7.2 Linear probing

Algorithm for Collision Handling: Chaining

The algorithm for resolving collisions by chaining differs from **linearprobing** in that the hash table is not searched. If the hash address is not empty, then a linked list of keys hashed to the same address is searched instead. Either the key value is found in the list, in which case the appropriate action is taken, as in **linearprobing**, or the key is not found and other actions are called for. Pointers are required to get to the next element on a list. A counter is not needed; the end of a list is signaled by a special symbol (nil in Pascal) in the pointer field of a list element. For the sake of simplicity, assume each element in the lists and in the table consists of two fields, the first for a key and the second for a pointer. The key field in the table contains a string of blank characters at all times. Thus, table entries are really listheads. Of course, the key field could contain information about the list, and one or more fields could be added to each list element to hold the rest of the record.

Algorithm chaining

    Variables: newkey, the key to be hashed (and inserted if an insert operation is to be done).
    newaddress, the address to be inserted if an insertion operation is done, or the address of the record whose key was supplied if a find operation was done.
    table, the hash table.
    tablesize, the size of table.
    key, a key value already in a linked list.
    next, the pointer to the next element in a linked list.
    n, the number of keys.
    hashindex, the hash table index generated by the address calculation method, division in this case.

Input: newkey.
Output: The newaddress associated with newkey, if the operation specified is find, otherwise an updated table with the entry corresponding to newkey deleted if the operation was delete, or newkey and newaddress inserted if the operation was insert.

Using the division hash method, find hashindex for newkey.
Search the linked list beginning at table[hashindex].
If a key with the same value of newkey is found
    then delete or return the addrress, depending upon the operation requested.
If no matching key value is found, and the operation is insert,
    add newkey and newaddress to the end of the list.

Programs for Collision Handling: Chaining

The Pascal procedure for the algorithm to resolve collisions by chaining uses pointer variables. It needs elements, or nodes, containing four fields: the key value, the address of the record associated with the key value, a flag for deleted records, and a pointer to the next element in the chain. One way to implement nodes and pointers in linked lists is to take advantage of the Pascal feature that permits the user to define data types by declaring a pointer type, *ptrtype* and a node of type *nodetype*. Data items of type *ptrtype* point to nodes declared to be of type *nodetype*. The following declaration in Pascal accomplishes this goal:

```
type
  string = packed array[1..8] of char;
  ptrtype = ^nodetype;
  nodetype = record
               key : string;
               fileaddress: addresstype;
               deleteflag: boolean;
               next : ptrtype
             end;
```

The procedure assumes this declaration. Note that additional fields could be included in *nodetype* to keep frequently used fields from the record more easily accessible.

```
procedure chaining (var table : hasharray;
                    var errorcode: 0..4;
                    opcode: (insert, delete, find);
                    newkey : string);

{ Chaining calls the function divisionhash to
calculate an address, hashindex, from the input
newkey, then searches a linked list. If a key value
equal to newkey is found, and a delete or find
opcode is specified, then the operation is carried
out Otherwise newkey is inserted at the end of the
list. }

var
  p,q : ptrtype;
  hashindex = 1..tablesize;
```

```pascal
begin     { chaining }
          { Calculate the index for the hash table. }
   hashindex := divisionhash(newkey);

                    { Search the appropriate list. }
   p := table[hashindex]^.next; { Initialize a
                                  pointer to point
                                  to where the
                                  listhead points. }
   while (p^.key <> newkey) and (p^.next <> nil) do
     p := p^.next;  { Move to the next node in the
                      list. }

   if p^.key = newkey   { A key with value equal to }
     then               { newkey is found. }
        case opcode of
           insert:  errorcode:= 1; { insertion error:
                                     duplicate keys }
           delete:  p^.deleteflag := TRUE;
           find  :  address := p^.fileaddress;
        end; { case }

     else {No value equal to newkey is in the list.}
        case opcode of
           insert:  begin
                      new(q);
                      p^.next := q;
                      q^.key := newkey;
                      q^.fileaddress := address;
                      q^.next := nil
                    end
           delete:  errorcode:=2; { deletion error:
                                    no matching key }
           find  :  errorcode:=3; { find error: no
                                    matching key }
        end;  { case }
end;   { chaining }
```

Pascal Program 7.3 Chaining

COBOL does not include the concept of dynamic memory allocation; there is no equivalent to the Pascal command "new" which requests a memory location for the program. There is also no pointer feature which stores the address of a memory location. Therefore, all the space needed for the hash table and chains must be reserved in advance as a fixed-size table.

In this example implementation, the table contains 400 rows, of which 103 make up the hash table, and the others are for chains. Each row corresponds to one key value, and includes the key value, the address of the corresponding record, and a pointer to the next table entry whose key value produces the same hash value. A section of the table, shown below, illustrates this implementation of linked lists (chains) using a fixed-size table:

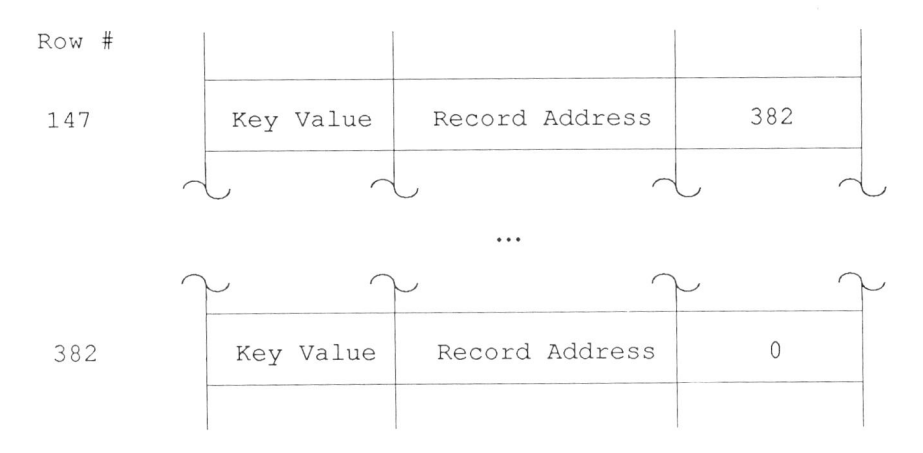

Row #			
147	Key Value	Record Address	382
...			
382	Key Value	Record Address	0

In this case, the "pointer" is a subscript value for the row in the table containing the next chain position, that is, the position containing the next key value that produces the same hash value. Pointer value 0 indicates the end of the chain.

```
DATA DIVISION.
WORKING-STORAGE SECTION.
01 CONSTANT-VALUES.
    03 HASH-TABLE-SIZE       PIC 9(3)      VALUE 103.
    03 FULL-TABLE-SIZE       PIC 9(3)      VALUE 400.

01 HASH-TABLE.
    03 HASH-TABLE-ENTRY OCCURS FULL-TABLE-SIZE TIMES.
        05 TABLE-KEY         PIC X(8). (or whatever
                                        is appropriate)
        05 TABLE-DELETE-FLAG PIC X.
        05 TABLE-ADDRESS     PIC <whatever is
              appropriate for the file being addressed.>
        05 TABLE-POINTER     PIC 9(3).
```

```
01 POINTERS.
    03 HASH-INDEX              PIC 9(3).
    03 TABLE-POSITION          PIC 9(3).
    03 NEW-CHAIN-POSITION      PIC 9(3).
        88 TABLE-FULL VALUE ZERO.

01 FLAGS.
    03 OPERATION-CODE          PIC X.
        88 INSERT-KEY          VALUE IS 'I'.
        88 DELETE-KEY          VALUE IS 'D'.
        88 FIND-KEY            VALUE IS 'F'.
    03 SEARCH-ENDER            PIC X(5).
        88 PLACE-FOUND         VALUE IS 'FOUND'.
        88 SEARCH-FAILED       VALUE IS 'FAIL'.

PROCEDURE DIVISION.

CHAINING.
    PERFORM INITIALIZE-POINTERS
        VARYING TABLE-POSITION FROM 1 BY 1
        UNTIL TABLE-POSITION > FULL-TABLE-SIZE.
    PERFORM DIVISION-HASH.
    PERFORM SEARCH-TABLE.

INITIALIZE-POINTERS.
    MOVE ZERO TO TABLE-POINTER(TABLE-POSITION).
    MOVE SPACE TO TABLE-DELETE-FLAG(TABLE-POSITION).

SEARCH-TABLE.
    PERFORM FOLLOW-CHAIN
        UNTIL PLACE-FOUND
        OR SEARCH-FAILED.
    PERFORM USE-TABLE.

FOLLOW-CHAIN.
    MOVE TABLE-POINTER(HASH-INDEX) TO HASH-INDEX.
    IF TABLE-KEY(HASH-INDEX) = NEW-KEY
        MOVE 'FOUND' TO SEARCH-ENDER
    ELSE IF TABLE-KEY(HASH-INDEX) = ZERO
        MOVE 'FAILED' TO SEARCH-ENDER.

USE-TABLE.
    IF DELETE-KEY
        IF PLACE-FOUND
            MOVE 'D' TO TABLE-DELETE-FLAG(HASH-INDEX)
        ELSE PERFORM DELETION-ERROR.
    IF INSERT-KEY
        IF NOT SEARCH-FAILED
            PERFORM DUPLICATE-KEY-ERROR
```

```
            ELSE
                MOVE NEW-KEY TO TABLE-KEY(HASH-INDEX)
                MOVE NEW-ADDRESS TO
                                TABLE-ADDRESS(HASH-INDEX)
                IF TABLE-FULL PERFORM FULL-TABLE-ERROR
                    ELSE MOVE NEW-CHAIN-POSITION TO
                             TABLE-POINTER(HASH-INDEX)
                         ADD 1 TO NEW-CHAIN-POSITION
                         IF NEW-CHAIN-POSITION >
                             FULL-TABLE-SIZE
                             MOVE ZERO TO
                                 NEW-CHAIN-POSITION.
    IF FIND-KEY AND SEARCH-FAILED
        PERFORM FIND-ERROR-MISSING
        ELSE MOVE TABLE-ADDRESS(HASH-INDEX) TO READ-ADDRESS.
```

COBOL Program 7.3 Chaining

Divison hash is used to convert any key to a number. The hash table is searched by following a chain that begins at the location specified by the hash value (HASH-INDEX), until the new key is found or the end of the chain is encountered. If a new key value is being inserted, a new piece is added to the chain for this hash index, and the key value and address are inserted. If a key value is being deleted, the corresponding entry is marked. (No attempt to recover the space previously occupied by a deleted key is included.) If a key is being searched for (in order to do a read operation on the file), the chaining process stops when the key has been found, and the address at that location is copied to a data name (READ-ADDRESS) for use by the READ statement. The program that uses the chaining code then continues with the READ operation.

Error conditions are tested, but error treatment is not specified. Generally, an error code is set to a particular value. The program that uses this process checks this code before continuing. An error message may be written to a program log also.

Analysis of Collision Handling Methods

An analysis of hashing is really an analysis of collision handling. Because every address calculation technique is designed to be $O(1)$, the number of probes after a collision is the only variable which significantly influences the time required for a hash technique.

Only the average case of collision handling merits analysis. The best case occurs when there are no collisions. The worst case—when all keys hash to the same address—is untenable; a different choice of hash function would be made. A complete analysis of the average case is

Load Factor α	Linear Probing $(1-\alpha/2)(1-\alpha)$	Random Probing $-(1/\alpha)\log(1-\alpha)$	Chaining $1+\alpha/2$
0.1	1.06	1.05	1.05
0.5	1.50	1.34	1.25
0.75	2.50	1.83	1.38
0.9	5.50	2.56	1.45

Figure 7.11 Expected number of probes in collision handling methods for different load factors α.

outside the scope of this book. Only the results of three collision methods—linear probing, random probing, and chaining—are discussed. Dynamic hashing is also considered.

The expected number of probes in collision handling is a function of how full the hash table is. Let k be the number of keys in the hash table of size n. Then the **load factor** $\alpha = k/n$ is a measure of the fullness of the table. A complete analysis can establish the fact that the expected number of probes to find a key with linear probing, random probing, and chaining is $(1 - \alpha/2)(1 - \alpha)$, $-(1/\alpha)\log(1-\alpha)$, and $1 + \alpha/2$, respectively. Some representative values of the formulas are shown in Figure 7.11. It is apparent that chaining is consistently better than the other two methods, and that there is little difference in the methods until the table is over half full. Then linear probing deteriorates due to the effects of primary clustering.

Dynamic hashing is especially efficient when the entire hash table is in memory, including the binary trees resulting from collisions. Then, all records can be accessed with one file access. If any part of the table or trees is in external storage, then the number of file accesses increases. When all binary trees are in memory, the amount of time to search them is relatively small, a function of the depth of the tree. In the worst case, the search time is $O(\log n)$. This occurs when all key values hash to the same index and the hash table takes on the appearance of a binary tree, an undesirable and unlikely situation. The best case is $O(1)$, when no collisions occur. For each collision, additional time is required for rehashing and relocating records.

Summary

The advent of storage devices such as the disk opened the door to additional ways to process large files. Because individual records can be accessed directly on disks, records in a file do not have to be physically contiguous, nor must they be processed in any predefined order. Other means than sequential are possible for organizing and accessing files of records. Some preliminary processing in memory determines a record's actual or relative location before it is read from external storage.

Records that are physically organized as direct (relative) or indexed files can be processed in this way. Both organizations allow random as well as sequential access of records. The proper selection of sequential, relative, or indexed file organization depends on how records are accessed in a specific application. Access time and overhead should be minimized. A good understanding of trade-offs among possible file organizations and access methods is essential.

Sequential file organization and accessing methods are treated in Chapter 6. Relative file organization and accessing by hashing are topics in this chapter. Hashing methods include address calculation and collision handling techniques. Computations on key values produce relative addresses in a directory (hash table) where key values and corresponding record addresses are stored (or produce the relative address of a record in the file). A collision occurs when a relative address produced by hashing a key is occupied by a record whose key is different from the one used to produce the address. Records are found with one comparison in most cases. This chapter treats two general types of hashing methods: static, in which the hash table size does not change; and dynamic, in which the table size grows as locations are needed.

The third type of file organization, indexed, and its implications for sequential and random access methods, are the subjects of Chapter 8.

EXERCISES

1. List the major criteria for choosing a relative file organization over a sequential file organization.
2. List three applications in which sequential processing is preferable to random processing.
3. List three applications in which random processing is preferable to sequential processing.
4. Describe how the Pascal compiler at your installation implements relative addressing.
5. Design an algorithm to create a relative master file using a division remainder hashing function and chaining with one overflow area. The algorithm should handle insertions, deletions, and changes.
6. Given a tape containing a sequential file of 5000 records, create a random access file using relative file organization. Assume each record contains 120 bytes (characters) beginning with an automobile license number (3 letters followed by 3 digits) as key field. The remainder of the record can be treated as one string for purposes of

creating the file. Use one of the hashing methods discussed in this chapter.

7. Assume the key values of 8 records are to be hashed into relative locations numbered 100–110. The key values are:

    4522010 3795521 4522001 3600063 3794251 4522008 3600081 4501054

    a. Show the completed hash table for each of the following methods:
       (1) Folding, using the sum of the first three and last three digits, with linear probing.
       (2) Midsquare, using the middle three digits, with linear probing.
       (3) Division Remainder with $n = 11$ and linear probing.
    b. Compare the methods in (a). in terms of scattering of key values, number of collisions, collision handling, and appropriateness for the data.

8. Using the division remainder hashing function with chaining, show the contents of the hash table after storing the 24 key values given in the section "Dynamic Hashing." Let table size = 11 and primary bucket size = 3. Assume one overflow area.

9. Compare the hashing method of Exercise 8 with the dynamic hashing example in the chapter in terms of scattering of key values, number of collisions, and collision handling.

10. Using dynamic hashing with bucket size one, show the hash table after storing the 8 key values given in the section "Division-Remainder."

11. Develop an algorithm and program to implement dynamic hashing with bucket size 3. Test the program with the 24 key values given in the section.

CHAPTER 8

INDEXED SEQUENTIAL ACCESS

INTRODUCTION

The previous chapter dealt with random access techniques, by which the location of each individual record of a file can be made available. The methods discussed included storing the address in a table, along with a key identifying the record. The table is then searched until the key is found, or the key is used in a hashing function to find the table entry without searching. Once the table entry for a record is found, the record is read from the storage device directly, using the address found in the table entry. Hashing methods are also used to calculate directly the address of a record in a relative file, without need of a table. In such cases, the consequences of collisions are much greater than when hashing into a table. Every hash function "miss" becomes a wasted input/output operation and seriously impacts the running time of the program.

This chapter treats access in indexed sequential files. The principal difference between random access to these files and access to those with direct (or relative) organization is the ability to access directly only a portion of the records—those that are indexed. Other records are accessed by progressing sequentially from the nearest indexed record. One advantage of this method is that far fewer addresses must be maintained. A disadvantage is that most records cannot be accessed directly.

The chapter begins with an overview of the general indexed sequential organization technique. Specific examples—ISAM, VSAM, and SCOPE—follow. All indexed sequential methods depend on an effective strategy for maintaining the index, which acts like a road map through the file. A class of structures—B-tree, B^+-tree, and B^*-tree—have become the standard approach to maintaining the index, and these structures are the subject of the final sections of the chapter.

OVERVIEW

Indexed sequential organization is a compromise between direct and sequential organizations. Like direct organization, it requires that a directory be maintained that contains the location of records identified by their keys. However, the locations of only some of the records are kept in the directory. Most records are found by sequential search after access to an index record.

An everyday example of this method is the use of page indices in a telephone book. Printed at the top of each page are the first and last names on the page. If the desired name is between these two index names, then it belongs on that page. If it is not on that page, the index values tell us whether to look on earlier or later pages.

In order to make the example correspond more closely to an indexed sequential file organization, we would need to modify the telephone book. Instead of appearing at the top of each page, the index entries would occupy a special section of the book. In that section, each index name would appear with its page number.

Of course, the index would not list the first and last names of each page, since the last name of one page is so closely related to the first name of the next. Only the last name of each page and its page number appear. Finding a name in the phone book requires first turning to the index and locating the first name in the index that does not come before the one sought. For example, with the following index entries:

    Handel, Arthur — p. 27
    Hendrix, Susan — p. 28

the search for

    Hastings, William

proceeds to page 28. The names on page 28 are scanned. The name "Hastings, William" will be on that page if it is in the book at all.

Consider what happens to the index if the phone book is updated. A change near the beginning of the book may make all index entries for later pages invalid. All the index entries must be changed, along with the individual page entries. If the telephone book is updated often, such changes become burdensome.

One way to prolong the validity of the index and most pages is to underfill pages. Then a new name can be added in the extra space on the correct page, and revising that page does not affect any other pages or the overall index. Instead of reproducing a page each time a name is deleted from the list, the name is marked in the master copy and omitted the next time the page is changed for other reasons.

This approach wastes some space on each page. However, it allows the phone book and its index to remain stable for a much longer time than if each page were filled. Making full use of this reserved space requires that new names be added uniformly over the pages. Suppose that, initially, there is space for five additional listings per page. The sudden addition of a group of entries with the same or similar last names overruns the space left on the page. That page becomes full and there is no room for another entry.

The extra name could be moved to the next page, where there is still extra room. However, that movement requires an index change as well, because the last name on the current page is no longer the same as shown in the index (since that last name has been moved to the next page). One alternative is to provide an overflow area to hold such extra listings until a complete update of the phone book and indices is necessary. All such overflow entries are placed at the end of the book's section for their first letter. (If there is a sudden influx of families named Schwab, extras go at the end of the S section until it is time to redo the whole book.) The index needs an entry to indicate which names could be found in the overflow area and where that area is located. (All the Schwab entries have to be locatable, even though they are not in the expected place.)

Overall, this arrangement is somewhat complex. However, such a system allows an entry to be found simply, by first looking in the index and then turning directly to the correct page.

The organization just described is an indexed sequential organization. It works in the same general way as computerized indexed sequential files. All that remains now is to consider where the indices and overflow areas are kept and how records are allocated to parts of the storage device. For very large files it is also necessary to subdivide and index the index itself.

Descriptions of two approaches to indexed file access follow. One incorporates details of the storage device in the distribution of the records (ISAM), and the other keeps the logical grouping of records independent of physical storage (VSAM and SCOPE).

INDEXED SEQUENTIAL ACCESS METHOD (ISAM)

The indexed Sequential Access Method (ISAM), introduced by IBM in the early 1960s, uses overflow areas, much like the telephone book example. The use of ISAM in the IBM environment has largely been supplanted by the Virtual Storage Access Method (VSAM). ISAM is included here

Track 0				
Track 1	Record	Record	Record	Record
Track 2	Record	Record	Record	Record
Track 3	Record	Record	Record	Record
Track 4	Record	Record	Record	Record
Track 5	Record	Record	Record	Record
Track 6	Record	Record	Record	Record
Track 7	Record	Record	Record	Record
Track 8	Record	Record	Record	Record
Track 9				

Figure 8.1 A cylinder opened out

because of its use of overflow areas, because similar products are still widely used, and because it is relatively easy to understand. It provides a good introduction to other approaches to indexed sequential access.

Primary Data Area

ISAM is oriented toward the actual storage device on which it is implemented. For explanation and illustration, a file is assumed to be stored on a disk pack that has ten surfaces for holding data. Each cylinder contains ten tracks, numbered 0 through 9.

Some amount of disk storage space must be allocated for the file. For now, assume that the data fits easily on one cylinder. The file system, then, allocates one cylinder in response to programmer specification. The system also enters some information about the file, including its name, location and access privileges, into a directory, so that it can find the file when it is requested to do so. Now consider the one cylinder assigned to the file. Figure 8.1 illustrates the cylinder "unwrapped" to show all of the data it holds.

Track 0 of the cylinder is used for indexing and does not hold data. We return to it shortly. During file creation, data is written sequentially, beginning with track 1. Figure 8.2 contains a sample set of key values for records in a file to be created under ISAM organization. Each record has a particular field to be used as a key to the record. Only record keys are shown in illustrations, because showing complete records introduces too

```
1403   1440   1513   1524   1586   1590   1598   1610
1634   1652   1673   1690   1735   1746   1780   1810
```

Figure 8.2 Key values to initial records for an ISAM file

Track 0				
Track 1	1403	1440	1513	1524
Track 2	1586	1590	1598	1610
Track 3	1634	1652	1673	1690
Track 4	1735	1746	1780	1810
.				
.				
.				
Track 9				

Figure 8.3 Initial entries in the cylinder

much clutter. Though the rest of the record is not shown explicitly, it is assumed to be stored where its key is shown. Records are initially distributed over the available space. Some space—the last track(s) of the cylinder—is not used in storing data, but is reserved for later use as an overflow area.

The Track Index

Figure 8.3 shows the initial distribution of the sample data. An index into this file is placed on track 0. The index entry for each track identifies the highest key value to be found on that track. The initial track index is shown in Figure 8.4. For each track in the cylinder, there are two entries: a normal entry and an overflow entry. Each of these entries contains the location of the track that is described and the value of the highest key associated with that track. While there is no data in the overflow area, the overflow entry and the normal entry both have the same value for the highest key to be found on the track. The normal entry contains the track address, and the overflow entry contains a special value (a byte of all 1s, equal to 255 in decimal notation) to indicate that there is no data for this track in the overflow area.

When a record is read from an indexed sequential file, the track index is consulted. The first entry in the track index whose maximum key is greater than or equal to the key of the record being sought is located. The track associated with the key is then searched, in order to find the record. For example, reading the record with key equal to 1673 requires first

Track 0	1:1524	*:1524	2:1610	*:1610	3:1690	*:1690	4:1810	*:1810

Figure 8.4 Initial track index

searching the track index for the lowest maximum key that is greater than or equal to 1673; in this case, that is 1690. The track associated with that key is track 3 of the cylinder. On track 3, the records with keys equal to 1634 and 1652 are passed over and the record with key equal 1673 is found. An attempt to read a record with a nonexistent key proceeds in the same way: a search for a record with key equal to 1595 still begins by searching the track index. The smallest key greater than 1595 is 1610, and that points to track 2 of the cylinder. Track 2 contains records with keys 1586, 1590, 1598, and then 1610. Finding the record with key equal to 1598 implies that there is no record with key 1595. The read operation fails.

Record Insertion

When an ISAM file is updated, a record may be added to the primary storage area. Assume that the reason for attempting to read record 1595 is to establish that there is no record with that key prior to adding it. Once the read fails, it is safe to write the new record. The record is inserted on track 2 between the records with keys 1590 and 1598. The records with keys 1598 and 1610 must be moved to make room for the addition. There is no more space on the track, so record 1610 is moved to an overflow area. Record 1610 is placed on track 9 of the cylinder, the record 1598 is moved, and the new record is inserted.

Cylinder Overflow

Now, however, the track index is no longer correct. The highest key value associated with the track has been moved to the overflow area, and the highest key value found on the primary track is now 1598. The index is adjusted accordingly in Figure 8.5. The original maximum key value, 1610, remains the maximum key associated with track 2. It does not change unless the file is reorganized. However, the maximum key values for the primary and overflow areas associated with track 2 are now different. The index for the primary area shows the new maximum key on track 2. The overflow index shows where the overflow area is and what the maximum key value in the overflow area for track 2 is. (The first overflow position associated with track 2 is position 1 of track 9. The maximum value associated with track 2, now in the overflow area, is 1610.)

A read operation now occurs in the following way. To read record 1598, the system must first find that the appropriate maximum index key is associated with the primary area for tract 2. The record, if it exists, is on tract 2. An attempt to read 1608 reveals that that key is associated with track 2 but is larger than the maximum key on the primary track. If the

Track 0	1:1524	*:1524	2:1598	9-1:1610	3:1690	*:1690	4:1810	*:1810
Track 1	1403	1440	1513	1524				
Track 2	1586	1590	1595	1598				
Track 3	1634	1652	1673	1690				
Track 4	1735	1746	1780	1810				

.
.
.

Track 9	(2) 1610:#

Figure 8.5 *A cylinder with overflow*

record exists, it is on the overflow area. The overflow record pointer gives the location of the first record from track 2 in the overflow area. A search of that location reveals record 1610. Since 1610 is greater than 1608, the record does not exist. The # represents a null pointer in the area, indicating that there are no further records in the overflow area associated with track 2—none that are known, anyway, since this record has the key value identified as the maximum for track 2. However, if there were additional records for track 2 in the overflow area, the pointer field would be used to indicate the location of the next one.

The record with key value 1608 is added directly into the overflow area and becomes the first overflow record associated with track 2. It is placed in the next available space on track 9 and is given a pointer field value of 1, indicating that it is followed by the record in position 1 of the overflow track. The index for track 2 overflow records is adjusted to show the location of this new record as the beginning of the overflow list for track 2.

Records in the overflow area are associated with any of the tracks in the primary area. Therefore, they cannot simply be moved aside to add the new one. The overflow area is organized as a collection of linked lists. There is a separate linked list for each full track that is using the overflow area. Each entry in the overflow area comprises the record itself, including its key (shown with the key only), and a pointer to the next record belonging to the same track (see Figure 8.6).

If many additions are made and the linked lists become very long, the time required for finding a particular record may become unacceptably long. Furthermore, the overflow area itself may become full. When either of these conditions occurs, the file must be reorganized. During file reorganization, all records are written in primary storage areas, and the overflow area is cleared. A volatile file, one requiring frequent changes such as a list of subscribers or customers, may need frequent reorganizations.

226   Chapter 8

Track 0	1:1513	9-2:1524	2:1598	9-3:1610	3:1690	*:1690	4:1810	*:1810
Track 1	1400	1403	1440	1513				
Track 2	1586	1590	1595	1598				
Track 3	1634	1652	1673	1690				
Track 4	1735	1746	1780	1810				
⋮								
Track 9	(2) 1610 #	(1) 1524 #	(2) 1608 1					

Figure 8.6   *Overflow linked lists*

Independent Overflow Area

Many files are larger than one cylinder. In such files, each cylinder is organized as indicated previously. As an option, an additional type of overflow area can be allocated for such files. This area, called an independent overflow area, is located away from the prime data area, and is used to hold overflow records from all tracks of all cylinders. The advantage of the independent overflow area over overflow areas on each cylinder is that no space has to be reserved on cylinders that do not need overflow space. The disadvantage is that, since the area is separate from the prime data areas, a seek operation (head movement) is required for accessing the area. In most ISAM files, some cylinder overflow space is allocated, and an additional independent overflow area is available to use when the overflow area of some cylinders becomes full. The existence of the independent overflow area allows reorganization to be postponed, but does cause deterioration of access time for overflow records.

Record Deletion

When a record is deleted from an ISAM file, other records are not moved into the space that has been created. Instead, the record is marked as deleted by putting a byte of all 1s in a position recognized by the file system. The record is logically deleted, though it is still physically present. An added record may overwrite the deleted one only if it has the same key value as the deleted record. If a deleted record is bumped from prime storage, it is not copied to the overflow area unless it has the highest key value associated with the track. During sequential access to an ISAM file, a deleted record is skipped. However, random access to a record that has been deleted returns the record. The program must check the status of the record. (It is possible to "undelete" a record by changing the indicator byte.)

ISAM files may contain records of fixed or variable length. Fixed-length records can be processed more efficiently because it is easy to calculate where the next record begins. When a track full of records is read into main memory to be searched for a particular record whose key has been specified, it is possible to use a binary search on the records by their keys. If the records are of variable length, this cannot be done because the boundary between records cannot be determined. The length field from each record must be read before the starting location of the next record is known. On the other hand, fixed-length records can cause wasted space if the amount of data to be stored in each record varies greatly. For example, if a record of transactions against checking accounts is designed to be of fixed length, the length has to be large enough to accommodate the most active account. Space is wasted in the lightly used and average accounts. Processing efficiency and storage efficiency must be balanced in deciding when to use fixed- or variable-length records.

Cylinder Index

When a file requires multiple cylinders, it is necessary for the file system to know which cylinder to access for a particular record. Since different cylinders require different positions of the read/write head (seeks), it is important to locate the correct cylinder at once. A separate index is maintained to guide the file system to the correct cylinder. This is called the **cylinder index** and is organized much like the track index of each cylinder. The cylinder index shows the largest key value associated with each cylinder and the cylinder on which it is to be found. The cylinder index is maintained in an area separate from the cylinders.

Master Index

In very large files, the cylinder index itself becomes excessively large. It may, in fact, fill a number of tracks. Searching through the cylinder index becomes a time-consuming operation. A master index is then used to index the cylinder index. The master index contains the location of the track in the cylinder index and the maximum key associated with the cylinder index entries on that track. The master index is kept in main memory during file processing in order to minimize the time required to search it (see Figure 8.7).

Summary of ISAM Index Levels

In summary, the ISAM file organization forms a hierarchy of indices into a file. The most detailed index gives information about a single track of

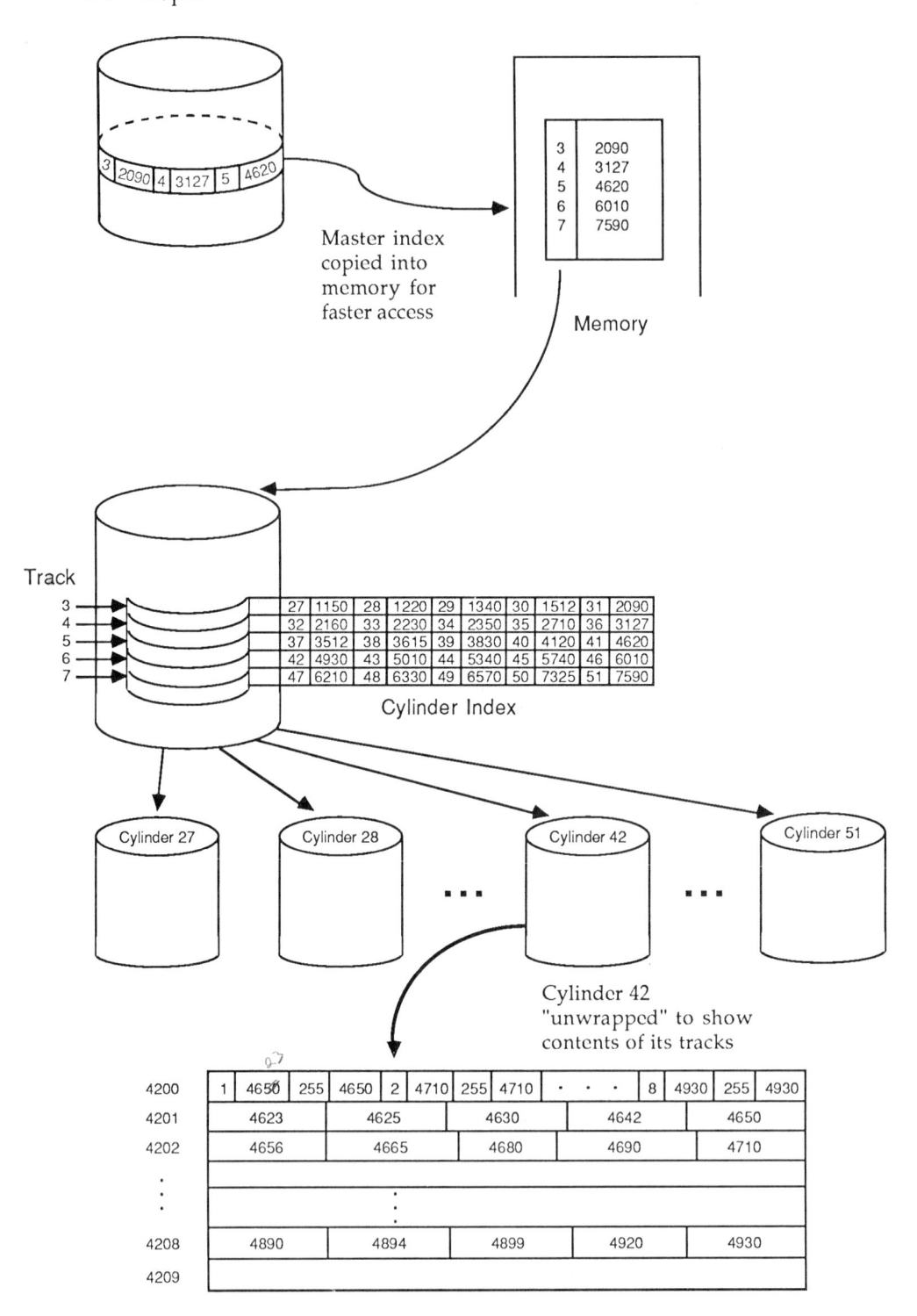

Figure 8.7 *A schematic view of an ISAM file with master, cylinder, and track indices*

data records. The cylinder index summarizes characteristics of entire cylinders. The master index contains maximum key values associated with multiple cylinders. The entire system is influenced by the size of each track and cylinder in the file storage device in use.

VIRTUAL BULK STORAGE

This section describes an approach to indexed file storage that separates the details of the storage device from the file organization. At some level, the exact location of the record in terms of cylinder and track must be known. However, these details can be left to modern disk management systems that can be altered when the storage devices in use are changed, without affecting the logical organization of the file.

Both VSAM of IBM and SCOPE of Control Data Corporation specify file organization in these logical terms, leaving the physical details to an underlying system. In both systems records are collected together in groups. A group of records stored together as a unit is called a SCOPE Indexed Sequential (SIS) Data Block by CDC, and a Control Interval by IBM. Both systems organize the block, or interval, into three parts: the data records are placed at the beginning of the storage area; information about the records is stored at the end of the area; and the middle section is empty and available for the addition of more records. Originally, when the file is created, the amount of space to be left empty for additions is specified.

SCOPE Indexed Sequential (SIS) Files

SIS files are indexed by SIS Index Blocks. A SIS Index Block contains pairs of values: a key and an address. The key is the lowest key associated with a group of records stored in a particular data block. The address indicates where that data block begins. Higher levels of index blocks may be used to form a tree of key/pointer pairs. At each level, an index block contains pointers to a smaller portion of the file than the level above, allowing the record to be more precisely located. A file with three levels of index is shown in Figure 8.8. A SIS file may have up to 63 levels of indexing.

Virtual Storage Access Method (VSAM) Files

VSAM control intervals themselves are collected into control areas. Each control interval may have empty space to allow for file expansion. Each control area may have empty control intervals also. When a control interval does become full, it is split. Half of the records remain in the original control interval and the rest are moved to an empty control

230 Chapter 8

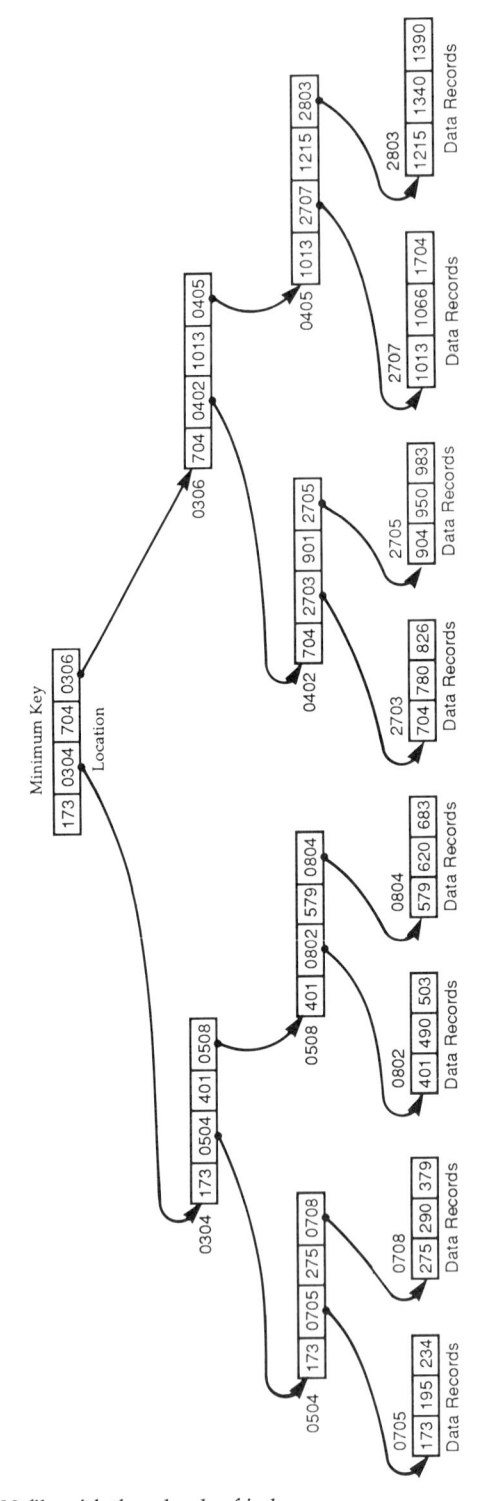

Figure 8.8 A SIS file with three levels of index

interval in the control area. Each of the resulting control intervals then has space left for further expansion. Locating records within the control area is accomplished with the use of a control index. Each control area has an entry in the control index. Within the index entry are key/address pairs. The key is the largest key associated with a particular control interval, and the address is the location of the beginning of the control interval.

When the number of control areas becomes large, the number of index entries to search becomes too large and access is slow. Thus, like ISAM and SIS files, VSAM files have levels of indexing. Higher-level indices point to lower-level indices until the pointer to the control interval is found. VSAM files can have up to three levels of indexing.

Entry Sequenced and Relative Record Data Sets

Three types of VSAM files are defined: KSDS (Key Sequenced Data Set), ESDS (Entry Sequenced Data Set), and RRDS (Relative Record Data Set). ESDS and RRDS are VSAM implementations of sequential organization and relative organization, respectively. In an ESDS, records are loaded sequentially in contiguous storage locations. An individual record can be accessed directly if its RBA (Relative Byte Address) is known. The RBA is the displacement of the record from the beginning of the space allocated to the file. However, sequential access is most convenient for ESDS files, and this form of organization is used to provide the advantages of sequential organization and access in files created under the VSAM system. Similarly, RRDS is provided to allow relative file organization techniques to be used within the VSAM system. A record is accessed by providing its relative position in the file, just as in the relative organization considered in the last chapter.

Key Sequenced Data Sets

Control Intervals and Control Areas

By far, the most common form of VSAM file is the KSDS. In a KSDS, records are initially loaded into control intervals. The control intervals are themselves parts of a **control area**. A control area is never larger than a cylinder on the storage device used. The data control interval size is a multiple of 512 bytes and may be up to 32K bytes long. Figure 8.9 illustrates a VSAM KSDS organization.

Control Interval Definition Field, Record Definition Field

Figure 8.10 shows the content of the Control Interval Definition Field and the Record Definition Fields found in each control interval. The purpose of the CIDF is to keep track of space used within the control interval, for instance, the amount of unused space. An RDF appears for each record in the control interval if the records are of variable length; if

232   Chapter 8

Data Records (Keys shown)						Unused Space	RDF= for records whose keys are shown						CIDF
27	35	42	50	58	63		63	58	50	42	35	27	

Figure 8.9   Data control interval with six records

(a) CIDF (Control Interval Definition Field)

(Binary value) = total displacement in bytes to beginning of unused space in the control interval	(Binary value) = total number of bytes of unused space in the C.I.
0 15	16 32

(b) RDF (Record Definition Field)

```
          0                        1              2
┌──────┬──────┬──────┬──────┬──────┬──────┬─────────────────────────────────┐
│Unused│Paired│Spanned│Length/│RRDs │Unused│ Length of data record OR number │
│      │      │Record│Count │Only │      │ of consecutive records of the   │
│      │      │      │      │     │      │ same length                     │
└──────┴──────┴──────┴──────┴──────┴──────┴─────────────────────────────────┘
```

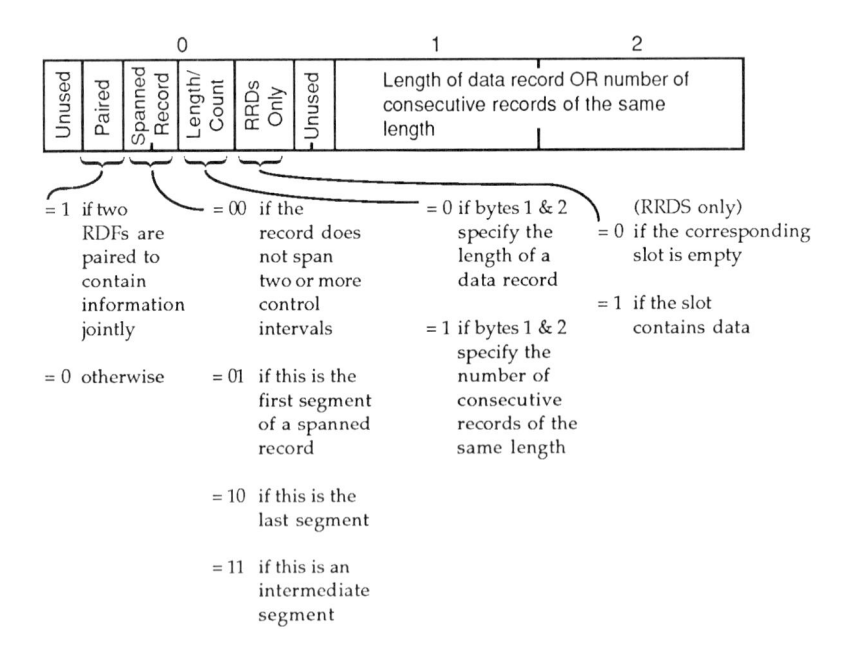

= 1 if two   = 00 if the   = 0 if bytes 1 & 2   (RRDS only)
     RDFs are   record does   specify the   = 0 if the corresponding
     paired to   not span   length of a   slot is empty
     contain   two or more   data record
     information   control   = 1 if the slot
     jointly   intervals   = 1 if bytes 1 & 2   contains data
                                                           specify the
= 0 otherwise   = 01 if this is the   number of
                                  first segment   consecutive
                                  of a spanned   records of the
                                  record   same length

                             = 10 if this is the
                                  last segment

                             = 11 if this is an
                                  intermediate
                                  segment

Figure 8.10   CIDF (Control Interval Definition Field) and RDF (Record Definition Field)

the records are of fixed length, only two RDFs are needed for each control interval.

Index Control Intervals

The index level that contains pointers to the data control intervals, and therefore to the records of the files, is called a **sequence set**. Figure 8.11 shows the details of an index control interval. The header field in an index control interval includes:

- The level number for this index (1 for the sequence set; successively higher for higher-level indices)
- A displacement value that tells where in this index record the pointers to control intervals are to be found
- The length of the index record
- The amount of space in the index record taken up by pointers to free control intervals
- A horizontal pointer.

The horizontal pointer is used in sequential record retrieval. Records within a data control interval are sequentially ordered by key, but the control intervals are not necessarily in any sequential order. Sequential processing, beginning with any particular record, proceeds as follows: The various levels of index are traversed until a pointer is found to the data control interval containing the specified record. Successive records are processed in order until all the records in the data control interval have been used. The horizontal pointer of the sequence control interval that pointed to this data control interval is then used to locate the next logical control interval, and processing continues.

Random Access

Random access to a record in a KSDS VSAM file consists of following the index pointers until the data control interval containing the specified record is found. The records within the control interval are then examined in sequence to find the one whose key matches the key specified for the access. The process is like that used for ISAM file access. The differences are in the organization and use of storage areas, and in the maintenance of record keys. The methods for organizing keys and maintaining the indices

Header	Pointers to unused control intervals in a control area	Unused space in this Index control Interval	Pointers to control Intervals with data in a control area	RDF for this Index CI	CIDF for this Index CI
	PTR PTR PTR PTR PTR		PTR PTR PTR PTR PTR		

Figure 8.11 Structure of an index control interval

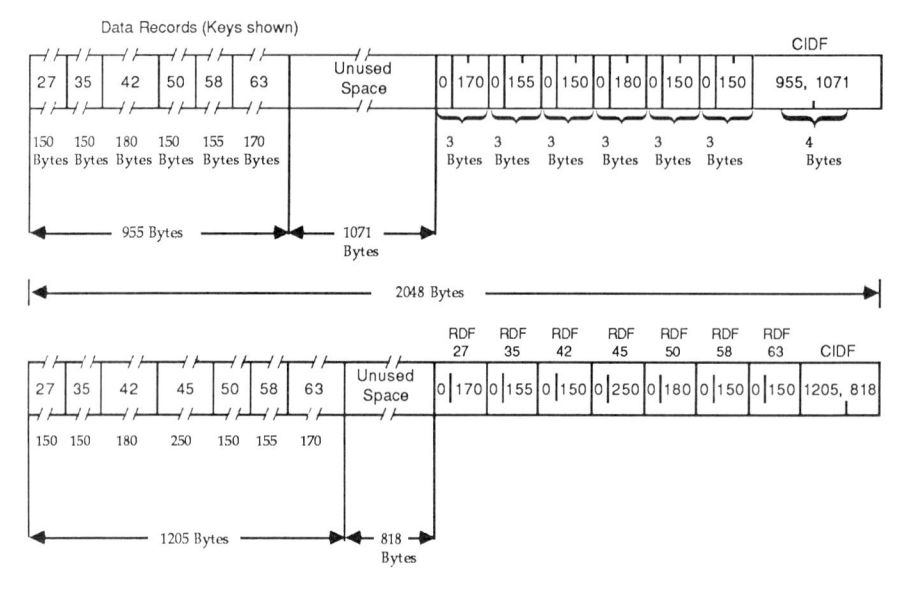

Figure 8.12 A data control interval before and after inserting record 45 (the first byte of each RDF is 0. See Figure 8.10.)

in a form that supports efficient use of the file are described in the B-Trees section of this chapter.

Insertion and Deletion

Addition of a record to a data control interval maintains the sequential order by key of records within the interval. After the appropriate control interval for the record is identified by searching the index, the CIDF of the control interval is examined to see if there is room for an additional record. If there is room, the existing records are examined to find the proper location for the new record. When the right location has been found, any records that have higher key values than the new record are moved over. In addition, if the records are of variable length, and thus have individual RDFs, the RDFs corresponding to the records that are moved must also be moved. The new record and its RDF are then inserted. Figure 8.12 shows the insertion of a variable-length record into a control interval. When a record is deleted from a KSDS VSAM file, the space is recovered and available for use with future additions.

Control Interval Split

If the control interval does not have room for the new record, an additional control interval in the same control area is used. Half of the records of the full control interval are moved to the new control interval. The new record is inserted in its proper position, after any necessary movement of records has been completed. Figure 8.13 shows the insertion of a variable length record into a control interval when a split is required. Using a new control interval requires updating the index entry as well.

Control Area Split

If no other control interval is available in the control area when a split is required, a new control area is needed. When this happens, a request is made to the file system to allocate space for an additional control area and assign it to this file. (VSAM uses the term **cluster** to refer to all the parts of a file, including the data control intervals, the control areas, and the index areas.) A partial control area cannot be allocated. When a new control area is allocated, the full control area is split; half of its control intervals are moved to the new control area and half remain. Now both the new and old control areas are half full and have room for additions before another split is needed. Index entries are updated accordingly.

VSAM-SIS Overflow Handling

The type of file organization illustrated by SIS and VSAM has no overflow areas for adding records. Instead, each record is incorporated into the prime storage area. When the prime storage area is full and can accept no

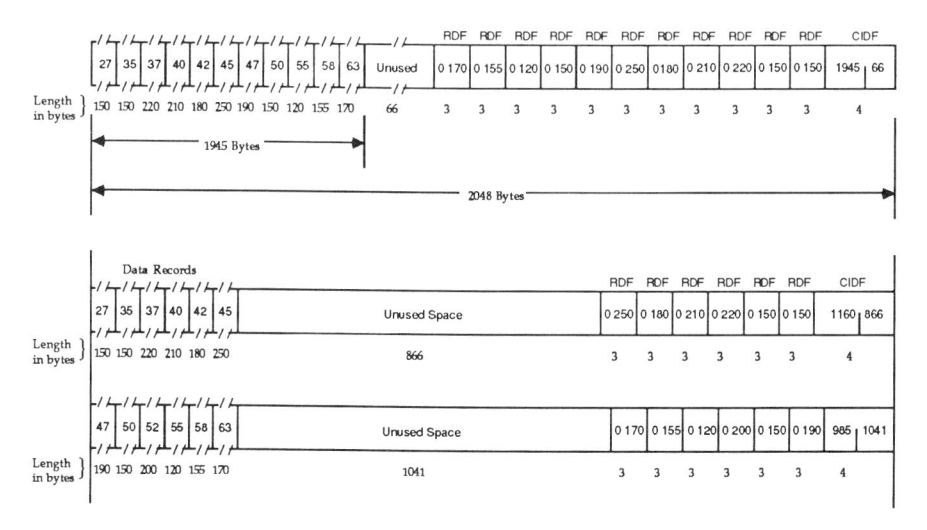

Figure 8.13 A data control interval split. Splitting a data control interval is possible only if an unused control interval exists in the control area. If no empty control interval exists, the control area must split, producing two control areas, each with empty control intervals. The control interval then splits as shown.

more records, the prime area is split. The splitting of the prime area involves a time-consuming process—copying half the records in one area into another area. However, although this is time-consuming, it is done only when a new record causes a split, and it produces additional space that allows more records to be added before another split will be needed.

In contrast, the organization typified by ISAM, which uses overflow areas, does not require time-consuming, prime area splits, but does require chained searching of the overflow area for reading records. When the number of records in the overflow area becomes large, the time required for each read operation becomes significant. Since reading is much more common than an addition that causes a split, the expanding organization of SIS and VSAM results in better performance. That performance, however, is completely dependent upon the efficiency with which the indices can be searched and the location of the record determined. A great deal of attention has been directed toward methods for organizing and maintaining indices. Some fruits of that work are the subjects of the next section.

B-TREES

Throughout this text, methods are featured that arrange keys in a tree structure to reduce the time needed to search for a record or sort a file. Another method for storing and processing files based on a tree structure, and two variations, are introduced in this section. The fundamental organization is called a B-tree. Its modifications, the B*-tree and especially the B$^+$-tree, are the current *de facto* standards for index maintenance and access in database systems. All three techniques feature limited search time and reasonably simple updating procedures.

Balanced Trees

In illustrations of trees of record keys and associated pointers there is a balance in the distribution of records throughout the space allocated for the file and in the distribution of keys in various levels of indexing. The benefits of this hierarchical arrangement of keys come from the fact that at each level in the tree, there is a substantial reduction in the number of file records still in consideration for accessing. These benefits are only realized when the balance for the distribution of keys is maintained throughout the life of the file, regardless of additions and deletions.

In Figure 8.14 a small file of six records is shown with two levels of indexing. Figure 8.15 shows the result of adding two records (key values 12 and 20) and deleting two records (key values 39 and 64) without balancing. The file still has six records, but now the two-level index is nearly useless. The first level of index, instead of dividing all the records

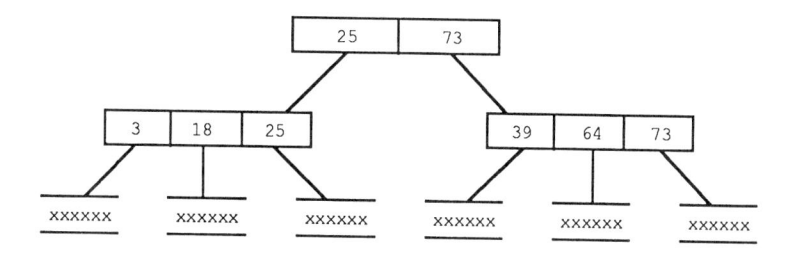

Figure 8.14 Two levels of indexing for a small file

into two groups of approximately equal size, only separates one record from the five others. The group of records indexed by the record containing keys 3, 12, 18, 20, and 25 includes nearly the whole file.

When a similar situation arises in large files, all the benefits of the multiple-level indices are lost, but the overhead involved in storing, updating, and stepping through them remains. Efficient use of multi-level indices requires rules for maintaining a balanced tree structure. A B-tree meets this requirement because it is always balanced.

One of the important characteristics of a binary search tree as an efficient search method is that the number of comparisons needed to find a particular entry is related to the height of the tree. Each time the search moves down a level from the root toward the terminal or leaf nodes, the number of entries still to be considered is cut in half. This characteristic takes a more general form in a B-tree and its two modifications.

Although similarities exist between B-trees and binary trees, there are also significant differences, such as the requirement of the binary tree that no node have more than two descendants. The maximum number of descendants from a node of a B-tree is usually more than two; it is determined by the "order" of the B-tree.

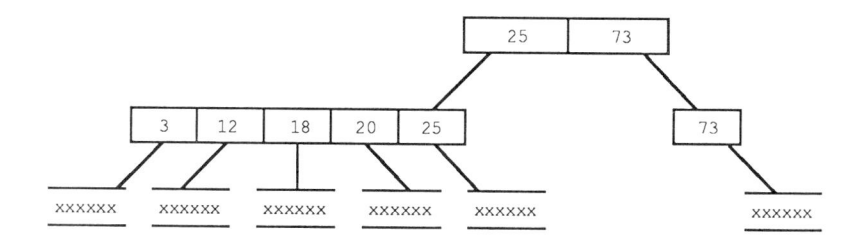

Figure 8.15 Unbalanced indices

B-Tree Properties

In general, a B-tree of order n has the following properties:

1. The root has at least two descendants, or is a leaf.
2. Each node has no more than n descendants.
3. Each node that is not a root or a leaf has at least $\lceil n/2 \rceil$ descendants.
4. All leaf nodes are at the same level
5. A nonleaf node with k descendants contains $k-1$ key values.

A B-tree of order 5 is shown in Figure 8.16. It has the following properties:

- Each node contains key values, addresses of their records in the file, and pointers to nodes at the next level. The node format is
  $P_0\ K_1\ A_1\ P_1\ K_2\ A_2\ P_2 \ldots K_j\ A_j\ P_j$,
  where $0 < j < n$, P = a pointer, K = a key value, and A = the address of the record with key value K. Pointers P in leaf nodes are null.
- The root has at least two descendants (rule 1) and no more than five descendants (rule 2).
- Each interior node (that is, not a leaf and not the root) has at least three descendants (rule 3), but no more than five (rule 2).
- Any node with k descendants contains $k-1$ key values, $k=3,4,5$ (rule 5).

Each node of a B-tree is stored as a record in an index file.

Retrieval

Retrieving a record from the indexed data file consists of several steps. First, the root node of the B-tree is read into memory from the index file. The index entries in the root node are searched. Since the entries are in sorted order, a high-speed binary search can be used. If the key value of the record being sought is found in the root node, the address of the corresponding record is found with it and the desired record is read from the file storage device. If the key value is not found in the root, it may be in one of the root's descendants. The root contains a pointer (address) to an index file entry that indexes records whose key values are less than the first entry in the root, another pointer to a different index entry that indexes records whose key values are less than the second key in the root, but greater than the first, and so on. Finally, there is a pointer to the index entry that indexes all key values greater than the last key value in the root.

Indexed Sequential Access 239

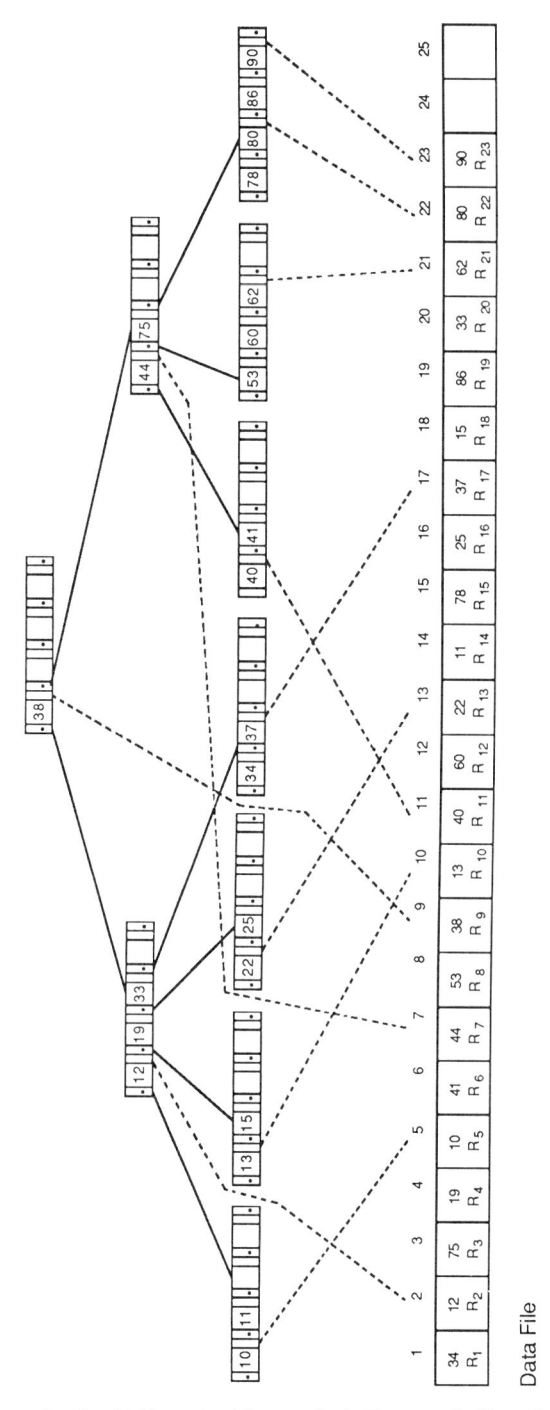

Figure 8.16 B-tree of order 5. Record addresses in indices are indicated by dotted lines to the records in a data file. (Only some record addresses are included.)

If the desired record key is not in the root, the appropriate next-level index entry is read into memory. It is searched and the desired key value is found or another index entry is read. The process continues until the value is found or a leaf node is read. Pointers in a leaf node are null, indicating no additional index records. Thus, if the desired key is not found by the time the leaf node has been examined, the record is not in the file.

Reading the records containing index information is a time-consuming process. The fewer such records that must be read and searched, the faster the desired record is available for the program. Increasing the number of entries in each index record reduces the number of index records that must be processed, because it decreases the height of the B-tree. However, the index entries must be stored together on the file system as a block to be read into memory at one time. Constraints imposed by the system on block size and I/O operations determine the appropriate index record size.

Tree Capacity

Consider a B-tree of order n. What is the smallest number of nodes that such a tree will have if it is of height m? The root is a node and it must have at least two descendants. Each of those two must have at least $\lceil n/2 \rceil$ descendants. Each of those descendants must also have at least $\lceil n/2 \rceil$ descendants, and so on. Thus, at level zero there is one node, the root. At level 1 there are at least two nodes; at level 2, at least $2 * \lceil n/2 \rceil$ nodes; at level 3, at least

$$(2 * \lceil n/2 \rceil) * \lceil n/2 \rceil = 2 * (\lceil n/2 \rceil)^2$$

nodes. At level 4 there are at least

$$(2 * (\lceil n/2 \rceil)^2) * \lceil n/2 \rceil = 2 * (\lceil n/2 \rceil)^3$$

nodes. Since the root is at level zero, the leaves are at level m of a tree of height m. The total minimum number of interior nodes is the sum of all the levels from 0 (the root) to $m-1$:

$$1 + \sum_{j=1}^{m-1} 2 * (\lceil n/2 \rceil)^{j-1}$$

The descendants of level $m-1$ are the leaf nodes. Thus there are

$$2 * (\lceil n/2 \rceil)^{m-1}$$

leaf nodes. The total minimum number of nodes in a B-tree of order n and height m is then

$$1 + \sum_{j=1}^{m} 2 * (\lceil n/2 \rceil)^{j-1}$$

As an example, suppose a B-tree of order 8 has height 5. Then $\lceil n/2 \rceil = 4$ and the minimum number of interior nodes is

$$1 + 2*4^0 + 2*4^1 + 2*4^2 + 2*4^3 = 171.$$

The minimum number of leaf nodes is

$$2 * 4^4 = 512.$$

Of principal interest is the number of records that are accessible by a B-tree of a particular height. That depends on the number of key values contained in the tree. Each node of the tree, except the root and the leaves, contains at least $\lceil n/2 \rceil - 1$ key values. The root and the leaf nodes each contain at least one value. Therefore, a B-tree of height m contains at least the number of key values indicated by

$$k = 1 + \sum_{j=1}^{m-1} [2 * \lceil n/2 \rceil^{j-1}) * (\lceil n/2 \rceil - 1)] + 2 * \lceil n/2 \rceil^{m-1}$$

Simplifying the summation yields

$$k + 1 = 4 * \lceil n/2 \rceil^{m-1}$$

as the minimum number of key values contained in a tree of height m. If the number of key values is specified, then the maximum height of the tree needed to address them is found by solving the above equation for m:

$$m <= 1 + \log_{\lceil n/2 \rceil} \left(\frac{k+1}{4}\right)$$

To get a firmer idea of what this means, suppose a file with 39,062,499 different key values is indexed with a B-tree of order 50. Then the largest number of times required to read an index record is

$$1 + \log_{\lceil \frac{50}{2} \rceil} \left(\frac{39,062,499+1}{4}\right)$$

which is

$$1 + \log\lceil 25\rceil 9{,}765{,}625 = 1 + 5 = 6$$

since $9{,}765{,}625 = 25^5$. As another example, suppose a B-tree of order 200 stores (4,000,000 - 1) key values. Then any value can be found in no more than

$$1 + \log\lceil 200/2\rceil ((4{,}000{,}000{,}196\ 1 + 1)/4) = 1 + 3 = 4 \text{ key searches}$$

since $1{,}000{,}000 = 100^3$.

In order to retain the advantages of the B-tree, the indices must remain in B-tree form throughout all insertions and deletions to the file. This requires a balancing procedure as part of the insertion and deletion algorithms. The B-tree is organized to facilitate these processes.

The following examples illustrate insertion and deletion in B-trees. The two modifications, B^+-trees and B^*-trees, are then described and insertion and deletion are exemplified. Of the three versions, B^+-trees are the most common in applications. For that reason, algorithms are included only for B^+-trees.

Insertion

Consider the B-tree of order 3 in Figure 8.17. For convenience, address fields are not included. Each node contains at least one but not more than two key values. Each node except the leaf nodes has at least two but not more than three descendants.

First, add a key value of 340. Take the left branch from the root, the middle branch from the next node, and the right branch from the next. The leaf node has room for an additional key, so 340 is inserted. Figure 8.18 shows only the nodes along the path taken to insert 340.

Next, insert a key whose value is 460. Again take the left branch from the root, then the right branch, and again the right branch to reach the leaf node containing values 446 and 481. There is no room here for another key value. To make room, the leaf node splits. Half the leaf node key values go in the left node after splitting, half go in the right node, and a value moves up to the parent node to separate the two leaves (see Figure 8.19). In this case, the inserted value, 460, falls in the middle, and it is the one to move up to the parent. Since there is room for another value in the parent node, the key is inserted.

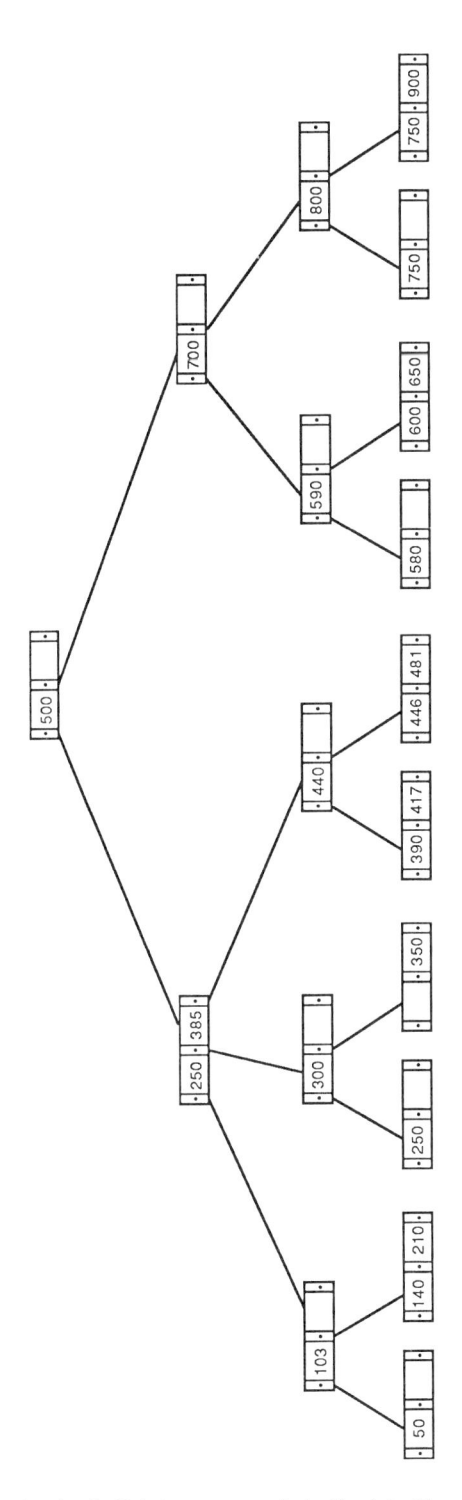

Figure 8.17 *B-tree of order 3. Pointers to records in the data file are not shown.*

244   Chapter 8

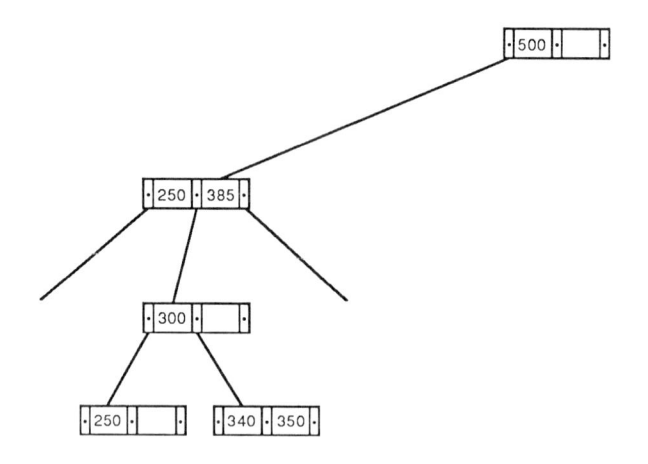

Figure 8.18 Insertion of 340. Only the search path is shown.

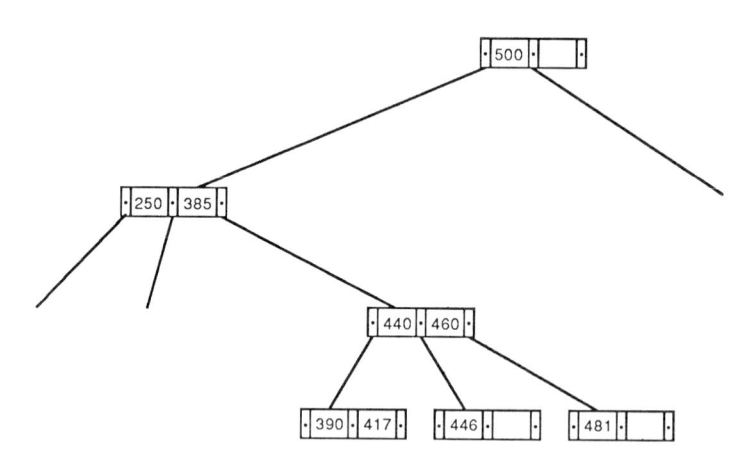

Figure 8.19 Insertion of 460. Only the search path and nodes affected by the split are shown.

Finally, consider the insertion of key value 425. In Figure 8.19, follow the branches to the leaf node containing 390 and 417. The node is full and must be split. This time the added value goes in the new right node and the value 417 moves up to the parent node. The parent is also full (it contains 440 and 460). It splits into

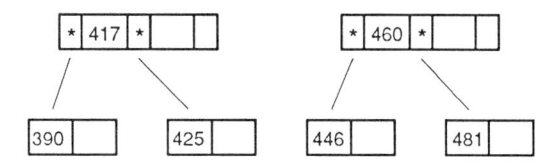

```
   *|417|*              *|460|*
   /      \             /      \
 |390|   |425|        |446|   |481|
```

and key value 440 moves up to the next parent. However, that parent node is also full (it contains 250 and 385). The parent splits and the key value 385 is moved up one level. This time the node in which a new key is inserted is the root. The root node has space and the insertion is made, yielding the tree of Figure 8.20. Had there been no space in the root, it would have split just as the other nodes did. The result, in that case, is an additional level added to the tree.

Notice that each time a node splits, two nodes that are only half full replace it. After a split it is unlikely that the node is split again for some time. Of course, the more room there is in each node (that is, the higher the order of the B-tree) the more empty space is produced by each split.

Deletion

Deleting a key from a B-tree is slightly more complex than adding a key. In order to maintain balance the B-tree structure rules must be followed.

Again refer to Figure 8.17. If the record whose key value is 210 is deleted from the file, the altered index is easily produced. The node containing 140 and 210 becomes a node containing only 140. No other change is required.

Suppose, however, that the key value 103 must be removed. Simply removing that value from its node leaves a node with no key and no way to choose the correct path to its descendants. The value 103 is replaced by the next highest key value in the file. This is found by following the branch to the right of 103 and then following all left branches from there to a leaf node. In the example, the first node encountered is a leaf, and so its leftmost value (140) becomes the replacement for 103.

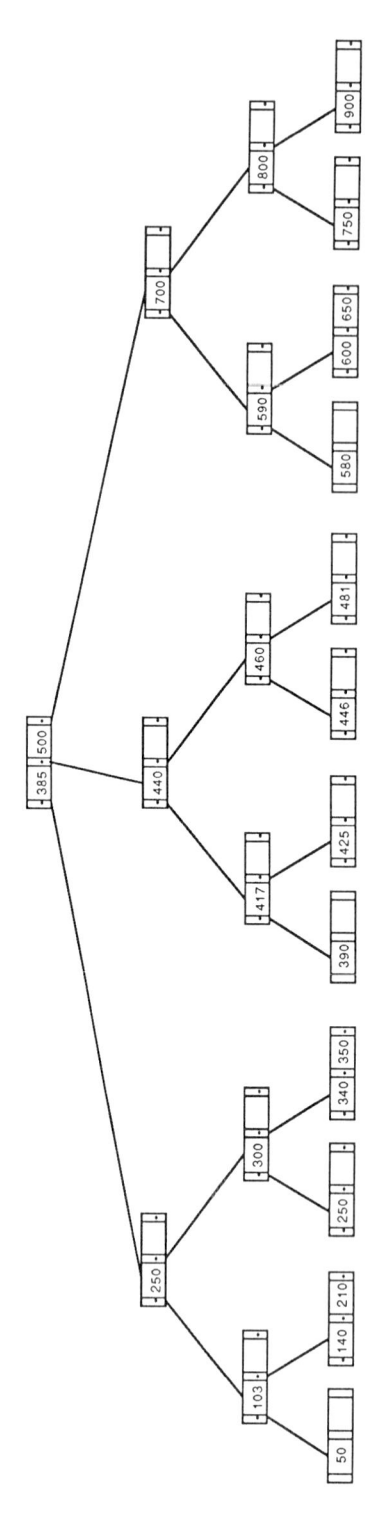

Figure 8.20 B-tree of Figure 8.18 after insertion of 425. Pointers to records are not shown.

Thus, the three nodes

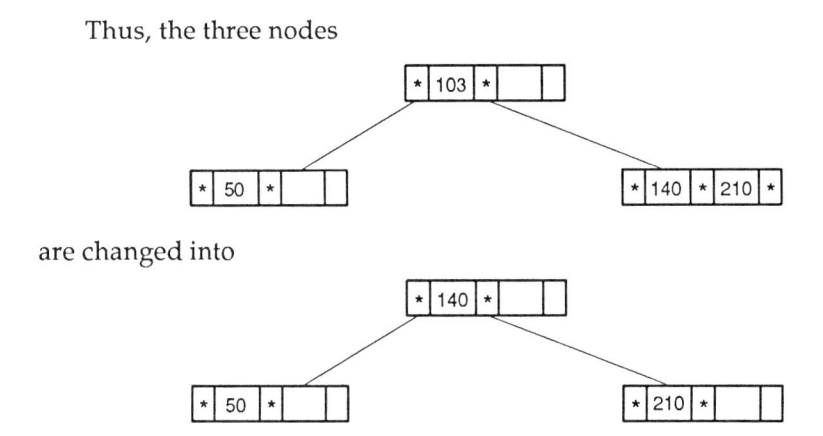

```
              * 103 *

    * 50 *              * 140 * 210 *
```

are changed into

```
              * 140 *

    * 50 *              * 210 *
```

Sometimes moving a key from a leaf node to a higher level may leave the leaf with fewer than the minimum required values (one for the order 3 tree). Consider what happens if key 580 is deleted. Key 590 replaces 580, producing an empty node. The other descendant of the parent node is used to provide values so that the key value in the parent is between the two descendants. Thus, 600 is in the parent node, 590 in the left descendant, and 650 in the right descendant.

Deletions in a very sparsely populated tree can lead to very extensive redistribution of key values. In general, however, the redistribution causes each node to have more than its minimum number of entries and thus reduces the likelihood of further adjustment. This cannot be shown convincingly with the small order 3 example, but can be seen by working through an example with a higher order, such as 5.

B^+-TREES

An important variation of a B-tree is called a **B^+-tree.** It is implemented frequently in databases and applications such as CDC's SIS files and IBM's VSAM files, where an index to a large file is required. Nonterminal nodes constitute the index which is stored separately from the file. Terminal (leaf) nodes contain blocks of records in the file or the addresses of records.

Like a B-tree, the B^+-tree has nodes at least half full. One of the differences is that leaf nodes are linked in order of key values. This linkage permits sequential processing of the values. The other difference is that the interior nodes do not contain addresses of records in the file. The nodes simply facilitate locating the desired key value and its record address contained in a leaf node. As a consequence, all key values must appear in leaf nodes. Another consequence is fewer file accesses, and therefore shorter search time, because B^+-tree interior nodes can contain more key values in the same amount of space than B-tree nodes. In the same space occupied by two addresses in a B-tree interior node, a B$^+$-tree can hold an additional key value and pointer.

B$^+$-trees are commonly implemented without the P_0 pointer. Thus, all nonterminal nodes contain the same number of key values as pointers. The order of the B$^+$-tree is the maximum number of pointers (and key values) a node can contain. For example, each interior node and leaf of a B$^+$-tree of order 5 has at least $\lceil \frac{5}{2} \rceil -1 = 2$, and at most 5, key values. A root has one to five values.

The nonterminal node format is

$c\ h\ K_1\ P_1\ K_2\ P_2 \ldots K_j\ P_j,$

where c is a counter that indicates the number of key values in the node ($c = j$) and h is an integer determined as follows. For each leaf node, $h = 1$. Parents of leaf nodes have $h = 2$. Parents of those parents have $h = 3$, and so on. The root contains the largest value of h. Each K_i is the largest value in the descendant pointed to by P_i. The extra pointer P_0 is not stored in the node, but is often defined in programs to point to a value smaller than any possible key value. The space in the node is used to hold the c and h fields.

The leaf node format is

$c\ h\ K_1\ A_1\ K_2\ A_2 \ldots K_j\ A_j\ P$

where $0 < j < n$, as in leaf nodes of B-trees, c and h are the same as above, and the A's are addresses of records in the file. P is a pointer to the leaf node containing the next larger key value.

Insertion

Insertion of a record into a B$^+$-tree requires searching through the indices until a specific leaf node is encountered. A search of this node either produces the key value and the address of the corresponding record, or identifies where in the node the key value and record address are to be inserted. The process can be as straightforward as adding the value and address to the leaf node and making no other changes in the B$^+$-tree. At the other extreme, however, insertion could require node splitting and changes in every index level. Usually, insertions cause relatively little disruption of indices.

Suppose the file of records with key values

20, 10, 90, 60, 40, 50, 70, 30, 80, 25, 55, 65, 95

```
    ┌─┬─┬──┬─┬──┬─┬──┬─┬──┬─┬─┐
    │4│1│10│·│20│·│60│·│90│·│*│
    └─┴─┴──┴─┴──┴─┴──┴─┴──┴─┴─┘
```

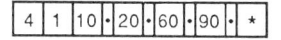

(a) Leaf node after inserting first four key values

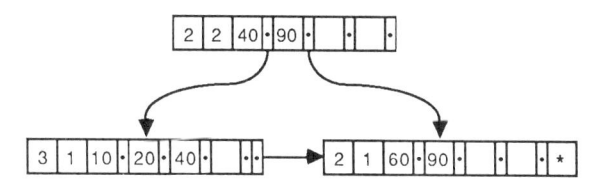

```
              ┌─┬─┬──┬─┬──┬─┬─┬─┐
              │2│2│40│·│90│·│·│·│
              └─┴─┴──┴─┴──┴─┴─┴─┘
              /                 \
┌─┬─┬──┬─┬──┬─┬──┬─┬─┬─┐   ┌─┬─┬──┬─┬──┬─┬─┬─┬─┐
│3│1│10│·│20│·│40│·│·│·│──▶│2│1│60│·│90│·│·│·│*│
└─┴─┴──┴─┴──┴─┴──┴─┴─┴─┘   └─┴─┴──┴─┴──┴─┴─┴─┴─┘
```

(b) Splitting after inserting 40

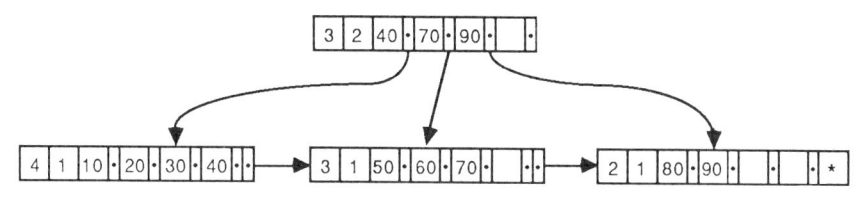

```
                    ┌─┬─┬──┬─┬──┬─┬──┬─┬─┐
                    │3│2│40│·│70│·│90│·│·│
                    └─┴─┴──┴─┴──┴─┴──┴─┴─┘

┌─┬─┬──┬─┬──┬─┬──┬─┬──┬─┬─┐  ┌─┬─┬──┬─┬──┬─┬──┬─┬─┐  ┌─┬─┬──┬─┬──┬─┬─┬─┬─┐
│4│1│10│·│20│·│30│·│40│·│·│─▶│3│1│50│·│60│·│70│·│·│─▶│2│1│80│·│90│·│·│·│*│
└─┴─┴──┴─┴──┴─┴──┴─┴──┴─┴─┘  └─┴─┴──┴─┴──┴─┴──┴─┴─┘  └─┴─┴──┴─┴──┴─┴─┴─┴─┘
```

(c) Splitting after inserting 50, 70, 30, 80

Figure 8.21 (a)-(c) Growth of a B^+-tree of order 4

is to be stored as a B^+-tree of order 4. The first value, 20, is inserted into an empty leaf node because the tree grows from the bottom up, as indicated in the sequence in Figure 8.21(a)-(f). After four insertions, the leaf appears as in part (a) of the figure, where the * indicates a null pointer. Addresses to the records in the file are omitted to show the process more clearly.

Figure 8.21(b) shows the effects of inserting the next key value, 40. The counter in the leaf is 4, which is its maximum value. An empty node is linked to the leaf, and the four key values 10, 20, 60, and 90, and their record addresses, are distributed between the two leaves. The left node contains the $\lceil 4/2 \rceil = 2$ lowest key values, and the right node gets the remaining two values. This process is called **splitting**. The new value, 40, is inserted in the appropriate node. Counter and pointer fields are adjusted and the h field in the new right leaf is set to 1. An empty node is made the parent of the two leaves and the largest value from each leaf is inserted. Pointers to the leaves, but no record addresses, are added. The counter and h fields are set to 2. The new node is the root of the tree.

Figure 8.21(c) shows the tree after the next four key values are inserted. The value 50 is inserted by comparing it to the values 40 and 90 in the root. Since $40 < 50 \leq 90$, the pointer associated with 90 is followed to

250   Chapter 8

(d) Splitting after insertion of 25

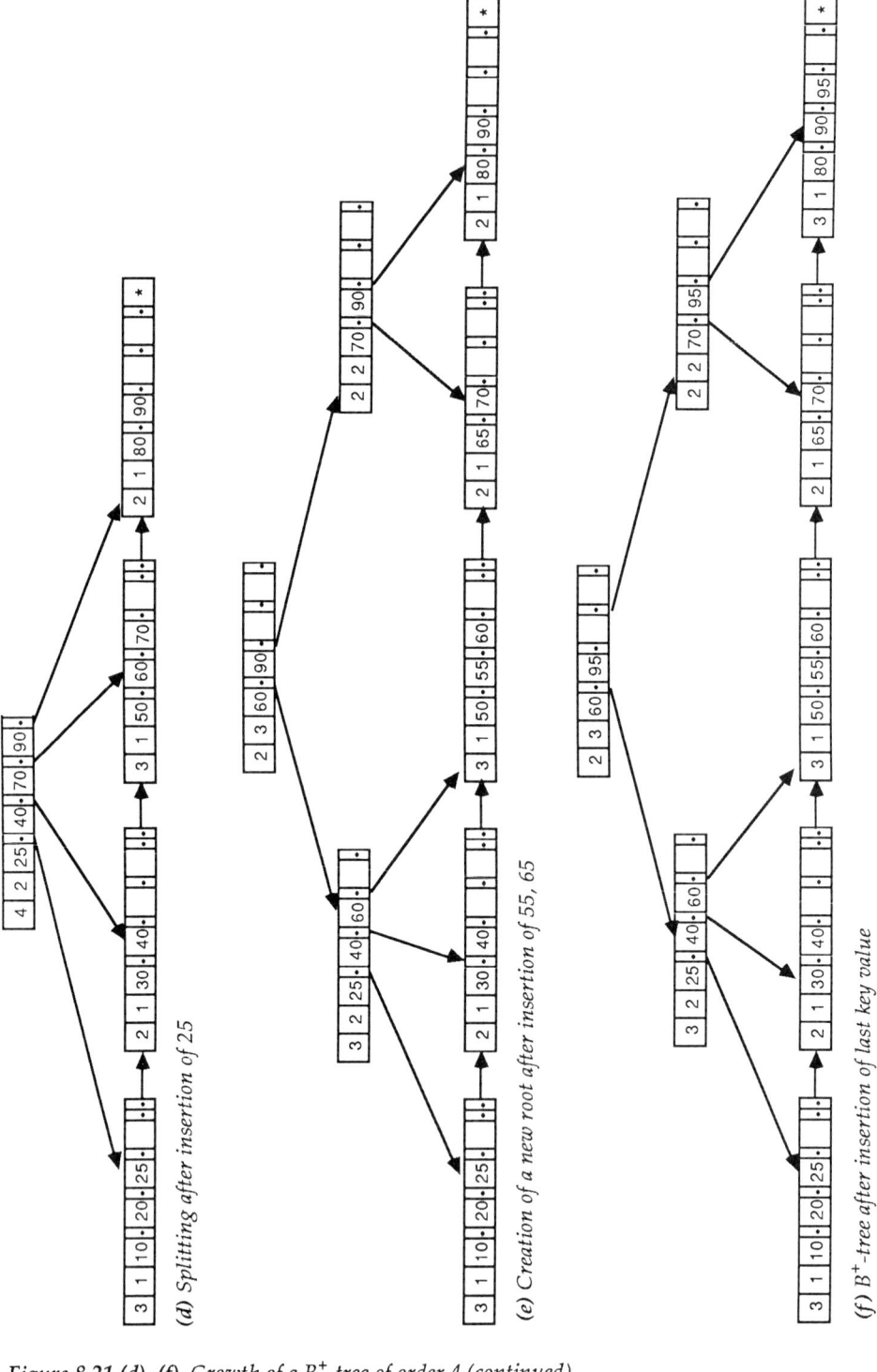

(e) Creation of a new root after insertion of 55, 65

(f) B$^+$-tree after insertion of last key value

Figure 8.21 (d)–(f) Growth of a B$^+$-tree of order 4 (continued)

the leaf and 50 is inserted in order. The leaf's counter is incremented to 3, but no other changes are necessary. The same process places 70 in the right leaf. The key value 30 goes into the left leaf because 30 < 40. When 80 is inserted, the right leaf splits and the key value 70 is copied into the parent, incrementing its counter to 3.

Insertion of the next value, 25, causes the leftmost leaf to split and 25 is also added to the parent as shown in Figure 8.21(d). The key value 55 is inserted between 50 and 60 in the leaf and no splitting occurs. When 65 is inserted into the same leaf, a split directs the value 60 to the parent. There is no space in the parent so it splits, creating a new root containing 60 and 90, as depicted in Figure 8.21(e). The new root's h field is set to 3. If there were more levels of the tree, splitting could propagate through all of them.

Insertion of the value 95 illustrates the last type of change to consider, shown in Figure 8.21(f). The value 95 is greater than the values in the root, so it will replace 90. The rightmost pointer in the root indicates the next node in which 95 will replace 90. Following this node's pointer locates the leaf containing 90. The value 95 is inserted in that leaf, and the changes are made to the higher index levels.

Algorithm for Insertion

An algorithm to insert a key value into a B^+-tree is in three main parts: search, addkey, and split. A search is conducted to see if the value is already present. If it is, then return to the algorithm to do whatever processing is required, if any. Otherwise, addkey is invoked. If there is space in the node for the value, add the key value and record address in the leaf node, update other fields in the node, update ancestors as necessary, and return to the algorithm. If no space is available, split the node. The process of node splitting involves adding a key value to the parent. Thus, the splitting part of the algorithm contains a recursive call to addkey which, in turn, calls the splitting part again. In this way, adding and splitting work their way up the indices to the root, and split it when necessary.

Thus, to insert a key value,

    Search:
        Search down to a leaf for the key value.
        If the key value is present, then return.
        If new key value will be the largest in the node, then replace
            largest values in higher index levels with the new key value.
        Add the key value.

    Add Key:
        If node is full, split the node.
        Insert key value in sorted list in node.

Split:
   Get a new node.
   Leave keys from positions 1, 2, ..., $\lceil n/2 \rceil$ in original node and place remaining keys in new node.
   If nodes are leaves, insert into linked list.
   Update other fields in nodes.
   Add a key value to the parent.

Deletion

Deleting a record from a B^+-tree requires searching through all levels of indices until a specific leaf is found. The key value and record address are deleted from the leaf and the record is deleted, either by returning the record block to the system (that is, making it available for later use) or by marking it "deleted" in the file. If the key value is the largest value in the leaf, then it must be replaced in all index nodes in which it appears by the next largest value in the leaf. If the node has too few values when the largest value is deleted, then additional processing is necessary to maintain the B^+-tree structure

To delete the record with key value 90 from the B^+-tree of Figure 8.21(f), fetch the root from external memory and search it for 90. Since $90 \leq 95$, follow the pointer associated with 95 to the next level (that is, retrieve from external memory the index node at the next level). Search that node for 90. Since $70 < 90 \leq 95$, follow the pointer associated with 95 to the next level, which happens to be a leaf (the h field contains 1). Find the key value 90 and the record address. Delete 90 and the record address, and reduce the counter in the leaf by 1. No other change is necessary in the structure. Deleting the record with key value 25 involves the same search procedure and the same processing in the data file and leaf node. However, one other change occurs: 25 is deleted from the parent and replaced there by the next largest value (20) in the leaf. Figure 8.22 reflects the deletions of 90 and 25.

Suppose the record with key value 65 is deleted next. Removing 65 reduces the counter to 1, signaling that the number of key values in the leaf is below the minimum for the tree structure. The node at the same level and to the left is fetched from external memory. Its counter field contains a value greater than $\lceil \frac{4}{2} \rceil - 1$, so the largest key value (60) and its pointer are deleted, and then inserted into the node from which 65 was deleted. Counter fields in both nodes are changed. The value 60 is replaced by 55 in the parent and in the root. The result is shown in Figure 8.23.

When 95 is deleted, significant changes are made in the structure. The value 95 is deleted from the leaf and all ancestors in which it appears, and is replaced by 80, the value remaining in the leaf after deletion of 95. The

Indexed Sequential Access   253

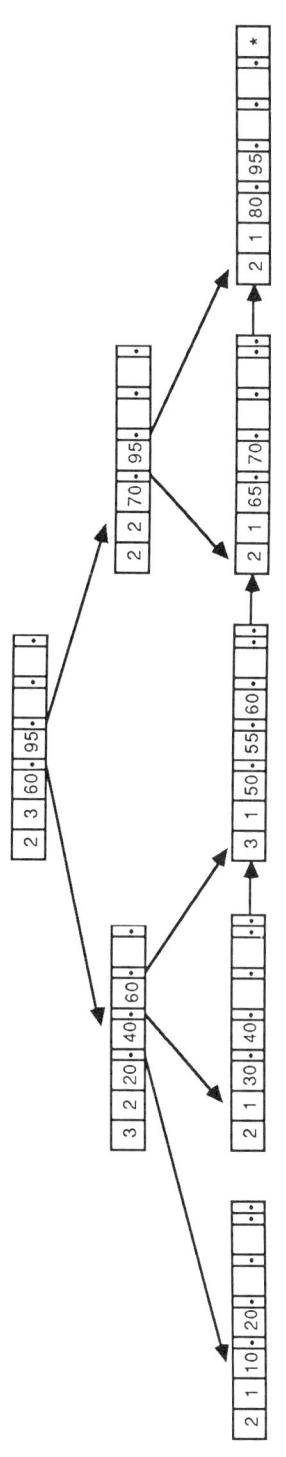

Figure 8.22 *Deletion of 90 and 25*

254   Chapter 8

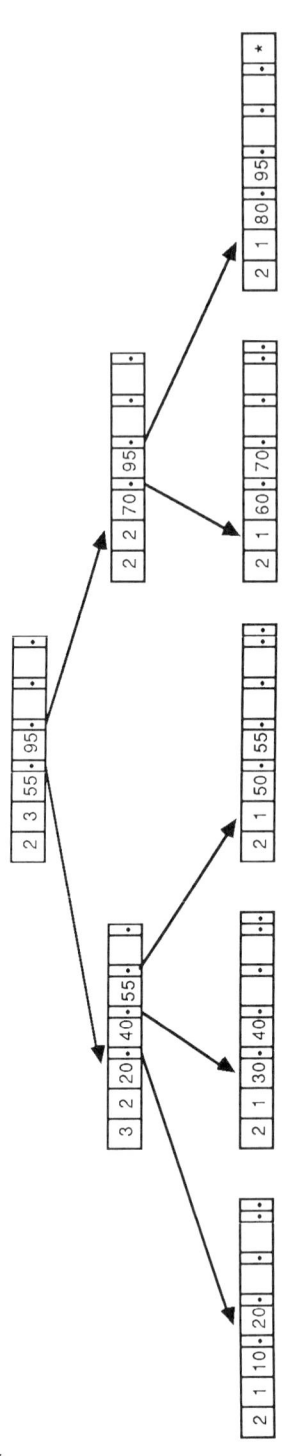

Figure 8.23 Deletion of 65

counter is 1 in the leaf, so the left sibling is fetched. It contains two values. The values in the two nodes are combined into one node containing 60, 70, and 80. The counter is set to 3, and 70 is deleted from the parent, reducing its counter to 1. The left sibling is fetched and its maximum key value (55) is deleted and inserted into the node. Counters are changed and the largest remaining value in the left sibling (40) replaces 55 in the root. See Figure 8.24(b).

Algorithm for Deletion

An algorithm for deletion of key values from B^+-trees is in three parts: search, removekey, and adjustindex. The search part invokes the removekey part when the key value is found and terminates when the value is not found. Removekey invokes Adjustindex to restore balance to the B^+-tree and correct any indices affected by the deletion. Both Removekey and Adjustindex invoke Removekey recursively to propagate the effect of the deletion up the tree as far as necessary.

Thus, to delete a key value,

> Search: Search down to a leaf for the key value.
> If the key value is not present, return.
> Otherwise, remove the key value.
>
> Removekey:
>   To Remove a Key Value (K) and its address from a Node (N)

{Remove the key K (K.value and K.address) from the node (N) in which it was found}
  m = m −1 {count of keys in the node}
  if N = Root
     then if K.value is not the largest key in the node
            then move other keys down to fill its place
          return.
  if K.value is largest key value in N
     then RemoveKey (K) from Node (parent_of_N)
          Insert next highest key into parent_of_N
     else move larger keys down to replace K.
  Adjustindex.

> Adjustindex: {Adjust balance and correct indices}

  if m < $\lceil n/2 \rceil - 1$
     then if there is a left sibling
            then if the left sibling m > $\lceil n/2 \rceil$
                   then RemoveKey (max key) from node (left sibling)
                        Insert max key of left sibling into N

               else RemoveKey (max key of left sibling) from
                       node (parent_of_N)
               move all keys from N to left sibling
          else if the right sibling m ≤⌈n/2⌉
               then RemoveKey (max key of N) from node (parent_of_N)
               Insert min key of right sibling into parent_of_N
               move all keys in right sibling down to replace min
               else RemoveKey (max key of N) from node (parent_of_N)
               move all keys from right sibling to N.

B*-TREES

The insertion process for B-trees can be made more efficient with a different procedure for handling overflow. In B-trees, an attempt to insert a key value into a filled node causes overflow which can trickle up through a number of levels in the tree structure. In their 1972 paper (see Reference list), Bayer and McCreight introduced a method that limits the effect to nodes at two levels: leaves and their parent. This overflow technique is one of the two main differences between B*-trees and B-trees.

The other difference is that nonroot nodes of B*-trees must be at least two-thirds full; in B-trees they are at least half full. Two consequences of this condition are that a B*-tree has fewer nodes to search, and insertions are more likely to cause overflow. Processing a B*-tree is more efficient than processing a B-tree because fewer external records are read, and overhead due to splitting nodes is reduced.

Properties

Formally, a B*-tree of order n has the following properties:

1. The root has at least two, and at most $2*\lceil(2n–1)/3\rceil + 1$ descendants, unless the root is also a leaf.
2. Each node has no more than n descendants.
3. Each node that is not a root or a leaf has at least $\lceil(2n–1)/3\rceil$ descendants.
4. All leaf nodes are at the same level.
5. A nonterminal node that has k descendants contains $k-1$ key values. A leaf contains at least $\lceil(2n–1)/3\rceil - 1$ values.

Indexed Sequential Access 257

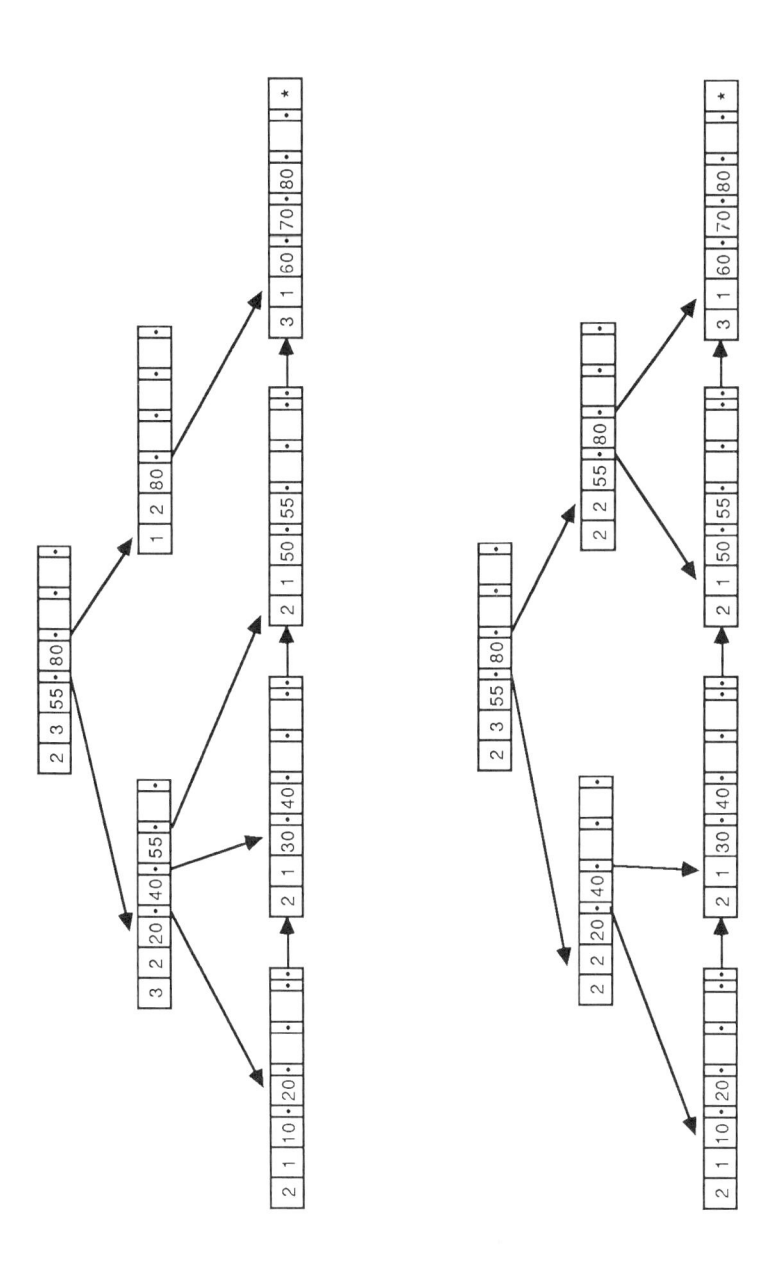

(a) First stage

(b) Final result

Figure 8.24 Deletion of 95

Capacity

Both B-trees and B*-trees contain approximately the same number of key values in nodes for orders of $n \leq 5$, but there is a significant difference for higher values of n. For example, when $n = 50$, the root of a B-tree contains between 1 and 49 key values, and nonroot nodes contain between 24 and 49 key values. The corresponding numbers for B*-trees are 1 and 66 for the root, and 33 and 49 for nonterminal nodes. This means that a B*-tree could have as many as 67 descendants at the first level, each with 24 to 49 key values, or a range of 1608 (67*24) to 3283 (67 *49) values available with one access of an external file. For a B-tree, the range is 1176 (49*24) to 2401 (49*49), or about 25 percent fewer key values.

Overflow Handling

Overflow handling represents the other advantage of B*-trees over B-trees. The overflow technique during insertion into a B*-tree of order 5 is illustrated in the sequence of Figure 8.25(a)–(c). Suppose the root and two leaf nodes are as shown in Figure 8.25(a). An attempt to insert the key value 350 into the right descendant of the root causes overflow because the node is full. Redistribution of values rotates the key values locally among the three nodes to a sibling that is not full. The value in the antecedent (root) is moved to the left descendant, and the first value in the full node is moved to the antecedent. The value 350 is then inserted into the right descendant. The result appears in Figure 8.25(b).

Both leaf nodes are now full. When a new value, 180, is inserted, a different phenomenon occurs—rotation is accompanied by a split into three leaf nodes, with the number of values in each node satisfying the minimum and maximum requirements for a B*-tree. The left descendant is full, but rotation as in Figure 8.25(b) cannot take place because the right descendant is also full. Instead, the left descendant gets the values 125 and 140, the antecedent gets 150 from the left descendant, the new middle descendant gets 180 and 200, the antecedent gets 230, and the right descendant gets the remainder of the values 290, 310, 350, and 400. Figure 8.25(c) shows the result.

In general, when splitting is necessary at the time insertion is attempted (all leaf nodes are full), assignment of values to leaf nodes follows a set of rules:

1. The leftmost descendant gets the minimum number of lowest key values, that is, $\lceil (2n - 1)/3 \rceil - 1$ values.

2. The antecedent gets the next higher value. (Note that the pointers on either side of this value point to the left and middle leaf nodes, respectively.)

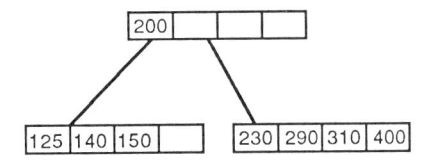

(a) B*-tree of order 5

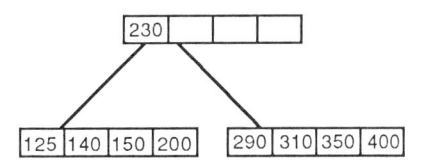

(b) B*tree after insertion of the key value 350

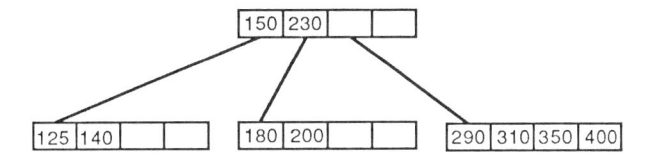

(c) B*-tree after split when 180 is inserted

Figure 8.25 (a), (b), (c) Insertion in a B*-tree

3. The new middle descendant gets the minimum number of next higher values, that is $\lceil (2n - 1/3 \rceil - 1$ values.
4. The antecedent gets the next higher value. (Note that the pointers on either side of the value point to the middle and right leaf nodes, respectively.)
5. The right node gets the remaining values.

SEARCH TIME COMPARISON

Comparisons of search time between B^+-trees and either B-trees or B*-trees is complicated by the fact that a B^+-tree may have fewer levels than the other structures (because there is space for more key values in each nonterminal node), but every search must continue to the leaf nodes. In B- or B*-trees, search terminates at the level where the key value is found, because the address of the record is in the same node as the key value.

SUMMARY

This chapter concludes the discussion begun in Chapter 6 of three major file organizations:—sequential, direct, and indexed. Historically, sequential file organizations appeared first, fitting well with the physical characteristics of magnetic tape. Random organizations became popular after random access devices such as disks were made available. Indexed organizations combine features of both sequential and random organizations.

An indexed organization is characterized by an index stored in external memory as blocks of key values and pointers. Block size is usually determined by physical characteristics of storage media. Successively, blocks corresponding to a given key are located through random access by means of pointers associated with key values. Eventually, the location of the key is identified. Its pointer is the storage location of the record with that key value. Sections of the data file of records are stored sequentially, but each record (or block of records) is directly accessible. The data is also accessible in sequential order.

ISAM, VSAM, SIS, and B-, B^+-, and B*-trees use the indexed organization. ISAM is the basis for a number of indexed sequential organizations. VSAM has largely replaced ISAM in IBM installations. SIS is CDC's implementation. All three of these methods permit sequential as well as random processing of the data file.

The COBOL language includes features such as the ACCESS, ORGANIZATION, and KEY clauses that interface with the computer's file system and simplify use of file access methods. Pascal was not designed with such emphasis on input/output operations; programs written in Pascal require the programmer to specify the file access process more directly.

The B-tree structure combines features of indexed organization and balanced search trees. By requiring a minimum number of key values in each node, B-trees guarantee a balanced structure as insertions and deletions of records are made. B*-trees impose a higher minimum number of key values per node than B-trees require: $\lceil (2n - 1)/3 \rceil - 1$ versus $\lceil n/2 \rceil - 1$. Both structures allow addresses to records in the index nodes, but neither structure directly implements sequential processing of the data file.

In B^+-trees, only leaf nodes contain record addresses. Leaf nodes are linked to allow sequential processing of the data file. More key values are possible in index nodes, reducing the search length. Because each access of an index node is done by retrieving the node from external memory, a reduction in search length can significantly improve processing time. B^+-trees are frequently used to store and maintain records in databases and in applications in which records are accessed by more than one key. Methods for multiple key processing are discussed in the Chapter 9; databases, in Chapter 10.

… Indexed Sequential Access 261

EXERCISES

1. Refer to Figure 8.7.
   (a) Where would a record with key value equal to 4675 be found?
   (b) Assuming only the Master Index is in memory (and that all the records on a track are read at one read operation, as a block), how many reads must be executed to retrieve a record with key value equal to 5210?
   (c) Show revisions to the figure that would be required (i) if a record with key value equal to 4660 were inserted; (ii) if record 4650 were deleted; and, (iii) if record 4640 were inserted after record 4650 was deleted.
   (d) How many reads are needed to discover if record 7830 exists?
   (e) How many reads are needed to discover if record 1325 exists?
2. SIS files keep the value of the lowest key in a data block in the index entry for that data block. VSAM files keep the value of the largest key value in the index entry for a particular control interval. What effect does this difference have on the operations required to find a record?
3. Revise Figure 8.12 to show the data control area as it would appear if all the data records were of the same length, 200 bytes each.
4. What is the maximum size record that could have been added to the original control interval of Figure 8.13 without causing a control interval split?
5. What is the advantage of dynamically-sized control intervals (or data blocks) as used in VSAM (SCOPE) over the use of overflow areas by systems such as ISAM?
6. For each of the following numbers of key values k find the maximum number of comparisons required to find a given value in a B-tree of order n.
   (a) $k = 39,062,499; n = 5$
   (b) $k = 4,000,000 - 1; n = 10$
7. Find the maximum number of key values possible in a B-tree of order n and height m. (*Hint*: First find the largest number of nodes possible at each level, then for all levels.)
8. Design algorithms for insertion and deletion in B-trees.
9. In the B-tree of Figure 8.16, insert the following key values in the order given: 70, 82, 65, 42, 43, 39.
10. From the B-tree of Figure 8.16, delete the following key values in the order given: 37, 19, 44, 38.
11. Cite an example of a query that could be answered best by sequentially searching the key values in the leaves of a B^+-tree.

12. In the B^+-tree of Figure 8.21(f),
    (a) Insert the following key values in the order given: 52, 98, 85, 15, 22, 58.
    (b) Insert additional values until the root splits (that is, until the height of the tree is increased by one).
    (c) What are maximum and minimum numbers of key values required to split the root?
13. In the B^+-tree of Figure 8.21(f), delete the following key values in the order given: 90, 40, 30, 60, 80, 95.
14. Develop programs to implement the insertion and deletion algorithms for B^+-trees. Test the programs with the data used to generate Figure 8.21(f).
15. Contrast insertion in a file stored as an ISAM-type indexed sequential organization, a B-tree, and a B^+-tree. Consider all cases.
16. Repeat Exercise 15 for deletion.

CHAPTER 9

MULTIPLE-KEY FILE ORGANIZATIONS

INTRODUCTION

Every file organization introduced in previous chapters was based on accessing records through a primary key. Hashing techniques and B-tree structures were introduced to simplify a user's task of getting data from a record with a specific primary key value. One record key does not always provide sufficient access to the information that could be obtained from a file, however. For example, consider the file illustrated in Figure 9.1. If an index provides the address of the first record for each faculty member, a university administrator readily obtains responses to queries such as, "What courses did Dr. Jones teach?" or "How many students were in Dr. Brown's courses?"

However, answers to the following queries are not easily provided:

- What is the grade distribution in MA 290?
- Who taught MA 290?
- What CS courses were offered last semester?
- Was Kretz a student in EN 105?
- What courses were taken by the student with ID number 122345654?
- Did Dean take both a CS and an EN course?

Answering such queries from this file requires accessing each record sequentially and testing appropriate fields. Processing is sequential

FACULTY	COURSE	STUDENT	ID	GR	STUDENT	ID	GR
Abel	MA 290	Kingle	132465798	B	Porter	777564343	C ...
Abel	MA 420	Fisk	212345675	C	Marten	268947562	A ...
Fox	EN 190	Dean	122345654	A	Frankes	345234121	D ...
Voigt	PH 402	Henry	432123432	D	Patrick	262354354	A ...
Voigt	PH 250	Hunter	321123321	C	Lunt	777665555	C ...
Carson	CS 360	Patrick	262354354	A	Tretnor	112223333	D ...
Carson	CS 220	Gomez	543345543	B	Kim	131242353	B ...
Smith	EN 105	Kingle	132465798	C	Monk	543345543	A ...
Green	CS 200	Porter	777564343	B	Raker	322245111	C ...
Brown	EN 333	Patrick	262354354	D	Tron	357468579	B ...
Nelson	MA 150	Jones	445546647	B	Patrick	262354354	C ...
Garcia	EN 200	Dean	122345654	A	Jones	445546647	C ...
Garcia	EN 410	Archer	421675988	B	Baker	222786954	A ...

...

Figure 9.1 Some of the records in the faculty file

because a file that is ordered on one key is an unordered file with respect to any other attribute used as a key. To obtain responses to any of the queries directly from the file, it is necessary to restructure the file or create additional index records to relate each other key to the primary key.

Methods for accessing records on keys other than the primary key are the topics of this chapter. Two techniques are examined: **Inverted lists**, which reverse the role of the key and the record attribute data, and **multilists**, which are linked lists embedded in a file. The first five queries call for the use of inverted lists; the sixth indicates the need for a multilist structure. Algorithms to query a file that is organized for multiple-key accessing follow the discussions of inverted lists and multilists.

Inverted Lists

When records in a file are stored according to a primary key, all other keys are considered secondary. Accessing a record through a secondary key requires processing the records sequentially until the key value is found or determined not to be in the file. If searches on values of a secondary key are frequent, then time is wasted repeatedly conducting sequential searches of the file. For large files stored in external memory, overhead is exorbitant for this kind of processing.

The usual way to avoid this problem is to create an additional index of the secondary key values. This secondary key index can be structured in various ways. The most direct method sets up an **inverted list**—an index consisting of the value of the secondary key of each record and its corresponding primary key.

Figure 9.2 shows an inverted list for the courses in Figure 9.1 sorted on the secondary key. It is used to answer the query, "What is the grade distribution in MA 290?" in the following way. Find the secondary key value MA290 in the inverted list and read the corresponding primary key value "Abel". Then access the record with that primary key. A count of the number of each letter grade in the record yields the answer. Note that a response to the query, "Who taught MA 290?" is obtained from the inverted list without accessing any records in the file. This is one of the advantages of inverted lists. The same inverted list is useful in dealing with the third and fourth queries, namely, "What CS courses were offered last semester?" and "Was Kretz a student in EN 105?"

An application can have as many inverted lists as there are secondary attributes in the file's records. Each inverted list can be a sequential (sorted or unsorted) file, an indexed sequential file, or any other structured file introduced in previous chapters. It is stored separately from the records in a file and from the primary key index. If the inverted list is small enough to fit into memory, then an internal search method can be used to find a specified value in the list. When an inverted list is organized as in Figure 9.2, no pointers are necessary because the secondary key value is located in the same node as its corresponding primary key value. This arrangement provides immediate access to the primary key value once the secondary one is found, but does not allow access to a record directly from a secondary key value.

Duplicate Keys

Duplicate values of the secondary key often occur. To avoid including a value more than once in an index, all primary key values corresponding to the same secondary key value are collected in the same node, just as different keys that hashed to the same address are stored in the same bucket. Figure 9.3 shows a partially inverted list for ID numbers. This

COURSE	FACULTY
CS 200	Green
CS 220	Carson
CS 360	Carson
EN 105	Smith
EN 190	Fox
EN 200	Garcia
EN 333	Brown
EN 410	Garcia
MA 150	Nelson
MA 290	Abel
MA 420	Abel
PH 250	Voigt
PH 402	Voigt
...	...

Figure 9.2 An inverted list for courses

ID	FACULTY			
112223333	Carson			
122345654	Fox	Garcia		
131242353	Carson			
132465798	Abel	Smith		
212345675	Abel			
222786954	Garcia			
262354354	Brown	Carson	Nelson	Voigt
268947562	Abel			
321123321	Voigt			
...	...			

Figure 9.3 A partially inverted list for ID numbers

structure facilitates finding all records that contain a specific ID number as a secondary key value.

In particular, this inverted list deals efficiently with the query, "What courses were taken by the student with ID number 122345654?" The answer is obtained by locating 122345654 in the secondary key index. The corresponding values FOX and GARCIA are read; they are the primary key values for finding the appropriate records. Once the records are found, the COURSE fields yield the desired results.

Structures for Inverted Lists

Any one of a number of structures can hold a secondary key index. Some possibilities include a sequential file, an array, a linked list, an indexed sequential file, or a tree structure. In a sequential or indexed sequential file organization, records must be large enough to hold the secondary key value and multiple primary key values, or pointers to the primary key values. The number of primary key values is not the same in all records, indicating that variable-length records are needed. Alternatively, fixed-length records are used, in which the size of the primary key field is specified to hold the maximum number of values for any given entry. Space is wasted because most records are likely to contain fewer primary key values than the maximum for which space is allotted. For example, if the inverted list in Figure 9.3 is stored in fixed-length records, all primary key fields must have space for four key values, even though only one record contains that many. In an array representation, such as that shown in Figure 9.3, the primary keys constitute additional columns.

Linked lists are dynamic structures; they avoid the problem of specifying a maximum size of primary key field. As each record is read, the secondary and primary key values are added to linked lists and the inverted list is stored as a linked structure. The data from Figure 9.3 is stored as a linked structure in Figure 9.4. Each node containing a

Multiple-Key File Organizations 267

KEY VALUE	POINTERS	PRIMARY KEY	POINTER			
112223333	•——→	Carson	null			
122345654	•——→	Fox	•——→	Garcia	null	
131242353	•——→	Carson	null			
132465798	•——→	Abel	•——→	Smith	null	
212345675	•——→	Abel	null			
222786954	•——→	Garcia	null			
262354354	•——→	Brown	•——→	Carson	•⤵	
	⤷	Nelson	•——→	Voigt	null	
268947562	•——→	Abel	null			
321123321	•——→	Voigt	null			

Figure 9.4 Inverted list stored as a linked list structure

secondary key value also has two pointers—one to the next secondary key node and one to the first primary key node. Each node containing a primary key value also has a pointer to the next primary key node. An inverted list in a linked structure requires extra space for pointer fields, but does not require the amount of space for the entire file to be allocated in advance. After the list is created, it can be converted into a sequential file and placed in external memory. Figure 9.5 shows a sequential version of the list structure in Figure 9.4. The sequential nature of the file

RECORD NUMBER	RECORDS		
1	| 112223333	| 2	|
2	| Carson	| null	|
3	| 122345654	| 4	|
4	| Fox	| 5	|
5	| Garcia	| null	|
6	| 131242353	| 7	|
7	| Carson	| null	|
8	| 132465798	| 9	|
9	| Abel	| 10	|
10	| Smith	| null	|
11	| 212345675	| 12	|
12	| Abel	| null	|
13	| 222786954	| 14	|
14	| Garcia	| null	|
15	| 262354354	| 16	|
16	| Brown	| 17	|
17	| Carson	| 18	|
18	| Nelson	| 19	|
19	| Voigt	| null	|
20	| 268947562	| 21	|
21	| Abel	| null	|
22	| 321123321	| 23	|
23	| Voigt	| null	|

Figure 9.5 The structure in Figure 9.4 stored sequentially in external memory

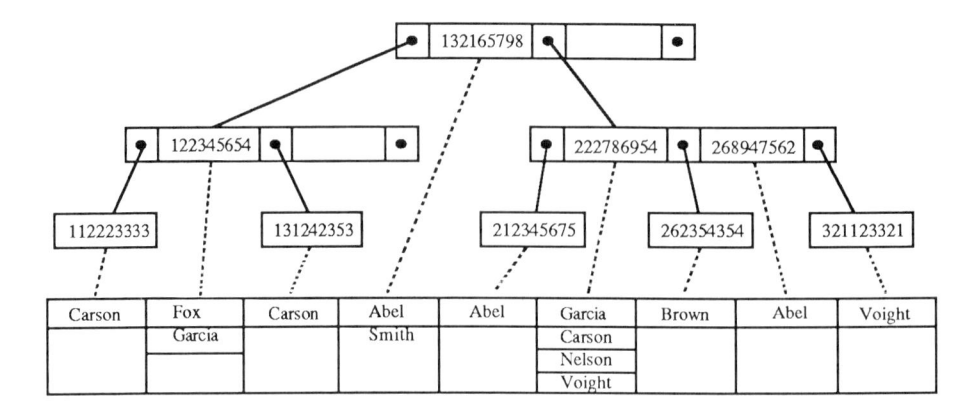

Figure 9.6 Inverted file with secondary keys stored as a B-tree

eliminates the need for pointers to the next secondary key. Relative addresses replace pointer values. When needed, the file is read into main memory and the linked structure is recreated.

Search Time

Search time can be excessive when large files are organized sequentially or as linked lists. A tree-structured organization can be searched and modified more quickly. Consequently, indexed sequential and B-trees are frequently used to store the secondary key values of an inverted list. A B-tree of order 3 is shown in Figure 9.6. Indices of the directory contain one or two secondary key values and pointers to the next level of indices, as usual, but also contain, for each key value, a pointer to primary key values. Only slight modifications of the B-tree algorithms in the previous chapter are required.

Maintenance

Maintenance of an inverted list in a file organization depends upon the structure of the list and the operation being performed. Each time an insertion, deletion, or update is made in the file, all inverted lists must be modified. Changes are carried out as in the primary key index. Additional overhead is required to modify inverted lists, but no new maintenance concepts arise. The overhead can be considerable, especially in volatile files.

Inverted Lists in Indexed File Organizations

Generation and maintenance of inverted lists can be accomplished in indexed file systems such as VSAM through use of the **alternate index** facility. The VSAM file system creates and maintains the inverted lists without need for intervention by the programmer. The alternate index is specified when the file is created. After that, any update operation performed on the file is automatically applied to any inverted lists as well.

Program Access to Inverted Lists in Indexed File Systems

COBOL includes statements that interact with the file system to facilitate creation of and access to records. Options in the SELECT statement specification allow use of inverted lists to access a file through secondary keys.

Consider a file of videotape library data for use at a rental company. Each film has a unique identifier assigned by the company, which serves as the primary key. In addition, the record for each film includes the year the film was released, an indication of the story type, and the principal actor and actress. Each of these fields can be defined as an alternate key and used to retrieve information about films. A small sample file is shown in Figure 9.7, and the appropriate inverted lists in Figure 9.8.

MOVIE-ID	MOVIE-TITLE	ACTOR	STORY-TYPE
01049	Search for the Lost Ark	Harrison Ford	Adventure
02310	The Color of Money	Paul Newman	Drama
03220	Indiana Jones and the Temple of Doom	Harrison Ford	Adventure
.			
.			
.			

Figure 9.7 MOVIELIST file (only selected fields shown)

```
ACTOR Inverted List:
Harrison Ford     01049      03220
Paul Newman       02310

STORY-TYPE Inverted List:
Adventure         01049      03220
Drama             02310

MOVIE TITLE Inverted List:
Search for the Lost Ark                  01049
The Color of Money                       02310
Indiana Jones and the Temple of Doom     03220
```

Figure 9.8 Some of the inverted lists defined for the movie list file

COBOL statements required to access the file follow. (Pascal does not have special statements to interface with the file system, and thus each of the steps described in the previous section would be programmed explicitly.)

```
SELECT MOVIELIST ASSIGN TO <device>
     RECORD KEY IS MOVIE-ID
     ALTERNATE KEY IS MOVIE-TITLE
     ALTERNATE KEY IS RELEASE-YEAR WITH DUPLICATES
     ALTERNATE KEY IS ACTOR        WITH DUPLICATES
     ALTERNATE KEY IS ACTRESS      WITH DUPLICATES
     ALTERNATE KEY IS STORY-TYPE   WITH DUPLICATES
```

MOVIE-TITLE is shown as an alternate key so that a record can be accessed without knowing its identification code. None of the other alternate keys are unique, and the clause WITH DUPLICATES causes the file system to treat them appropriately. If the file is created by this program, appropriate inverted lists are created. If the program is accessing a file that was created previously, it can only reference keys that were established when the file was created.

Random access to a file requires the use of the KEY clause in the COBOL START statement. When an alternate key has multiple entries in the file, the READ statement returns the record corresponding to the first inverted list entry for that key value. Subsequent READs return other records with the same key value. When all records with the desired key value have been read, additional READs return TRUE to the AT END condition. The clause NEXT RECORD causes the file system to return the record corresponding to the next key in the inverted list, not the next record in the file.

```
          MOVE SPACES TO SEARCH-STATUS.
          MOVE ACTOR-NAME-IN TO ACTOR.
          START MOVIELIST
               KEY = ACTOR
               INVALID KEY MOVE "DONE" TO SEARCH-STATUS
                    PERFORM SEARCH-FAILED.
          PERFORM LIST-FILMS UNTIL SEARCH-STATUS = "DONE".

     LIST-FILMS.
          READ MOVIELIST NEXT RECORD
               AT END MOVE "DONE" TO SEARCH-STATUS.
          IF SEARCH-STATUS NOT = "DONE"
               PERFORM WRITE-A-LINE.
```

Though access appears direct, it actually involves all the steps described in the previous section. START traces through the various levels of indexing to find the entry corresponding to the current value of

ACTOR-NAME-IN—Harrison Ford, perhaps. READ then uses the first primary key found and begins the process of accessing the actual data file. The second time the READ statement is executed, it uses the second primary key found in the ACTOR list for Harrison Ford, and another access to the data file, through its various index levels, is begun. After the last primary key has been used, the next attempt to READ causes the AT END condition to be set to true. If there had been no entry for Harrison Ford in the inverted list, the START statement would have terminated with an INVALID KEY condition.

Use of the ALTERNATE KEY and WITH DUPLICATES features of COBOL is available only when the underlying file access system supports inverted list access to the file, as does VSAM. Such access is not provided by ISAM.

LINKED LISTS IN FILES

Inverted lists are created and maintained separately from a file. An alternate approach is to provide secondary key access to records from within the file. In particular, records having equal values of a secondary key are linked together. To accomplish this, every record must have an extra link (pointer) field for each secondary key. The term multilist (multiple-threaded list) is given to this kind of file organization. In the following section, multilist organizations are examined, including two variations that limit the length of the linked lists.

Multilists

To get an idea of how a multilist is created, consider the file in Figure 9.9. Suppose all courses in the same discipline are to be linked. Then COURSE is a reasonable choice for the secondary key. In the first record, the value of the key is MA 290. Insert MA in one field of a listhead and a pointer to the first record in a second field. Actually, the primary key value could be used instead of a pointer. The listhead should have at least a third field, to hold an integer representing the number of items on the list.

The second record has MA 420 in the secondary key field. Add the record to the linked list headed by the MA listhead. The third record contains EN 190. Insert EN and a pointer to the record in a listhead. The next record contains PH 402. Create a listhead for PH and insert a pointer to the record. Insert the next record, with key value PH 250, into the PH linked list so that the course numbers are in increasing order. Continue through the file until all records are on linked lists. The result is a multiplicity of linked lists, or multilist, on one secondary key and an index of listheads. In Figure 9.9, some of the records' fields are left out so

RECORD NO.	FACULTY	COURSE	LINK
1	Abel	MA 290	2
2	Abel	MA 420	null
3	Fox	EN 190	12
4	Voigt	PH 402	null
5	Voigt	PH 250	4
6	Carson	CS 360	null
7	Carson	CS 220	6
8	Smith	EN 105	3
9	Green	CS 200	7
10	Brown	EN 333	13
11	Nelson	MA 150	1
12	Garcia	EN 200	10
13	Garcia	EN 410	null

LISTHEAD INDEX

DISC.	LINK	LENGTH
CS	9	3
EN	8	5
MA	11	3
PH	5	2

Figure 9.9 Multilist for courses

that the multilist structure is highlighted. Notice that the entire multilist, except for the index of listheads, is contained within the records.

The LENGTH field in the listhead index is useful for responding to queries such as, "Did Dean take both a CS and an EN course?" From the index it is clear that there are three CS and five EN courses. This suggests that it is more efficient to search for Dean in the CS list before looking in the EN list. If Dean is not in the CS list, then there is no need to search the longer list. In general, when different lists in two or more multilists are to be searched in response to a query, the LENGTH fields are compared and the shortest list is searched first, then the next shortest, and so on. This improves search efficiency because the least number of records is accessed to determine a response.

Maintenance

Maintenance of multilists is similar to that of any linked list. Each time a record is inserted into the file, lists must be updated within each multilist structure. If the lists are not ordered, then the new data is simply inserted at the head of each list. If the lists are ordered by the number of times a record is accessed, then the data is appended to the end of each list. In such cases, it is helpful to keep a pointer to the end of each list in the listhead. If the lists are ordered by other means, then a search and several pointer changes are required to insert data in the proper order in each list. When a record is deleted from the file, it is usually more efficient to mark the corresponding entries in multilists, rather than to delete them. At a later time, all of the marked entries can be deleted and necessary changes can be made in the multilists. Record updating could be handled as a deletion followed by an insertion in the multilists.

Doubly Linked Lists

Maintenance efficiency may be improved by using doubly linked lists in the multilist structures; that is, in addition to the pointer to the next item in the list, another pointer is kept to the previous list entry. Thus, it is possible to traverse the list in either direction. Deletions are faster because of the backward pointers in doubly linked lists, as are insertions in ordered lists. However, more space (for another pointer) is required.

Controlled Length Multilist

Searching and maintaining a multilist can become time-consuming when the lists grow in length. Much of this overhead can be avoided by restricting their length. One way to do this is to specify a maximum number of items that can be in a list. Then the first item to exceed the maximum begins a new list. The structure is called a **controlled-length multilist**. The example in Figure 9.10 has the maximum length of two. Notice that the structure is similar to the multilist in Figure 9.9. The only differences are that the entire contents of the COURSE field appear (to facilitate searching), additional entries appear in the listhead index, and pointers are adjusted accordingly in the list.

The main advantage of the controlled-length multilist structure is that searches involve less record movement between external and main memories. For example, data about EN 333 can be obtained by searching the listhead index to find EN 200 and then reading two records, corresponding to EN 200 and EN 333. In the multilist structure, the first four records of EN courses are read. A disadvantage of the controlled-length multilist structure arises from the redundancy of the entries in the listhead index and the values in the secondary key fields of

RECORD NO.	FACULTY	COURSE	LINK
1	Abel	MA 290	null
2	Abel	MA 420	null
3	Fox	EN 190	null
4	Voigt	PH 402	null
5	Voigt	PH 250	4
6	Carson	CS 360	null
7	Carson	CS 220	null
8	Smith	EN 105	3
9	Green	CS 200	7
10	Brown	EN 333	null
11	Nelson	MA 150	1
12	Garcia	EN 200	10
13	Garcia	EN 410	null

LISTHEAD INDEX

COURSE	LINK	LENGTH
CS 200	9	2
CS 360	6	1
EN 105	8	2
EN 200	12	2
EN 410	13	1
MA 150	11	2
MA 420	2	1
PH 250	5	2

Figure 9.10 Controlled-length multilist structure

records. This redundancy increases as lists get longer or when the maximum length is made smaller.

Cellular Multilists

Another method for limiting the length of lists is based on the physical placement of records on storage media. Groups of records on direct access storage media are separated or partitioned into cells (for instance, tracks, sectors, or cylinders on disks, or blocks on tape). The boundaries of these cells provide a hardware oriented means of restricting list length in a multilist organization. For each distinct value of a secondary key, the length of a list is the number of records containing that value which are stored in a cell. This organization, called **cellular multilist**, prevents linked lists from crossing cell boundaries. Its listhead contains the same three fields as a controlled-length multilist index, except that the LINK field contains, for each cell, both the cell number and the relative position of the first record in the cell which contains the secondary key value. Cellular multilist should be considered when many records are in the same cell. If no more than a few records with the same key values are in any cell, then inverted lists are more efficient.

Both a controlled-length multilist of length 1 and a cellular multilist in which, for each distinct key value, there is no more than one record with that value in each cell, are inverted lists. A controlled-length multilist of infinite length and a cellular multilist in which, for each distinct key value, all records with that value are in one cell, are multilist structures. Consequently, the advantages and disadvantages of controlled-length and cellular multilists fall somewhere between the two extremes: inverted lists and multilists. The main advantage of cellular multilists over controlled-length multilists is that several read operations can be started at the same time and can be overlapped with other actions such as queries or responses.

By this time, it should be clear that file designers have an extensive collection of techniques available to them. As demonstrated in Chapters 7, 8, and 9, file organizations can be sequential, random, or indexed. A choice of structures is possible within each category of organization. The choices apply to secondary and primary keys. Only secondary key structures are discussed in this chapter. Many of those structures contain pointers to primary key values, but the structure for storing primary keys is not specified. Designers have the same choices for structuring primary keys, however. For example, secondary key values stored as a B-tree can contain pointers to primary key values stored as a sequential file, a hash table, or a B^+-tree. File maintenance is a major factor in the choice of organization or structure.

QUERY ALGORITHMS

Responses to the queries in previous sections of this chapter require searching in one inverted list or multilist. Frequently, however, queries are not that simple. They may contain values of several distinct secondary keys and require searching more than one list. For example, a reasonable query of a file of employees is, "Find all employees who are system analysts, earn more than $39,000, have been employed at least five years, and work in the Cincinnati office." This section includes efficient algorithms for obtaining responses to these kinds of queries. In particular, the section concentrates on the following types of queries:

1. All values of attributes must be satisfied.
2. At least one attribute value must be satisfied.
3. A combination of (1) and (2).

Conjunctive Queries

Queries which require all attribute values to be satisfied are referred to as **conjunctive queries.** They consist of a list of attribute values (operands) separated by the Boolean operator AND. The following query is conjunctive:

"Find all system analysts who work in Cincinnati."

The query can be written in either of the following forms:

    (JOBTITLE = "system analyst") AND (OFFICE = "cincinnati")

or

    (JOBTITLE = "system analyst") ∧ (OFFICE = "cincinnati")

where the symbol ∧ is the Boolean operator AND.

Conjunctive queries are readily handled by processing partially inverted lists in which the primary keys corresponding to a secondary key are sorted, say, in ascending order. Figure 9.11 (a)–(e) shows part of a large corporation's file of employees sorted on the primary key IDNUMBER, and partially inverted files on employees' job titles, salary levels, numbers of years employed, and branch offices where they work. The query initiates a search of the JOBTITLE list for the value "system analyst" and of the OFFICE list for "cincinnati". This produces two sorted lists of employee IDNUMBERs. The lists are merged in the same way the master and transaction files are merged in Chapter 6—by using the

IDNUMBER	JOBTITLE	SALARY	YEARS	OFFICE
101234050	programmer	$36,700	7	new york
121445775	system analyst	$43,500	9	newark
145678932	secretary	$18,500	9	cincinnati
173884950	system analyst	$40,000	7	pittsburgh
191282373	programmer	$31,000	6	new york
200104210	system analyst	$36,700	5	cincinnati
202141516	system analyst	$43,500	6	new york
205647586	manager	$43,500	9	cincinnati
210364833	secretary	$14,600	5	newark
211537912	system analyst	$43,500	7	baltimore
222554678	programmer	$31,000	4	pittsburgh
234785431	programmer	$31,000	6	newark
268463749	secretary	$18,500	7	pittsburgh
300213450	programmer	$33,900	6	newark
321558899	programmer	$31,000	6	newark
...				

(a) A file of employees with primary key IDNUMBER.

JOBTITLE	IDNUMBER			
manager	205647586			
programmer	101234050	191282373	222554678	234785431
	300213450	321558899		
secretary	145678932	210364833	268463749	
system analyst	121445775	173884950	200104210	202141516
	211537912			

(b) A partially inverted list on JOBTITLE

SALARYLEVEL	IDNUMBER			
...				
3	210364833			
4				
5	145678932	268463749		
...				
8	191282373	222554678	234785431	321558899
9	300213450			
10	101234050	200104210		
11	173884950			
12	121445775	202141516	205647586	211537912
...				

(c) A partially inverted list on SALARYLEVEL. The salary level values represent ranges. For example, 9 represents all salaries greater than $33,000 and less than or equal to $36,000.

Figure 9.11 An employee file and partially inverted lists (continued on the next page)

YEARS	IDNUMBER				
...					
4	222554678				
5	200104210	210364833			
6	191282373	202141516	234785431	300213450	321558899
7	101234050	173884950	211537912	268463749	
8					
9	121445775	145678932	205647586		
...					

(d) A partially inverted list on YEARS.

OFFICE	IDNUMBER				
baltimore	211537912				
cincinnati	145678932	200104210	205647586		
newark	121445775	210364833	234785431	300213450	321558899
new york	101234050	191282373	202141516		
pittsburgh	173884950	222554678	268463749		

(e) A partially inverted list on OFFICE.

Figure 9.11 (continued)

balance line algorithm. The algorithm is simply modified so that, instead of a record being updated whenever a match occurs, each record whose primary key IDNUMBER is the same in both lists is accessed. Instead of each key being read, a pointer is moved down the key values. The algorithm must also be modified to terminate when no more key values remain on one of the lists. In particular, if one of the attribute values is not in a partially inverted list, then there are no records in the file that satisfy the query. An algorithm for handling conjunctive queries is given in Figure 9.12. Notice that multilists could be used in place of partially inverted lists.

Longer conjunctive queries—those with more than two attribute values as operands—are processed in a similar way, by moving pointers along the lists (or reading key values) until all pointers point to the same primary key value. For example, the response to the query

```
(JOBTITLE = "programmer") ∧ (SALARYLEVEL = "8") ∧
(YEARS = "6") ∧ (OFFICE = "newark")
```

produces the records with primary key values 234785431 and 321558899. The response to the query

```
(JOBTITLE = "programmer") ∧ (SALARYLEVEL = "8") ∧
(YEARS = "3") ∧ (OFFICE = "newark")
```

Assume that a partially inverted list exists for each attribute value (operand) in a conjunctive query.
    Search each partially inverted list for the operand.
    If any operand is not found, then terminate.
    For each operand, read the corresponding list of primary key values.
    Set a pointer to the head of each list.
    Until one of the lists is empty, do the following steps:
        Set MINKEY = smallest value pointed to.
        If MINKEY = every value pointed to, then get the record.
    Increment every pointer that points to a value = MINKEY.
    Terminate.

Figure 9.12 Conjunctive Query Algorithm

indicates that no records satisfy the query (because 3 is not a value in the YEARS list). The response to

```
(JOBTITLE = "programmer") ∧ (SALARYLEVEL = "12") ∧
(YEARS = "6") ∧ (OFFICE = "newark")
```

also indicates that no records satisfy the query (because no programmer in the original file is at salary level 12). The process is similar to the n-way merge introduced in Chapter 6, except that the algorithm terminates when any list is empty.

In the preceding example, each partial list contains relatively few entries for each key value. The JOBTITLE list, for example, has six IDNUMBERs for the value programmer. When the number of entries gets large, as in a major corporation, a different structure allows more efficient query processing. That structure involves converting the partially inverted list to a collection of lists, with the key values in the partially inverted list becoming the titles of the lists. Figure 9.13 shows lists that are used instead of the JOBTITLE and OFFICE partially inverted lists.

Information from lists of this type can be obtained with queries such as

```
system analyst ∧ cincinnati
```

The query triggers a search of both lists. IDNUMBERs common to both lists are produced. In this case only one value, 200104210, is found. It is then used as a primary key to locate the record.

MANAGER	PROGRAMMER	SECRETARY	SYSTEMS ANALYST	
205647586	101234050	145678932	121445775	
	191282373	210364833	173884950	
	222554678	268463749	200104210	
	234785431		202141516	
	300213450		211537912	
	321558899			

BALTIMORE	CINCINNATI	NEWARK	NEW YORK	PITTSBURGH
211537912	145678932	121445775	101234050	173884950
	200104210	210364833	191282373	222554678
	205647586	234785431	202141516	268463749
		300213450		
		321558899		

Figure 9.13 Lists of employees by job title and place of work

Disjunctive Queries

Queries requiring that at least one attribute value be satisfied are called **disjunctive queries**. They consist of a list of attribute values (operands) separated by the Boolean operator OR. The following query is disjunctive:

"Find the employees at salary level 9 or who have five years of service."

The query can be written in either of the following forms:

    (SALARYLEVEL = "9") OR (YEARS = "5")

or

    (SALARYLEVEL = "9") ∨ (YEARS = "5")

where ∨ is the Boolean OR.

The response to this query produces the records with primary key values 200104210, 210364833, and 300213450. The records are found by searching the two partially inverted lists, SALARYLEVEL and YEARS. When the key value 9 is matched by a value on SALARYLEVEL, and the value 5 is matched on YEARS, then the two lists of primary keys corresponding to 9 and 5 are merged by a modified balance line

Assume that a partially inverted list exists for each attribute value (operand) in a disjunctive query.
Search each partially inverted list for the operand.
If no operand is found, then terminate.
For each operand, read the corresponding list of primary key values.
Set a pointer to the head of each list.
Until all of the lists are empty, do the following steps:
    Set MINKEY = smallest value pointed to.
    Get the record.
    Increment every pointer that points to a value = MINKEY.
Terminate.

Figure 9.14 Disjunctive Query Algorithm

algorithm. Every record with a key on the merged list is produced as the query response. Suppose the SALARYLEVEL key value were 4 instead of 9. Then there is no match; its list of primary keys is empty. In such a case, the merged list is the same as the list corresponding to the value 5, that is, 200104210 and 210364833. The same procedure is followed when the disjunctive query has more than two secondary key values. An algorithm is given in Figure 9.14. For example, the query

```
(JOBTITLE = "secretary") ∨ (SALARYLEVEL = "10") ∨
(YEARS = "3") ∨ (OFFICE = "cincinnati")
```

produces records with the IDNUMBERs 101234050, 145678932, 200104210, 205647586, 210364833, and 268463749.

As noted before, if the lists in Figure 9.13 are available, some queries can be expressed differently. In particular, the query

```
manager ∨ baltimore
```

produces the IDNUMBERs 205647586 and 211537912.

Compound Queries

A third type of query is called a **compound query.** It consists of both AND and OR operators. For example,

> "Find all employees who are system analysts working in Newark or who are programmers working in Pittsburgh"

is a compound query. It is written in either of the following forms:

```
((JOBTITLE="system analyst") AND (OFFICE="newark")) OR
((JOBTITLE="programmer") AND (OFFICE="pittsburgh"))
```

Assume that a partially inverted list exists for each operand in a compound query.
    Search each partially inverted list for the operand.
    Read all lists of primary key values corresponding to the operands.
    Set a pointer to the head of each list.
    For each conjunctive query part of the compound query, identify the shortest list of primary key values corresponding to the operands.
    Until all shortest lists are empty, do the following steps:
        Set MINKEY = the smallest primary key value on the shortest lists.
        In the conjunctive query part containing MINKEY, if all key values pointed to = MINKEY, then get the record.
        Increment all pointers that point to key values = MINKEY.
    Terminate.

Figure 9.15 Hsiao-Harary Algorithm for compound queries

or

```
(system analyst ∧ newark) ∨ (programmer ∧ pittsburgh)
```

depending on whether the partial list or job title and place of work lists are available. In either case, the response produces the records with IDNUMBERS 121445775 and 222554678.

    The algorithm for handling compound queries is a combination of the algorithms for conjunctive and disjunctive queries. In the example, each of the conjunctive queries and then the disjunctive one are treated to obtain the records satisfying the compound query. An algorithm of this kind, however, does not take advantage of list length during processing, so it is not efficient. A modification known as the Hsiao-Harary Algorithm is more efficient. It is given in Figure 9.15. It works in the following way.
    Consider the query

```
(JOBTITLE="programmer" ∧ SALARYLEVEL="10" ∧ YEARS="7") ∨
(JOBTITLE="secretary" ∧ OFFICE="new york")
```

The length of each list is shown here:

programmer	6
salary level 10	2
years 7	4
secretary	3
newyork	4

For each conjunctive query, choose the shortest list, that is, salarylevel10 for the first query and secretary for the second. Any record that is on the three lists programmer, salarylevel10, and years7 must be on the shortest of the lists. Similarily, any record on the two lists secretary and newyork must be on the shorter of the lists. Using the algorithm for conjunctive queries, access the records on the lists salarylevel10 and secretary. As each record is accessed, its fields are examined to determine if it satisfies the conjunctive query. Those records meeting the requirements are produced as the response to the original query. In the example, the only records produced have IDNUMBERs 101234050 and 268463749.

There are also queries that request ranges of values rather than single values. The query given at the beginning of the section

> "Find all employees who are system analysts, are above salary level 10, have been employed at least five years, and work in the Cincinnati office"

is an example. This is a conjunctive query. Simply modify the Conjunctive Query Algorithm so that the search of the SALARYLEVEL list looks for all values greater than 11 and the search of the YEARS list looks for all values greater than or equal to 5. The algorithm for disjunctive queries and the Hsiao-Harary Algorithm can be modified in a similar way.

Summary

We now have seen methods for accessing records on any field, not just the one containing the primary key values. With this capability, files are organized to suit the application that requires them. There is a choice of primary and secondary keys. That choice, of course, depends on the nature of the data in the file and what kind of queries are made to obtain records from the file.

Multiple-key access to records allows more efficient access to information in files than when access was limited to primary keys. Creating indices on secondary keys permits record access with little additional expenditure of time and relatively little extra memory requirements. Most importantly, no file duplication is required. This means that updating records is less complicated and time-consuming, as well as less susceptible to error.

The structures introduced in this chapter, inverted lists and multilists, facilitate record access on secondary keys. A principal reason for using these structures is to access records by specifying particular key values in queries. This goal led to algorithms for processing queries involving multiple key values. In the next chapter these ideas are extended to include methods of obtaining information from collections of files, or databases.

Exercises

1. Create a table of advantages and disadvantages of inverted lists, multilists, controlled-length multilists, and cellular multilists.
2. Use data in Figure 9.11(a) to create each of the following structures:
   a. a multilist on OFFICE
   b. a controlled-length multilist (length 4) on JOBTITLE
3. Design and develop an algorithm and program to implement a multilist structure. Use the data in Figure 9.9 to test the program.
4. Construct an order 3 B^+-tree representation of the secondary key index for the data in Figure 9.3. Compare your result with Figure 9.6. Discuss advantages and disadvantages of each structure.
5. Modify the n-way sort merge algorithm to provide responses to conjunctive queries. Can the algorithm be modified to handle disjunctive queries? Use examples in this chapter to test your algorithms.
6. Write a program to modify the balanced line algorithm to handle conjunctive queries. Use the data in Figure 9.11(a)-(e) and the query examples in this chapter to test your program.
7. Repeat Question 6 for disjunctive queries.
8. Write a program to implement the Hsiao-Harary Algorithm of Figure 9.15. Run the program with the test data and query examples in Exercises 6–7. Compare the efficiency of your program with the programs in Exercises 6–7.
9. Express each of the following queries in logical notation. (For example, "Find the IDNUMBER of all programmers in the New York office" is written (programmer ∧ newyork).
   (a) Find the IDNUMBER of all secretaries in the Pittsburgh office who have worked at least three years and have a salary level greater than 2.
   (b) Find the IDNUMBER of all secretaries in the Pittsburgh or New York office or who have worked at least six years.
   (c) Find the IDNUMBER of all programmers or system analysts who either have salary level less than 11 or have worked five or more years.
10. Use the Hsiao-Harary Algorithm to determine the response to each of the queries in Exercise 9.
11. Design a system to implement cargo handling control at a large airport, given the following specifications:

    Each item entering the airport has a numbered label stuck to it. A record for each item is in a large file on disk and contains at least the following fields: Label number, Time (time and date of arrival),

Customs Indicator (set if customs clearance is needed), Shipper, Destination Indicator (to tell whether the item is bound inward, outward, or for trans-shipment), Airline Inwards, Airline Outwards.

The disk file forms a basis for all processing. User requirements are:

Airport staff. Need to find details of any item, given its label number. Also responsible for inserting and deleting records as cargo arrives or leaves.

Customs. Need to know what items require customs clearance. Items are cleared as they arrive, not in label number sequence.

Shippers. Need to know what items are ready to be collected.

Airlines. Need to know, for each destination, what items are in the airport.

All users can query the file at any time. Include a discussion of record layout, file organizations, query processing, and advantages of your choices.

CHAPTER 10

DATABASE PROCESSING CONCEPTS

INTRODUCTION

The file processing concepts, techniques, algorithms, and programs introduced in earlier chapters were considered from the viewpoint of a user or an application program requiring data from a single file. That file was organized so that access with the primary key was most efficient. The logical aspects of data and data structures were included in the application program. In the last chapter, multiple-key organizations were introduced. They allow other users to use the file for different applications and to view the file differently from the way in which it was organized for the primary application. A file organization based only on a primary key is efficient for one application but generally causes inefficient file processing in a different application. For example, suppose a hospital's patients file were organized with the patient's name as primary key. Then a nurse or doctor could interact readily with that file from a nurse's station, but the file would be of little or no use to the following people:

- Someone conducting a hospital utilization study and wanting to determine the percentage of beds occupied on specific days
- An administrator wanting to know which patients were seen by a specific doctor or given a particular medication

A more common example is the impracticality of searching a telephone book for the name or phone number of a person who lives at a known address.

One way to alleviate this problem is to duplicate and restructure some or all of the data in the original file for access by another application. This duplication of records or files results in **data redundancy**. It usually leads to **data inconsistency**, that is, failure to maintain the same data in two or more files. The issue of data redundancy was avoided in the previous chapter by creating separate indices which provided access to a single file through secondary keys.

One of the serious constraints inherent in file processing systems like the one in the previous chapter is that they do not provide **data independence**, the ability to separate the representation of data from the application programs that use the data. When data independence is lacking, a change made in the logical record description of a file requires the entire file to be reloaded into storage and every application program using the file to be rewritten. Some file systems such as VSAM and SCOPE handle the physical rearrangement of data for the applications programmer; but changes in a file's physical structure—for instance, the size of each field and the ordering of fields—and changes in record contents require altering application programs. For example, changing from five- to nine-digit zip codes involves changing all programs that access records containing zip codes.

Reprogramming is expensive, especially for large applications. Similarly, the inefficiencies of maintaining separate files containing the same data or of providing only one logical data organization for separate users can become expensive, aggravating, and error-prone. A common way to minimize these problems is to create a general-purpose system (hardware and software) to manage a collection of files containing interrelated data. The collection of integrated files is referred to as a **database**, and the system as a **database system**. The term **database management system (DBMS)** refers to a specific collection of software or applications programs in the database system. These topics are the focal points of this chapter.

Early in this text, data storage at low levels—physical characteristics of storage devices, and detailed representations of numbers, characters, and strings—is the focus. Then higher-level organizations of these representations are considered as records and files. Operating system features that provide storage and access capability, while relieving the programmer of the need to know details of the file system, are highlighted. In this chapter, database management systems are considered; they insulate the programmer and end user of data still further from file organization details.

Some of the fundamental terminology, characteristics, and concepts of database systems are introduced in this chapter, primarily by means of examples. An in-depth treatment of database systems is beyond the scope of this book, however. Design considerations and architectural approaches, including the three common database models, are identified. Query languages to enable users to interact with a DBMS are illustrated. Applications such as online systems and expert systems, as well as the role of fourth-generation languages, are cited. Important issues such as privacy, security, and integrity, discussed in Chapter 5, are applied to databases.

BASIC TERMINOLOGY AND CONCEPTS

A Database's Three Levels of Abstraction

One of the most fundamental ways to think of a database system is in terms of its structure. Usually three layers, or levels of abstraction, are identified: the physical database (or physical level), the conceptual database (or conceptual level), and the user's view. They are shown in Figure 10.1. Of these three levels, only the physical database actually contains data. The other two levels are logical in nature and sometimes reduce to just one level, when the user's view coincides with part of the conceptual database.

This separation of physical and logical levels occurs frequently. For example, when a customer calls in an order to a department store clerk, the customer has a logical view of how the store's stock is maintained. This view may be similar to or distinct from that of the clerk. Both logical views are different from the way the stock is physically stored. In particular, the item the customer wants may be in the store called, or may be in another store or in a warehouse. The customer doesn't know (or care) where the item really is, but simply wants to know whether or not the item is available. Another concern is that the store has a system for processing the order efficiently and accurately. A customer is more comfortable if the system allows interaction with the procedure to remain the same even when the store's stock is rearranged (that is, data independence is built into the system). Of importance to both the customer and store personnel is the fact that data is accurate (data integrity) and protected against accidental or malicious tampering (data security).

Aspects of all three levels of abstraction are depicted in Figure 10.1. For simplicity, only one file constitutes the database system. The physical database refers to the way in which records are organized and the file is actually stored—that is, sequentially on disks, with field and record length specifications, including fields for store number, item, retail price, and cost. The conceptual database includes the logical specification of data and relations among data items, shown as tables (resembling inverted lists). This is a logical model of the physical database that provides structures for obtaining responses to user queries. Most of the

288 Chapter 10

User View

- Customer: All chairs with price < $400
- Customer: Men's suits, 44L, with price < $200
- Clerk: Number of 44L suits < $200 in stock
- Manager: Profit from sale of suits

Conceptual Database

Department	Item
⋮	⋮
Furniture	Chair
⋮	⋮
Furniture	Sofa
⋮	⋮
Men's Clothes	Hat
Men's Clothes	Suit
⋮	⋮
Men's Clothes	Tie
⋮	⋮

Item	Stock #	Quantity
⋮	⋮	⋮
Chair	C214	2
⋮	⋮	⋮
Chair	C976	3
⋮	⋮	⋮
Suit	S297	8
Suit	S574	4
⋮	⋮	⋮
Suit	S841	5
⋮	⋮	⋮

Stock #	Retail Price	Cost
⋯	⋯	⋯
C214	245.50	140.00
⋯	⋯	⋯
C976	389.95	260.00
⋮	⋯	⋯
S297	195.00	105.00
S574	325.00	195.00
⋯	⋯	⋯
S841	74.50	55.00
⋮	⋯	⋯

Physical Database

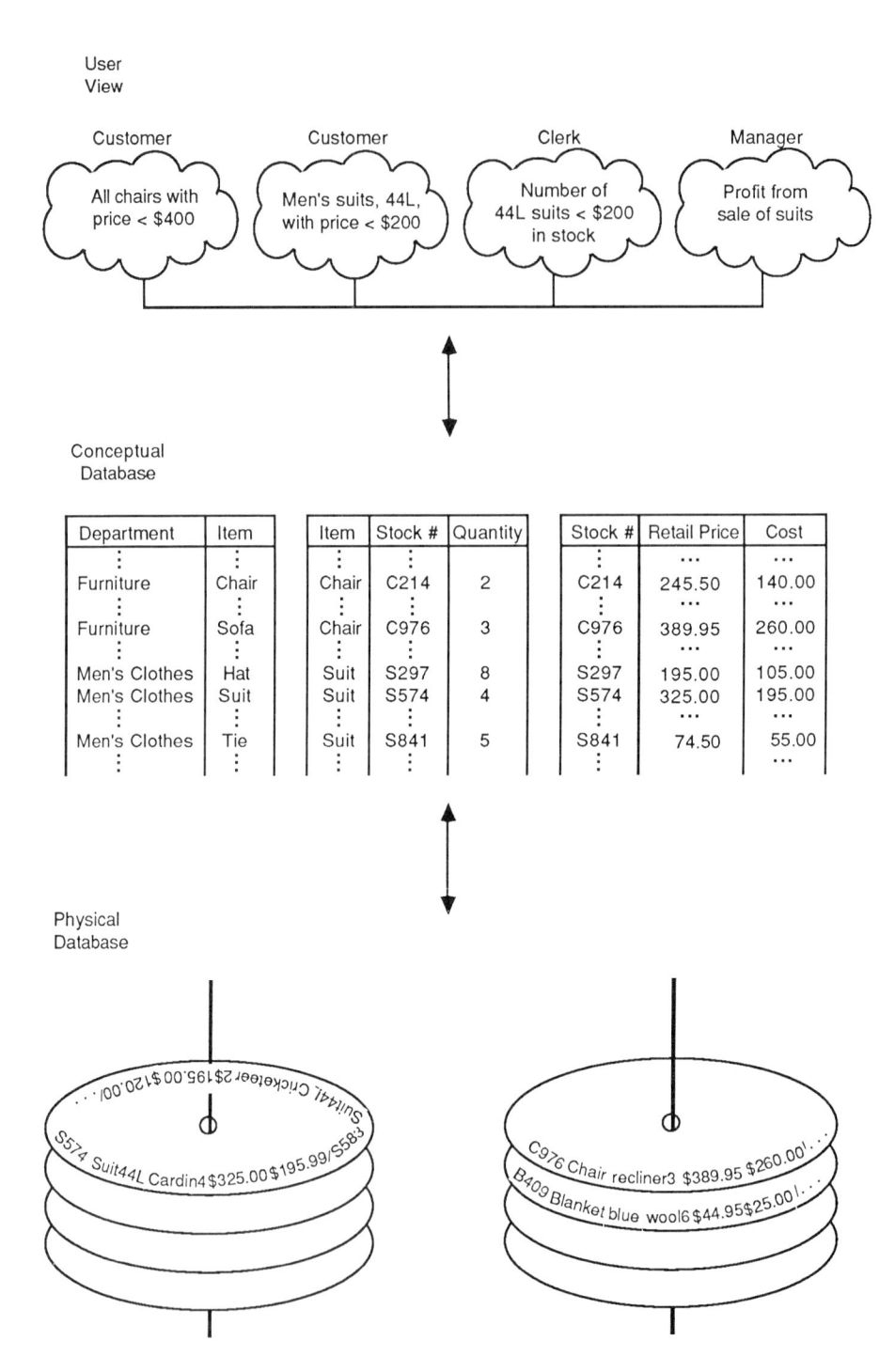

Disk 1: ...S583/Suit44L Cricketeer 2 $195.00 $120.00/...
       S574 Suit44L Cardin 4 $325.00 $195.99/S583...

Disk 2: ...C976 Chair recliner 3 $389.95 $260.00/...
       B409 Blanket blue wool 6 $44.95 $25.00/...

Figure 10.1 Three levels of a database

material in the first ten chapters of this text gives the database designer tools for implementing the physical and conceptual databases.

There are many different users' views of parts of the conceptual database. Customers, for example, see merchandise as items within a price range; clerks see quantities of items on hand; and managers see the difference between retail price and cost to the store.

The Internal Level

The **physical database**, or **internal level**, pertains to the actual data and how it is stored on physical devices. It consists of two major parts: (1) a set of programs that interact with the operating system to help manage the database; and (2) the records and files stored in external and main memory. Data types in Chapter 1, sorting, searching, and merging techniques in Chapters 2, 3, and 6, and physical characteristics of storage media in Chapter 4 pertain to the physical database. Ideally, the physical database is totally hidden from users so that changes in it do not affect their interaction with it (that is, data independence is maintained).

The Conceptual Level

The **conceptual database**, or **conceptual level**, has a relationship to both the physical database and the application environment. As exemplified earlier, it presents a logical model of the physical database to the users. Structures in Chapters 6–9, such as hash tables, B-trees, indexed sequential files, and multikey organizations, pertain to the conceptual database.

The conceptual database makes use of a high-level language referred to as a **data definition language (DDL)** which specifies how the physical database should look. The DDL consists of notation and statements that describe the kinds of distinguishable items, called **entities**, in the database and the kinds of relationships that exist among them. When the description is processed, a stored data description, called a **schema**, is produced.

The DDL does not manipulate the database. A **data manipulation language (DML)** carries out that function. Only the actual database design, and any design modifications, are achieved with the DDL. This separation of functions, design from implementation, is one of the characteristics (and conveniences) of a DBMS. It enables changes to be made to the physical database without altering programs or affecting a user's communication with the database. The separation is possible because the data and structures in a database are maintained apart from the software required to manipulate them.

The External Level

A **user's view**, or **external level**, is a logical representation of part of the conceptual database. Just as the term implies, a view is the way in which a particular user sees the conceptual database. There is a view for each user with a different application of the database. For example, nurses may need to get information on a patient, such as medications, symptoms, when doctors saw the patient, when physical therapy is scheduled, and what care the patient needs, from a hospital database. The hospital's billing personnel have a very different view of the database; they need to know the length of stay, what kind of room the patient was in, the cost of medications, and the patient's mailing address.

The special facility for describing the statements and definitions in a view is called a **subschema data definition language (SDDL)**. The descriptions are usually given in terms compatible with a specific programming language, such as COBOL. When an SDDL is processed, a **subschema** is produced. The SDDL defines how the conceptual database should look to each user, but provides no manipulation capability. Another special facility, called a **subschema data manipulation language**, allows the user to make queries and specify operations on views.

The Human Components

Before exploring the conceptual and external levels in more detail, we consider two important aspects of database systems: people and a DBMS. Three categories of people are crucial to an efficient and effective database system: users, applications programmers, and the database administrator.

Database systems are created for **users**. More than one user may access a database on a minicomputer or mainframe through terminals or on a shared file system through a network of computers of various types. A single user may have access to a database on a microcomputer. Conceptually there is little difference. In each case, a user appears to have sole access to the database. If access or interaction is inconvenient, then, the database is poorly designed or implemented.

The two most common ways for a user to access a database system are through (1) an applications program and (2) a query language processor. Applications programs are written in a language like COBOL or Pascal, or in a fourth-generation language (4GL). They enable a programmer to store, retrieve, and update data in the database by issuing requests to a DBMS. The **query language processor** is built-in as an integral part of the database system. It is interactive and easier to use than COBOL or Pascal because it enables a user to give more English-like commands to the DBMS. Some systems provide an even higher-level interface, a **menu** of commands from which a user simply makes a choice.

An **applications programmer** writes the programs to access the database. These programs are specific to the applications environment. For example, a specific business requires inventory and billing programs with particular features appropriate for that business; a college needs a program to produce a transcript. The applications programs receive data as input, in either online or batch mode (for instance, groups of drop/adds after the beginning of a semester), and interface with the DBMS.

The **database administrator (DBA)** may be one person or a group of people. The title really signifies a set of duties and responsibilities primarily directed to the care of the database and the satisfaction of its customers, the users. More specifically, the DBA manages the activities and resources of the database and controls its structure. This provides an element of centralized control over one of the most valuable resources of an organization, its data. Without this control, data would be scattered throughout the organization in localized, nonintegrated files and databases. Under those decentralized conditions, sharing data is considerably more difficult, and duplication of data, as well as inconsistencies among various sets of data, are costly.

The DBA role in managing the resources of a database includes:

(a) *Interfacing with users.* This involves seeing that users' needs are met and that no user interferes with any other user, for example, by erasing or modifying the other's data or making an unauthorized access to data. The DBA (and possibly the user) also writes applications programs and defines the mappings between the external and conceptual levels.

(b) *Defining security and integrity checks.* This is part of the conceptual schema. The kinds of checks are included in the discussion of privacy, security, and integrity in Chapter 5 and later in this chapter.

(c) *Monitoring the database's performance.* See (c) below.

(d) *Establishing a back-up and recovery strategy.* Data is backed up so that it can be recovered after all or part of the original data is lost due to human error or system failure.

The aspects of a DBA's responsibilities that pertain to controlling the structure of a database include:

(a) *Designing the physical database.* This involves determining the representation and physical storage of data as well as defining the mappings of this representation between the internal and conceptual levels.

(b) *Designing the conceptual database.* This involves defining the entities relevant to the organization and what information about them must be included in the conceptual schema.

(c) *Adapting the database as requirements change.* This requires keeping up-to-date with the organization's needs and monitoring the database's performance to see that it fulfills the needs. Also, when changes to the physical database are made, the mappings in (a) must be modified to maintain data independence.

Utility programs included in a database system enable the DBA to carry out these duties. Utilities include programs to create the original database, to rearrange data in the physical database, to dump and restore programs and data for recovery purposes, and to provide statistical analysis to help evaluate performance of the database. The **data dictionary** is a major utility in a database system. It can be thought of as a database of information about the system. It includes:

- Definitions of records, their fields, and interrelationships.
- Descriptions of mappings between physical and conceptual levels, and between conceptual and external levels.
- Which parts of the database are used by each program.
- Which users need what reports compiled from data in the database.
- Which terminals have access to the database.

The DBMS

The **database management system** is the software part of a database system that is visible to users. The DBMS takes a user's request, analyzes it, and then processes it. The request, or query, may be written in COBOL, Pascal, a 4GL, or some other language. Processing entails checking the user's external schema and its mapping to the conceptual schema, then looking at the conceptual-to-internal schema mapping and the definition of the storage structure, and finally executing on the physical database the operations that were generated by the user's request.

The schematic of a database system in Figure 10.2 shows the DBMS in relation to the user, other software, and the physical database. The **data communications manager**, or **communications control program**, is software that conveys messages between various users and applications programs. How it operates is beyond the scope of this book. The operating system controls all programs. One particular function of the operating system is to handle I/O requests from the DBMS.

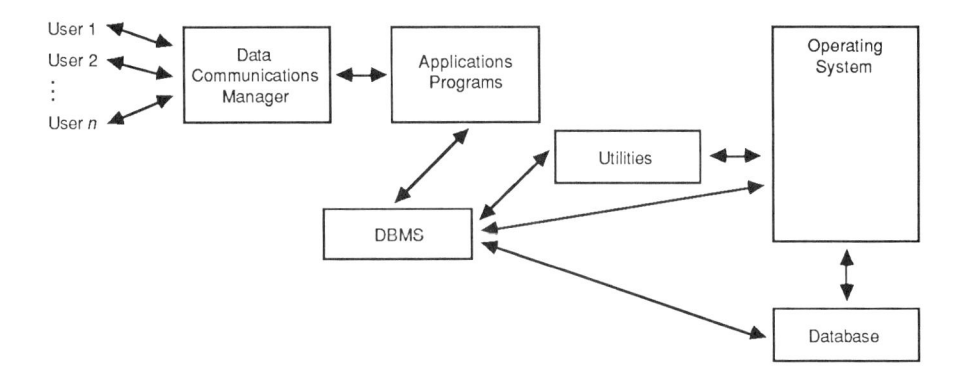

Figure 10.2 Software components of a database system

DATA MODELS

A DBMS typically is characterized by the data model it uses. A **data model** consists of a structure for organizing data and a set of operations. The structure provides a logical representation of the data for the user. The operations enable the user to access and manipulate the data. Data models are at the conceptual level. Their purpose is to describe a database in such a way that a physical organization can be constructed which will respond promptly to users' queries.

There are hundreds of DBMS products available, but practically all of them are based on three data models: hierarchical, network, and relational. Actually, most DBMSs are relational, especially recent ones. Historically, hierarchical systems appeared first, followed closely by network systems. Our treatment of the models will be in the order of their development, and will concentrate on the structure and operations that pertain to each type.

Hierarchical Models

In a hierarchical data model, the basic structure is a tree. In general, a number of different trees are included in the model. In each tree, records appear as nodes, and relationships are "parent-child" in nature. Not all nodes have the same record type. Access to any node is through the root and along a unique path. The ordering of nodes in a tree is an essential feature of a hierarchical model. All trees in the model can also be ordered by defining a root such that its children are the roots of every tree. In that sense, a hierarchical data model is a single-tree structure.

To illustrate a hierarchical data model, consider a hypothetical shop that sells and repairs bicycles. The owner carries several sizes of bicycles (that is, 24-inch, 26-inch, 28-inch, and specialty types) made by different manufacturers in various styles, and obtained from distributors. To repair bicycles, the owner maintains an inventory of parts from various suppliers. The sales part of the operation has a database which includes the following specifications:

- The record for each size contains a size and a pointer to information about manufacturers.
- The record for each manufacturer contains a name, a pointer to information about distributors, and a pointer to information about styles of bicycles.
- The record for each distributor contains a name, a state where located, and a telephone number.
- The record for each style contains an identification number, gender, grade, weight, and a pointer to information about assemblies.
- The record for each assembly contains a frame assembly number, a wheel assembly number, and an accessory package number.

Specification of additional records involves the repair part of the operation. For example, each wheel assembly number is a reference (pointer) to information about the kinds of rims, spokes, tires, and other parts of the assembly; any subassemblies of a specific part; and the suppliers. Each subassembly record contains information about individual parts (nuts, gears, etc.).

The tree type in Figure 10.3 shows the hierarchical structure of the bicycle shop database. A **tree type** is a logical representation of the relationships in the hierarchical data model. It consists of a root record

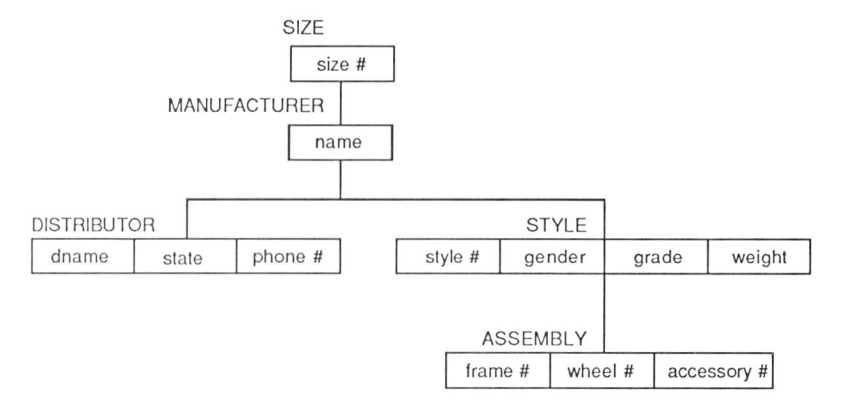

Figure 10.3 A tree type for the bicycle shop database

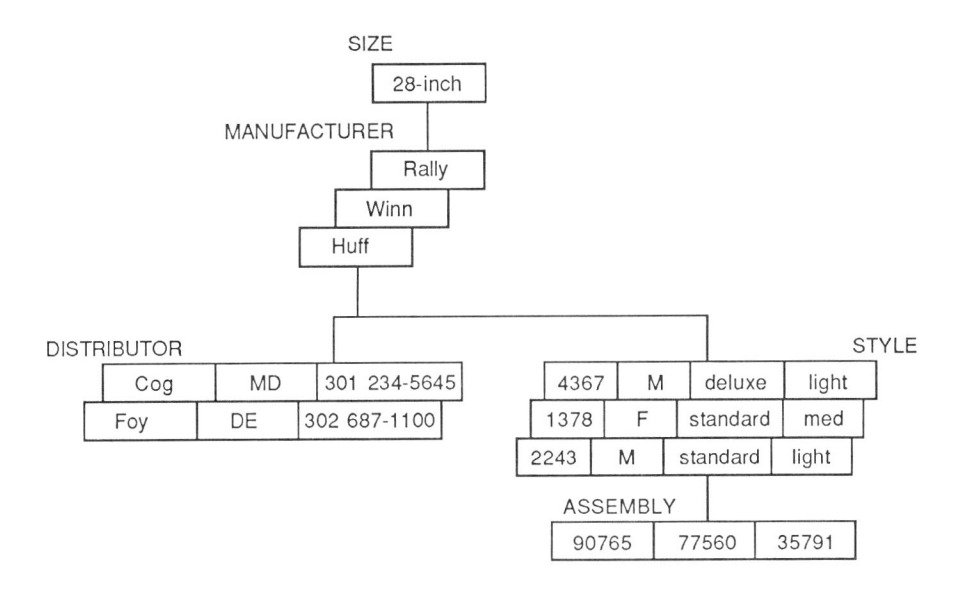

```
                        SIZE
                     ┌─────────┐
                     │ 28-inch │
                     └─────────┘
        MANUFACTURER      │
                     ┌─────────┐
                     │  Rally  │
                  ┌─────────┐──┘
                  │  Winn   │
               ┌────────┐──┘
               │  Huff  │
               └────────┘
                    │
    ┌───────────────┴───────────────┐
DISTRIBUTOR                                          STYLE
  ┌──────┬────┬──────────────┐   ┌──────┬───┬──────────┬───────┐
  │ Cog  │ MD │ 301 234-5645 │   │ 4367 │ M │ deluxe   │ light │
  ├──────┼────┼──────────────┤   ├──────┼───┼──────────┼───────┤
  │ Foy  │ DE │ 302 687-1100 │   │ 1378 │ F │ standard │ med   │
  └──────┴────┴──────────────┘   ├──────┼───┼──────────┼───────┤
                                  │ 2243 │ M │ standard │ light │
                                  └──────┴───┴──────────┴───────┘
                                         ASSEMBLY │
                                  ┌───────┬───────┬───────┐
                                  │ 90765 │ 77560 │ 35791 │
                                  └───────┴───────┴───────┘
```

Figure 10.4 Sample occurrences of the bicycle shop database.

type and an ordered set of subtree types. There are multiple **occurrences** of a tree type in a hierarchical data model—that is, trees with specific values for each record. Figure 10.4 contains occurrences of the tree type SIZE in Figure 10.3.

The tree in Figure 10.4 contains one occurrence of SIZE. That is all it can contain because SIZE is the root of the tree. As a parent node, SIZE has one child, MANUFACTURER, but three occurrences of the child. One of the occurrences, HUFF, is a parent of DISTRIBUTOR, with two occurrences, and of STYLE, with three occurrences. One of the STYLE occurrences is a parent of an ASSEMBLY occurrence. Other occurrences of trees with root SIZE (= 28-INCH) are not shown in Figure 10.4. For example, there is a tree in which RALLY is the child of 28-INCH, and occurrences of DISTRIBUTOR and STYLE are children of RALLY. Similarly, there is a tree including WINN. Children of the other occurrences also are not shown.

A DBMS incorporating this data model has a **data dictionary** (a portion of which is shown in Figure 10.5), which includes descriptions of record types and their interrelationships. The dictionary helps the owner enter data to create the database and is instrumental in responding to queries by the owner. When the owner is ready to enter data, the DBMS commonly presents a template (a listing of fields with space to enter a value for each field) based on the definitions in the data dictionary. As the owner enters values, the DDL translates them into formats which the DML uses to store the records in the physical database. Later, when the

296   Chapter 10

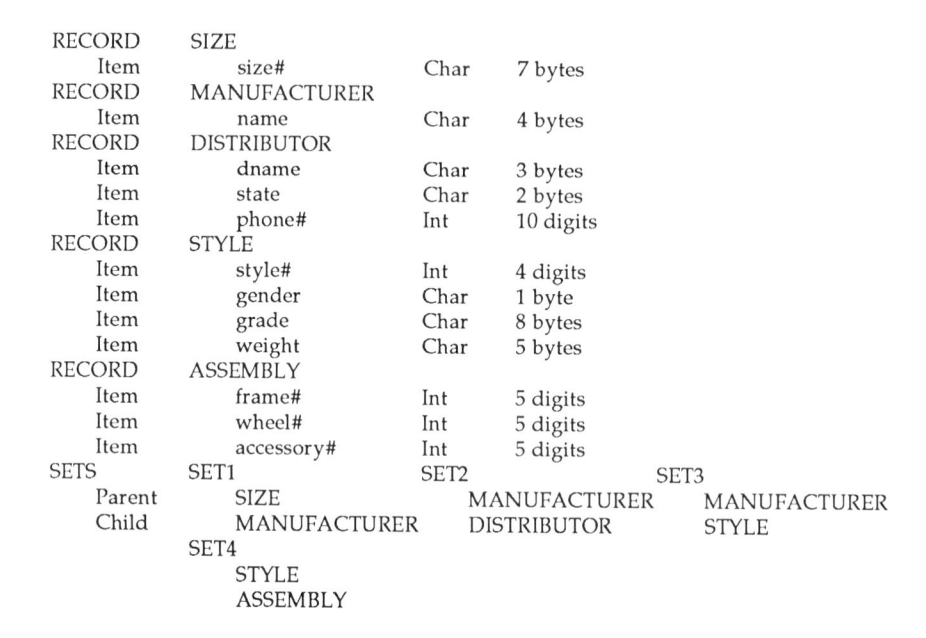

RECORD	SIZE		
Item	size#	Char	7 bytes
RECORD	MANUFACTURER		
Item	name	Char	4 bytes
RECORD	DISTRIBUTOR		
Item	dname	Char	3 bytes
Item	state	Char	2 bytes
Item	phone#	Int	10 digits
RECORD	STYLE		
Item	style#	Int	4 digits
Item	gender	Char	1 byte
Item	grade	Char	8 bytes
Item	weight	Char	5 bytes
RECORD	ASSEMBLY		
Item	frame#	Int	5 digits
Item	wheel#	Int	5 digits
Item	accessory#	Int	5 digits

SETS	SET1	SET2	SET3
Parent	SIZE	MANUFACTURER	MANUFACTURER
Child	MANUFACTURER	DISTRIBUTOR	STYLE
	SET4		
	STYLE		
	ASSEMBLY		

Figure 10.5 Sample data dictionary for the bicycle shop hierarchical database.

owner queries the system (by means of a language understood by the DBMS), the query is checked against the data dictionary. The query is then translated by the DBMS into directions for the DML to search storage and for the operating system to output a response—a value of a record, for example.

During this process, the owner communicates only with the DBMS at the conceptual level, not with the storage structures at the physical level. Because the system exhibits data independence, the DBA can rearrange data in storage, for example, by using a hash table instead of an inverted list or by creating a new index for a B-tree, and the owner is completely unaware of the changes.

Various operators are required to process data in a hierarchical model. Not surprisingly, they correspond to the ones for tree structures. These include operators to perform the following operations:

- Locate a specific occurrence of a tree.
- Move from one tree to another.
- Move from record to record.
- Insert/delete/update a record.

A hierarchical data model (or hierarchical DBMS) is especially appropriate for applications, such as payroll and inventory, in which relationships among entities are generally **one-to-many**. These relationships are conveniently represented by the parent-children organization of a tree. The menu portion of menu-driven systems, such as a bibliographic retrieval system, is an example. When a selection is made from the main menu (a list of subject headings like fine arts, sports, and medicine, for example), a secondary menu appears which is a list of subcategories of the previous selection (for instance, basketball, baseball, sailing, etc., for sports). The process can continue through a number of menu levels.

The most common hierarchical database system is IBM's IMS (Information Management System). It is used extensively on mainframes. IMS appeared in 1968 (as IMS/360 Version 1) and was the first database system to become commercially available. Currently, there is a virtual storage version (IMS/VS).

A hierarchical model is easy to understand, but not every collection of data can be arranged conveniently into tree structures as required by the model. Therefore, hierarchical data models and database management systems are not suitable for all applications requiring a database. Their disadvantages—data redundancy, updating records, and inability to handle many-to-many relationships directly—result from constraints of the tree structure. In the bicycle shop example, the same manufacturer is likely to make several sizes of bicycles, or the same distributor might handle two or more manufacturers' bicycles. Because of the unique path restriction, multiple copies of each manufacturer's or distributer's record must be stored. In a large database, this redundancy can take considerable storage space. If we had continued the subtree of parts assemblies, for example, the same part (a nut or a gear) would appear for almost all of the bicycles. Some systems do provide mechanisms to reduce the amount of data redundancy.

Deleting or updating records also can be troublesome. All copies of a record must be updated or deleted; otherwise data inconsistency occurs. When changes are made, only the occurrences of record types which pertain to that record should be updated or deleted. The network data model considered next overcomes some of these disadvantages of a hierarchical model.

Network Models

A network data model has a directed graph as its underlying structure. A **directed graph**, or **digraph**, consists of two sets, the nonempty set V of vertices and the set E of edges, together with a function from an edge e in E to an ordered pair of vertices p,q in V. The edge e goes from p to q. An edge may also go from q to p, but it is different from e. Figure 10.6 shows a digraph with five vertices p,q,r,s,t and six edges a,b,c,d,e,f. The arrows

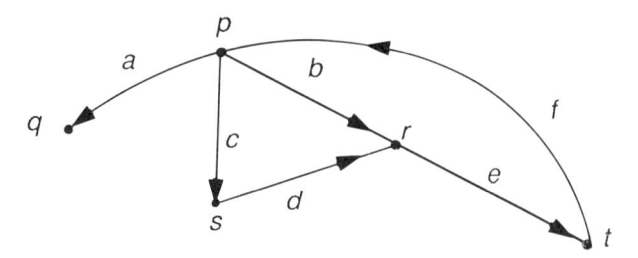

Figure 10.6 A sample directed graph

indicate the direction of the edges. For example, the edge a goes from p to q. In mathematical notation, $V=\{p,q,r,s,t\}$, $E=\{a,b,c,d,e,f\}$, and $f:E\to V\times V$ is defined by $a=(p,q)$, $b=(p,r)$, $c=(p,s)$, $d=(s,r)$, $e=(r,t)$, $f=(t,p)$.

A digraph resembles a tree, but with a significant difference: there is not always a unique path between any two nodes. This feature makes a digraph more versatile than a tree (which is a special case of a digraph) and an appropriate structure for a network data model. Not only can each parent have many children, but each child can have any number of parents. As a result, the network data model handles many-to-many relationships better than the hierarchical model, but still not directly.

In the bicycle shop example, a distributor record could contain pointers (directed edges) to each record bearing a distinct name of a manufacturer; a manufacturer record could contain pointers to each record with a distinct size of bicycle. The data dictionary of a network DBMS holds descriptions of these relationships. Programs in the DBMS translate the descriptions to gain access to data in storage structures. One of these structures may be a multilist relating distributors to manufacturers. Other structures are possible for the same relationship, but the user of the DBMS does not know how the data is stored.

This network of relationships facilitates response to queries like the following:

- What size bicycles does Winn make?
- Which manufacturer's bicycles does Cog distribute?

Neither of these queries is handled readily by the hierarchical model. Other more complicated queries are also possible in a network model, provided links (directed edges) exist from children of one parent to children of another parent, or from children to parents.

Network data models originated in 1971 with the final report of the Data Base Task Group (DBTG) of the Programming Language Committee of the Conference on Data Systems Languages (CODASYL), the organization which defined COBOL. The proposals of the DBTG spawned a number of network databases, commonly referred to as "CODASYL systems." One of the best known of these systems is IDMS (Integrated Database Management System), produced by Cullinet Software primarily for IBM mainframes.

Network systems are more complicated structures and require more complicated operators than hierarchical systems. Although both kinds are still in use, new development of them has all but halted in favor of the third general type of data model—relational. For that reason, and because of their similarity to hierarchical models, our treatment of network systems is cursory.

Relational Models

The most common databases currently in use are **relational**. They offer the user more flexibility and convenience than the other two models. The fundamental ideas on which they are based first appeared in print in 1970 by E. F. Codd (see Reference List). Relational databases implementing these ideas did not occur immediately, because hierarchical and network models had already gained a foothold among users. Now, however, relational databases are in demand, so much so that vendors of hierarchical and network databases are providing relational front-ends for users.

The underlying structure of a relational database (RDB) is a table in which each row is a record and each column is a field. The external level—that is, what the user perceives—represents data in tabular form. Operators create new tables from old. Tables are supported at the conceptual level, even though data may not be stored in tables at the internal level. For example, indexed sequential structures may store data, but the database software must convert related data into tables for the user.

Tables, in general, can have variable-length records with more than one data value within fields. However, in tables of an RDB, every occurrence of a record type has the same number of fields, and each field contains a single data value. These record types are said to be in **first normal form**. The process of restructuring records to meet specific requirements such as these is called **normalization**. We will identify other normal forms and say more about normalization after we consider an example.

To illustrate the relational model, the records in the bicycle shop example (Figure 10.4) are reorganized and more data is added. Figure 10.7 contains the unnormalized data, and Figure 10.8 shows the tables (with records in first normal form) as perceived by the user of a relational database system.

SIZE	MANUFACTURER	DISTRIBUTOR
28-inch	Huff	Cog MD 3012345645
		Foy DE 3026871100
	Rally	Foy DE 3026871100
	Winn	Cog MD 3012345645
26-inch	Rally	Foy DE 3026871100
24-inch	Huff	Cog MD 3012345645
		Foy DE 3026871100

SIZE	MANUFACTURER	STYLE	ASSEMBLY
28-inch	Huff	1378 F	Standard Medium 90765 77560 35791
		2243 M	Standard Light 90755 77123 35464
		4367 M	DeLuxe Light 90745 77342 35112
	Rally	8686 F	Standard Heavy 15532 56784 77987
	Winn	6653 M	Special Light 44465 21321 65454
		7734 F	Regular Heavy 44497 21765 65888
26-inch	Rally	8675 M	DeLuxe Medium 15477 54668 75333
24-inch	Huff	2045 F	Standard Light 90533 74190 32498

Figure 10.7 Data for the bicycle shop example

The following tables are included in Figure 10.8:

- DISTRIBUTOR. Each distributor record has fields for DNAME, STATE, and PHONE#.
- STYLE. Each style record has fields for STYLE#, GENDER, TYPE, and WEIGHT.

DISTRIBUTOR, and STYLE are regarded as **entities**. The remaining tables represent **relationships**. They include:

- MANUFACTURER-DNAME
- MANUFACTURER-STYLE#
- SIZE-MANUFACTURER
- STYLE#-ASSEMBLY

Each relationship is in the form of an inverted list.

Figure 10.8 illustrates one of the characteristics of an RDB, namely, that all of the information content of the tables is given explicitly, not through pointers to other tables. In particular, relationships are visible to users as rows in tables. For example, row 3 of the SIZE-MANUFACTURER table gives the information that a 28-inch bicycle is made by Winn. It is not necessary to read the value of a field and then follow a pointer to data related to the value.

SIZE	MANUFACTURER
28-inch	Huff
28-inch	Rally
28-inch	Winn
26-inch	Rally
24-inch	Huff

MANUFACTURER	STYLE#
Huff	1378
Huff	2045
Huff	2243
Huff	4367
Rally	8675
Rally	8686
Winn	6653
Winn	7734

DISTRIBUTOR

DNAME	STATE	PHONE#
Cog	MD	3012345645
Foy	DE	3026871100

MANUFACTURER	DNAME
Huff	Cog
Huff	Foy
Rally	Foy
Winn	Cog

STYLE

STYLE#	GENDER	TYPE	WEIGHT
1378	F	Standard	Medium
2045	F	Standard	Light
2243	M	Standard	Light
4367	M	DeLuxe	Light
......			
8686	F	Standard	Heavy

STYLE#	ASSEMBLY (FRAME#	WHEEL#	ACC#)
1378	90765	77560	35790
2045	90533	74190	32498
2243	90755	77123	35464
4367	90745	77342	35112
...			
8686	15532	56784	77987

Figure 10.8 Some of the tables in an RDB system for the bicycle shop

All record types in the tables in Figure 10.8 are in first normal form. Second through fifth normal forms are also defined for relational models. All five normal forms can be applied to hierarchical and network models as well. Only definitions and examples are included; detailed treatments are contained in books on databases.

First normal form. All occurrences of a record type contain the same number of fields. Variable-length records, including those with variable-length fields (that is, fields that contain more than one data value), are not in first normal form. Figures 10.7 and 10.8 contain examples of record types violating and satisfying, respectively, first normal form.

Second normal form. The record type satisfies first normal form, and a nonkey field pertains only to the entire key. Second normal form is violated when the key consists of two or more fields and at least one of the nonkey fields contains data about only one of the fields in the key. For example, consider the record type

MNAME | STYLE# | DNAME | GRADE | WEIGHT

with key MNAME-STYLE#. Assume the distributer's name (DNAME) pertains to both the manufacturer's name (MNAME) and the style number (STYLE#), but GRADE and WEIGHT pertain only to STYLE#. Then the record type violates second normal form because GRADE (and WEIGHT) is data about part, but not all, of the key. By reorganizing, the record types

MNAME | STYLE# | DNAME   and   STYLE# | GRADE | WEIGHT

with MNAME_STYLE# and STYLE#, respectively, as keys, satisfy second normal form.

Third normal form. The record type satisfies first normal form, and no nonkey field may pertain to another nonkey field. For example, the record type

MNAME | DNAME | STATE

with key MNAME violates third normal form because STATE contains data about DNAME and not MNAME. The reorganized record types

MNAME | DNAME   and   DNAME | STATE

satisfy third normal form.

Fourth normal form. The record type satisfies third normal form and may not contain two or more independent multivalued facts about an entity. For example, the record type

NAME | DNAME | STYLE#

violates fourth normal form because there are more than one DNAME and STYLE# for each occurrence of MNAME. The reorganized record types

MNAME | DNAME   and   MNAME | STYLE#

satisfy fourth normal form. Each of the record types can have additional fields, provided the fields are single-valued and do not violate third normal form.

Fifth normal form. The record type satisfies fourth normal form, and its information content cannot be reconstructed from record types which have fewer fields. For example, suppose the following rule exists: if a distributor sells a certain size of bicycle to a shop and the distributor represents the manufacturer of that size, then the distributor sells that size for that manufacturer. Consider the following table:

DNAME	MNAME	SIZE
Foy	Huff	28"
Foy	Huff	26"
Foy	Winn	28"
Foy	Winn	26"
Cog	Huff	26"

This record type is not in fifth normal form because all of the true facts (information content) can be reconstructed from three record types, each containing only two fields:

DNAME	MNAME
Foy	Huff
Foy	Winn
Cog	Huff

DNAME	SIZE
Foy	28"
Foy	26"
Cog	26"

MNAME	SIZE
Huff	28"
Huff	26"
Winn	28"
Winn	26"

All of these three record types satisfy fifth normal form and have the form of inverted lists.

The term **normalization** refers to any of the normal forms. Record types may be normalized according to the third normal form but not the fourth, for example. In general, normal forms and normalization are important guidelines for designing records in a database system. Normalization tends to prevent data inconsistencies and various problems associated with updating fields. It facilitates the updating of nonkey fields, but may cause extra retrievals to obtain all fields pertaining to a given key. Thus, tradeoffs exist between maintenance and performance. Consequently, complete normalization, especially with respect to the fourth and fifth normal forms, is not always implemented.

Operations performed on RDBs relate to the tables that constitute the underlying structure of the relational model. In the data definition language (DDL), tables are created, changed, and deleted. In the data manipulation language (DML), items in tables are updated, selected, inserted, and deleted. The DML works with as many tables as necessary—for example, to retrieve phone numbers of all distributors of a specified manufacturer and size of bicycle. Also, various built-in functions are provided for counting, finding sums, and so forth. Specific examples of some of the possible queries and operations common to RDBs are included in the section on query languages.

As indicated earlier, the basic concepts on which relational database systems are built originated in a paper by E. F. Codd in 1970. Actual development of RDBs occurred in the mid to late 1970s. Two significant efforts during that period were in California—"System R" at the IBM Research Laboratory in San Jose, and "INGRES" at the University of California, Berkeley. System R was a prototype of the language SQL (pronounced "sequel" and originally spelled that way), which is supported by several relational database systems, including DB2, SQL/DS, ORACLE, UNIFY, PDQ, and QINT/SQL. Some vendors of systems not based on SQL have indicated that they are developing SQL interfaces for their products. INGRES (originally standing for "Interactive Graphics and Retrieval System") was also a prototype and supports the language QUEL (QUEry Language) rather than SQL. It gained initial popularity in university environments before becoming a commercial product. Other nonSQL-based relational database systems include RUBIX, IDMS/R, dBASE II, dBASE III, R:BASE, NOMAD, and INFORMIX.

The most prominent advantage of the relational model, especially when compared to the hierarchical or network models, is its capability to represent many-to-many associations among record types. These relationships are implemented conveniently as tables. Because the information content in tables is explicit (that is, no pointers are involved), the user can more readily identify relationships. The nonkey fields in an RDB are easy to update. However, processing in an RDB is less efficient than in a network database. Another disadvantage is that all records within the same table must be fixed-length with single-valued fields.

CREATING A DATABASE

Suppose the bicycle shop owner decides to create and maintain a SALES database. After analyzing relationships among distributor, style, assembly, and any other parameter, the owner concludes that each sale has attributes

VOUCHER, DATE, and AMOUNT

and that the relationships for each sale are

SIZE, MANUFACTURER, DISTRIBUTOR, STYLE, and ASSEMBLY

Schematically, these attributes and relationships are shown in Figure 10.9. Attributes are in parentheses and relationships are indicated by lines. In a real application, at least three other databases can be created: DISTRIBUTOR, STYLE, and ASSEMBLY (SIZE and MANUFACTURER also are possible). Assume that three databases exist for purposes of this example.

```
SALES (Voucher, Date, Amount)
       ├── SIZE
       ├── MANUFACTURER
       ├── DISTRIBUTOR (name, state, phone#)
       ├── STYLE (style#, gender, grade, weight)
       └── ASSEMBLY (frame#, wheel#, accessory#)
```

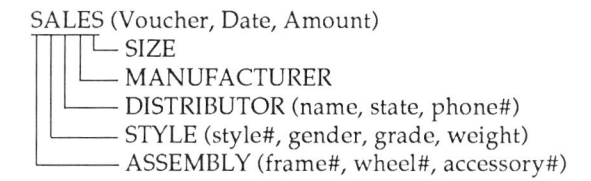

Figure 10.9 Relationships and attributes in SALES database

The owner must decide the physical characteristics of each attribute. Field lengths, whether or not a value in a field is optional, and which attributes are keys, are some of the issues that require decisions. For simplicity, Figure 10.10 contains only the length and key characteristics.

Data can now be loaded into the SALES database. Specific data for SALES are shown in Figure 10.11. The data in Figure 10.7 is also loaded (or already exists) in the DISTRIBUTOR, STYLE, and ASSEMBLY databases. Actually, ASSEMBLY needs one additional field to contain a value for the entire assembly if it is a separate database.

After the initial loading, additional data can be inserted. This is done with the help of a database language, a menu, or a program. Each insertion contains values for the mandatory fields in a SALES record, plus the primary key values in each of the databases related to SALES. A sample insertion is

```
VOUCHER        P94321
DATE           112587
AMOUNT         376.12
SIZE           26-inch
MANUFACTURER   Huff
STYLE#         2243
ASSEMBLY#      31313
```

Relationships are established and data is entered. Figure 10.8 contains the kind of data and relationships that pertain to this example. Other relationships are VOUCHER and STYLE#, VOUCHER and ASSEMBLY#, and so on. Update, deletion, and other operations can now be performed. Provisions for report generation, security, and integrity are included as necessary.

If the owner can find an appropriate database applications program, then only the data and relationships indicated above need entering. The program takes care of structuring and storing data, and hides all of the details from the user (in the conceptual and physical levels). If a program is not available, then the owner must decide which data structures and file organizations to incorporate, and how data is stored on physical devices.

SALES	Length	Key
voucher	char(6)	yes
date	char(8)	yes
amount	real(8)	yes
size	char(6)	yes
manufacturer	char(8)	yes
dname	char(8)	yes
state	char(2)	no
phone#	char(10)	no
style#	char(4)	yes
gender	char(1)	no
grade	char(8)	no
weight	char(6)	no
frame#	char(5)	no
wheel#	char(5)	no
accessory#	char(5)	no

Figure 10.10 Physical characteristics of data for SALES

Voucher	Date	Amount	Size	Manufacturer
A46325	102986	195.83	26inch	Rally
A55555	012087	219.95	24inch	Rally
...				
R69741	091987	142.64	26inch	Huff

Figure 10.11 Data for the SALES database

Programs to implement the decisions must be written. The first ten chapters of this book give the kind of information the owner needs to accomplish the task.

QUERY LANGUAGES

Users most commonly access a DBMS by a menu- or forms-driven interface, a data manipulation language (DML), or a query language. In the menu- or forms-driven system, users pick items from a succession of lists or fill in forms. Programming is required to use a DML to communicate with the software in a DBMS. The hierarchical implementation IMS and the network-oriented IDMS use data manipulation languages. Query languages provide interactive, high-level commands such as SELECT and are easier to learn and use than DMLs. Query languages are more popular as means of access to a relational database. Some of the facilities of a SQL-based system such as DB2 are illustrated. Similar capabilities are found in nonSQL-based systems such as the dBASE series. The object is to give a flavor of query languages, not to give sufficient details to use or design them.

SQL-Based Systems

A user of SQL has data definition language facilities to create, change, and delete tables. To create the "style" table of Figure 10.8, we enter

```
CREATE TABLE style
     ( style#     INTEGER(4)   NOT NULL,
       gender     CHAR(1),
       type       CHAR(8),
       weight     CHAR(6) )
```

This statement establishes a table named "style" with four columns headed "style#", "gender", "type", and "weight". Data types (INTEGER, CHAR) and field widths also are specified. When entries are made, a field marked NOT NULL must not be empty; other fields may be left blank. A new column is added to the right of the columns in "style" with the command ALTER TABLE:

```
ALTER TABLE  style
      ADD    color(8)
```

The command DROP TABLE deletes the table:

```
DROP TABLE style
```

Data manipulation facilities of SQL include the statements SELECT, UPDATE, DELETE, and INSERT. Examples of SELECT and INSERT follow. SELECT may be used to answer the query "Get the type and weight for style numbered 1378." The statement

```
SELECT  type, weight
FROM    style
WHERE   style# = '1378'
```

gives the result "standard" "medium". A list of all style numbers is obtained with the statement

```
SELECT  style#
FROM    style
```

An INSERT command enters data into a table:

```
INSERT
INTO    style
VALUES  ( 1378, f, standard, medium )
```

This statement provides values for all four fields in the table. The statement

```
INSERT
INTO    style ( gender, weight )
VALUES  ( f, medium )
```

adds values only to the two fields specified.

The SELECT command implements a "join", an operation that distinguishes relational systems from other systems. It is a query to obtain data from two or more tables. One example of its use is to get all combinations of size and distributor information having the same manufacturer. The statement

```
SELECT  size.*, distributor.*
FROM    size, distributor
WHERE   size.manufacturer = distributor.manufacturer
```

causes a search of the two tables "size" and "distributor" and produces the result

28-inch	Huff	Cog	Huff
28-inch	Huff	Foy	Huff
28-inch	Winn	Cog	Winn
28-inch	Rally	Foy	Rally
26-inch	Rally	Foy	Rally
24-inch	Huff	Cog	Huff
24-inch	Huff	Foy	Huff

Many variations of this small sample of basic statements are possible. SQL and other query languages also have an extensive repertoire of built-in functions, Boolean operators (such as AND, OR, and NOT), and other commands which allow repetition (DO-WHILE) and choice

(IF-THEN). Complex programs may be written in the language, or may be embedded in high-level languages, such as COBOL and Pascal. A user should become familiar with the facilities of a query language and then prepare a preliminary design of a problem solution before attempting an application.

SECURITY AND PRIVACY MEASURES

Databases contain vast amounts of information about people, company matters, and national and international affairs. Multiple users have access privileges. Greater security precautions than in one-user systems are essential to protect an individual's right to privacy, a company's confidential data, and military secrets. Integrity, or accuracy, of data also is a vital concern. Measures discussed in Chapter 5 to increase security (for example, passwords and encryption) and integrity apply to databases. Special care is necessary, however, because many related files are involved, rather than just a single file. An update, for example, must be processed in every affected file. Also, an authorized user of one file must not be allowed access to related tables or files to which authorization has not been given.

Database languages such as SQL and NOMAD contain statements directed toward the security of a database. Specifically, a SQL user must gain authorization to perform operations, access, or create a table file. Otherwise, the system assumes the user is not authorized.

Initially, database administrator authority (DBA authority) is given to a person who can then perform any operation in the system and grant authorization to users. The DBA issues SQL statements like

```
GRANT SELECT ON STYLE TO A49652
```

to allow user A49652 to perform SELECT operations on the table STYLE. User A49652 cannot delete, insert, or update items in STYLE, nor perform SELECT on any other table. Other SQL statements such as

```
GRANT INSERT,DELETE ON STYLE TO A49652
GRANT SELECT,UPDATE ON STYLE TO A49652
GRANT UPDATE ON STYLE TO A49652
```

allow user A49652 to perform only the operations specified, and only on the designated file or table. A user can get authorization to CREATE tables. That user can perform any operation on each table he or she creates. In addition, authority can be granted to access specific records (rows) or columns of a table, and to obtain summary information only. All authorizations are maintained in a system file and are accessible to the DBA. Authority can be revoked with statements like

```
REVOKE UPDATE ON STYLE FROM A49652
```

Most database languages, including SQL, do not have statements to support integrity. Users can include their own integrity support within programs, as indicated in Chapter 5, or use a database language like NOMAD, that does provide statements. For example, NOMAD allows the user to specify a pattern, or mask, that must be satisfied by any insertion or update. The statement

```
MASTER PERSONNEL INSERT KEYED(SSN)
    ITEM SSN  . . . HEADING 'PERSONNEL' MASK '999-99-9999'
```

ensures that entries in the primary key field SSN of table PERSONNEL are of the form 225-96-4015. Entries in any of the forms 225964015, 22A-96-4015, or 225-96-401 are rejected. The statement does not prohibit entries of incorrect SSNs that are in the proper form.

The statement

```
MASTER PERSONNEL INSERT KEYED(SSN)
    ITEM SSN . . .
```

prevents insertion of a new value of SSN if the same value is already in the table. The statement

```
MASTER PERSONNEL INSERT KEYED(SSN)
    ITEM SSN  . . . MEMBER 'JOBTITLE'
```

indicates that JOBTITLE is a table containing SSN, but not as the primary key. NOMAD checks INSERT and UPDATE (but not DELETE) operations on table JOBTITLE to make sure that the value of SSN is already in the table PERSONNEL.

NOMAD also provides statements to specify ranges of acceptable values for keys. The statement

```
MASTER PERSONNEL INSERT KEYED(SSN)
    ITEM JOBTITLE  . . . LIMITS (PROGRAMMER, SYSTEMANALYST)
```

restricts entries in JOBTITLE to the two values PROGRAMMER and SYSTEMANALYST. The statement

```
MASTER PERSONNEL INSERT KEYED(SSN)
    ITEM SALARY . . . LIMITS (10000:90000)
```

allows entries in SALARY only if they are greater than 10000 and less than or equal to 90000.

These examples illustrate the kinds of security and integrity measures provided by database languages. In general, there is a great need to improve language facilities to increase security and integrity of data in databases.

APPLICATIONS AND TRENDS

This section takes a brief look at online databases and expert systems, two general areas in which databases are having a major impact in the marketplace. Comments are given on the movement toward fourth generation languages for interacting with databases.

Online Databases

A wealth of information is available in databases that are accessible through terminals. The number of electronically marketed databases is estimated to be around 3000, with a recent increase of 30 percent annually. Contents of these databases range from research abstracts in scientific fields to newspaper stories; from legislative activity to credit data. Some of the most popular or valuable ones and an indication of their contents include:

- *ADI/INFORM.* Indexes and abstracts of 550 management-oriented journals. An 8000-word vocabulary facilitates searching.
- *Disclosure II.* SEC (Securities Exchange Commission) filings on approximately 9000 companies by geographic location, sales level and product category.
- *International Software Database.* Product descriptions and published reviews of over 55,000 software packages.
- *Legi-Slate.* Daily Federal Register announcements. Status and schedules of national legislation.
- *Nexis.* Full text of *The New York Times* since 1980, the *Washington Post* since 1977, and approximately 100 business publications.
- *NTIS (National Technical Information Service).* Index of most publicly available reports on government-sponsored research, development, and engineering projects.
- *Official Airlines Guide Electronic Edition.* Daily schedule and fare updates on 650 carriers worldwide.
- *SiteSelects.* Descriptions of facilities, meeting places, and surrounding areas for corporate meeting planners.

- *Westlaw.* Full text of opinions covering state court cases reported in the National Reporter System since 1967 and Supreme Court opinions since 1932.

The cost of a search can vary from several dollars to hundreds of dollars. Users pay for each minute of connect time and for each citation, as well as a communications charge for each minute. These systems can be expensive to use, but that cost should be compared to alternatives for obtaining similar information. Many companies are finding the online services to be very good investments.

Expert Systems

Knowledge-based or **expert systems** are those systems that behave like a human expert within a particular subject domain. They usually require years to be developed, field-tested, and accepted. In general, they are programmed to respond to queries as an expert would. Knowledge and inference mechanisms in a specific area of application, such as disease diagnosis, tax preparation, or estate planning, must be reduced to vocabulary and rules. Effective systems require a blend of techniques and concepts from fields such as artificial intelligence, mathematics, and databases.

Relational databases are being used in expert systems because tables provide a feasible structure for relating items according to specified rules. However, relational models alone do not provide an adequate basis for determining what data *means*. For example, database systems do not provide the meaning, or semantic difference, that prohibits adding an integer representing a style number to one that represents a telephone number. Nor do tables expressing parent-child relationships provide the necessary inferences to interpret the query, "Who are the grandparents of John?"

Rules of inference also are required. Special languages such as PROLOG are needed to express the rules conveniently. Heuristics, or rules of thumb, are employed for those cases not completely covered by rules. Mathematical concepts from relational algebra, logic, and analysis should be incorporated. So, too, are probability and statistics needed to help determine when particular rules or conclusions are reasonable. Integrating all of these concepts with appropriately designed databases is a potentially fruitful area of research and development.

Fourth-Generation Languages

Applications programs constitute part of the software in a DBMS. They enable users to interact with the database system without writing programs. Invariably, however, an occasion arises for which an applications program is not available. Then the user must provide a program. This may be done in the traditional sense of writing a program in a high-level language such as COBOL. Alternatively, it may be done by interfacing with an **application generator,** a software tool built into a DBMS to help users develop applications programs. An application generator is called a "fourth-generation" tool because it is considered an advancement over other languages (machine and assembly languages of the "first and second generation," respectively, and "third-generation" languages like COBOL or Pascal). Users interact with an applications generator through a form of dialog, rather than the usual program. The interface between users and an application generator is a **fourth-generation language (4GL).**

Because applications of databases vary considerably, the kinds of 4GLs that are available differ both syntactically and semantically. Most 4GLs may be used with more than one database system and contain facilities that support query handling and report writers. But there are 4GLs oriented toward developers of large programming systems (ADS/O, Mantis, Natural), information center users (Focus, Nomad2, Ramis II), and programmers involved in management applications such as project planning and documentation (APS, Pacbase, Telon). Also, 4GLs may be menu-driven, procedural-oriented, or nonprocedural in nature. They may be designed for programmers or for nontechnical users. They also differ in ease of use and in the applications for which they are best suited. Details of the languages and their differences are beyond the scope of this book.

Summary

This chapter represents a departure from the study of concepts and techniques for handling separate files. The focus is on two or more related files in a database. All of the topics in previous chapters provide an extensive tool kit for the design of effective systems to store and manipulate records in a database. Applying those topics requires a knowledge of the database environment. An introduction to that environment is provided, including basic terminology and concepts for the three architectural levels of databases—external (user), conceptual, and internal (physical)—and relationships and roles of users, applications programmers, and database administrators.

A database management system is characterized by the data model on which it is based. Of the three general types of models—hierarchical, network, and relational—relational models are the most prevalent today. Many relational database systems are based on, or interface with, the query language SQL, designed to make user interaction more convenient. Fourth-generation languages have also been developed to facilitate user interaction with database management systems.

Immense quantities of data are stored in databases, many of which are extremely large. Business, government, the legal and medical professions, and others are dependent on database systems to store, process, and retrieve data. The popularity of online database services is one indication of this dependence. Another indication is the extensive effort to develop expert systems for better decision-making based on data in database systems. Yet another significant development is the implementation of database systems spread throughout a number of interconnected computers in a computer network or distributed system. Although this topic is beyond the scope of this book, the reader should understand some of the basic issues and concepts involved in processing files in distributed systems after studying the next chapter.

Exercises

1. Why is data independence important in databases?
2. Give an advantage and a disadvantage of data redundancy in a database. Under what conditions is it better to have redundancy than to eliminate it?
3. Why are data structures and file organizations hidden from users of database systems?
4. What database systems are available at your computer installation? How are they accessed? Who is the DBA? What languages are available for interacting with the database systems? What security and integrity measures are there?
5. What advantages do indexed sequential files have over inverted lists and direct files for answering queries? What are the disadvantages?
6. For each of the following descriptions, state whether inverted lists, direct files, or indexed sequential files are most appropriate. Give a reason for each answer.
   (a) Data is highly variable and dynamic. Responses must be timely (for example, a customer requests an airline ticket for a specific flight).
   (b) Records are small and fixed in size. Fast access is required (for example, a supermarket manager wants to change the price of an item).
   (c) A daily inventory list is required. Changes to the file are accumulated and made periodically (for example, during registration period, a registrar of a large university wants course enrollment data, in order of course mnemonic and number; drops and adds are processed at the end of each day).

7. Describe an application for which each of the following database systems is best suited:
   (a) Hierarchical
   (b) Network
   (c) Relational
8. In the bicycle shop RDB example, how would each of the following queries be processed?
   (a) What styles come in 26-inch size?
   (b) What is the phone number of each distributor of 24-inch bicycles?
9. For the bicycle shop RDB example, construct a table to facilitate response to the query, "What accessory sets are available for deluxe bicycles?"
10. Describe how the Hsiao-Harary Algorithm can be used to obtain information from the tables in Figure 10.8.

CHAPTER 11

FILE PROCESSING IN COMPUTER NETWORKS

INTRODUCTION

In earlier chapters a number of aspects of the storage and retrieval of records stored in files are considered. Some of the files discussed were stored in contiguous storage locations, and others had records distributed over the available storage space and retrieved more or less directly. In some cases, all of the information of interest was stored in one file, and in other cases, related files or a database contained the data. In all cases, however, only one computer was involved in the file system at any one time. Access to a file was accomplished through the I/O processing subsystem of a single computer.

In many modern computer installations, file systems are distributed not only over multiple file storage devices, but also over completely separate computers. Such systems create new problems that need to be solved in order to provide for the accessibility and integrity of data. In this chapter, these problems and some of the solutions currently available are addressed.

DEFINITIONS

A **computer network** is a collection of independent computing devices that are able to communicate with each other. A necessary characteristic of a computer network is that each computing device be able to function and perform tasks without communicating with the others. In contrast, a distributed system is a collection of computing devices that, taken together, form a computing system. Parts of the system may be distributed over a wide area, perhaps including several countries, or may be limited to several machines in the same room.

In a computer network, each computer may offer somewhat different features. For instance, a typesetting program and a laser printer may be available to the users of one computer in the network. Another computer may include a particular statistical package. Still another may provide access to other computer networks and the ability to send and receive mail to and from a large community of colleagues. Each computer in the network may have some amount of storage space available for files, or all of the storage may be attached to one computer and shared by all the users of all the computers in the network.

In both computer networks and distributed systems, a primary application for the communication system that links the machines is the transfer of data from one computer to another. Among the concerns in this application are the accurate transfer of the data over a communication link, the security and privacy of data that is transferred, and the possible existence of multiple copies of a file with the attendant concern that the copies may not be consistent.

Not all the computers on a particular network need to be of the same type, nor have the same capability. A single network may include one or more supercomputers, mainframe computers, several minicomputers, and perhaps hundreds of microcomputers. Microcomputers may participate in the network either as independent computers or by attaching to another computer as an "intelligent" terminal.

COMPUTER NETWORKS

The geographic spread of a computer network determines the network type. A **local area network (LAN)** is built from high-capacity, highly dependable communication links. Current technology limits the total length of these networks to a mile or less. **Wide area networks (WAN)** employ a variety of communication methods, including leased and dial-up telephone lines, microwaves, and satellites. There is no restriction on the length of a WAN, and several are spread over more than one nation.

Because of their limited geographic dispersement, LANs can be managed and controlled. Though a number of different types of computers, perhaps from different vendors, may be part of the same local network, a single type is often used. Whether there are multiple types of machines or not, the exact configuration of the network is known to those responsible for its management, and the task of controlling the use of the network is manageable. Decisions involving the purchase of additional equipment can be made with knowledge of the needs of the user community. Growth of the system can be controlled and carefully monitored. Such control is more difficult in the environment of a WAN and, as we shall see, may be impossible when networks are connected.

The difference in communications capabilities between LANs and WANs influences the types of applications that may be suitable for each. LANs are connected by extremely dependable, high-speed, and high-information-carrying communications systems. WANs, on the other hand, are characterized by far less dependable, and much slower communication links. These links are, however, capable of spanning great distances. More processing time is required for computers in a wide area network to determine whether or not a communication attempt has succeeded. Applications requiring a rapid, dependable response are not appropriate in such a system. As an example, some LANs are composed of workstations with little or no disk storage. One or more stations on the network act as disk servers and provide all of the disk storage needed by all of the other computers. Each time a program running on one of the work stations needs to access a disk, it sends a message over the network to the disk server. Data that is to be stored or retrieved must be sent over the network. This configuration has an advantage in that it is not necessary to allocate disk space to the individual work stations and try to have the right amount of storage available to each station. Any such effort is likely to result in unused space at some stations and a shortage at others. The disadvantage of the disk server configuration is that all disk access is necessarily slower, since it must use the network. Adequate service can be provided in very high-speed local networks, but such an application would not be appropriate in a wide area network.

The capacity of WAN connections, in bits per second, is usually significantly less than the capacity of LANs. A given WAN may employ many different types of links; two messages sent from one station to another may travel by different routes, using different media. (A **message** in a computer network is the unit of data that is sent from one computer to another. A message may contain a command to be executed on the other computer, or a response to a command given by another computer. A message is frequently a section of a file that is in transit.) Because of the wide displacement of stations, overall control of the network is more difficult. It is common to find different types of computers at different locations. Files transferred from one computer to another often require some amount of translation.

Finally computer networks are frequently connected to other computer networks. Thus, a local area network with high channel capacity and good local management and control may be connected to another local network, which may in turn be connected to a wide area network. In such cases, a user on a computer in the first LAN has access to many resources and may be able to communicate, via electronic mail and bulletin boards, with colleagues around the country or the world. Data collected locally may be supplemented by similar data collected in a different environment. Results calculated at one site may save time and work elsewhere and allow progress to be made much more quickly. The implications are significant for research, product development, and sales projections.

File transfer

An important application of computer networks, both local and wide area, is the transfer of data from one computer to another. As more users are connected by networks, it becomes more common to share data by transferring copies of all or a part of a file to a colleague. The other person may be using a different type of computer, with a different set of file-handling capabilities. In order for the data to be shared, programs must exist on both computer systems. These programs must interact with the local file access system to retrieve (and store) data, and must be able to send (and receive) the data on the network. If the two file access systems are the same, the task of communicating is not complex. However, if very different storage methods are used by the cooperating computers, some translation must be done. The steps necessary to provide accurate transfer of files over a network are usually hidden from the average computer user in file transfer programs. The user needs only to know that the same (or compatible) file transfer programs are available on both computers that are to be involved in the transfer.

A frequent use of file transfer programs is to upload data from a microcomputer to a host computer, perform manipulations, and download the result. The reverse is also common: a file stored on a host is downloaded to a microcomputer, manipulated with one of the popular user-oriented programs, and returned to the mainframe.

Security, Integrity, and Privacy

Network architecture and file transfer methods have serious implications for the security, integrity, and privacy of data. Both the sources of error in transit and the opportunities for the data to be seen by others are matters of concern to the users of data in a computer network. The common architectures for computer networks are discussed in this chapter, partly to demonstrate the vulnerability of data on the network. Encryption methods can be used to make data difficult to read by an eavesdropper, but complete security is extremely difficult. This topic was addressed more fully in Chapter 5.

Requirements of File Sharing
Movement of Files

Communication between computers that are of different types, or are attached to networks that operate differently, involves translations at many levels. One computer may use 8-bit EBCDIC codes and another, 7-bit ASCII. Numeric values may be encoded in 16-bit words on one, and 32- or 48- or 60-bit words on the other. The file systems are likely to be very different. One computer may use the VSAM system considered in Chapter 8, while the other may treat every file as a long string of bytes (the Unix operating system view). The message to be transferred may begin on a local area network that carries ten million bits per second (10 Mbps), then travel onto a wide area network that transmits 56,000 bits per second (56 Kbps), and finally be delivered over a dial-up connection at 1200 bits per second (1200 baud). Flow control and translation between every possible pair of computers would seem to be impractical.

The approach taken in the development of the ARPAnet, and now the basis of the ISO standards, is the use of an intermediate form for communications between networks. A transmission that is to initiate on an IBM MVS system and terminate on a DEC computer running Unix, for instance, would require that the internet access program be running on both systems. The IBM version would take the message from the IBM system and translate it into the intermediate form and put it on the network with the address of the destination DEC system. The DEC computer would include within its Unix operating system a program to accept the transmission from the network in the intermediate form and translate it into a form acceptable to itself.

The result of this approach is that, instead of requiring each computer system to accept from and translate to each other possible computer system, each must be able to receive from and translate to only one system—the defined internet standard.

A user with access to the TCP/IP programs can send a file to another computer that also has TCP/IP and can receive a file from such a system. The program within the collection of programs known as TCP/IP (Transport Control Protocol interaction with the Internet Protocol), which is responsible for file transfer, is called FTP (file transfer protocol). A user wishing to transfer a file executes the FTP program and must specify the name or address of the other computer to be used. Whether the other computer is in the same room or 3000 miles away will not be noticeable to the user. The user will be requested to provide suitable access information—an account and password. The user will then be communicating with the file transfer facility of the other computer and will have the ability to request a number of services. The user may ask for a list of files, change directory on the remote computer, "get" a specified

322   Chapter 11

```
Dewey[22] ftp nemo
Connected to nemo.
220 nemo FTP server (Version 4.7 Fri Oct 24 04:58:13 EDT 1986) ready.
```
[Start ftp, requesting contact with a computer called "nemo".]

```
Name (nemo:cassel): cassel
Password (nemo:cassel):
331 Password required for cassel.
230 User cassel logged in.
nemo-sun > help
Commands may be abbreviated.  Commands are:
```

!	dir	mget	quit	trace
append	form	mkdir	quote	type
ascii	get	mls	recv	user
bell	glob	mode	remotehelp	verbose
binary	hash	mput	rename	?
bye	help	open	rmdir	
cd	lcd	prompt	send	
close	ls	sendport	status	
delete	mdelete	put	struct	
debug	mdir	pwd	tenex	

[A list of the commands accepted by ftp.]

```
nemo-sun > help dir
dir            list contents of remote directory
nemo-sun > help mdelete
mdelete        delete multiple files
nemo-sun > help verbose
verbose        toggle verbose mode
nemo-sun > help mkdir
mkdir          make directory on the remote machine
nemo-sun > help ascii
ascii          set ascii transfer type
```
[Meanings of some ftp commands.]

```
nemo-sun get main.tex
200 PORT command okay.
150 Opening data connection for main.tex (192.5.39.2,1463) (594 bytes).
226 Transfer complete.
610 bytes received in 0.03 seconds (20 Kbytes/s)
nemo-sun > get udreport.sty report.1
200 PORT command okay.
150 Opening data connection for udreport.sty (192.5.39.2,1464) (7023 bytes)
226 Transfer complete.
7238 bytes received in 0.37 seconds (19 Kbytes/s)
```
[Get file *main.tex*, store it on the computer where ftp was started, using the same name.]
[Get file *udreport.sty*, store it as *report.1*.]

```
nemo-sun > get references.bib  ref.b
200 PORT command okay.
150 Opening data connection for references.bib (192.5.39.2,1473) (22146 bytes)
226 Transfer complete
22876 bytes received in 1.01 seconds (22 Kbytes/s)
nemo-sun > pwd
251 "/usa/cassel" is current directory.
nemo-sun > quit
221 Goodbye.
Dewey[25]
```
[Get a larger file.]
[Print the directory name of the remote computer.]

Figure 11.1 An ftp file transfer session, on a 10-Mbps Ethernet

file or group of files which will be transferred to the local computer and stored in suitable format, or "put" one or more local computer files on the other computer. The user may be able to rename or delete files on the other computer if the files are structured to allow such access by this user. A typical FTP session is shown in Figure 11.1.

File transfer is a somewhat well-defined task and is frequently carried out successfully. A much more difficult problem is that of file access between incompatible file systems. When the home office simply wants to know the volume of business for a particular day or month, transfer of an entire file is a burden. However, if the file systems are very different, random access to a file between machines is generally not possible.

Microhost Connection

While internetworking considerations are growing in importance, cooperation between a microcomputer and a host is often a more immediate need. Programs and hardware have been developed to facilitate the transfer of files between machines. A popular example is **Kermit,** developed at Columbia University Center for Computing Activities and distributed free. Kermit is one of a number of protocols for reliable transfer of sequential files over ordinary serial telecommunications lines. Files can be transferred between PCs, between host computers, from host to PC, and from PC to host. A file transfer using Kermit is shown in Figure 11.2.

Storage Limitations

When a computer is part of a network, users of other computers on the network have access to its storage resources. Similarly, local users have the ability to store some of their data at remote sites where extra storage is available. This leads to concern about the dependability of the network connections, in addition to the performance of the local computer. If a computer user is dependent upon storage on another computer, the local computer, the storage computer, and the network must all be working correctly in order for the user to do work.

THE NETWORKED COMPUTER ENVIRONMENT

In Chapter 4, the physical details of common file storage devices are described so that the behavior of file access system requirements becomes more meaningful. Most programmers do not have to use detailed knowledge of the physical system very often, but such knowledge often makes requirements of file access systems meaningful and therefore easier

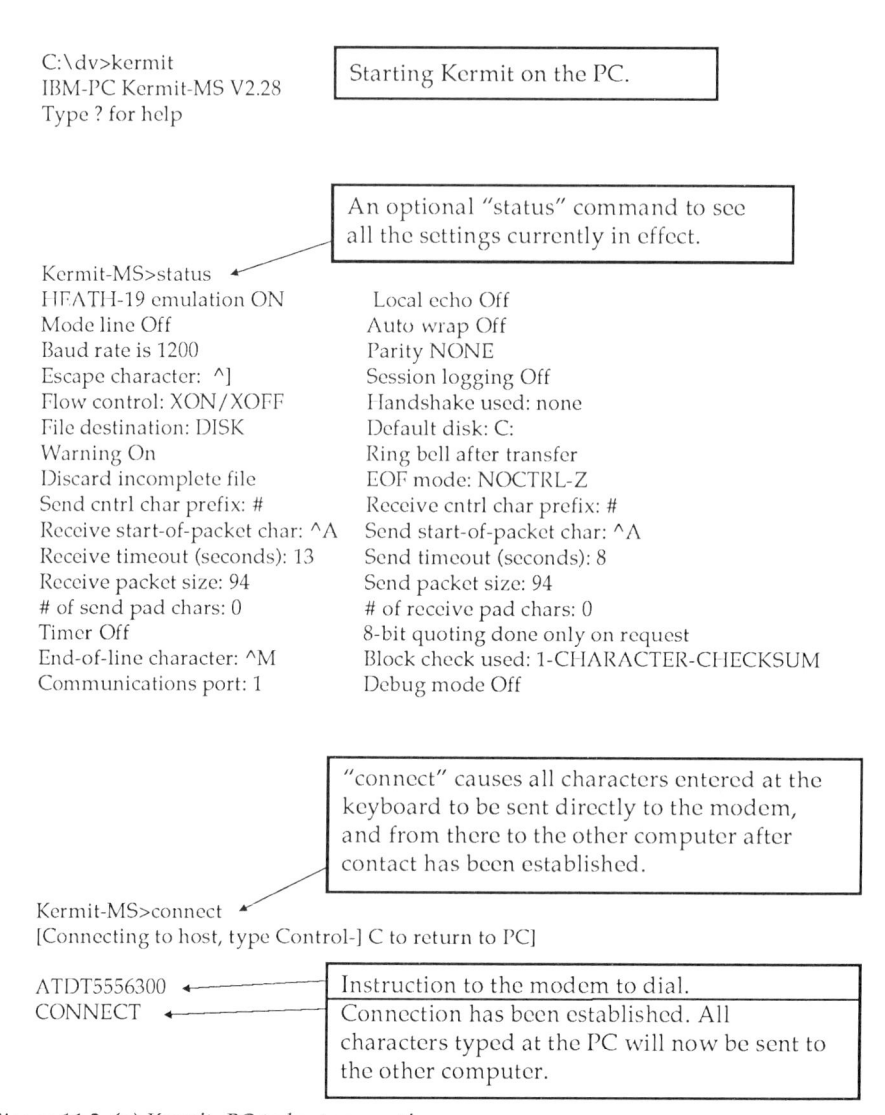

```
C:\dv>kermit
IBM-PC Kermit-MS V2.28         Starting Kermit on the PC.
Type ? for help


                                 An optional "status" command to see
                                 all the settings currently in effect.

Kermit-MS>status
HEATH-19 emulation ON        Local echo Off
Mode line Off                Auto wrap Off
Baud rate is 1200            Parity NONE
Escape character:  ^]        Session logging Off
Flow control: XON/XOFF       Handshake used: none
File destination: DISK       Default disk: C:
Warning On                   Ring bell after transfer
Discard incomplete file      EOF mode: NOCTRL-Z
Send cntrl char prefix: #    Receive cntrl char prefix: #
Receive start-of-packet char: ^A   Send start-of-packet char: ^A
Receive timeout (seconds): 13      Send timeout (seconds): 8
Receive packet size: 94            Send packet size: 94
# of send pad chars: 0             # of receive pad chars: 0
Timer Off                          8-bit quoting done only on request
End-of-line character: ^M          Block check used: 1-CHARACTER-CHECKSUM
Communications port: 1             Debug mode Off


                                "connect" causes all characters entered at the
                                keyboard to be sent directly to the modem,
                                and from there to the other computer after
                                contact has been established.

Kermit-MS>connect
[Connecting to host, type Control-] C to return to PC]

ATDT5556300          Instruction to the modem to dial.
CONNECT              Connection has been established. All
                     characters typed at the PC will now be sent to
                     the other computer.
```

Figure 11.2 (a) Kermit: PC to host connection

to meet. This section is a brief introduction to the low-level details of common computer network systems. Its purpose is also to establish some understanding of the underlying system so that use of the system from higher levels will be more meaningful.

Local Nets: Tokens versus Contention

Though many ways of connecting computers to form local networks have been designed and implemented, three particular strategies have been

File Processing in Computer Networks 325

> Next, the user logs into the host computer as usual.
>
> To transfer a file from the host computer to the PC, the following steps are taken:

> Kermit is started on the host computer (called Dewey here)

Dewey[23] kermit
C-Kermit, 4C(056) 12 Jul 85, 4.2 BSD
Type ? for help
C-Kermit>send security

> "C-Kermit" is the prompt from Kermit on the host computer, which in this case is running the unix operating system and a version of Kermit programmed in the "C" language.

Kermit-MS>receive security

> After telling the host side of Kermit to send a file (named security), the user returns to the PC side of Kermit (by typing control-] C) the PC side of kermit is told to receive a file and name it security.

File name: SECURITY.
KBytes transferred: 1

Receiving: In progress

> PC-Kermit displays the status of the transfer as it occurs.

Number of packets: 16
Number of retries: 0
Last error: None
Last warning: None

File name: SECURITY.
KBytes transferred: 13

Receiving: Completed

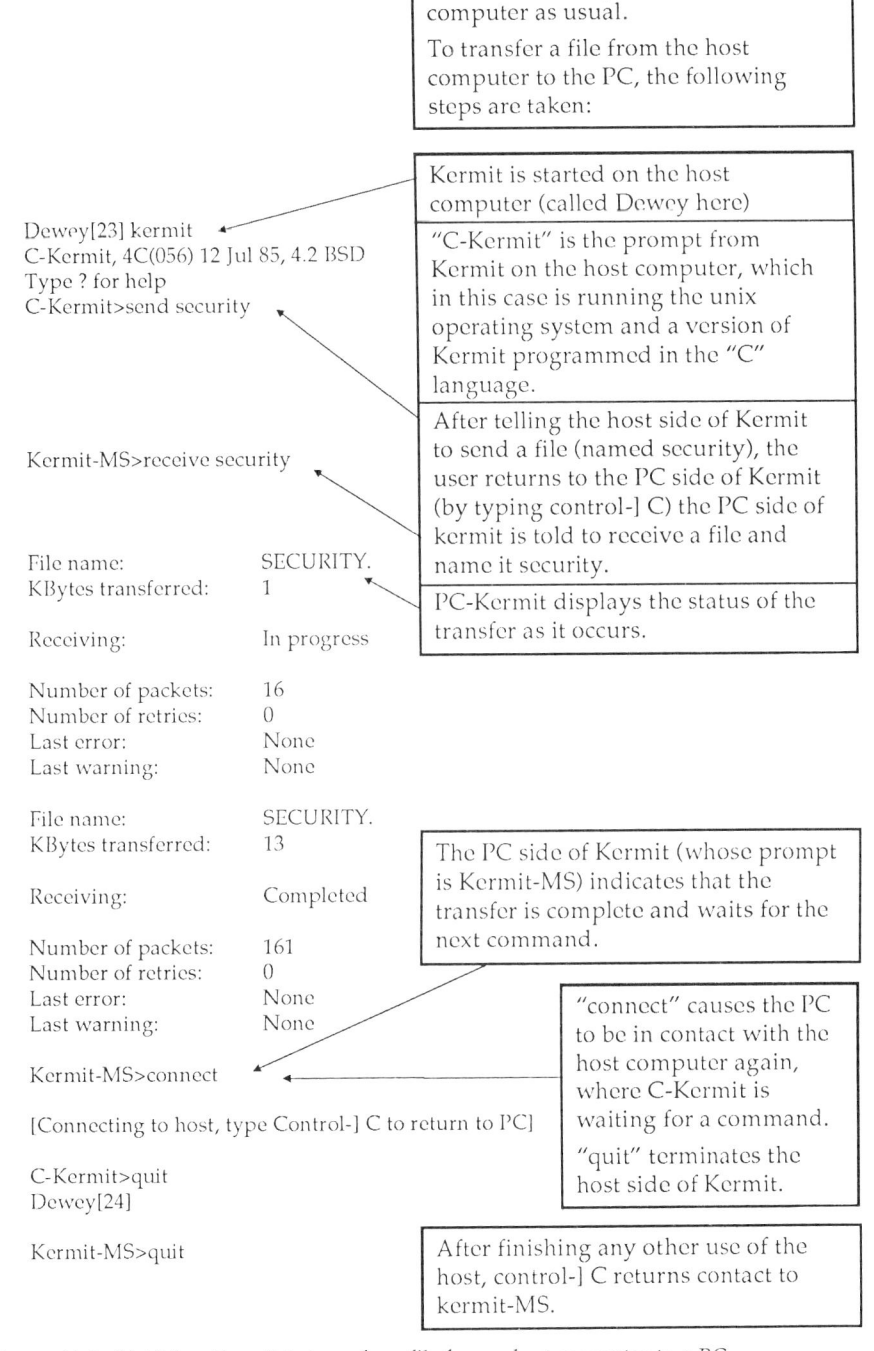

> The PC side of Kermit (whose prompt is Kermit-MS) indicates that the transfer is complete and waits for the next command.

Number of packets: 161
Number of retries: 0
Last error: None
Last warning: None

Kermit-MS>connect

[Connecting to host, type Control-] C to return to PC]

> "connect" causes the PC to be in contact with the host computer again, where C-Kermit is waiting for a command.
>
> "quit" terminates the host side of Kermit.

C-Kermit>quit
Dewey[24]

Kermit-MS>quit

> After finishing any other use of the host, control-] C returns contact to kermit-MS.

Figure 11.2 (b) Using Kermit to transfer a file from a host computer to a PC

Figure 11.3 Bus-type local area network

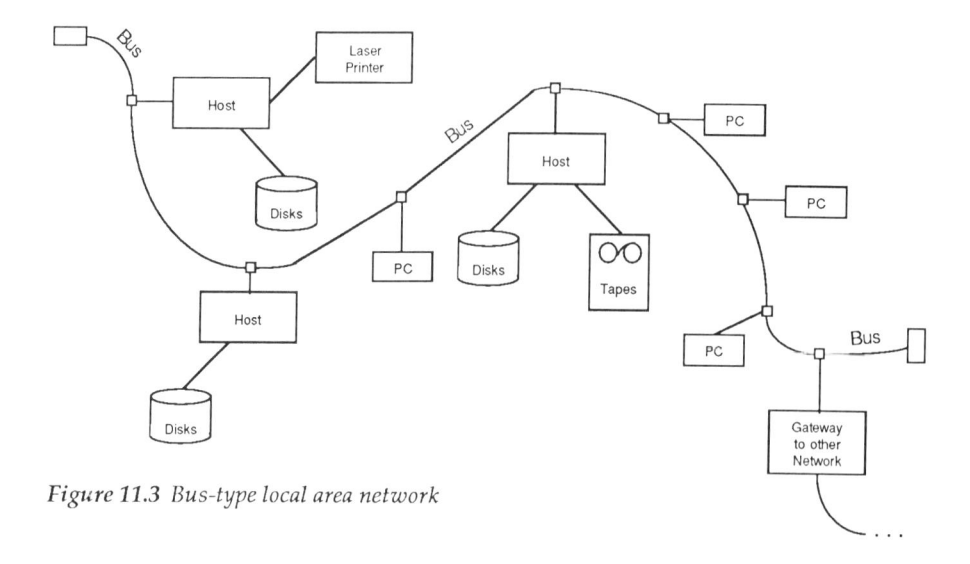

standardized: the token ring, the token bus, and the contention-based systems.

The **token bus** and **contention** systems use a common communication medium called a **bus.** All transmissions are placed on the bus, and all computers attached to the bus receive all transmissions. Figure 11.3 shows a common configuration.

The **token ring** arrangement is characterized by point-to-point connections between computers arranged in a ring. In the ring architecture, shown in Figure 11.4, each transmission goes from a sending computer to a receiving computer and is not received by any other computer on the network. However, a message can be sent only to a computer that is adjacent in the ring. In order to communicate with any other computer on the net, the sender depends on the other computers to pass on the message until it reaches the intended recipient.

Each computer is attached to a network by means of a **network interface unit (NIU).** To the computer, the interface appears as a type of input/output unit. Programs interact with the network interface in much the same way as with other I/O devices. There is one significant difference, however. When the computer receives input from a disk, the data remains on the disk. The computer receives a copy of the data as a result of its own request. The data arrives in a quantity requested by the computer and at a time when the computer has requested it.

In contrast, a message arriving on the network may or may not have been requested by the computer. The time of its arrival is not entirely predictable, and the data does not stay on the network. Because the arrival of a message is not under the control of the receiving computer, the computer may be busy at the time of the arrival. Each network interface has at least one buffer to hold a message until the computer is able to

File Processing in Computer Networks 327

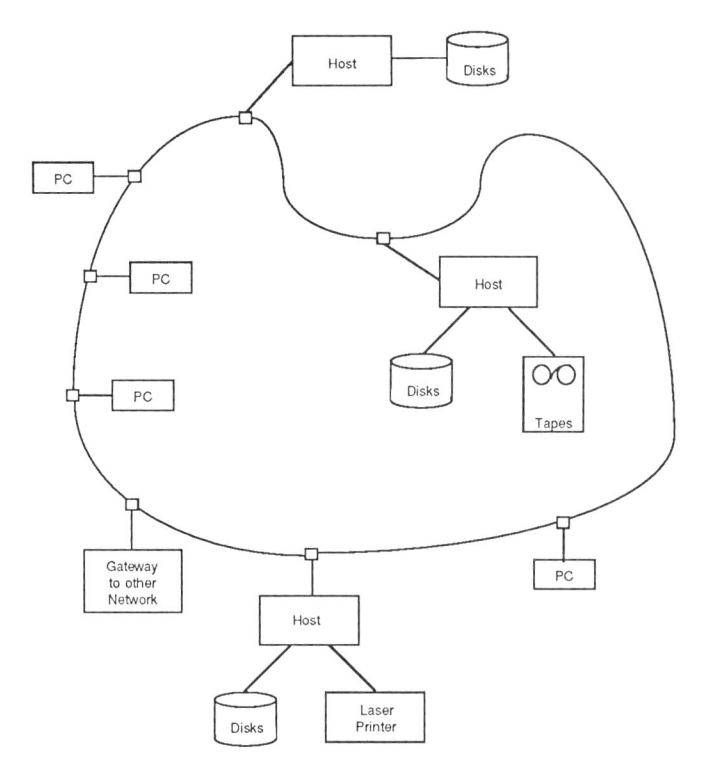

Figure 11.4 Ring-type local area network

accept it. If another message arrives before the first is accepted by the computer, the new message will be lost. Thus, part of the processing time of any computer attached to a network must be used to monitor the network interface, checking for new messages and moving them to main memory locations for processing by appropriate programs.

When the arriving message is a request for service, such as a directory listing, or a remote login, or the initiation of some program execution, the requester will generally wait for a response before sending another message. Though another, unconnected request may arrive almost immediately, there is a high probability that the station will have adequate time to accept the message and process it before having to accept another.

When the two communicating computers are participating in a file transfer, however, the message reception burden is greatest. The computer that is sending the file breaks the file into **packets** of a size suitable to the network and sends them in rapid succession. The receiving computer examines each packet as it arrives to confirm that it is part of the file transfer (as other messages may arrive at any time), and reassembles the packets into a complete file. In any network, there is some possiblity that an individual packet will not arrive uncorrupted at its destination, so a method is required to identify consecutive packets to prevent a hole from forming in the reconstructed file. Furthermore, in a wide area network, it is possible that different packets in the file transfer will travel by different routes from the sender to the receiver. Thus, packets may arrive out of order. The receiver must check sequence and reassemble the file correctly. **Flow control** is the process of coordinating the speed of the sender and receiver so that the receiver does not get swamped with more messages than it can handle, and the sender is not unnecessarily delayed.

The differences among the three primary types of local area networks are contained in the network interface units and in the network access programs. An application program or a user of the system need not know which type of network is in use. Briefly, the three standard local network systems work as follows.

Token-based systems share the right to transmit a message by passing a token—a special pattern of bits interpreted by the network interface as permission to send. When a station receives the token, it checks to see if a message is ready to send. If so, the message is sent; if not, the token is sent on to the next station.

In the token ring, when a station receives a transmission that is not a token, it checks a field in the message that contains the destination address of the message. If the address matches the station's own, the network interface copies the message into its own storage (buffer). It notifies the computer that a message has arrived on the network (by setting a particular bit in a register), and sends a copy of the message on to the next station on the network. If the address of the message destination does not match its own address, the network interface passes the message on to the next station, but does not copy it into its own buffer.

When the station that sent the message receives it again, it knows that the message has been around the ring and presumably has been received by the intended destination. (In some ring systems, the receiving station changes a special bit in the message to indicate that it has been received.) The station that originated the message then removes the message from the ring and passes the token to the next station. A station that receives the token is allowed to use the ring and send a message of its own.

A special address is used to indicate a message that is to be received by all stations. This allows messages to be broadcast to all computers at once, rather than having to be sent to each computer individually. Thus, each interface must recognize its own address and also the broadcast address.

In a contention-based system, a station that wishes to transmit a message puts the message on the communication channel where all other network users can hear it. The most popular such system, Ethernet, is an example of a network system known as CSMA/CD (Carrier Sense Multiple Access with Collision Detection).

In order to send a message, a station first listens to the channel to determine that no one else is using it. The station then sends its message and continues to listen. If another station also sent a message at nearly the same time, the two messages will collide and become garbled. Both sending stations hear the garbled message, stop transmitting (back off) for a randomly determined amount of time, and then try again. If a message collides again, the station concludes that the channel is carrying a lot of traffic and backs off for a random time that is allowed to be much longer than the previous back-off.

Because of the randomness of the back-off time and the undetermined number of times that back-off may occur, it is impossible to say exactly how long it will take to get a message transmitted. Though it is extremely unlikely, there is some possibility that the message will never get through at all.

A token bus is a combination of the token ring (in which a station cannot transmit until it has the token, but then has exclusive use of the channel) and a bus system (in which all stations share a common transmission media and must compete for its use). In a token bus system, the bus is used as a common transmission medium for all message-passing, but the stations pass a token from one to another in order to give and receive the right to use the channel. There is no contention for the common bus. The token passes from one station to another in a well-determined order, effectively forming a logical ring.

The token bus is easier to manage than the token ring. When a station on the ring goes down, a break in the ring could occur. To prevent such breaks, bypass connections are included in the configuration, allowing a malfunctioning station to be skipped. When a station goes down in a token bus, it does not affect any other communication. The station that precedes it on the ring notices that the station is not responding and sends its messages to the next station in the logical ring instead. The adjustment is made in the addresses used by the computing stations and does not depend upon the physical transmission medium. Adding a new station is also simple: an adjustment to the sending address of one station is all that is required.

On the other hand, the token ring has the advantage of not needing an address for each station-to-station transmission. Each station sends a message to the only other station to which it can send. Adding a station to the ring involves breaking a connection and inserting the new computer.

Network monitors are useful tools for network management. They can be used to collect information on how much traffic is travelling on the network, what types of data are being sent, which computers are sending and receiving large portions of the network traffic, when error conditions occur, and other important information about network performance. Such monitors are built by using a specially configured network interface unit that recognizes not only its own address and the broadcast address, but also all others. Actually, the interface receives all messages without checking the destination address. All messages sent over the network are accessible to the monitoring computer.

In a token ring, the monitor acts like any other computer in the net: it receives a message that is travelling on the ring and passes it on. However, it always copies the message into its own buffer and passes it to a program for examination. In the bus systems, the monitor does not need to be an active participant in network activity. It simply "listens" to the net and copies all transmissions.

The existence of a monitor on a network is important for network management. It is also significant in the context of the security and privacy of messages sent over the network. Users involved with applications of sensitive data need to be aware of the existence of monitors, and probably want to encrypt data when using the net.

More General Network Communication

In order for a program running on one network station to send a message over the network, it must be able to use the network access routines, just as it would use the I/O processing routines of the operating system to do other input/output operations. Since network operations imply the cooperation of two or more different computers, some agreement is needed about the nature of the network access programs. A number of different approaches have been taken to these questions. Among them are IBM's SNA (Systems Network Architecture), Digital Equipment Corporation's DECnet, and Xerox Network System (XNS). These have been used successfully for some years. They all require consistency among the machines attached to a network.

Communication is further complicated when the cooperation must be not only between different computers, but between different networks. Modern computing systems frequently involve interconnection of local networks to form a large communication system. For instance, Ethernet in one office, a token bus in another, and perhaps a token ring on the factory floor are all combined to allow the maximum in communication capability within a company. These linked local networks may be joined to others at distant company sites and become parts of a large wide area network.

Networks are joined by computing devices called **bridges** or **gateways**. Bridges are used to join similar networks where messages that come from one net can be passed to the other without modification. The chief function of the bridge is to determine which messages must be passed through to the other net. It may have to choose among several possible networks as the next destination for a message that is travelling to a distant net. A gateway is a more complex device. A gateway connects dissimilar networks and must make a message compatible with the destination net protocols before passing it on. This may involve appending extra information in the form of a header, splitting a long message into smaller packets that can be managed by the destination net, and other tasks. In addition, the gateway must also determine the most appropriate path for the message to take to reach its final destination. A bridge or gateway is most often a dedicated computer whose only function is to provide for communication between and among networks.

Open Systems Interconnection

In order to foster flexibility and interoperability among networks, the International Organization for Standardization (ISO) has developed the Open Systems Interconnection (OSI) standards. These standards define the operations necessary to allow communication between cooperating user applications on incompatible computers and a variety of network types. The OSI standards define seven layers of protocols separating the details of physical connection to the transmission medium from addressing and routing decisions, and from data representation and program interactions. The OSI model is shown in Figure 11.5

Many of the goals of the OSI standards have been met in a set of protocols developed for the ARPAnet under sponsorship of the Defense Advanced Research Program Agency (DARPA). The TCP/IP protocols have provided the ability to exchange files through FTP (File Transfer Protocol), send and receive mail, and logon to a remote computer. This suite of protocols has a well-established user base and is the most common internetwork communication in use today. Though most users will migrate to the OSI standard when programs have reached a suitable development, the ARPA protocols will be most common for some time. The ARPA protocols also provide a solid base of experience for use in developing new standards.

Summary

With network protocols to transfer files among connected computers, and protocols such as Kermit for transferring files over serial connections, including dial-up lines, file sharing and moving are practical, straightforward operations. They are likely to become more important as use of networks and interconnected networks becomes more common.

In this chapter we introduce local and wide area networks and the considerations necessary to access data from more than one computer in a network. We note that it is now feasible to transfer a file from one computer system to another over a communications network, even if the

Application
Access to the OSI environment for users; also distributed system support services.
Presentation
Conversion among different representations of data, different characteristics of terminals, and file system organizations.
Session
Establishes communication between applications, maintains the connection and terminates it when appropriate. (Includes providing login steps for one system using another.)
Transport
Moves data and control information from one computer system to another. Includes adjusting sending speed to accommodate limitations of receiver; resends what does not arrive correctly at the other side. All is transparent to the user, who can just assume that everything gets sent successfully.
Network
Establishes a path over which information is exchanged between two communicating systems. Makes any decisions necessary in regard to routes to use. All is transparent to the user.
Data Link
Concerned with the reliability of data units sent over a network. Appends and checks extra bits to detect transmission errors.
Physical
Moves bits over the physical connection between communicating systems. Concerned with cables, and signal encoding

Figure 11.5 The 7-layer Reference Model for Open Systems Interconnection of the International Organization for Standardization.

computers are of different types and their file systems are incompatible. On the other hand, direct access to file records from an incompatible computer is not yet available in general.

Interconnection of computers over dial-up lines and through local and wide area networks presents significant opportunities for file sharing, data collection, and information dispersement. Soon they will be normal components of most computer systems, and important aspects of file processing.

EXERCISES

1. Consider a file of 100,000 records, each of which contains 150 bytes. Assume that the file is to be transferred from one computer to another, and that both computers are on the same local area network. Assume that the network channel capacity is 10 Mbps (ten million bits per second). If the NIUs of both computers are able to operate fast enough to use the network channel at its full capacity, how long would it take to transfer the file?

2. Consider the file in Question 1 again. NIUs do not operate that fast. How long would the file transfer take if the NIUs send and receive data at 200 Kbps?

3. Just as a chain is only as strong as its weakest link, a network is only as fast as the slowest component on the path to be taken. Suppose the file in Question 1 is to be transferred between computers on different networks. How long would the file transfer take if the networks were each 10 Mbps, but were connected by a gateway at a link capable of handling 56 Kbps? How long would it take if the link were 19.2 Kbps?

APPENDIX A

COBOL FROM PSEUDOCODE

Throughout this text, algorithms are described in commonly used pseudocode. The purpose of this descriptive tool is to remove the question of the syntax of various statements and allow the programmer to concentrate on the logic of what needs to be done. As it happens, the form used in this pseudocode for the basic control structures can be adapted easily to Pascal but is very unlike the corresponding COBOL program statements. This appendix presents a mapping between the pseudocode statements in the text and the corresponding COBOL statements.

The basic control structures of structured programming are the following:

1. Sequence
2. Selection
3. Repetition

Sequence is accomplished in COBOL, as in other languages, by putting statements one after another in the order in which they are to be executed. The only difference between the pseudocode and COBOL is the way in which it expresses what the statement is to accomplish. There are really no rules in pseudocode, except that the intention be clear. In COBOL, of course, the syntax is completely specified. Some examples follow.

336   Appendix A—COBOL from Pseudocode

Pseudocode	COBOL
Total ← Total + amount	ADD AMOUNT TO TOTAL
	or
	COMPUTE TOTAL = TOTAL + AMOUNT
read X, Y, Z	FD INFILE . . .
	01 INRECORD.
	03 X PIC 99.
	03 Y PIC X(5).
	03 Z PIC 9(11).
	. . .
	READ INFILE AT END PERFORM
	FINISH-UP.
POS ← ⌈n/2⌉	03 POSITION PIC 99.
	03 N PIC 99V9.
	COMPUTE POSITION = (N + 0.5)/2

Selection is implemented in COBOL in much the same form as in other languages and is similar to the usual pseudocode version. Selection is accomplished with an IF statement, as shown here:

Pseudocode	COBOL
If age > 62 and	IF AGE EXCEEDS 62 AND
years-of-service > 10	YEARS-OF-SERVICE > 10
then	MOVE 'TRUE' TO
eligible = true	ELIGIBLE-FLAG
generate letter	PERFORM SEND-LETTER
else	ELSE
eligible = false.	MOVE 'FALSE' TO
	ELIGIBLE-FLAG.

It is in the Repetition commands that COBOL and pseudocode descriptions vary most. Several cases are shown below.

Pseudocode	COBOL
for i = 1 to n do . . .	PERFORM . . . VARYING I FROM 1
	BY 1 UNTIL I > N.
while j > 0 do . . .	PERFORM . . . UNTIL J NOT > 0.
case k of	IF K = 1 PERFORM . . . .
1: . . .	IF K = 5 PERFORM . . . .
5: . . .	
end case	
repeat . . .	PERFORM . . .
until delta < .01	UNTIL DELTA < 0.01.

A common part of a pseudocode specification is a reference to a procedure or function. The procedure or function is a section of program code that is given a name so that it can be referenced as needed. The point is twofold: to allow the same set of statements to be included in the whole problem solution at several places while being written only once, and to allow a program to be easier to read by separating clearly defined portions of code from the main body of the solution. A procedure is simply a set of program steps to be executed. It may calculate one or more values; it may perform input and/or output operations; it may rearrange elements in an array. In fact, it may do anything that any complete program could do. A function is a set of program steps that calculates a single value. The function name takes on the value that the function steps produce. For example, to sort an array into ascending order requires a procedure. A function is used to calculate the numerical average of the array elements.

Procedures and functions are used frequently in the pseudocode and Pascal programs in this text. There is no direct implementation of a function in COBOL. The function is implemented by using a paragraph or subroutine and assigning the result of the computation to a particular data-name defined for the purpose.

Procedures are available in COBOL in two forms. Procedures that do not use parameters can be implemented by paragraphs and appropriate PERFORM statements. Thus the pseudocode

```
Begin New District
```

becomes the COBOL statement

```
PERFORM BEGIN-NEW-DISTRICT.
```

Sometimes a procedure requires parameters. For instance, if a program includes an array sort, the sort routine needs to be told what array to sort and how many elements are in the array. In pseudocode, the information is specified as a parameter list:

```
bubble-sort(A, N)
```

In COBOL there are two approaches. First, an array, which is always the array to be sorted, can be defined in working storage. Also, a data-name, which is always interpreted as the number of elements to be sorted in the array, can be defined. Then to sort any array, the program first moves all of the elements of the array to the sorting array location, and moves the number of elements in the array to the location set aside to indicate how many elements are to be sorted. The sort routine is then PERFORMed, and the resulting array is moved back to the original location. In other words, the programmer specifically codes the parameter associations.

An alternative is to use the COBOL subprogram facility. This involves writing two separate programs: one for the subprogram and one for the main program. A LINKAGE SECTION is defined to allow the two programs to communicate. An array sort, for example, requires the following coding:

```
Subprogram:

<Usual IDENTIFICATION and ENVIRONMENT DIVISIONs including
     (PROGRAM-ID. BUBBLESORT.)>

DATA DIVISION.
   <usual FILE and WORKING-STORAGE SECTIONs.>

   LINKAGE SECTION.
   01 NUMBER-OF-ELEMENTS     PIC 99.
   01 ARRAY-TO-SORT.
      03 ARRAY-ELEMENT OCCURS 1000 TIMES INDEXED BY INDX.

PROCEDURE DIVISION USING NUMBER-OF-ELEMENTS,
                        ARRAY-TO-SORT.

<statements required to perform the sorting>

SPECIAL-PARAGRAPH.
    EXIT PROGRAM.
```

The "EXIT PROGRAM" statement causes control to be returned to the main program that invoked this subprogram.

```
Main Program:

<Usual IDENTIFICATION, ENVIRONMENT, and DATA DIVISIONs,
including definitions of the array or arrays that are
going to be sorted.>

PROCEDURE DIVISION.
      .
      .
      .
      CALL "BUBBLESORT" USING NUMBER-OF-SCORES, SCORE-LIST.
      .
      .
      .
```

where NUMBER-OF-SCORES is the count of the number of elements in the array SCORE-LIST, which is to be sorted.

Procedures and repetition are often combined in a technique called recursion. Recursion is the calling of a procedure from within the procedure itself. Every recursive procedure consists of two parts: the base and the recursive part. The base is a section of the procedure that does not ever call itself. The recursive part is the part that does call itself. The base part of the procedure is executed if some condition is met. The recursive part calls its own procedure, but each call is closer to the condition in the base part than the previous part. An example of a problem that responds well to the recursive procedure approach is the binary search:

Binary Search: (first position, last position, search object, location where found)

Base Part: Look at the element in the array halfway between the first and last position. If that element matches the search object, put its position in the "location where found" parameter and stop. If the first and last positions are the same, put "null" in the location where found parameter and stop.

Recursive Part: If the search object is less than the element halfway between the first and last positions, then call binary search again, using the same first position, last position equal to the position before the halfway point, the same search object, and the same variable to store the location where found. If the search object is greater than the element halfway between the first and last positions, then call binary search again, using the position after the midpoint for the first position, the same last position, the same search object and variable to store the position where found.

Recursion is not part of standard COBOL. Some COBOL implementations (Burroughs COBOL, for instance) will allow a paragraph to include a statement to PERFORM itself, or a subprogram to CALL itself. When recursion is not available, the same problem can be solved using an iterative technique. Unfortunately, the iterative solution is often more complex and more prone to programming error. In the text, recursive solutions are often used, because of their simplicity and clarity. In several cases, the equivalent iterative solution is coded in COBOL, while the recursive version is shown in Pascal.

APPENDIX B

COBOL FOR PASCAL PROGRAMMERS: AN INTRODUCTION

The purpose of this appendix is not to teach the COBOL language fully to programmers familiar with Pascal, but to point out some of the characteristics of COBOL programs that differ from Pascal programs and to make COBOL programs readable to a Pascal programmer.

The first thing that a Pascal programmer notices about a COBOL program is its length. There are no short COBOL programs by the standards of other languages. To appreciate a COBOL program, one should understand some of the goals of the language designers and the role that COBOL was designed to play. Among the requirements for COBOL programs was the ideal of self-documentation. In theory, a COBOL program could be read and understood by someone with knowledge of the application area, but little or no programming knowledge. This goal accounts for the large number of business English-like words found in the average COBOL program. COBOL was also designed to facilitate the most common activities associated with commercial data processing: input and output. COBOL is rich in statements that allow files and records to be defined, and reports to be formatted.

COBOL has no function definition facility, and the use of subprograms (procedures) is somewhat awkward and not commonly used. With the exception of functions and procedures, structured programming concepts are well supported. Of course, it is possible to write bad programs in any language, but COBOL has provided support for good programming style since long before structured programming became the fashion.

Every COBOL program consists of four distinct divisions, shown below, only two of which are very substantial.

IDENTIFICATION DIVISION. Descriptive material about the program, who wrote it when, and what it is expected to do.

ENVIRONMENT DIVISION. Associative material between this program and the environment in which it is to be run—in particular, the file system.

DATA DIVISION. Descriptive material about the variables used in the program.

PROCEDURE DIVISION. All the executable statements of the program.

The remainder of this introduction to COBOL is arranged in sections by these division.

IDENTIFICATION DIVISION

This division is strictly documentation; it is not translated by the compiler at all. A program name is required. Other entries include the author's name, the date the program was written, the date it was last compiled, notes on security, and remarks about the program's purpose.

ENVIRONMENT DIVISION

The most important section of this division is the INPUT-OUTPUT SECTION. In this part of the program, each file used in the program is associated with an external name, generally denoting the device on which the file is to be found or will be placed. A file may be assigned to a printer, to a disk area, or to the console or keyboard of a terminal, for instance. The organization and access to be used with the file are specified. The names of keys to be used in random access are declared. An example follows:

```
SELECT PERSONNEL-FILE ASSIGN TO <system disk name>
    ORGANIZATION IS INDEXED
    ACCESS MODE IS RANDOM
    RECORD KEY IS EMPLOYEE-ID
    ALTERNATE RECORD KEY IS DEPT-NUMBER WITH DUPLICATES.
```

DATA DIVISION

The division consists of all the declarations of variable names to be used in the program (variables are usually called data names in COBOL). Each data name is associated with a description, equivalent to a type declaration in Pascal. There is a difference in the types that can be declared in COBOL, however: There is virtually no limit to the descriptions that can be used. Integers and reals can be declared as in Pascal, though the descriptions look strange:

```
COUNT-1    PICTURE 999        USAGE IS COMPUTATIONAL.
SUM-1      PICTURE 9(5)V99    USAGE IS COMP-1.
SUM-2      PICTURE 9(10)V99   USAGE IS COMP-2.
INDEX-1    PICTURE 9(11)      USAGE IS INDEX.
```

COUNT-1 is defined as an integer stored and used in binary. SUM-1 is a single-precision floating-point value, and SUM-2 is a double-precision floating-point (real) value. INDEX-1 is also a binary integer, and is the preferred form for array indices and subscripts. The PICTURE clauses are redundant when usage is defined to be a computational form. However, the PICTURE clause is a critical element of most data-name descriptions.

The most common use of COBOL data names is to DISPLAY their values in printed form. The default USAGE of each data name is DISPLAY. DISPLAY usage means that each individual character in the value of the data name is stored as an EBCDIC or ASCII code. The number 123 is not stored as the binary equivalent of one hundred twenty-three, but as three characters: "1", "2", and "3". Such characters cannot be used in computations, and any number involved in computations is transformed by the compiler into one of the computational forms.

Some COBOL systems include an additional COMPUTATIONAL form: COMP-3. Numbers in COMP-3 form are used in computations as decimal values, using decimal arithmetic. Though this system is not efficient in terms of computational speed, it is very well suited to handling precise decimal fractions. In applications requiring calculations in dollars and cents, decimal arithmetic provides the advantage of exact representation, with no rounding errors introduced by the use of the binary system.

PICTURE (PIC) clauses describe, character by character, what the value associated with each data name looks like. Meanings of the most common PICTURE clause elements and some examples follow:

Picture Element	Meaning
9	A digit
V	A decimal place indicator
.	A decimal point inserted in output
X	Any character—alpha, numeric, or other

Examples

99V9	A three-digit number that is to be treated as having one decimal place
9(11)V99	A thirteen-digit number with two decimal places
X(35)	A string of any 35 characters

Level Numbers: Most data names are assigned a structure. The level number associated with each name indicates its place in the structure. These structures are similar to the Pascal record structure.

Examples

```
01 EMPLOYEE-RECORD.
    03 EMPLOYEE-NAME.
        05 EMPLOYEE-LAST-NAME     PIC X(20).
        05 EMPLOYEE-FIRST-NAME    PIC X(10).
    03 EMPLOYEE-DEPARTMENT        PIC XXX.
    03 EMPLOYEE-JOB-TITLE         PIC X(20).
    03 EMPLOYEE-HIRE-DATE.
        05 EMPLOYEE-HIRE-DAY      PIC 99.
        05 EMPLOYEE-HIRE-MONTH    PIC 99.
        05 EMPLOYEE-HIRE-YEAR     PIC 99.
```

In this example, the employee record consists of four fields: the employee's name, department, job title, and hire date. Name and hire date, in turn, are composed of other subfields: last and first names for name; day, month, and year, for date. A data name with a high-level number is a subdivision of the data name with a lower-level number that immediately precedes it. The lowest-level number (01) indicates a top-level definition. This is a data name that is not part of any other entity. When a data name has components, it does not have a PICTURE clause. The PICTURE is reserved for the lowest-level data entities. The "picture" of the higher-level entity is a composite of the pictures of its subfields. In the preceding example, EMPLOYEE-RECORD consists of 59 characters: EMPLOYEE-NAME consists of 30 characters; and the EMPLOYEE-HIRE-DATE is made up of 6 characters.

The closest equivalent to a Boolean variable in COBOL is the use of a condition-name. A condition-name is declared by using a special level number (88) in the description of the field. A name is assigned to a value.

The name takes on the value "true" when the data name at the previous level takes on the named value. For example:

```
01 FLAGS.
   03 SEARCH-STATUS   PICTURE XXX.
      88 SEARCH-DONE  VALUE "YES".
```

SEARCH-DONE is equal to TRUE when SEARCH-STATUS is equal to YES.

There are many more details to be learned in order to be able to use a DATA DIVISION effectively, and to declare any variable to be the type wanted. These few have been included to give an idea of COBOL data declarations, and to permit a programmer familiar with Pascal to follow the sample COBOL programs given in the text.

PROCEDURE DIVISION

The PROCEDURE DIVISION of COBOL is used to specify the steps to be taken in the program execution. The PROCEDURE DIVISION is organized into named paragraphs. Paragraphs can be thought of as procedures without parameters, although the analogy is not exact. Paragraphs listed in order will be executed in the order shown, unless some other statement changes the order of execution. The most common statements of the PROCEDURE DIVISION follow.

Input/Output

```
OPEN INPUT <filename>
     OUTPUT <filename>
     I/O <filename>
```

(The file is opened, that is, the file system locates the file in the system directory, determines the access rights of this user, and establishes appropriate buffers and pointers. If the file is indexed sequential, its top-level index is read into memory. A file opened as I/O can be used for both input and output—that is, can be updated—in the same program.)

```
READ <filename> AT END <statements to be executed>.
          or INVALID KEY
```

(The file named is read and one record retrieved. If the read fails because of end of file being reached, or because the key used does not appear in the file, the statements that follow the AT END or INVALID KEY clause are executed. There are no begin ... end groupings in COBOL. A group of statements to be executed are set off by a key word at the beginning, like AT END or INVALID KEY here, and another key word or a period at the end. The use of the period in COBOL programs is very important. Statements do not have to end with a period unless the statement is the last one in a paragraph, or is the last statement in a group to be executed when a particular condition occurs.)

```
WRITE <record name> FROM <data name>.
```

(Move the contents of data name to the area defined for the record name, which is declared in association with a file name, and write the record onto the file.)

```
CLOSE <filename>.
```

(The file is closed. No further access in this program is permitted unless another OPEN is executed. Buffers and index space occupied by this file are released.)

Data Manipulation and Computation.

The most common statement in most COBOL programs is the MOVE statement:

```
MOVE <data name> TO <data name>.
```

MOVE is actually a copy statement. Values are frequently moved from the input area into which they were read to an area in the WORKING-STORAGE SECTION (part of the DATA DIVISION that serves as a scratch pad). The values are then moved from the work area to an output field description area. The reason for all the moving is that the input/output operations are carried out in terms of records. A COBOL READ or WRITE statement always refers to a record at a time; it is not possible to provide a list of individual fields to be read or written. All the elements of a record are defined together, and their descriptions are included. Thus, when a file is read, all the fields of the record defined for that file become available. Input field descriptions are usually very general; most PICTURES of input fields are composed of Xs. This is so that a typing error in preparing input will not cause a program to fail as a result of having an L where a 1 is expected, for instance. (If a PICTURE clause of an input field is described with 9s, only digits may appear in the field. If a non-digit appears, the program will halt. This is like the Pascal program action when a nonnumeric value is entered in a field declared to be integer or real.) After the data is read, the field can be tested for consistency (IF field-name NUMERIC). If the field is found to be numeric, it is then moved to a working area that is defined with 9s, and perhaps a COMPUTATIONAL USAGE. The value can then be used in computations. After the value has been changed as required by the program, it is then moved to a field defined as part of an output record. The record can then be written. Notice that MOVE does not just copy the value, but also transforms it, if required by the format of the receiving field. Editing is specified by the PICTURE clause of the receiving field and can be used to increase or decrease the number of decimal places carried in the value, or to insert editing characters for printed output.

Computations can be done in COBOL in either of two ways. The COMPUTE verb allows specification of assignment statements that are much the same as Pascal assignment statements:

```
COMPUTE RESULT = 3 * A ** 2 + B / 5.
```

This symbol ** indicates "raise to the power of".

COBOL also includes "arithmetic verbs," which are sometimes more convenient for specifying computations:

```
ADD 1 TO COUNTER.
SUBTRACT QTY FROM INVENTORY.
DIVIDE TOTAL BY COUNT GIVING TEAMS
               REMAINDER EXTRA-PLAYERS.
```

The first two examples do just what the English suggests. The third divides the total by count and stores the result in the data name TEAMS, and the remainder in the data name EXTRA-PLAYERS. The Pascal mod function gives the remainder after division and is equivalent to the REMAINDER specification in COBOL. The Pascal div function gives the integer result after dividing, without regard to the remainder. It is equivalent to the GIVING clause of COBOL. Care must be taken to consider the number of decimal places specified for the data names used in COBOL arithmetic statements. All arithmetic is applied to the value as described, including all of its decimal places. Thus, if a number is described with two decimal places, the remainder is a number of hundredths.

Control Structures

Sequence: As in Pascal, statements are executed in the order seen, unless otherwise indicated.

Selection: The IF statement in COBOL is like the IF statement in Pascal, except for the following two differences:
    (a) COBOL does not use the word THEN in an IF statement. Everything from the condition to the first ELSE or period is considered to be part of the "then" part of the IF statement. (Punctuation is sometimes optional in COBOL, but the period to end an IF is critical.)

(b) COBOL has a statement, NEXT SENTENCE, that allows a jump from within a deeply nested IF statement to the statement that follows the IF.

Repetition: The COBOL PERFORM verb accomplishes all loop types in COBOL programs. See Appendix A for a description of the proper form of PERFORM for each type of loop.

Recursion: Recursion is not part of standard COBOL. It is available in some systems that allow a statement in a paragraph to perform the same paragraph, or a subprogram to call itself. It is seldom seen, however. The iterative version of the algorithm must usually be used in COBOL programs.

APPENDIX C

PASCAL FOR COBOL PROGRAMMERS: AN INTRODUCTION

The purpose of this appendix is not to teach the Pascal language fully to programmers familiar with COBOL, but to point out some of the characteristics of Pascal programs that differ from COBOL programs and to make Pascal programs readable to a COBOL programmer.

Like COBOL programs, Pascal programs have a particular structure. Each Pascal program is in the following form:

```
program <program name> (list of files used);
<declarations of constants, types, variables,
functions and procedures>
  begin
      <main program statements>
  end.
```

The first line corresponds to the IDENTIFICATION and ENVIRONMENT DIVISIONs of a COBOL program. Though there is no formal structure in the language for specifying programmer name, compile date, etc., in Pascal as there is in COBOL, these are frequently put in comment form immediately following the "program" line.

The declarations correspond to the COBOL DATA DIVISION. The declarations are quite different from COBOL PICTURE clauses, as will be described below. Functions and procedures are blocks of Pascal program statements that can be invoked in the main program, or in other functions and procedures, whenever needed. Each function or procedure has the same structure as an entire Pascal program, except that the first line identifies this block of code as a function (which takes on a value) or a procedure (which is just a block of code to be executed). Variables in a function or procedure are one of three kinds. Variables declared for the main program can be accessed by the function or procedure. These are called global variables because they are available to every routine within the program. Variables declared within the procedure or function can be used only within that routine. They are called local variables and are not seen by the main program or other procedures or functions. The third kind of variable is a parameter. A parameter is a local name for a global variable. The list of parameters used by the function or procedure is included in the first line of the declaration. When the function or procedure is invoked, a list of global variables to be substituted for the parameters must be provided. The advantage of this method is that the procedure or function can be invoked at different times using different global variables. For example:

```
program demo (input, output);
  var x, y, z    : array[1..50] of integer;
      nx, ny, nz:integer;

  procedure bubblesort(var a:array[1..50]of integer;
                       max: integer);
    var i, holder: integer;
      begin
          <bubblesort code, using i as the loop
          counter and holder for temporary storage
          during exchanges. The array sorted is
          called a and it has max values to be
          sorted.>
      end;

  begin {main program}
    bubblesort(x,nx);
    bubblesort(y,ny);
    bubblesort(z,nz);
  end.
```

Comments are enclosed in braces {} and are used frequently in Pascal programs to make the code easier to read.

A further description of Pascal declarations is needed. First, it should be understood that the Pascal programmer and the COBOL programmer have a different logical view of the way in which values are stored in a computer, and therefore of the way in which these values are manipulated. In general, the COBOL programmer sees a value as a string of characters or digits, sometimes digits with a sign and/or an implied decimal place. A Pascal programmer, on the other hand, sees data in terms of a small number of defined data types: integer, real, boolean, char, array, and pointer. Integer is a whole number, with no decimal places. It takes up one full computer word (or two 8-bit words in older microcomputers). The range of values that can be represented in an integer variable is determined by the number of bits in a word on the computer in use. (For 16-bit machines the range is ±32,767; for 32-bit machines the range is ±2,147,483,647). The integer with value 1 takes up the same amount of space as the integer with the largest value possible on the machine.

Real numbers are floating-point numbers. Each number has a whole number part and a fractional part. Reals are stored in two separate parts: a mantissa and an exponent, as well as a sign for each part. Computations with real numbers are much more complex than computations with integers, and are used only when there is a need for the greater range of values provided by reals, or when a fractional part is required in the value.

There are strict rules about combining numbers. An integer cannot be added to a real, for instance, because of the difference in the ways in which they are represented internally. A conversion of the real to integer format can be made for the sake of carrying out the computation, but the Pascal programmer is required to request the transformation explicitly.

A variable declared to be of type char can contain a single character. Any character in the character set is allowed. The declaration is equivalent to a COBOL PICTURE X. Each such variable can hold only one character. A character variable can be used in read and write statements, can be compared to other character variables or a character constant, and can be copied to or from other character variables or a character constant. In some versions of Pascal, variables can be of type string, where string is a sequence of characters. A string variable can be used in read and write statements, and can be compared to, and copied to or from, other string variables or a string constant. A string can also be concatenated to another string, and can be checked for length.

A boolean variable can take on only the value TRUE or FALSE. Boolean variables are used in Pascal as flag variables are used in COBOL, and are approximately equivalent to condition names.

An array type is equivalent to the COBOL table. The Pascal array declaration:

```
var keys: array[1..25] of integer;
```

says that the variable named keys consists of 25 integers, and the positions of these integers are numbered 1 through 25. The equivalent COBOL declaration would be:

```
01 KEY-VALUES.
   03 KEYS OCCURS 25 TIMES.
```

Pascal arrays can be numbered any way the programmer chooses, unlike COBOL table entries, which are always numbered beginning with 1. Thus,

var count: **array**[-10, 10] **of integer**;

allows the count to consist of 21 integers numbered from -10 through 10. This numbering scheme is convenient if the program is counting occurrences of something on each day for ten days before and after a particular day. The count for the particular day is count[0], the count for the day before is count[-1], and so on.

Higher dimensional arrays are declared in either of two ways. For the COBOL table declaration,

```
01 INVENTORY-TABLE.
   03 SIZE-OF-SHIRT OCCURS 3 TIMES.
      05 STYLE-OF-SHIRT OCCURS 5 TIMES.
         07 COLOR-COUNT OCCURS 4 TIMES PICTURE 99.
```

the Pascal equivalent is

var shirtcount: **array**[1..3,1..5,1..4] **of integer**;

or

var shirtcount: **array**[1..3] **of**
                      array[1..5] **of**
                              array[1..4] **of integer**;

A variable of type pointer is a special entity in Pascal that has no equivalent in COBOL. The value contained in a pointer variable is the address in main memory where another variable is stored. A particular advantage of pointer variables is the ability to request that a new memory location be assigned to the program while it is executing. Thus, if p is a pointer variable, the statement

new(p)

requests that a new memory location be assigned to the program and the address of that memory cell be placed in the variable p. Memory that is no longer needed can be returned to the system also. This facility allows the efficient use of such structures as linked lists, where the length of the list is not known in advance. The list grows and shrinks as it is used.

Records are defined in Pascal, similar to records in COBOL. There are no level numbers, but the subordinate structure is indicated by the use of the word "record":

```
var employee: record
           id: integer;
           empname: record
                       last name: packed
                           array[1..20] of char;
                       firstname: packed
                           array[1..10] of char;
                    end;
           hiredate: record
                        month,
                        day,
                        year: integer;
                     end;
        end;
```

A packed array is just a more efficient way to store characters in words of storage.

In addition to the data types that are defined by Pascal, the programmer may define types appropriate for the program. For instance, if there is a need to define a data record structure in several places, the programmer may choose to define that as a new type, and then use it where it is needed:

```
type date = record
            month, day, year: integer
         end;
     name = record
            lastname: packed array[1..20] of char;
            firstname:packed array[1..10] of char;
         end;
var employee: record
           id: integer;
           empname: name;
           hiredate: date;
        end;
```

Control structures

Sequence: A Pascal program consists of a main program, much like the PROCEDURE DIVISION of a COBOL program, and usually some number of functions or procedures. The purpose and use of functions and procedures is discussed in Appendix A. Functions and procedures are not executed unless specifically called for by a statement in the main program. Within the main program, statements are executed in the order in which they appear, unless another order is specified.

Selection: The Pascal IF statement is like the COBOL IF statement with the following exceptions. The general form of the IF statement is

```
if <condition> then <block of code>
    [else <block of code>];
```

The else clause, shown in [ ]s, is optional, just as ELSE clauses are optional in COBOL. The IF statement is terminated by a semicolon, instead of the period of COBOL. A block of code is any number of statements. If the block of code has more than one statement, they must be enclosed in begin ... end.

Example:
```
if (age > 62 and years > 10)
    then
        begin
            eligible := true;
            writeletter;
        end
    else
        eligible := false;
```

A single statement, such as eligible := false, can be enclosed in **begin ... end**, but does not require the enclosure.

Repetition: Pascal includes the **for ... do, while ... do,** and **repeat ... until** loop forms. The for loop is a counted loop equivalent to the PERFORM ... VARYING .... The form of the for loop is

```
for <var> := <start value> to <end value> do
        <block of code>;
```

or

```
for <var> := <start value> downto <end value> do
        <block of code>;
```

The <var> is called the loop index. Its value changes by 1 (if the "to" form is used) or by –1 (if "downto" is used) each time the loop body is repeated. The equivalent COBOL PERFORM statements include VARYING ... BY 1 (or –1).

Example:
```
for j := n downto k do
    begin
        x[j+1] := x[j];
    end;
```

The **while ... do** loop is similar to PERFORM ... UNTIL, except that the condition is reversed. Thus, the COBOL

```
PERFORM READ-CHECK UNTIL REC-ID = CODE-SOUGHT.
```

becomes, in Pascal

```
while rec-id <> codesought do
    readcheck;
```

The Pascal **repeat ... until** corresponds most closely to the COBOL PERFORM ... UNTIL .... The difference is that in Pascal the statements to be executed appear between the words repeat and until; in COBOL the statements are in a paragraph referred to by name in the PERFORM statement. The Pascal program may have a procedure name in the repeat statement, as shown for the while statement above.

One final control structure is the use of procedures and functions. These can be invoked as needed anywhere in the program. The use of parameters to share values between the calling and called program module provides flexibility. A very powerful control structure implemented in Pascal is the use of recursion. Recursion is the calling of a routine, such as a procedure of function, by itself. This often allows a process to be described in much simpler terms than is the case if such calls are not permitted. Appendix A contains further description of the use of recursion, and there are many examples in the text. Pascal supports recursion in all implementations.

REFERENCES

Aho, A. V., J. E. Hopcroft, and J. D. Ullman. *Data Structures and Algorithms.* Reading, MA: Addison-Wesley, 1983.

Austing, Richard H., and Lillian N. Cassel. *Computers In Focus*, Monterey, CA: Brooks-Cole, 1986.

Bayer, R. and E. McCreight. "Organization and Maintenance of Large Ordered Indexes." *Acta Informatica*, 1(3):173–189, 1972.

Bouros, Michael P. *Getting into VSAM: An Introduction and Technical Reference.* New York: John Wiley & Sons, 1985.

Bucholz, W. "File Organization and Addressing." *IBM Systems Journal*, 2(6):86–111, 1963.

Chaturvedi, A. "Tree Structures: A Tutorial on Using Tree Structures for Random Data Storage and Retrieval." *PC Tech Journal*, (2):78–87, 1985.

Chaturvedi, A. "Tree Structures: Part 2." *PC Tech Journal*, (3):131–142, 1985.

Claybrook, Billy G. *File Management Techniques.* New York: John Wiley & Sons, 1983.

Codd, E. F. "A Relational Model of Data for Large Shared Data Banks." *Communications of the ACM*, 13(6):377–387, June 1970. Republished in *Communications of the ACM*, 26(1), January 1983.

Comer, D. "The Ubiquitous B-Tree." *ACM Computing Surveys*, 11(2): 121–137, June 1979.

Dale, N., and C. Weems. *Pascal*, 2nd ed. Lexington, MA: D. C. Heath, 1987.

Dale, N., and S .C. Lilly. *Pascal Plus Data Structures,* Lexington, MA: D. C. Heath, 1985.

Date, C. J. *An Introduction to Database Systems*, Vol. 1. 4th ed. Reading, MA: Addison-Wesley, 1986.

Date, C. J. *Database: A Primer.* Reading, MA: Addison-Wesley, 1983.

Deasington, J. J. *X.25 Explained: Protocols for Packet Switching Networks.* New York: Halsted Press, 1985.

de Cruz, Frank, ed. *Kermit User Guide 1985*. New York: Columbia University Center for Computing Activities, 1985.

Diffie, W., and M. E. Hellman. "Multiuser Cryptographic Techniques." *AFIP Proceedings of the National Computer Conference*, 1976, pp. 109–112.

Dijkstra, E. W. *A Discipline of Programming*. Englewood Cliffs, NJ: Prentice-Hall, 1976.

Fagin, R. "Normal Forms and Relational Database Operations." *Proceedings ACM SIGMOD International Conference on Management of Data*, May 1979, pp. 153–160.

Fife, D. W., W. T. Hardgrave, and D. R. Deutsch. *Database Concepts*. Cincinnati, OH: South-Western, 1986.

Grossans, D. *File Systems Design and Implementation*. Englewood Cliffs, NJ: Prentice-Hall, 1986.

Hanson, Owen J. *Design of Computer Data Files*. Rockville, MD: Computer Science Press, 1982.

Hoare, C. A. R. "Quicksort." *Computer Journal*, 5(1):10–15, April 1962.

Hoffman, Lance J. *Modern Methods for Computer Security and Privacy*. Englewood Cliffs, NJ: Prentice-Hall, 1977.

Horowitz, E., and S. Sahni. *Fundamentals of Computer Algorithms*. Rockville, MD: Computer Science Press, 1978.

Hsiao, D. K., and F. D. Harary. "A Formal System for Information Retrieval from Files." *Communications of the ACM*, 13(2):67–73, February 1970.

Inmon, W. H., and T. J. Bird, Jr. *The Dynamics of Database*. Englewood Cliffs, NJ: Prentice-Hall, 1986.

Jensen, Kathleen, and Niklaus Wirth. *Pascal User Manual and Report*, 3rd ed. Revised by A. B. Mickel and J. F. Miner. New York: Springer-Verlag, 1985.

Johnson, L. F., and R. H. Cooper. *File Techniques for Database Organization in COBOL*. Englewood Cliffs, NJ: Prentice-Hall, 1981.

Kay, Russell. "Computer Security Information Services." *Computer Security Journal*, IV(1):29–40, 1986.

Kent, W. "A Simple Guide to Five Normal Forms in Relational Database Theory." *Communications of the ACM*, 26(2): 120–125, February 1983.

Knuth, Donald E. *The Art of Computer Programming; Vol 1: Fundamental Algorithms*, 2nd ed. Reading, MA: Addison-Wesley, 1973.

Knuth, Donald E. *The Art of Computer Programming; Vol. 3: Sorting and Searching*, Reading, MA: Addison-Wesley, 1973.

Lakshmivarahan, S. "Algorithms for Public Key Cryptosystems: Theory and Applications." *Advances in Computers*, Vol. 22. New York: Academic Press, 1983, pp. 45–108.

Lefkovitz, D. *File Structures for On-Line Systems*. New York: Spartan Books, 1969.

Loomis, Mary E. S. *Data Management and File Processing*. Englewood Cliffs, NJ: Prentice-Hall, 1983.

Lum, V. Y. "General Performance Analysis of Key-to-Address Transformation Methods Using an Abstract File Concept." *Commuications of the ACM*, 16(10):603–612, 1973.

Lum, V. Y. "Key-to-Address Transform Techniques." *Communications of the ACM*, 14(4):228–229, 1971.

Maurer, W. D. and T. G. Lewis. "Hash Table Methods." *ACM Computing Surveys*, 7(1):5–20, 1975.

Miller, Nancy E. *File Structures Using Pascal.* Menlo Park, CA: Benjamin/Cummings, 1987.

Moulton, Rolf T. *Computer Security Handbook.* Englewood Cliffs, NJ: Prentice-Hall, 1986.

Neufeld, M. L. and M. Cornog. "Database History: From Dinosaurs to Compact Discs." *Journal of the American Society for Information Science,* 37(4), July 1986, pp. 183–190.

Parker, Donn B. "A Strategy for Preventing Program Theft and System Hacking." *Computer Security Journal,* III(1):21 32, Summer 1984.

Philippakis, A., and B. Kazmier. *Structured COBOL,* 3rd ed. New York: McGraw-Hill, 1986.

Popkin, Gary S. *Comprehensive Structured COBOL,* 2nd ed. Boston, MA: Kent, 1986.

Prause, P. N., and G. I. Isaacson. "Protecting Personal Computers—A Checklist Approach." *Computer Security Journal,* III(2):13–24, Winter 1985.

Ranade, Jay, and Hirday Ranade. *VSAM Concepts, Programming, and Design.* New York: Macmillan, 1986.

Reynolds, J., and J. Postel. "Official ARPA Internet Protocols." (RFC 944). Marina del Rey, CA: Network Working Group, Information Sciences Institutue, 1985.

Scholl, M. "New File Organization Based on Dynamic Hashing." *ACM Transactions on Database Systems,* 6(1):194–211, 1981.

Smith, P. D. and G. M. Barnes. *Files and Databases: An Introduction.* Reading, MA: Addison-Wesley, 1987.

"Special Issue on Database." *ACM Computing Surveys,* 8(1), March 1976.

Stallings, William. *Data and Computer Communications,* New York: Macmillan, 1985.

Stonebraker, M., et al. "The Design and Implementation of INGRES." *Transactions on Database Systems,* Vol. 1:189–222, September 1976.

Stubbs, D. F., and N. W. Webre. *Data Structures with Abstract Data and Pascal.* Monterey, CA: Brooks/Cole, 1985.

Tanenbaum, Andrew S. *Computer Networks.* Englewood Cliffs, NJ: Prentice-Hall, 1981.

Tremblay, Jean-Paul, and Paul G. Sorenson. *An Introduction to Data Structures with Applications.* New York: McGraw-Hill, 1984.

Ullman, Jeffrey D. *Principles of Database Systems.* Rockville, MD: Computer Science Press, 1982.

Wiederhold, Gio. *File Organization for Database Design.* New York: McGraw-Hill, 1987.

Williams, J. W. J. "Algorithm 232 Heapsort." *Communications of the ACM,* 7(6):347–348, June 1964.

Wirth, Niklaus. *Algorithms + Data Structures = Programs.* Englewood Cliffs, NJ: Prentice-Hall, 1976.

INDEX

Absolute address, 184–186, 194
Access
  control of, 125
  direct, 144, 159, 185
  dynamic, 184
  random, 184, 185, 226, 233, 270, 342
  real time, 144
  relative file, 194
  sequential, 144, 159, 184, 185, 226, 231
  virtual storage, 229
Access control
  capability, 126
  list, 126
  files, 127
  matrix, 125, 126
Access time, 94, 96, 105, 181, 182
  blocking, 142
  files, 142
Address, 183, 187, 195, 198, 219
  absolute, 184–186, 194
  associated with key, 206
  calculation, 189, 203, 210
  collision handling, 189
  directory, 194
  indexed, 184, 185
  open addressing, 195, 197–199
  relative, 184–186, 189, 191–193

Addressability, 94
ADI/INFORM, 311
Administrative security, 120
ADS/O, 313
ALGOL 60, 3
Algorithms, 32, 38
  address calculation, 203
  array, 38
  balance line, 159, 170, 277, 279
  binary search, 53
  chaining, 209, 210
  conjunctive query, 278
  deletion, 255
  disjunctive query, 280
  divisionhash, 204
  hashing, 204
  heapsort, 86
  Hsiao-Harary, 281
  insertion, 251
  insertion sort, 43
  largest key, 38
  linear probing, 205, 206
  query, 275
  quicksort, 69
  search, 31, 34
  sequential search, 32
  sort, 47
  sort merge, 162

Algorithms *(continued)*
  two-way merge, 146
  two-way sort merge, 150
Alternate index, 269
Alternate key, 270, 271
Applications programmer, 291
Application generator, 313
APS, 313
Archives, 98
ARPAnet, 320, 331
Arrays, 3, 8, 13, 16, 17, 187, 266, 337
  attributes, 9
  binary search of, 58
  COBOL subscripts, 11
  COBOL table, 34
  data types, 351
  dimension subscripts, 10
  memory locations, 17
  packed, 353
  searching, 31
  three-dimensional, 9
  two-dimensional, 8
ASCII, 7, 16, 101, 203, 320, 343
Attributes, 3
  arrays, 9
  databases, 305
  records, 12

B-tree, 219, 237–248, 268, 296
  capacity, 258
  overflow handling, 258
  search time comparison, 259
B*-tree, 219, 236, 242, 256, 259
B+-tree, 219, 236, 242, 247, 249, 274
  after split, 259
  insertion algorithm, 251
  record deletion, 252
  record insertion, 248
  splitting after insertion, 250
Back-up strategy, 291
Balance line algorithm, 159, 170, 277
Balanced merge, 154
Balanced *n*-way merge, 155
Balanced sort merge, 160
Balanced trees, 236
Balanced two-way merge, 155
BASIC, 3, 97
Batch mode, 130
Batch processing, 143, 144
Bayer and McCreight, 256

Bell Laboratories, 127
"Big-oh" notation, 36
Binary, 19
Binary file, 18, 27
Binary search, 52, 66, 89, 145, 238, 330, 339
  analysis of, 57, 65
  array, 58
  COBOL program, 57
  efficiency, 58, 61
  key, 57
  linked list, 58
  method, 53
  Pascal program, 56
  recursive, 54
  tree version, 65
Binary tree, 61–67, 80, 81, 90, 201, 202, 216, 237
  complete, 81, 83, 89, 90
  definition of, 64
  depth of, 65, 68
  full, 65, 66, 81, 82
  heap, 82, 83
  level, 65
  nodes, 65, 68
  root of, 65
  search, 65, 237
  sort phase, 151
  subtrees, 64
Block, 108, 109
  of data, 105
  size, 104
Blocking, 142
Blocking factor of files, 104
Boolean data type, 351
Branch nodes, 63
Bridges, 330, 331
Broadcast, 328, 330
Bubble sort, 47, 58
  algorithm, 48
  analysis of, 52
  COBOL program, 51
  Pascal program, 50
Bucket, 200–202, 265
  overflow, 200–202
  primary, 200–202
Buffer, 103–105, 171, 172
Bulletin boards, 320
Burroughs Corporation, 96, 339
Byte addressing, 96

Cache, 95, 97
Calculation of address, 203
Capacity of B-trees, 258
Card, 105, 106, 107
  readers, 105
  zones in, 106
Carrier Sense Multiple Access with Collision Detection (CSMA/CD), 329
Cascade merge, 157
Cellular multilists, 274
Chaining, 195, 199, 203, 205
  algorithms, 210
  collision handling, 209
  number of probes, 216
Character, 3, 7, 14, 17, 351
Check digit, 131, 132
CIDF (Control Interval Definition Field), 232–235
Cluster, 235
  primary, 197, 198, 216
  secondary, 197
Coalesce, 197, 199
Coalescing of collision sequences, 198
COBOL, 290, 292, 298, 309, 313, 349, 350, 351
  access to inverted lists, 270
  alphabetic and numeric tests in, 130
  alternate key, 271
  buffer space, 105
  characteristics, 341
  computations in, 347
  data integrity, 129
  division in, 342–346, 349
  file description entry, 100
  file organization, 183
  level numbers, 344
  linkage section, 338
  listings, 23
  merge statement, 149
  records, 13, 353
  recursion, 339, 348
  repetition, 355
  secondary keys, 269
  sorting files, 30
  store objects, 27
  tape-label, 101
  use of period, 346
COBOL arrays, 11, 352
  array subscripts, 11
  search array (table), 34, 35
COBOL data types, 26
  character, 7
  declare integers, 5
  fixed-point numbers, 6, 15
  integer, 4, 14
  packed decimal, 15
  string, 8, 16, 17
COBOL divisions
  data division, 342–346, 349
  environment division, 342, 349
  identification division, 342, 349
  procedure division, 342, 345, 354
COBOL programs
  binary search, 57
  bubble sort, 51
  chaining, 213
  collision handling: chaining, 213
  control break, 164
  editing, 20
  division hashing, 205
  for sorted files, 33
  hashing, 205
  insertion sort, 46
  linear probing, 209
  listings, 23
  merging two files, 148
  pseudocode, 335–337
  quicksort, 73, 78, 79
  sequential file update, 175
  sort merge, 153
  straight selection sort, 41
  structured programming, 342
  subprogram, 338
CODASYL (Conference on Data Systems Languages), 298, 299
Code file, 18, 19, 21, 23, 27
Codd, E. F., 299, 303
Collating sequence for character set, 7
Collision, 191–198, 200–203, 206, 219
Collision handling, 189
  algorithm, 205
  analysis of, 215
  chaining, 209
  linear probing programs, 207
  number of probes, 216
Columbia University Center for Computing Activities, 323
Communications control program, 292

Comparison tree, 68
Comparison-based sort, 66, 67, 80, 90
Composite data types, 7, 13, 26
Compound query, 280, 281
Computer networks, 317–320, 324
Computer Output Microfilm, 98
Conceptual database, 287, 289, 292
Conceptual level, 289
Conference on Data Systems
 Languages (CODASYL), 298
Conjunctive query, 275, 277, 278, 281
 algorithm, 278
Contention, 324, 326
Contention-based system, 328
Controlled length multilist, 273, 274
Controller disk, 112
Control area, 231
Control area split, 235
Control break, 158–160
 COBOL program, 164
 Pascal program, 167
Control Data Corporation (CDC), 96, 229, 247
Control Interval Definition Field (CIDF), 231, 232
Control interval split, 234
Control of access, 125
Core storage, 96
Cost, 94
Createheap, 85, 86
 procedure in Pascal program, 88
CSMA/CD (Carrier Sense Multiple Access with Collision Detection), 329
Cullinet Software, 299
Cylinder, 141, 184, 222–226
 disk, 112, 114
 index, 227, 228, 229
 overflow, 224

DARPA (see Defense Advanced Research Program Agency)
DASD, 108
Data, 94
 back-up and recovery strategy, 291
 independence, 286, 289, 292
 models, 293
 objects, 3
 primary area, 222
 text, 18
 transfer rate, 110, 111, 182
 within fields, 17
Data array, 27, 351
Data Base Task Group (DBTG), 298
Data communications manager, 292
Data Definition Language (DDL), 289, 295, 303
Data dictionary, 292, 295, 296, 298
Data encryption standard, 123
Data field, 17
Data integrity, 117, 118, 128, 132, 133, 291
 check digit, 131, 132
 in COBOL, 129
 inconsistency, 286
 in Pascal, 129
Data Manipulation Language (DML), 289, 303, 306
Data pointer, 351
Data security, 110, 117, 133, 137, 291
 confidential, 118
 encryption of, 122, 123
 privacy, 117, 133, 134
Data redundancy, 286
Data types, 3, 353
 boolean, 351
 character, 3, 7, 14, 27, 351
 composite, 7, 13, 26, 27
 fixed-point, 14
 floating-point, 14
 integer, 3, 14, 27, 351
 in COBOL, 7, 8, 13, 26
 in Pascal, 7, 8, 11, 27
 numeric, 131
 real, 3, 6, 14, 27, 351
 simple, 4, 26, 27
 string, 3, 7, 8, 11
Data validation, 131
Database Administrator (DBA), 291, 292, 296, 309
Database integrity, 311
Database Management System (DBMS), 286–298, 306, 307, 312, 313
Database network, 299
Database privacy, 135, 309
Database query, 134
Database security, 309, 311
Database system, 286
Database types, 117, 134, 285–306
 conceptual, 287, 289, 292

hierarchical, 299
network, 299
online, 311
physical, 287, 289, 291, 292, 295
relational, 307, 312
DB, 310
DB2, 304, 307
DBA (see Database Administrator)
DBASE, 307
DBASE II, 304
DBASE III, 304
DBL, 296
DBMS (see Database Management System)
DBTG (Data Base Task Group), 298
DDL (Data Definition Language), 289, 295, 303
Decision tree, 68
DECnet, 330
Defense Advanced Research Program Agency (DARPA), 331
Deletion, 253, 254, 257
 algorithm for, 255
 doubly linked lists, 273
 key, 245
 multilists, 272
 random access, 187
 record, 234, 252
Department of Motor Vehicles, 133
Depth of trees, 63, 65, 68, 80, 81
DES, 124
Diffie and Hellman, 124
Digital Equipment Corporation (DEC), 96, 112, 113, 320, 330
Digraph, 297
Diminishing increment sort, 47
Directed graph, 297, 298
Directory, 183–189, 205
 address in, 194
 information in, 222
 searching, 206
Direct access, 144, 159, 182, 185
 storage device, 108, 142
Direct file organization, 186
Direct organization, 219, 220
Disclosure II, 311
Disjunctive queries, 279
 algorithm, 280
Disk, 187
 access speed, 112

controller, 112
cylinder, 112, 114
directory, 183, 184
fixed-block architecture, 109
gaps on, 109
server, 319
storage, 108
tracks, 109
Disk security, 110
Disk types
 drive characteristics, 112
 hard, 110
 floppy, 108, 113
 pack, 109, 112, 114
 rigid, 113
Displacement, 195
Distributed system, 318, 332
Divide and conquer sort, 68
Division, 192, 193, 196, 203, 207
Division-remainder, 192, 193, 196, 201
Division hash, 193, 196, 197, 204, 210, 215
DML (see Data Manipulation Language)
Double hashing, 198, 200
Doubly linked lists, 273
Dynamic access, 184
Dynamic hashing, 200, 201, 216
 after collision, 202
 after data entered, 203
Dynamic space allocation, 200

EBCDIC, 16, 101, 320, 343
Edit program, 20
Education Privacy Act, 136
Electronic mail, 320
Encryption, 122, 320
 control of access, 125
 Diffie and Hellman, 124
 key, 123
 public key, 124
 standard, 123
 substitution rule, 122
 United States National Bureau of Standards, 123
Enigma encoding device, 122
Entities, 300
Entry Sequenced Data Set (ESDS), 231
Environment division, 342, 349
ESDS (see Entry Sequenced Data Set)

Ethernet, 322, 328, 330
Exchange sort, 37, 47, 58
 algorithm, 48
 analysis of, 52
Expert systems, 311, 312
External
 files, 91, 144
 levels, 290, 292
 search, 144, 145
 sort, 30, 145

Fair Credit Reporting Act, 136
Federal Computer Systems Protection Act of 1983, 120
Fibonacci numbers, 156
Field, 12, 25
 data types, 17
 key, 30
 updating, 303
Fifth normal form, 302, 303
File, 13, 18–23, 141, 183, 187, 191, 199, 202, 206
 address, 183
 external, 91, 144
 header, 100
 index, 229, 238
 internal, 91
 inverted, 268
 key field, 30
 label, 101
 names, 19
 primary data area, 222
 runs, 156, 157
 searching, 29–32
 sharing, 320
 storage of, 98–101
 track, 141
 transfer, 320–323, 327, 328
 truncation, 190
 volatile, 225
File access, 127, 142
 direct, 182
 random, 182
 user, 125
File integrity, 320
File organization, 183
 blocked organization, 105
 blocking factor, 104
 direct organization, 186
 indexed organization, 183, 186, 269
 relative organization, 186, 219, 231
File privacy, 320
File processing
 batch, 143
 random, 186
File records, 29
 location of, 30
File security, 320
File sort/merge
 array used in sort operation, 38
 merging, 30, 148
 polyphase merge, 155
 sort/merge techniques, 21
 sorting, 30, 158
 two-way merge, 145–147
File Transfer Protocol (FTP), 320, 322, 323, 331
File types
 binary, 18, 19
 indexed sequential, 219, 265, 266
 listing, 21, 23
 master, 19, 20, 24–26, 135, 142, 159, 170–172, 275
 object, 23
 program, 21
 scratch, 21
 sequential, 140, 178, 266, 267
 source, 21, 25
 temporary, 19, 24
 text, 18, 19
 transaction, 19, 20, 21, 24, 159, 170, 275
 work, 171, 172
First normal form, 299, 301, 302
Fixed disk, 110
Fixed-block architecture, 109
Fixed-point numbers, 6, 14
Floating-point numbers, 6, 14, 15
Floppy disk, 98, 108, 109, 113
Flow control, 328
Focus, 313
Folding, 191, 192
Formatting, 160
Forms
 first normal, 299, 301, 302
 second normal, 301, 302
 third normal, 302
 fourth normal, 302
 fifth normal, 302
FORTRAN, 3

Fourth normal form, 302
Fourth-generation language (4GL), 292, 311–313
Freedom of Information Act of 1966, 135, 136
FTP (see File Transfer Protocol)
Full binary tree, 65, 66
Functions, 337, 349, 354, 356

Gap, 102, 104, 109
Gateways, 330, 331
Global variables, 350
Graphs
  digraph, 297
  directed, 297, 298
  trees, 62

Hard disks, 110
  data transfer rate, 110, 111, 182
  fixed, 110
  latency time, 110, 111, 182
  search time, 110
  seek time, 110, 111, 182
  winchester, 110, 113
Hash address, 196, 205, 209
Hash functions, 190–195, 198, 201, 215, 219
  division, 190, 197
  folding, 190
  key, 191
  multiplication, 190
  truncation, 190
Hash table, 189, 199–210, 213–216
Hash values, 197
Hashing, 188, 192–199, 202, 215, 265
  division hash, 210, 215
  division-remainder, 193, 196
  double, 198, 200
  dynamic, 200–203, 216
  linear quotient, 198
  open, 200
  techniques, 263
Heap, 81, 84, 89, 90
  createheap algorithm, 85
  creating, 83
  definition of, 82
Heapmaker
  algorithm, 86
  Pascal program, 87
Heapsort, 67, 68, 81, 85, 90
  algorithm, 86
  analysis of, 89
  createheap, 86
  efficiency, 61
  key, 85
  Pascal program, 87
  procedure in Pascal program, 88
Height of trees, 63
Hierarchical
  data model, 294, 296
  database, 297, 299
  models, 297–299, 301, 304
  systems, 293
Hoare, C. A. R., 68
Hoffman, 135
Hollerith, Herman, 106
Hsiao-Harary algorithm, 281
Human components, 290

IBM, 96, 106, 113, 221, 229, 247, 297, 299, 330
  Mass Storage Facility, 97
  MVS, 320
  Research Laboratory, 304
Identification division, 342, 349
IDMS/R, 304
IDMS (see Integrated Database Management System)
IMS (see Information Management System)
Independent overflow area, 226
Index, 185, 220, 221
  alternate, 269
  control intervals, 233
  cylinder, 227–229
  file, 238
  master, 227–229
  track, 223, 224, 228
Indexed
  addresses, 184, 185
  lists in file organizations, 269
  organization, 183, 186
Indexed sequential, 268
  access, 222
  file, 219, 223, 265, 266
  organization, 220, 221 266
Indexed Sequential Access Method (ISAM), 219–228, 231, 233, 236, 271
Information Management System (IMS), 297

INFORMIX, 304
INGRES, 304
Insertion, 310
  algorithm for, 251
  overflow, 256
  splitting after, 250
  with random access, 187
Inserting in
  B-trees, 242, 248, 251, 256, 259
  doubly linked lists, 273
  multilists, 272
  records, 234
Insertion sort, 37, 42, 58, 81
  algorithm, 43
  analysis of, 46
  COBOL program, 46
  efficiency, 52
  Pascal program, 45
Integer, 4, 14, 15, 17
  computations in, 16
  data type, 3, 351
Integrated Database Management
  System (IDMS), 299
Integrity, 118, 310, 311
  checks, 291
  of data, 117
  of files, 320
Interactive application, 159
Interactive, processing, 144
Internal file, 91
Internal level, 289
Internal Revenue Service, 133, 137
Internal sort, 30, 37, 90, 151
  exchange method, 37
  insertion method, 37
International Business Machines, 106
International Organization for
  Standardization (ISO), 331, 332
International Software Database, 311
Inverted file, 268
Inverted list, 264–267, 270, 271, 275,
  300, 303
  in indexed file organizations, 269
ISAM (see Indexed Sequential Access
  Method)
ISBN, 149
ISO (International Organization for
  Standardization), 320, 331
Iteration, 54, 70, 90
  in quicksort, 69, 73, 74, 78

Jacquard, Joseph Marie, 105
Join, 308

k-way merge, 157
Kermit, 323–325
Key, 31, 32, 196, 201
  address in directory, 194
  alternate, 270, 271
  associated record of, 195
  in B-trees, 242
  balance line algorithm, 277
  binary search, 57
  in bucket, 200, 202
  in collision handling, 189
  comparisons, 36
  comparison-based sort, 67
  deleted from coalesced list, 199
  deleting, 245
  in directory, 186, 187
  encryption, 123
  faster sorting, 61
  in field, 30
  finding address, 206
  for passwords, 122
  in hash functions, 190, 191, 219
  in hash table, 213, 215
  hashed to an address, 198
  in heapsort, 85
  in insertion sort, 42, 46
  largest remaining in sort, 37
  in linear probing, 210
  locating, 188
  locating in directory, 205
  for location of record, 223
  lowest maximum, 224
  in multiple-key organizations, 285
  number of values, 241
  in overflow handling, 258
  primary, 264–267, 271, 274–281, 285,
    310
  public, 124, 125
  queries, 275
  in quicksort, 68, 81
  relative address of, 192
  in search, 36, 145
  secondary, 264–275
  for security, 125
  in sequential files, 140
  in sorting files, 43
  in unordered files, 264

Index 369

value of, 30
when deleting records, 226
Key Sequenced Data Set (KSDS), 231, 233, 234
Key-to-address calculation, 188, 193
Knowledge-based systems, 312
KSDS (*see* Key Sequenced Data Set)

Lakshmivarahan, 125
Languages
  fourth generation, 311, 312
  query, 306, 307, 309
  subschema data manipulation, 290
LAN (*see* Local Area Network)
Latency, 110, 111, 182
Leaf nodes, 63
Legal security, 119
Legi-Slate, 311
Levels
  conceptual, 289
  external, 290, 292
  internal, 289
  in trees, 63, 65
Level numbers, 353
  in COBOL, 344
Linear probing, 195–198, 203, 210
  algorithm, 205, 206
  collision handling programs, 207
  number of probes, 216
Linear quotient, 197
  hashing with, 198
Linkage section, 338
Linked list, 187, 213, 225, 226, 266, 267, 272, 353
  binary sort, 58
  double linked, 273
  in files, 271
  search time, 268
Lists
  access control, 126, 127
  cellular multilists, 274
  coalesced, 199
  controlled length multilists, 273, 274
  doubly linked, 273
  inverted, 264–269, 270, 271, 275, 300, 303
  multilists, 264, 271, 277
  partially inverted, 266, 275–280, 281
Listing file, 21, 23, 27
Load factor, 216

Local Area Network (LAN), 318, 320, 326, 328, 330, 332
  contention, 324
  ring-type, 327
  tokens, 324
Local variables, 350
Logical record, 106
Log file in Pascal program, 173

Magnetic tape, 98
Mail, electronic, 320
Maintenance of, 303
  cellular multilists, 274
  doubly linked lists, 273
  inverted list, 268, 269
  multilists, 272
Main memory, 96, 97, 105
Mantis, 313
Many-to-many relationships, 298, 304
Master file, 19, 20, 24–27, 135, 159, 170–172, 275
  batch processing, 143, 144
  in COBOL program, 176
  in Pascal program, 173
  sequential processing, 142
Master index, 227–229
Matrix, 8
McCreight and Bayer, 256
Memory, 97
  buffer, 103
  byte addressing, 96
  core storage, 96
  word-addressable, 96
Menu, 290, 297, 305, 306
Mergesort, 149
Merging, 145, 158, 178
  algorithm, 146
  balanced, 154, 160
  cascade, 157
  COBOL, 148, 149, 153
  files, 30
  k-way, 157
  mergesort, 149
  n-way, 149, 278, 155
  natural, 150, 155
  polyphase, 155, 157
  runs, 150
  techniques, 21
  two-way merge, 145, 147, 155
  two-way sort merge, 150, 151

Merging *(continued)*
  sequential processing, 144
Message, 319, 326–329, 331
  security and privacy of, 330
Midsquare, 192
Models
  data, 293–296, 298
  hierarchical, 297–304
  network, 297–304
  relational, 299–304
  seven-layer reference, 332
Multilists (multiple-threaded
    list), 264, 271, 277
  cellular, 274
  controlled length, 273, 274
  maintenance of, 272
Multiple-key organizations, 285
Multiplication, 192

n-way merge, 278
National Crime Information
    Center, 133
National Technical Information
    Service (NTIS), 311
Natural merge, 149, 150, 155, 313
Network
  bridges, 330
  computer, 317–320, 324
  data model, 298
  database, 299
  gateways, 330
  local area, 318, 320, 324, 326, 330, 332
  management, 329, 330
  models, 297, 301, 304
  ring-type local, 327
  wide area, 318, 320 330, 332
  systems, 293
Network Interface Unit (NIU), 326,
    328, 330
Nexis, 311
NIU (Network Interface Unit), 326
Nodes, 63
  branch, 63
  leaf, 63
  nonterminal, 63
  terminal, 63, 67
  in trees, 63, 65, 68
NOMAD, 304, 309, 310
Nomad2, 313
Nonterminal nodes, 63

Normalization, 299, 303
NTIS (*see* National Technical
    Information Service)

Object code, 25
Object file, 23
Occurrences of a tree type, 295
OCR (Optical Character Reader), 140
Official Airlines Guide Electronic
    Edition, 311
Offline bulk storage, 98
Offspring, 63
One-to-many relationships, 297
Online bulk storage, 97
Online databases, 311
Open addressing, 195, 197, 198, 199
Open hashing, 200
Open System Interconnection
    (OSI), 331, 332
Optical Character Reader (OCR), 140
ORACLE, 304
OSI (*see* Open System Interconnection)
Overflow, 256
  handling, 258
  independent, 226
  bucket, 200–202
Overhead, 181, 182, 185, 237, 268
  controlled length multilists, 273

Pacbase, 313
Packed decimal, 15
  computations in, 16
  representation, 4
Packets, 327, 328, 331
Parent, 63
Parity, 101, 102
Partially inverted lists, 266, 276–278,
    280, 281
Partition, 63, 81
  in trees, 62
Pascal, 290–292, 309, 313, 343, 344,
    347–354
  access to inverted lists, 270
  address calculation, 203
  arrays, 10, 352
  characteristics, 341
  data integrity, 129
  declaring a record, 12
  field, 17
  files, 13, 183

Index 371

key in linearprobing, 210
operations on integers, 5
pseudocode, 335, 337
records, 353
recursion, 339, 356
recursive sort algorithm, 70
repetition, 355
sequential search of sorted file, 33
sorting files, 30
Pascal data types, 130
 character, 7
 integer, 4, 14
 real numbers, 6
 string, 8, 11, 16, 17
Pascal procedures
 createheap, 88
 heapsort, 88
Pascal programs
 binary search, 56
 bubble sort, 50
 control break, 167
 division hashing, 204
 for sorted files, 33
 hashing, 204
 heapsort, 87
 insertion sort, 45
 linear probing, 207
 quicksort, 72
 sequential file update, 173
 straight selection sort, 40
 two-way merge, 147
 two-way sort merge, 151
Passwords, 121, 122
 control of access, 125
 key, 122
 table look-up, 122
PDQ, 304
Physical database, 287, 289, 291–295
Physical record, 106
Physical security, 119
Pointers, 74, 81
 data type, 351
 in quicksort, 69
Polyphase merge, 155, 157
Primary clustering, 196, 197, 198, 216
Primary data area, 222
Primary key, 264–267, 271, 274–281, 285, 310
Primary bucket, 200–202
Printers, 107, 108

spooling, 107
Privacy, 118, 133, 137, 309
 of data, 117
 of files, 320
 of messages, 330
Privacy Act of 1974, 120, 136
Privacy Protection Study
  Commission, 136
Probing
 linear, 195–198, 203, 210
 quadratic, 198
 random, 197, 216
Procedure division, 342, 345, 354
Procedures, 337, 339, 349, 354–356
Program files, 21
Programs, 33
 address calculation, 203
 COBOL (*see* COBOL programs)
 Pascal (*see* Pascal programs)
 utility, 292
PROLOG, 312
Pseudo-random number, 197
Pseudocode, 335, 337
Public key, 124, 125
Punched cards, 106

QINT/SQL, 304
Quadratic probing, 198
Query, 134, 135, 144, 263–266, 272, 292, 295, 298, 303, 308
 algorithm, 275
 compound, 280, 281
 conjunctive, 275–278, 281
 disjunctive, 279, 280
Query languages, 306, 307, 309
 processor, 290
Quicksort, 47, 67, 68, 81, 90
 algorithm, 69, 70
 analysis of, 80
 COBOL iterative version, 78
 COBOL program, 73, 79
 efficiency, 61
 iterative version example, 74
 key, 68
 Pascal program, 72
 stack, 68
Quotient, linear, 197

R:BASE, 304
RAM, 97, 104

Ramis II, 313
Random access, 31, 182, 184, 185, 219, 226, 233, 270, 342
Random file processing, 186
Random probing, 197, 216
RBA (Relative Byte Address), 231
RDB (*see* Relational Database)
RDF (*see* Record Definition Field)
Real, 14, 17
Real data type, 3, 6, 351
Real time access, 144
Record, 3, 12, 13, 16, 17, 108, 109, 183, 186–191, 206, 219
  COBOL, 353
  fields, 12
  in a file, 29, 30
  logical, 106
  Pascal, 353
  physical, 106
  retrieval of, 238
  sequential search, 31
  storage location, 223
  truncation, 190
  updating in multilists, 272
Record Definition Field (RDF), 231, 232
Record deletion, 226, 234
  from B+-tree, 252
  from multilists, 272
Record insertion, 224, 234
  in B+-tree, 248
  in multilists, 272
Record gaps, 102
Recovery strategy, 291
Recursion, 54, 70, 90, 339
  COBOL, 348
  Pascal, 356
  Quicksort, 69, 73
Registers, 94, 97
Relational Database (RDB), 299, 307, 312
Relational models, 299, 301, 304
Relational systems, 308
Relationships, 300, 304
  in databases, 305
Relative address, 184–186, 189–195
Relative Byte Address (RBA), 231
Relative file, 219
  access, 194

addressing, 185
organization, 231
Relative organization, 183, 186, 191
Relative Record Data Set (RRDS), 231
Remote file storage, 98
Right to Financial Privacy Act, 136
Rigid disks, 113
Ring-type local area network, 327
ROM, 97
Root, 63, 65
RRDS (*see* Relative Record Data Set)
RUBIX, 304
Runs, 154–157, 160

Scatter storage, 188, 189
Schema, 292
SCOPE, 219, 221, 229, 286
SCOPE Indexed Sequential (SIS), 229–231, 235, 236, 247
Scratch file, 21
SDDL (*see* Subschema Data Definition Language)
Search, 32, 36, 58, 188, 199, 200, 219, 285
  algorithm, 31
  directory, 206
  files, 29, 30
  iteration, 54
  key, 145
  merging, 144
  more than one list, 275
  recursion, 54
  subtrees, 65
  time, 110, 187, 268
  track index, 224
Search table, 35, 206
Search types
  binary, 52, 66, 89, 145, 238, 330
  external, 144, 145
  random access, 31, 186, 187
  sequential, 31, 34, 52, 66, 140, 145, 220
Searching controlled length multilists, 273
Secondary clustering, 197
Secondary key, 264–268, 271, 274, 275
  in COBOL, 269
  in controlled length multilists, 273
Second normal form, 301, 302

Security, 98, 118–120, 309, 311
  access control, 125, 126
  administrative, 120
  checks, 291
  of data, 110, 117, 128
  encryption, 122, 123
  enigma encoding device, 122
  of files, 320
  legal, 119
  of messages, 330
  of passwords, 121, 122
  physical, 119
  of public key systems in
    networks, 124
  risk analysis, 119
  table look-up, 122
  technological, 120
  of transaction log, 121
Seek time, 110, 111, 182
Selection, 90
Selection sort, 37, 46, 58
  efficiency, 52
  memory requirements, 47
Sequence set, 233
Sequential access, 144, 159, 184, 185,
    226, 231
Sequential file, 140, 141, 266, 267
  access, 178
  addressing, 185
  indexed, 219, 265, 266
  key, 140
  organization, 184, 266
  processing, 139, 143, 158
  searching, 31
  update, 158, 159, 170, 173, 175
Sequential organization, 183, 186
Sequential processing, 143
Sequential search, 31, 34, 52, 66, 140,
    145, 220
  algorithm for, 32
  efficiency, 57, 58, 61
  key, 32
  of sorted Pascal file, 33
Sequential storage devices, 98, 107,
    108
Seven-layer reference model, 332
Shannon, Claude, 122
Shell sort, 46
Siblings, 63

Simple data types, 26
SIS (*see* SCOPE Indexed Sequential)
SiteSelects, 311
SNA (*see* Systems Network
    Architecture)
Social Security System, 133
Sort algorithms
  quicksort algorithm, 69
  search algorithm, 31
  sort phase of algorithm, 151
Sort array containing sorted file, 38
Sort file, 30
Sort key, 61
Sort methods, 58, 90, 158, 178, 337
  binary, 61
  bubble, 47, 58
  categorizing, 36
  comparison-based, 66, 67, 90
  diminishing increment, 47
  divide and conquer, 68
  exchange, 37, 47, 58
  external, 37, 145
  insertion, 37, 42, 58, 81
  internal, 30, 37, 90, 151
  quicksort, 47, 61, 67, 68, 81, 90
  random access, 187
  selection, 46, 47, 52, 58
  shell, 46
  sort/merge, 21, 144, 153, 154
  straight selection, 37, 42, 58, 81
  tree, 61
Sort programs
  heapsort, 61, 67, 68, 81, 85
  two-way sort Pascal program, 151
  quicksort COBOL program, 79
  sort/merge COBOL program, 153
  straight selection COBOL, 41
  straight selection Pascal, 40
Source code, 23
Source file, 21, 25, 27
Source file fields, 25
Splitting, 249, 251, 256, 258
  B+-tree, 250
  B*-tree, 259
Spooling, 107
SQL-based systems, 304, 307, 308,
    309, 310
SQL/DS, 304
Squaring, 192

374 Index

Stack, 69, 70, 74, 76–78, 81, 90
  in quicksort program, 68, 79
Stirlings approximation, 68
Storage
  direct access devices, 108, 142
  disk, 108
  offline bulk, 98
  online bulk, 97
  remote, 98
  scatter, 188, 189
  sequential devices, 98, 107, 108
  virtual access method, 229
  virtual bulk, 229
Straight selection sort, 37, 42, 58, 81
  COBOL program, 41
  Pascal program, 40
String, 3, 7, 11, 16, 17, 351
Structured programming, 341, 342
Subschema Data Definition Language
  (SDDL), 290
Subschema data manipulation
  language, 290
Substitution rule, 122
Subtree, 62–65, 67
Syntax, 335
Systems
  contention-based, 328
  database, 286
  database management, 292
  distributed, 318, 332
  expert, 311, 312
  hierarchical, 293
  knowledge-based, 312
  network, 293
  open interconnection, 331
  public key, 124
  relational, 308
  SQL-based, 307
  token-based, 328
Systems Network Architecture
  (SNA), 330
System R, 304

Tables, 11, 35
Table look-up of passwords, 122
Tape, 99, 102, 104, 108, 110
  capacity, 107
  compressed storage, 105
  density, 102
  drives, 99, 102

file header, 100
file label, 101
  label, 99, 101
  leader, 99
  mark, 99
  record gaps, 102, 103
  sorted files on, 158
  tracks, 101
  volume table of contents, 99
TCP/IP (Transport Control Protocol
  interaction with the Internet, 320,
  331
Technological security, 120
Telon, 313
Temporary files, 19, 24, 27
Terminal nodes, 63, 67
Text, 18, 19
Text files, 18, 27
Third normal form, 302
Token, 324, 328, 329
  bus, 326, 329, 330
  ring, 326, 328–330
Token-based systems, 328
Track, 101, 109, 141, 182, 184
  index, 223, 224, 228
Transaction, 159, 170–172
  files, 19–21, 24, 27, 159, 170, 275
  in COBOL programs, 176
  in Pascal programs, 173
  log, 121
Transport Control Protocol interaction
  with the Internet, 320
Tree, 63, 187, 266, 293, 298
  capacity, 240
  comparison, 68
  definition of, 62
  degree, 63
  depth, 63
  graphs, 62
  height, 63
  levels, 63
  partitions, 62
  properties and applications, 64
  sort, 61
Tree components
  nodes, 63
  offspring, 63
  parent, 63
  parent-children organization, 297
  root, 63

siblings, 63
Tree types, 294, 295
  B-tree, 219, 236
  B*-tree, 219
  B+-tree, 219
  balanced, 236
  binary, 61–67, 80, 81, 90, 201, 202, 216, 237
  decision, 68
  subtrees, 62, 63, 67
truncation, 191, 192, 193
two-way merge, 145, 147
  algorithm, 146
two-way sort merge, 152

UNIFY, 304
United States National Bureau of Standards, 123
UNIX, 127, 320
Update, 309, 310
Updating fields, 303
Updating records in multilists, 272
Users view, 287, 290
Utility programs, 292

Validation, 131
Values, key, 30

Variables, 350
Virtual bulk storage, 229
Virtual storage access method (VSAM), 219, 221, 229, 231, 233, 234, 236, 247, 269, 271, 286, 320
Volatile file, 225
Volume table of contents, 99
VSAM (*see* Virtual Storage Access Method)
VSAM-SIS, 235

WAN (Wide Area Network), 318–320, 328, 330, 332
Westlaw, 312
Wide Area Network (WAN), 318–320, 328, 330, 332
Williams, J. W., 85
Winchester disks, 110, 113
Word-addressable memory, 96
Workstations, 319
Work file, 171, 172

XNS (Xerox Network System), 330

Zones in punched cards, 106